THE

ATHENÆUM

COLLECTION

Decimus Burton
Architect

THE
ATHENÆUM
COLLECTION

HUGH TAIT

AND

RICHARD WALKER

WITH CONTRIBUTIONS FROM
SARAH DODGSON,
IAN JENKINS
AND RALPH PINDER-WILSON

THE ATHENÆUM

LONDON 2000

First published in Great Britain by The Athenæum, London 2000

Carole Green Publishing, 2 Station Road, Swavesey, Cambridge CB4 5QJ,
United Kingdom

A CIP record for this book is available from the British Library.

ISBN 0 95352 912 6

Designed, produced and typeset by Geoff Green Book Design, Cambridge

Printed in Hong Kong, by Midas Printing.

Frontispiece: Decimus Burton by E.U. Eddis (No. 123)

CONTENTS

PREFACE

WHEN I WAS ASKED by the Authors of this splendid book, if I, as Chairman of the Library Committee, would provide a Preface, I had no hesitation in agreeing to do so, as a tribute both to the book itself and to the scholarship, the indefatigable industry and the devotion of the honorary Authors.

Hugh Tait may well be described as the 'onelie begetter' of this volume as it was he who, some three years ago, identified the need for a definitive catalogue of the Athenæum Collection. He then proposed to the Library Committee that such a catalogue be produced for the membership and for others who could know little of this remarkable collection. The Library Committee unanimously endorsed this proposal – but how to do it? As well as Hugh Tait, the Club has another member who is an art historian of immense expertise, Richard Walker, whom Hugh Tait volunteered to engage in this enterprise. This engagement was considered and soon Richard Walker had generously agreed to undertake the catalogue itself – a work of infinite complexity and with not a few surprises.

In a project of this scope, where the editorial quality has to be matched by the quality of production, the question of finance immediately raises its head. Our proposed solution was to invite members to become subscribers to the volume and this invitation was quickly and warmly taken up by members sufficiently to guarantee financial security.

We were also fortunate to have the services of the Librarian, Sarah Dodgson, who, whilst continuing her normal duties, somehow found time to act as administrator, researcher, archivist and part author.

As Hugh Tait points out, the Athenæum from the beginning has put its glorious library before other works of art. The interesting and amusing story of the peripatetic portrait of George IV indicates this. Nevertheless, over the years an astonishing collection of some 2000 items of various categories has been acquired. To tell the story of this Collection, with detailed descriptions, illustrations and many colour plates, was the aim of Hugh Tait and Richard Walker. In that, they have succeeded wonderfully. They have captured the *genius loci* of the Club and its Collection so that we all may now be aware of what it is and how it has come about.

BRYAN BENNETT
CHAIRMAN OF THE LIBRARY COMMITTEE
July, 2000

LIST OF SUBSCRIBERS

Soloman Abramovich
Professor Andreas N. Adam
Dr Bernard Adams
J.K. Adams
P.M. Aichroth
Diana Allen
Leonard Allen
Michael Allmond
Bruce Allsopp
Kenneth Andrew
Dr James Appleyard
John A. Armitt
Dr William J. Arrol
Canon Adrian Francis Arrowsmith
George E. Assousa
Captain (RN) Julian Astbury
Roger Aylward
P.V. Baker
Dominic Baker-Smith
Sir Robert Balchin
Michael Baldwin
Sir Roger Bannister
Ashley Barker
Christopher Palgrave Barker
Dr David Barkham
John A. Barnes
Sir Ivor Batchelor
Professor R.W. Beachey
Peter Beesley
A.M. Behagg
Burton Benedict
Bryan Bennett
Peter Benton
Robert Berg
Francis J. Bergin
Leonard T. Berkowitz
John G. Bernasconi
R.L. Bickerdike
Professor P.M. Biggs
A.W. Bird
Malcom Bishop
Conrad M. Black
Guy V. Black
Mark Blackett-Ord

Colin Blackwell
R.M. Blackwell
David E. Bland
Professor T.C.W. Blanning
Professor Dr K-H. Böckstiegel
Sir Walter F. Bodmer
Dr Jeremy Bolton
Geoffrey Bond
Professor Sir Michael Bond
Professor Andrew D. Booth
Gary B. Born
Dmitry Bosky
Bruce Boucher
P.P. Bowcock
John Bowles
Sir Alan Bowness
H.R. Boyle
A. Kenneth Bradley
Professor Sydney Brandon
Lt. Col. Ian H. Branton
Patrick Brenan
Anthony J.E. Brennan
Allan Brent
Canon Brian Brindley
D.C. Britton
Dr Ivor Brodie
Rodney Brooke
Bernard Brook-Partridge
Arthur Brown
Dr David C. Brown
Robert G. Brown
Dr D.W. Budworth
Dr Nigel Buller
Nigel S.D. Bulmer
Professor Victor Bulmer-Thomas
Dr P.S. Bulson
Professor E.H. Burn
Sir John Burnett
Dominic Delisle Burns
I.M. Burns
D.P.G. Butler
James Calderwood
Professor John Caldwell
Michael J. Callewaert

Professor A.E. Campbell
Professor P.W. Campbell
Peter Cannon-Brookes
Harold Caplan
Dr M. Caplin
I.C. Carmichael
Colonel F.W.B. Carter
Reverend Charles T.S. Cavanagh
Desmond H. Cecil
Dr Alan Chadwick
Sir John Chadwick
John Charlton
Gerald Charrington
Professor Char-Nie Chen
Victor L.L. Chu
A. Trevor Clark
Dr Francis Clark
John Clark
Professor David Clayson
Dr J.T. Cliffe
Rabbi Professor D. Cohn-Sherbok
Professor George H.A. Cole
Professor Jonathan Coleman
James Collier
P.H. Collin
Martin Collins
Dr Peter Collins
Sir John Collyear
The Reverend Christopher Colven
His Honour Judge T.A.C. Coningsby
Charles A.G. Cook
Grahame D. Cook
Lodwrick M. Cook
David J. Cooper
Dr P.W.M. Copeman
Sir Alcon Copisarow
Dr Alec Coppen
Dr I.M. Corall
Professor John A. Corbett
Sir Patrick Cormack
Alan Cornish
David Cornwell
Sir Neil Cossons
Raymond J.R. Cousins

The Reverend Leonard W. Cowie
The Reverend Ronald Creighton-Jobe
David Crone
Dr John Crook
Peter M. Crystal
Lord Cuckney
Brian Currie
Professor Sir Alfred Cuschieri
Dr Lionel Dakers
David Dalgliesh
Dr George Daniels
David Darbyshire
B.W. Dartnell
Keith Davey
Derek L. Davies
Professor M.W. Humphrey Davies
Dr Royden Davies
Professor G.R. Davis
Ian Hay Davison
Gilbert de Botton
John Bedford Deby
Robert Delahunty
His Honour Keith Devlin
Philip Devlin
Gerald Dix
S.J. Dodgson
Michael Drake
Professor L. Dreyfus
James Owen Drife
Derek Drummie
Francis Duffy
The Reverend Canon Bruce Duncan
Dr Michael Simpson Dunnill
Hugo Dunn-Meynell
Dr John V. Dunworth
Dr H.D. Dupree
Dr David Dykes
Michael Eastwood
Dr Anthony Edridge
David A.O. Edward
J.H. Edwards
Wilfred T. Edwards
J.K. Eltringham
Professor Charles E. Engel
Dr John B. Enticknap
Professor Raul Espejo
The Reverend David Burton Evans
J.A. Everson
Michael J. Fairey
Dr Dennis Farr
Cecil Farthing
Honourable Justice Atanda Fatayi-Williams
David Wenlock Faull
Sir Bernard Feilden
Dr G.B.R. Feilden

Felipe Fernández-Armesto
Professor J.E. Ffowcs Williams
Professor Leon G. Fine
Leonid V. Finkelstein
Richard Fisher
R.J.H. Fleck
George Foggon
Professor Sir Hugh Ford
Jonathon Ford
Dr Ian Forgacs
Ian S. Forrester
J.Peter Foster
D.C. Freshwater
The Reverend Christopher Frey
Dr Michael J. Furness
J.G. Gaddes
Robert Edward Gage
G.F. Gainsborough
Dr Max Gammon
W.D.H. Gardiner
Peter Garland
Harry E. Gaylord
Dr David John Giachardi
N.C. Gibbon
Paul Gibbs
Professor R.E. Gibson
G.C.B. Gidley-Kitchin
Michael Gillingham
Brian Gilmore
Michael DeWitt Godfrey
T.F. Godfrey-Faussett
Martyn Goff
Dr Michael J. Goldsmith
Alfred Goldstein
Professor Anthony Goode
John Goodfellow
Sir Nicholas Goodison
Professor John F. Goodwin
Professor Laurence W. Gormley
John W. Gorrod
Professor Barry Gough
Dr John Gough
Alastair Graham
Kevin Grant
Dr A.C. Grayling
Peter J.StB. Green
Dr Frank Greenaway
Dr Peter Andrew Livsey Greenhalgh
Michael Gunningham
Dr W.M. Haining
The Reverend J.P. Haldane-Stevenson
Sir Basil Hall
Michael Hall
Dr Fred Hamblin
Sir David Hancock

J.R.A. Hanratty
Dr Wilfred G. Harding
William B. Harris
Dr P.D. Hart
Anthony F. Hatt
Richard O. Havery
Professor J.G. Hawkes
Simon Hawkins
Robert Hawley
Roger A.F. Heath
S.C. Heaven
Dr Barry Hemphill
Stuart Hibberdike
Professor F. Alan Hibbert
H.W. Higginson
Malcolm S. Higgs
Christopher Hill, Bishop of Stafford
Robin M. Hill
Professor Ian Hindmarch
Michael Brett Hockney
David Robert Holmes
Dr W.F. Holmes
Sinclair Hood
Ronald G. Hooker
Walter Hooper
Dr A.J. Hopkins
Dr Nigel W. Horne
Timothy Hornsby
Sir Robert Horton
Professor R.F. Hosking
David Howard
Christopher Howes
R.F. Hudson
The Right Reverend Peter F. Hullah
The Reverend Canon John Humphreys
Bruce Hunter
P.D. Hunter
Dr O.A.N Husain
N.S. Hush
Matthew Hutton
Sydney W. Jackman
Barry Jackson
Dr D. Geraint James
E.K.G. James
The Rt Reverend Graham James
Dr Ronald W. James
A.Geoffrey Jennings
Dr David Jewitt
Godfrey Jillings
The Reverend Malcom Johnson
W.P. Jolly
Sir Peter Jonas
Professor Gareth Jones
J. Clement Jones
John Ieuan Jones

Sir Paul Judge
Neil Kaplan
David R. Kaye
Michael Keall
Dr A.J. Kennedy
P.W. Kent
Sir Sydney Kentridge
Roeinton B. Khambatta
Professor P.J.H. King
Lady Kings Norton
Dr Henry Kinloch
Jonathan Kipling
J.S. Kirkham
Professor Stanley Kirschner
P. Kleeman
Rev. C.J. Klyberg
Dr Paul Knapman
Dr Roger Knight
Gordon A. Knights
Dr Ralph Kohn
Justin A. Kornberg
Christopher Lajtha
Dr N.G. Lambert
Sir Frank Lampl
Professor Peter T. Landsberg
Professor Peter Lantos
Brian A. Lavers
Jeremy Lawson
Anthony D. Lawton
Colin Leach
Dr Jeremy Lee-Potter
Dr Nigel J. Legg
Don E. Lennard
Derek Lennon
John Lenton
William M. Lese
Maurice Lessof
Eliot B. Levin
Dr Peter Lewis
Donald P.H. Liao
Professor G.M. Lilley
Roland Littlewood
B.D.S. Lock
Eur Ing Professor Brian Locke
Ian S. Lockhart
R.G.A. Lofthouse
David London
Jonathan H. Lourie
Professor Philip N. Love
E.W.B. Lyndon-Stanford
Sir George G. Macfarlane
Dr Neil Mackie
Roderick MacLeod
Professor Richard Macve
Chief (Dr) M.A. Majekodunmi

Michael J. Mallett
Leonard Sulla Manasseh
David F.C. Mann
Kingsley Manning
Professor John Marshall
Dr A.J. Martin
Professor John Martin
Dr J.F.A. Mason
His Honour Peter Mason
George Mathieson
Robert E. Mattock
Walter McCann
Dr D.P.J. McCarthy
The Rt. Reverend Nigel McCulloch
Brian McGeough
Vivian McIver
Dr John C. McKenzie
Henry B. McKenzie Johnston
Peter McKinley
James G. McMurtry III
Ian R. McNeil
Alexander S. McNeish
Dr James McQuaid
Professor Gwyn I. Meirion-Jones
Professor Anthony Mellows
The Reverend T.O. Mendel
Maurice Mendoza
Dr David Menhennet
Don Mentz
Colin Menzies
Dr T.J. Meredith
David S. Mitchell
Professor Dr John Warwick Montgomery
Professor Joseph R. Moore
Dr R. Milton Moore
Rodney Moore
Professor D.J. Morantz
Professor Gemmell Morgan
Professor Norbert R. Morgenstern
Sir Douglas Morpeth
David Morriss
The Very Reverend Dr John Moses
Professor John W. Mullin
Sir Kenneth Murray
The Reverend Gordon Mursell
Michael Napier
Clemens N. Nathan
Michael Cooper Neale
Dr Cyril Nemeth
Professor David E. Newland
Michael W.N. Nicholls
The Right Hon. the Lord Justice,
Lord Nicholls of Birkenhead
Frank Noah
James A. Noble

Robert Noel
Patrick Noon
The Rev.d Michael Northwood
C.M.G. Ockelton
P. N. O'Donoghue
John Older
Michael Ollerenshaw
Professor Eugenio Oñate
His Honour Judge Michael Oppenheimer
Sir David Orr
Michael Osbaldeston
Trevor Osborne
R.A. Oury
Lord Oxburgh of Liverpool
Felix de Marez Oyens
John Oyler
Roger Parker
Stephen Parks
Gordon Peacock
Professor M. Pepper
Professor Mark Perlman
Dr Peter J.C. Perry
Gordon Philo
Professor John Pickard
Joe Pilling
Patrick Pirie-Gordon
Jon Pither
The Very Reverend Stephen Platten
John Platts-Mills
Raymond J. Playford
Professor The Reverend Canon J.R. Porter
Dr George H. Poste
R. Potter
Professor John Poynter
C.N.R. Prentice
Brian D. Price
Terence Price
Professor Stefan Priebe
Peter H. Prowse
Anthony Pugh-Thomas
Geoffrey Purves
Ralph Quartano
John Rea
Geoffrey Redman-Brown
Dr Donald Rees
Professor W. Linford Rees
Brian C. Reid
William Reid
J.N. Reynolds
Michael Rice
Stephen J. Rice
Patrick Riley
Dr Colin N. Roberts
Stephen T. Roberts
The Reverend Charles Robertson

ACKNOWLEDGEMENTS

MEMBERSHIP OF THE ATHENÆUM involves access to a huge field of knowledge and expertise and the authors are deeply grateful to the many members of the Club who have expressed interest in this book and have helped in its production.

In particular, we would like to thank Bryan Bennett and Bruce Hunter for their faith in the idea at the outset, for their able 'piloting' of the project in its early stages and for their publishing skills. We are greatly indebted to Ian Jenkins, Ralph Pinder-Wilson and our Librarian, Sarah Dodgson, for agreeing to contribute to the volume with their specialised knowledge of the Henning frieze, the Oriental *objets d'art* and the political cartoons.

We wish to thank the Hon. Annabel Freyberg, Sir Stephen Runciman, Peter Sabine, Robert Weale and Derek Wiblin for expert advice and, in a more general way, Keith Davey, whose intimate knowledge of the Collection was acquired over some ten years or more, during which he, with the help of Helen Webb the former Librarian, organised the identification, cleaning, mounting and hanging of so much of the Collection. For their tireless labours in proof-reading, we offer thanks to David Barkham, Leonard Cowie, Peter Hart and Peter McKinley. We also greatly appreciate Peter Hart's permission to illustrate a design, possibly the earliest known record of the 'intended Club House' (Introduction Fig. A.)

This book would not have been completed within the tight schedule without the unfailing support of the staff of the Club, especially Jonathan Ford, Tom Weber, Stewart Ebbs, Denzil James and the Library team, including Kay Walters and Kate Gibson who created the photographic records of the Collection, and with the help of Anne Hegarty unearthed the hidden treasure that lies scattered in the Club archive. Our thanks are also due to Fiona Kimm and Susan Reynolds for their assistance during the final stages of compiling the Indices.

The staff of the London Library, the National Portrait Gallery library and the Victoria and Albert Museum have, as always, been most helpful; a special word of thanks must go to Mairead Dunlevy and her colleagues at the National Museum of Ireland, Dublin, to David Beesley, librarian of the Worshipful Company of Goldsmiths, to the Secretary and members of the Kipling Society, and to Dr Margrethe Floryan of Thorvaldsens Museum, Copenhagen.

The task of photographing the very varied objects in the collection was most ably undertaken, in two major sessions, by Simon Hawkins of Reeve Photography (Cambridge): we are most grateful to him and to our most co-operative book-designer, Geoff Green of Carole Green Publishing (Cambridge).

We are grateful for permission to reproduce a number of illustrations:

Brighton and Hove Council, Mr Andrew Barlow (No. 318)
The British Museum (Fig. 2 in Section IV and Fig. 3 in Section VI)
English Heritage, Crown Copyright (Fig. 1 in Section IV)
Manchester City Art Gallery (Fig. F in Introduction).
The photographs of the Duke of Wellington (Appendix I), Benedetto Pistrucci (Appendix II) and the design for the Club House (Fig. A in Introduction) were taken by A.C. Cooper Ltd.

Finally, we hope it is not too presumptuous to express the sensation that Athena and Apollo have watched over our labours. Certainly our wives, Audrey and Margot, have endured our preoccupation with this book, usually without complaint, and we thank them for their patience and encouragement.

LIST OF COLOUR ILLUSTRATIONS

HUGH TAIT

INTRODUCTION

For 176 years, the Athenæum Collection has been growing and almost every item has entered it through gift or bequest, largely due to the generosity of members and their families. As a result, the story of the Collection provides a fascinating – albeit incomplete – illustrated history of the changing nature of the Club.

The Club itself has no tradition of playing the role of 'patron' or, indeed, of 'collector'. When, in the early autumn of 1826, the members of the newly founded Athenæum gazed out of the windows of their Nash town house at 12 Waterloo Place, they had an uninterrupted view of the emptying of George IV's ornately furnished palace, Carlton House (Nos. 1106 and 1166). They will have been dismayed to find that this task would last until April, 1827, because only then could the demolition gang move in. By May, 1827, the Club's architect, Decimus Burton, had had his plans and specifications for the new Club House "submitted to competition of four of the most eminent builders of the metropolis" and the tender of Messrs Bennett and Hunt had been accepted (Fig.A). Consequently, the erection of the Club House was forced to overlap with the continuing demolition of Carlton House, an adjacent operation marred on two occasions by the fatal accidents suffered by two stone masons (see Fig.B). The earliest official confirmation that the whole of Carlton House had been taken down appears in a report dated 5th June, 1829 (PRO, Works 19/11/5, No. 58).

In that same month, the Committee of the Club met to consider Decimus Burton's schemes for the interior of the great room extending the full length of the building on the east side (100 ft long, 30 ft wide, and 27 ft high), which has long since been called the Drawing Room but which in 1829 was captioned the "LIBRARY" on two of Burton's water-colour designs (Pl. XX(a)). Most significantly, the Committee could have selected the scheme in which many pictures in gilt frames adorn the walls, but their rejection of it provides a far more revealing statement than any to be found in the *Minutes*. Moreover, most subsequent decisions confirm that there was a fairly consistent line of thinking on the subject throughout the 19th century.

The Committee made one exception – no doubt out of the deep respect they had for the memory of Sir Thomas Lawrence, P.R.A. and one of the Club's first three Trustees (Nos. 512-3). Before his death, they had accepted with gratitude, Lawrence's offer to present one of his flattering portraits of George IV (No. 318); indeed, in May, 1829, they had asked Lawrence "to choose the place for the picture…In consequence of this, Sir Thomas Lawrence attended at the Club and selected a space over the fireplace of the Library and desired that the book cases should be brought up so as nearly to touch the frame…". On 4th June, Lawrence signed the *Minute* recording that Decimus Burton, the Architect, had "submitted a plan for the fittings of the Library which was approved subject to such alterations as may be requested by Sir Thomas Lawrence for the introduction of his Picture". This room only became known as the "South Library" later on, when it was necessary to distinguish it from the newly created "North Library".

In the following six months, "the recess" for the picture was prepared and the problem of the "lighting of the Picture at night,…after a great deal of deliberation, trouble and expense, was finally arranged by Sir Thomas Lawrence himself". After one last inspection of the place in the Library on 5th January, 1830, Lawrence "expressed his general satisfaction" and agreed, again, that Saturday, 23rd January, would be the day for the installation of the picture, which he would have completed by then.

Lawrence died on 7th January, just two days after that visit to the nearly finished Club House. The Committee (with Croker in the Chair), at their first meeting in the new building (May, 1830), formally minuted their indebtedness to him for his past guidance "on all points connected with decoration and the Fine Arts", but there was still no sign of his picture of George IV. As reported in the *Gentlemen's Magazine* (Vol. 100, March, 1830, p.351), "over the fireplace of the Library is an empty space once destined by the Committee for the reception of Sir Thomas Lawrence's picture of the King, but which is now positively refused by the Executors". Lawrence had died with considerable debts and, consequently, his outstanding collection of old master drawings (including sheets by Raphael and Michaelangelo) had to be sold. The determined efforts of the Committee and, in particular, of Croker, finally resulted in the Executors selling Lawrence's

A: *The Athenæum : the earliest (?) design by Decimus Burton, 1827-8. (Discovered and acquired by our member, Mr. Peter Hart)*
The Minutes of 26 June 1827, show that the General Committee ordered an "engraving of the elevation of the intended Club House" to be made. This design does, indeed, correspond with the engraving signed by R.F. Cahusac (the engraver) and initialed, 'D.B.' (for Decimus Burton) that is pre-served in the Club's Collection. However, the engraving has previously been wrongly associated with a group of plans dating from the 1840–1 period. A related invoice and receipt (in the archives of the Club) confirms that Raphael F. Cahusac was being employed on this continuing project between 12 October and 23 December, 1828 (if not before) and that he received from Decimus Burton £10-17s in full settlement on 18 March, 1829.

unfinished painting to the Club in 1831 for £128-10s and they minuted their decision to have it "placed in the Library in the place for which it was intended by him with a flat rim or frame" and that Mr. G. Morant (of the firm of Picture Frame Makers in New Bond Street) should do the work "without delay".

Confirmation that the picture was not hung in 1831 in the Coffee Room, as previously published, can be found in *London Interiors* (2 Vols., 1841–4, p.166):

"Off the stairs, on the right of this balcony, is the Library…Above the mantle-piece is a portrait of George IV, painted by Sir Thomas Lawrence, upon which he was engaged but a few hours previous to his decease; the last bit of colour this eminent artist ever put upon canvass (sic) being that on the hilt and sword-knot of the girdle. Thus it remains unfinished, a pleasing yet painful memorial… Around the extent of one side of this room, is a gallery of peculiar elegance…"

The South Library, today, has a two-tier gallery around the four sides of the room and the space between the mantel-piece and the bottom gallery is filled by a long, low mirror.

The accuracy of the account in *London Interiors* (1841–4) is, in part, confirmed by the Club's Inventory of 1838, in which the picture of George IV is recorded as being in "The Library". However, in the next Club Inventory dating from 1856, the picture is listed among items in "The Coffee Room".

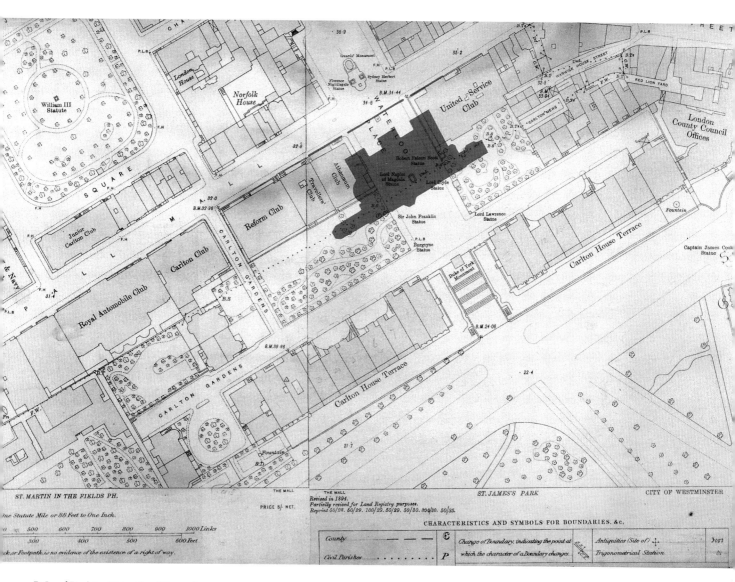

B: Land Registry Map, 1894 (No 1103)
The outline of George IV's Carlton House (demolished 1827-9) has been superimposed to show its relationship to Waterloo Place and the building of the Athenæum.

Consequently, the removal of the oil painting (approximately 8 ft high and 5 ft wide) from Lawrence's carefully chosen and meticulously prepared location in the South Library must have taken place after 1841-4 and before 1856.

By October, 1856, the painting had been once again taken down and the Committee resolved unanimously that this portrait "heretofore at the West End of the Coffee Room be not restored to its place". By January, 1857, the *Minutes* state that it was "now lying in a warehouse" and that it should "be presented, subject to the sanction of a General Meeting of the Club, to the Corporation of Brighton with a view to its being placed in the Pavilion…" The necessary approval was forthcoming at the Club's A.G.M. in May and by June, 1857, the

picture had become the property of the Brighton Town Council. Two months later, John Wilson Croker died suddenly and, although he had for some time not been closely involved with Club affairs, it is hard to believe that he was indifferent to these reversals. Both he and the Committee in 1830-1 had striven to honour the understanding that existed between the Club and Sir Thomas Lawrence at the time of his death. Their achievement had been negated within less than twenty-five years and the Club's only oil painting had now been ejected. If reasons were given, none is recorded.

Was the Club fundamentally opposed to the hanging of oil paintings on its walls? It is a fact that, in 1886, the Committee refused the famous collection of the Society of

Grove Street,
Lisson Grove North,
February 15, 1830.

The Committee of the Athenæum

To Chas. Rossi

		£	s	d
Dec. 22nd	For Cartage of Demosthenes to Pallmall (*sic*) from my place	0	5	0
	3 Masons ¾ of a day each placing Demosthenes in a nich (*sic*) on the Staircase	0	13	6
Dec. 31st	For Cartage back etc.			
	4 Men taking down and the use of Blocks and fall	0	14	6
		1	18	0

(on the reverse)

Mr. Rossi/Acct. for Demosthenes / £1-18-0.

The invoice was checked by the Club's architect and is endorsed:
"Certified to be correct / Decimus Burton / 22nd February, 1830". Furthermore, when
payment was made, the invoice was signed: "March 6, 1830 / Recd. Chas. Rossi".

Dilettanti (see Cowell, p.83). Apart from the Lawrence canvas, no oil painting entered the Collection during the first sixty-five years of the Club's existence. Furthermore, when the 19th century finally drew to a close, there was only one recorded oil painting in the Athenæum. It was the relatively small – and incredibly disappointing – version of John Opie's portrait of Dr. Samuel Johnson (1709–84), which had been presented by Humphry Ward in 1889 (No. 470). Framed and glazed, this inconspicuous painting was hanging in 1901 in the Writing Room, a small room that no longer exists but had been on the north side beyond the Morning Room. Throughout the 19th century, therefore, the absence of framed paintings from the walls of the Club House was a striking and consistent feature, quite uncharacteristic of the Victorian era but explicable in a Club faithfully respecting the Greek Revival or 'Athenian' qualities of the building.

Indeed, the Club's Committee had, from the start, shown a distinct preference for figure sculpture to adorn the interior of the new building, even before it was quite ready for occupation in the early spring of 1830. An unpublished document in the archives is quoted *in extenso* because it offers a unique glimpse of the admirable lengths to which the Committee were willing to go in order to choose a suitable sculpture for the commanding position on the Club Staircase. They had already commissioned, for the exterior, the figure of Athena and the Parthenon frieze and, iconographically, there were compelling arguments in favour of having the standing figure of the courageous Athenian orator, Demosthenes, whose eloquent opposition to the military might of Philip of Macedon had finally cost him his life in 322 BC. Furthermore, Demosthenes had lacked both wealth and position but, through his talents, had won fame in Athens and, therefore, was a particularly worthy candidate for the niche on the Staircase. The document is printed above, together with endorsements on the reverse and the receipt signed by Rossi.

In the light of this document, the decision to reject the figure of Demosthenes was clearly taken within those eight days around Christmas, 1829. Consequently, the erroneous version published more than a decade later (*London Interiors*, 1841–4, p.166) should now be disregarded: it stated that "the Demosthenes was originally designed for this place, but could not be sculptured in time for the opening of the House in 1830".

It now seems likely that Sir Thomas Lawrence's opinion had been sought within those eight days, since he is said to have recommended the casts of The Louvre's 'Diana' and 'Venus' for the two niches on either side of the Hall (Nos. 1259–60). Furthermore, it is probable that, prior to Lawrence's death, the suitability of the cast of the 'Apollo Belvedere' (No. 1258) had also been considered as an alternative to the Demosthenes (on the Staircase); Lawrence himself is known to have acquired an identical cast of the 'Apollo Belvedere', which he placed in his Private Sitting Room at No. 65 Russell Square. However, it was not until March, 1830, that

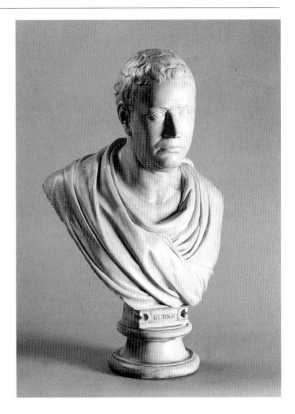

C: Plaster Bust of Sir Joshua Reynolds, P.R.A. (No 710).
Ordered by the General Committee "for the Drawing Room"
in February, 1830. This cast was supplied by Mr Sarte from a
marble by Joseph Ceracchi (1778).

D: Plaster Bust of Edmund Burke, M.P. (No 117).
Presented in 1829/30 by Burke's nephew, Thomas Haviland
Burke, who had also owned the marble bust by John Hickey
(destroyed in the Blitz, 1941, at the British Museum).

Decimus Burton was thanked for presenting it to the Club and, by then, it was in position on the Staircase.

Three other casts of figure-sculptures had been accepted (with thanks) at the previous meeting of the Committee in February, 1830, and these three were allocated a place facing Apollo on the balcony at the top of the Staircase (Nos. 1400 and 1409–10). They were a donation from the sculptor, E. H. Baily, and represented 'Poetry', 'Painting' and 'Eve at the Fountain'. Presumably, they had been previously selected by the Committee – but probably only after they had chosen the cast of the 'Apollo Belvedere' for the dominant position on the Staircase.

Two more pieces of statuary were placed in the Hall (on either side of the Staircase), bringing the total number in this central area of the Club House to eight large figures. The last two were casts of 'Milo' and 'Samson' by another contemporary sculptor, John Graham Lough (Nos. 1406 and 1413), and these two nudes can be seen in Radclyffe's engraving of 1841 published in *London Interiors* (No. 1266). Both were free-standing and mounted on large plinths, which in 1834, had

been altered in size, given "Siena Marble varnishes" and re-lettered with the inscription: "Presented by W. Sotheby, Esq., F.R.S." ; a bill for this work from G. Morant & Son, 88 New Bond Street, is dated 13th February, 1834 and totalled £17-1-6, which Decimus Burton counter-signed as correct in the following September. The involvement of the Club's architect in all matters relating to the statuary is highly significant.

When in 1833 Decimus Burton was asked to design the bookcases that the Committee had decided should be introduced into the "Great Room" (the Drawing Room), he crowned each one with a plaster cast of some portrait bust. These busts can be easily found in three near-contemporary pictorial records of the finished Drawing Room (Nos. 1263–5) and were described as "a curious collection of plaster casts – the ITALIAN IMAGES – of certain of Great Britain's great men" (*London Interiors*, 1841–4, p.166). This is an oblique reference to the London specialist workshops manned by Italian craftsmen that catered for the current demand for plaster casts of statuary.

Most significantly, two additional busts, each mounted on

a bracket on either side of the central fireplace and tall mirror, can also be clearly seen and it now seems that they are the pair of casts of the busts of Reynolds (Fig.C.) and Wren that had been ordered by the Committee on 23rd February, 1830, from a Mr. Sarte "for the Drawing Room" (Nos. 710 and 940). The Committee's intention to introduce sculptural – not pictorial – decoration into the Drawing Room is, therefore, documented from the moment the building of the Club House had been completed early in 1830.

Decimus Burton's choice of plaster busts for his bookcases in the Drawing Room in 1833 is not recorded – nor, indeed, if his selection was vetted by the Committee. However, the Club has a number of plaster casts with no known history or date of acquisition and the following seven were almost certainly among those acquired in 1833: William Harvey (No. 386), Samuel Johnson (No. 468), John Locke (No. 535), Lord Mansfield (No. 586), John Milton (No. 601), Isaac Newton (No. 628), and Shakespeare (No. 773). All seven 'Worthies' are commonly found among the portrait-busts decorating many an English library and would scarcely have justified the use of the phrase, "a curious collection". However, in addition to the busts of Reynolds and Wren, there may have been two more plaster busts in the Club at the time: David Garrick (No. 313) and Walter Scott (No. 760). Neither has a known history and whether either would have been deemed an appropriate subject for Decimus Burton's 1833 scheme is questionable. Of the two, Garrick seems the more acceptable, if only because he was a prominent eighteenth-century figure, who died in 1779 bequeathing his important library of early plays and literature to the British Museum. Sir Walter Scott, on the other hand, had become a member of the Club's first Management Committee in 1824 and had only died in 1832. Either bust could have been acquired at a later date but the archival evidence establishes that, by 1838, sixteen busts were located in the drawing room, though not more than ten would have been used to crown Burton's bookcases. Because his bookcases were considerably less tall than they are today, the busts would have had a far greater impact and the selection might, indeed, have invited comment from the members, one of whom – Thomas Haviland Burke – had presented a plaster bust of his uncle, Edmund Burke (Fig.D), even before the Club House had opened; he received the Committee's thanks on 26 January, 1830 (No.117). This plaster cast has acquired an added interest since the marble bust of Edmund Burke presented to the British Museum in 1825 by Thomas Haviland Burke was destroyed in a German air-raid on London in 1941 and, today, no photographic or descriptive record of its appearance survives. However, it is unlikely to have differed in appearance from this plaster version.

The Committee's other declared priority – initiated even before the building of the Club House – was to ensure that the Club built up a fine library of "useful works in the different provinces of Literature and Science". By 1832, the Library contained some 10,000 volumes, many donated by members but an increasing number were purchased, because as soon as the Club House opened, the Committee allocated £500 p.a. exclusively for the purchase and preservation of books and, by November, 1830, they had appointed the Club's first Librarian.

Like the libraries formed by English country gentlemen during the eighteenth century, the Library of the Athenæum quickly built up a collection of engravings. Similarly, none of these prints would have been framed or, indeed, hung on the walls. They were kept for inspection and study in solander boxes or in the special albums originally made for them. Where such libraries have survived, as at Chatsworth and Wilton, they now provide a rare sense of the rich scope that lay behind the eighteenth century concept of the library.

For the first 100 years of the Club's life, the strength of the Athenæum Collection was concentrated in the Library's rich holdings of prints. A shortage of space deprived the Library of the luxury of a Print Room, such as can be found at Chatsworth, but these engravings could always be consulted in the Library, where they were (and are) the responsibility of the Club's Librarian. As a result, they were regularly published (as they entered the Collection) in *The Catalogue of The Library of The Athenæum* (1845) and in the succeeding *Supplements and Additions*, where they were listed by subject in alphabetical order, having first been divided into two categories: 'Portraits' and 'Prints'.

Among the earliest albums of prints to be donated to the Club are *The Hundred Etchings* by Mary Dawson Turner, presented by her husband in August, 1830 (Appendix I). The most recent gift of an album of engravings came from Miss Constance Poll in 1929; it was a particularly welcome addition because it had been Decimus Burton's personal 'Portrait Album' (Appendix II). It contains a rare portrait of the Italian gem-engraver, Benedetto Pistrucci, who after the defeat of Napoleon, reached London in 1815 and, thereafter, made his home in England. His work as Chief Engraver at the Mint was outstanding and, in 1842, he was elected under Rule II (see Ward, pp.136–137).

Large albums of prints were received in 1865, 1884 and 1898 from George Richmond, R.A. and Henry Tanworth Wells, R.A. – both elected under Rule II in 1856 and 1873, respectively (see Ward, p.170 and p.242). These splendid additions have the added merit, today, of being in pristine condition. Furthermore, the 1898 donation contains an interesting group of portraits of some forty members of Grillion's, the famous dining club founded in 1812 (see *Grillion's Club, a chronicle 1812-1913*, Oxford, 1914); the two selected for illustration are the Cambridge historian, Lord

Acton, and the Viennese, Sir Joseph Edgar Boehm, R.A., who first came to England when he was 14 years old and became Sculptor-in-Ordinary to Queen Victoria and a member, elected under Rule II, in 1875 (see Ward, p.248).

Three artists, all of whom had been founding members – A.E. Chalon, R.A., James Ward, R.A., and Sir George Hayter, Portrait and History Painter to Queen Victoria – were between 1825–30 among the earliest donors of engravings; indeed, James Ward was thanked for his first gift of prints as early as 22 March, 1825, and within twenty-eight years the Club had 27 (or 29) of his engravings mounted in a giant album (see Appendix VI). Their example was matched in 1839 by the portraitist, Samuel Lane (elected 1838), and by several non-members, one of whom was William Skelton, the portrait engraver; his principal donation of engravings was made in 1831. In the interim, the Club had received gifts of prints from Sir Dominic Colnaghi and the firm of Colnaghi & Son (publishers, print-sellers and picture-dealers), one of which had been engraved just months earlier, in 1829, after the drawings of the Forum in Rome made by the architect, C.R. Cockerell, a founding member of the Club (No.1309). Undoubtedly, Colnaghi's most exceptional gift – received in March, 1828 – was the gilded relief specially commissioned from E.F. Watson to provide a worthy setting for Sir Thomas Lawrence's delicate miniature of Athena, which William Wyon had copied when making the Club Seal in 1825 (Nos.1279 and 1461–7; Pl. I (a)–(b)). Frustratingly, none of the documentation relating to the background story of this gift has yet been traced.

At the same time, the Athenæum's print collection was being enriched, on a more modest scale, by numerous individual members, like Lord Dover in 1830 (Nos.239–240) and the Bishop of Limerick in 1831–2 (No.462). Furthermore, as early as 1830 and 1831, ladies appear in the list of donors: Mrs Baillie (No.39) and Mrs Taylor (No.833). This pattern was to continue throughout the nineteenth century but, even so, there are, among the sitters, some surprising lacunae, of which the least understandable is the absence of any likeness of Anthony Trollope, a regular figure in the Club, especially in the whist room, and through his widow, the source of the marble bust of Milton (No.600).

Perhaps the most forgivable failure concerns Felix Slade (1790–1868), the creator of the Slade Professorship of the Fine Arts at the Universities of Oxford, Cambridge and London, and (at University College, London) of the Slade School of Art with its endowed scholarships, called 'The Slade Exhibitions'. Elected a member in 1825, he played a quietly active role in the Club and, under the directions of his will, enabled the Librarian (in 1869) to purchase a number of key, but expensively produced, reference works on art-historical subjects in various languages, all of which were then published in *Supplement and Additions to the Athenæum Library Catalogue* 1851-1880 under the special heading: 'The Felix Slade Collection: Books of Art' (pp.36–38). His collection of prints – just one facet of his activities as a collector – did not enter the Athenæum but was bequeathed to the British Museum, where the engravings are still valued not so much for their rarity, as for their superlative quality. However, he made one exception; in 1852, he presented the Club with a portrait of his elder brother, William (died 1858), engraved by J. Wallis in 1807 (No.782), but with characteristic modesty, none of himself. Indeed, when publishing my study of this enlightened – but rather elusive – early protagonist of Art education, the only portrait of Felix Slade I could find was the chalk and water-colour drawing done by Margaret Carpenter in 1851 and presented by her son, William, to the British Museum twenty-three years later (see *The Glass Circle Journal*, Vol.8 (1996), pp.70–87, Fig.2). Sadly, the Club may have to be content with a photograph in the case of Slade, but the filling of other gaps could be more rewarding.

In producing this book 'against the clock' to meet the deadline, every avenue could not be explored, but, undoubtedly, some donations to the Collection are now missing. Because the prints were kept in the Library, often in albums, fewer losses are recorded but, more recently, framed works hung in rooms and corridors have been more vulnerable, as in the case of the pen and wash drawing of 'The Flagellation', attributed to Sebastiano Ricci, which was given in 1941 by the Reverend Francis Palgrave. It had been presented to Francis Palgrave by the Rt. Hon. W.E. Gladstone in 1867, with an autograph inscription by the latter.

Certainly, by the turn of the century, there was a marked change in the Club's approach: graphic works were being acquired with the intention of displaying them on the walls. They were often inventoried soon after acquisition as "framed and glazed", as in the case of the eight prints of landscapes and narrative scenes given in 1901 by the Bavarian-born artist, Sir Hubert von Herkomer, R.A., who had been elected under Rule II in 1889 (see Ward, pp.297–8) and, from 1885–94, had been Slade Professor of the Fine Arts at Oxford.

This fundamental change of approach to the display of pictorial art in the Club House applied equally to drawings, water-colours and oil-paintings. Thus, as early as 1905, Percy Fitzgerald presented a framed drawing of Rudyard Kipling – a member from 1897–1936 – and it was hung in the Billiard Room (No.494). However, the real test must have come in 1911, when for the first time, a large canvas (more than 4 ft. × 3 ft.), complete with its original gilt frame, was being offered as a gift by a member. Furthermore, it was no ordinary portrait in oils; it was the picture of Frederick the Great that had been lent to Thomas Carlyle – at his request – while he was deeply engaged in writing his six-volumed *History of*

Friedrich II of Prussia, called Frederick the Great (No.300). He regarded Francke's portrayal of the King to be the most credible and, indeed, arranged for an engraved version (dated 1860) to be the Frontispiece of Volume V. As Carlyle had been elected a member, under Rule II, in 1853, it is not surprising that the Committee decided to accept this painting from The Hon. William Warren Vernon. It now hangs in the Front Hall – to the surprise of many a visitor – whilst, in the Library, the related correspondence from Carlyle is also preserved.

Within two years of that decision, the first oil-painting portraying a member of the Club entered the Collection. It was given by the widow and family of the late Professor John Hopkinson (1849–98), whose death, at 49, had been caused by a terrible Alpine accident (No.428).

Shortly afterwards, a purely decorative class of oil-painting was accepted by the Club: two landscapes given by Sir Squire Bancroft in 1916. Both depict popular eighteenth century riverside views, one at Chelsea and the other at Greenwich, but neither has any special relevance for the Club (Nos.1123–4). In the following year, there was another 'first': a large water-colour, 'The Lily Columns, St. Mark's, Venice', was presented by the artist, Reginald Barratt, who had been a member since 1908 (No.1230, Pl. XXIX). It is now displayed, with other water-colours, in the Ladies' Annexe, where the conditions are particularly favourable for their preservation.

Further changes came about in the 1920's, partly as a result of various gifts of pictures generated by the celebration of the Club's centenary in 1924; to quote from the printed Annual Report (May, 1925): "In view of the above [gifts of pictures] and the important bequest of Col. F.A. Lucas [died 1918], which included valuable collections of etchings by Meryon and Zeeman, the Committee took the occasion to request Sir Frank Dicksee, P.R.A., Mr. W.W. Ouless, R.A. and Mr. Cecil Hunt, H.R.W.S. to undertake, in addition to the hanging of the newly acquired pictures, a general re-arrangement by which all might be seen to the best advantage…" From the meetings of this small group was to emerge in 1929, the formally constituted 'Arts Sub-Committee' composed of the President of the Royal Academy (ex-officio) and four members who were artists: Sir Reginald Blomfield, R.A. (No. 86), Principal William Rothenstein (No. 733), Cecil A. Hunt, Esq., R.W.S. (Nos.437-8) and Mervyn O'Gorman, Esq., C.B. (Nos.646-7). They were "to advise in all matters concerning the artistic treasures of the Club, with special reference to the acquisition of portraits and prints of distinguished members, the Club's collection of which is very inadequate".

Apart from this radical development, the General Committee also took (in the summer of 1924) a decisive step in the direction of creating a permanent 'art exhibit' (to use a current American term) which members could show to guests. The Committee decided to authorise expenditure on

a specially designed revolving "swing-frame" (not unlike the one in the Ashmolean Museum) to house and, simultaneously, display the *pièce de résistance* of the Lucas Bequest: the exceptional collection of etchings by Charles Meryon and Reynier Nooms, called Zeeman. Before the end of the year, its installation was completed and members could, with a minimum of manual effort, look at as many as some 52 prints in 24 frames without jeopardising the condition of these rare and, in some cases, extremely valuable etchings (see Ward, 1926, p.88, and Cowell, 1975, p.83, for references to the "superb" and "splendid" examples of Meryon's work).

Charles Meryon, probably one of the greatest etchers of modern times, was born in Paris in 1821; his father was English but Charles worked mostly in Paris and died a comparatively young man in the asylum at Charenton in 1868. His works failed to achieve recognition during his lifetime and, in a fit of despair, he destroyed his copper plates; consequently, early impressions of almost all his etchings are very rare and, now, their quality is often compared with those of Rembrandt. Most remarkably, Colonel Lucas had acquired a set of eight etchings of Paris and its environs by a contemporary of Rembrandt, the Amsterdam-born artist, Zeeman, who died there in 1676. These Zeeman etchings had been a source of inspiration for Meryon and, in the Lucas Bequest, making comparisons between the mid-seventeenth century originals and the talented versions done by Meryon some 200 years later was a much-cherished experience for many a member and his guests. After World War II, the collection of etchings was returned to the revolving 'swing-frame' stand to be enjoyed by a new generation of members until, years later, the mechanism of the stand broke down. The withdrawal of the collection from exhibition was to prove more than a temporary measure; by the summer of 1984, all the Meryon etchings had been sold by the Committee, without reference to the members. However, the eight Zeeman etchings are still in the Collection (Nos.1187–94) and one of the signed views, 'The Château de Conflans' (Fig.E.) is reproduced to illustrate the accomplished technique of this Dutch artist that had attracted the discerning eye of Charles Meryon. Colonel Lucas, who was one of the Club's most generous benefactors in the field of etchings and engravings, had been elected a member in 1883 and, regrettably, the only likeness of Colonel Lucas in the Club is a photograph (No.548).

An entirely new dimension was added to The Athenæum Collection by the artists who were members during the Inter-War period. They were clearly encouraged by the Club's new policy, even if it was evident that wall space was strictly limited and always in competition with the Library's need for more book-shelves. Their donations, mainly of drawings and water-colours, but also some etchings, cartoons and, even preliminary sketches, have helped to trans-

E. *Château de Conflans, near Paris, by Zeeman, c. 1650 (No.1188).*
One of eight Zeeman etchings in the Lucas bequest (1918), which were a source of inspiration for Charles Meryon (1821-68), one of the finest etchers of modern times, but whose work is no longer represented in the Collection.

form the balance of the Collection. It now includes original works of such artists as Mervyn O'Gorman, D.S. MacColl (and of his friends, Philip Wilson Steer and Henry Tonks), Sir William Rothenstein, Sir Max Beerbohm, A.M. Hind, Charles March Gere, Randolph Schwabe and Francis Dodd. Of these painters, Philip Wilson Steer was a leading exponent of Impressionism in England; furthermore, he taught at The Slade, where Henry Tonks – one of the School's outstanding Professors – shared his enthusiasm. Together with D.S. MacColl (at the Tate Gallery), they became the three most influential figures in the development of English painting and art criticism and are to be found in Sir William Orpen's famous large oil-painting, 'Homage to Manet' (Fig F.), which he finished in 1909 (5 ft. 4 in. x 4 ft. 3 in.). Orpen, who was elected under Rule II in 1920, sold this canvas to the Manchester City Art Gallery within a year of completing it and it now hangs (on loan) in The Hugh Lane Municipal Art Gallery, Dublin, because it depicts a scene in Sir Hugh Lane's London home (in South Bolton Gardens) after Lane had bought Manet's 'Portrait of Eva Gonzales' in Paris. Portrayed beneath the Manet, from left to right, are George Moore (a powerful advocate of contemporary French painting),

Wilson Steer, D.S. MacColl, W.R. Sickert, Sir Hugh Lane and Henry Tonks (Fig.G.); however, it was Orpen himself who, in 1904, first led Lane to admire this work of Manet and to become an ardent collector of Impressionist paintings. In this painting, therefore, Orpen seeks to document an early significant stage in the story of English appreciation of the 'new' French phenomenon of Impressionism. The picture also has a certain relevance for the post-World War II saga of the much disputed Lane Bequest – now happily resolved – and of such publicity-seeking stunts as the theft from The Tate Gallery of one of the Lane pictures (Morisot's *Jour d'été*) – a news story that was then so wittily treated in *Punch* (25 April, 1956) by Norman Mansbridge, who later generously donated the original drawing to the Club (No.1004).

In the Club's Collection, Sir William Orpen figures in a humorous drawing that he himself had preserved (No.1028) and which in 1961, Mrs. Bodkin, the widow of the well-known Professor of Fine Arts at Birmingham University, Thomas Bodkin, gave – along with several other important drawings – to the Club in memory of her husband.

During this period, several benefactors contributed substantially, with works of high quality and interest. Two con-

F. *'Homage to Manet' by Sir William Orpen, 1909*
The scene is an historic gathering in Sir Hugh Lane's London home soon after he had purchased Manet's 'Portrait of Eva Gonzales';
those present were to become the most influential figures in London to advance the appreciation of 'new' French Impressionism in English circles.

Lent to the Hugh Lane Municipal Art Gallery, Dublin,
by the Manchester City Art Gallery, which had bought this large oil painting from the artist in 1910.
© Manchester City Art Galleries

G. 'Nymphs surprised' by Henry Tonks, 1934 (No. 1185).
The artist, portrayed on the extreme right of Orpen's 'Homage to Manet', went on to become one of
The Slade's most outstanding Professors. This late work of Tonks is the sole Impressionist oil painting
in the Collection. Through the generosity of his friend, D.S.MacColl (also portrayed by Orpen
beneath the Manet), the Collection now has three of Tonks's humorous watercolours (Pl.XI(b) and
Nos 1031 and 1041).

noisseurs, Marion Spielmann, elected in 1916 (Nos.801-802, Pl. VI (b)), and Arthur Jaffé, elected in 1918 (No.461), were both finding many desiderata and their gifts span nearly two decades. In 1938, there was received a remarkable gift of engraved portraits from a descendant of Joseph Jekyll, Barbara, Lady Freyberg (*neé* Jekyll). These prints were particularly welcome because it was in Joseph Jekyll's London home that preliminary meetings were held before the Club was formally launched in 1824.

From the first years of World War II, the Club has two large panels (made to protect the large mirrors in the Drawing Room), each decorated with an enlarged version of one of the mythological scenes painted on two Greek Vases. The work was executed by Lawrence Scarfe, a student from the Royal College of Art, under the supervision of the Art Panel but the panels are now in need of conservation. After the war, the Art Panel gradually met less frequently and, eventually, ceased to function. Nevertheless, artists like

Andrew Freeth and John Ward kept alive the inter-war tradition, whilst members and their families continued to make significant additions to the Collection. Perhaps the most recent gift is also one of the most impressive modern portraits : the charcoal drawing by Paul Benney, dated 1994, of Sir Isaiah Berlin (No 72). It is one of a number of studies made for the portrait group, "*The Supreme Court of Israel*", and was generously presented to the Collection by Lady Berlin in 1999.

The year 2000 has seen the Club re-introduce the Art Panel (with full Committee status) and already it has put in train the cleaning and restoration of Sir Thomas Lawrence's portrait of George IV prior to its return to the Athenæum, although not to its rightful position in the South Library. Such changes bode well for the future of the Collection, and the publication of this book will not only inform but will give greater protection to the contents – and, with foresight, a degree of permanency.

RICHARD WALKER

THE CATALOGUE

ABBREVIATIONS

Ath Ports	see Bibliography
BM	British Museum
Eng	see Bibliography
exh	exhibited
HL	half-length
HS	head and shoulders
NPG	National Portrait Gallery
O'D	see Bibliography
Ports	see Bibliography
repr	reproduced
RA	Royal Academy, Royal Academician
Richmond Coll.	see Bibliography
TQL	three-quarter-length
Wells-Grillion	see Bibliography
WL	whole-length

I PORTRAITURE

I(a) PORTRAITS

An 'original member' means one of the committee of fourteen which met on 16 February 1824; a 'founding member' indicates one of the five hundred candidates proposed and admitted later in the year.

SIR FREDERICK AUGUSTUS ABEL, Bt. FRS

1827–1902, chemist in the War Department; elected 1872 under Rule II.

By Alan Swinton, group photograph at Jesmond Dene, see **Groups** No. 958.

A different photograph, c. 1890, repr. Ward 1926, p. 232.

THE DUCHESS OF ABERCORN

1812–1905, Louisa Russell, daughter of the Duke of Bedford.

1   *By F C Lewis*, stipple engraving, 1833 (Ports I. 22, O'D 2), entitled 'Cottage Industry', after the picture by Landseer at Woburn Abbey.

LORD ABERDARE, GCB, FRS

1815–95, Henry Bruce, Home Secretary elected to the Club in 1853.

2   *By C. Holl, 1879,* stipple vignette, proof before letters (Wells-Grillion 11; O'D 2), from a drawing by H.T. Wells for Grillion's Club.
Presented by H.T. Wells, 1898.

THE EARL OF ABERDEEN, KG, KT, PSA

1784–1860, George Hamilton Gordon, 4th Earl of Aberdeen, Prime Minister; present at the Somerset House meeting, 16 Feb. 1824, and one of the first trustees of the Club.

3   *By S. Cousins, 1831,* mezzotint (Ath. Fol. I.17) after Lawrence's portrait commissioned by Sir Robert Peel, now in the Viscount Cowdray collection (Garlick 3).

4   *By E. Desmaisons,* lithograph published 1843.
Presented by Arthur Jaffé, 1931.

3

THE EARL OF ABERGAVENNY, KT

1755–1843, Henry Nevill, 2nd Earl, elected to the Club in 1844.

5   *By J. Thomson*, stipple engraving, private plate (Ports II. 9), after a miniature by A. Tidey.
Presented by Edward Walpole, 1838.

SIR WILLIAM DE WIVELESLIE ABNEY, KCB, FRS

1843–1920, photographic chemist, elected 1882 under Rule II.

By Alan Swinton, group photograph at Jesmond Dene , see **Groups** No 958.

RIGHT REV CHARLES JOHN ABRAHAM

1814–1903, Bishop of Wellington, New Zealand.

6 *By F. Holl*, stipple engraving in crayon manner, artists' names only (Richmond Coll. II. 28), after a drawing by George Richmond.
Presented by George Richmond, 1865.

VISCOUNT ACHESON, *see* GOSFORD, No. 338

SIR THOMAS DYKE ACLAND, Bt. MP

1787–1871, 10th baronet, politician, philanthropist; elected to the Club in 1831.

7 *By F. Holl*, stipple engraving in crayon manner, proof before letters (Richmond Coll. I. 19), after a drawing by George Richmond.
Presented by George Richmond, 1865.

8

LORD ACTON, KCVO

1834–1902, Regius Professor of Modern History, Cambridge; elected to the Club in 1860.

8 *By C. Holl, 1876*, stipple engraving, proof before letters (Wells-Grillion 8), from a drawing by H.T. Wells for Grillion's Club.
Presented by H.T. Wells, 1898.

WILLIAM DACRES ADAMS

1775–1862, secretary to William Pitt; elected to the Club in 1827.

9 *By W. Drummond, c.1836*, lithograph after Lawrence *c.1810*–15 (Garlick 12), published as *Athenaeum Portraits* no. 32.

ADOLPHUS FREDERICK

1774–1850, Duke of Cambridge, 7th s. of George III.

10 *By W. Skelton, 1808*, line engraving (Ports I. 8; O'D 1)
Presented by W. Skelton, 1831.

LORD ADRIAN, OM, PRS

1889–1977, Master of Trinity College, Cambridge, Nobel Prize (medicine) 1932; elected to the Club in 1932.

11 *After A R Middleton Todd*, photograph in the Nobel Prize book of an oil, 1955, in the Royal Society.

AGAR, *see* NORMANTON, No. 637

AGAR-ELLIS, *see* DOVER, Nos. 238–40

SIR WHITELAW AINSLIE

1767–1837, surgeon in the East India Company; elected to the Club in 1825.

12 By unknown artist, engraving.

ALBERT, PRINCE CONSORT

1819–61, m. Queen Victoria 1840

13 *By Louis Aristide, 1848*, line engraving (O'D 44), after the oil by Winterhalter in the Royal Collection, Windsor Castle (Millar 1992, no. 810).

ALBERT, KING OF THE BELGIANS

1875–1934, famous for his heroic resistance to the German invasion of 1914.

14 *By Georges Montinez*, line and stipple engraving from a photograph by Keturah Collins, London (Ports I. 15 and II. 11, 17).

JAMES ALDERSON, MD, *see* Appendix I, No. 1

ALEXANDER, GRAND DUKE OF RUSSIA

1818–81, succeeded his father in 1855 as Tsar Alexander II

15   *By Henry Cousins, 1841,* mezzotint after an oil by A.E. Chalon, painted in London in 1839.
Presented by A E Chalon, 1850.

HENRY ALEXANDER

Elected to the Club in 1830.

16   *By W. Drummond, 1836,* lithograph after Eddis, published as *Athenaeum Portraits* no.21.

QUEEN ALEXANDRA

1844–1925, Princess of Denmark and Queen of Edward VII.

17   *By Charles Laguillermie,* etching after an oil of 1894 by Sir Luke Fildes at Sandringham.

LORD ALVERSTONE, GCMG

1842–1915, Richard Everard Webster, created 1st Viscount Alverstone in 1913, Lord Chief Justice of England 1900–13; elected to the Club in 1883.

18   *By G.J. Stodart, 1888,* stipple vignette, proof before letters (Wells-Grillion 24), from a drawing by H.T. Wells for Grillion's Club.
Presented by H.T. Wells, 1898.

19   *After A. S. Cope, RA,* autogravure published by the Autotype Company, London, with facsimiles of signatures.

EARL AMHERST, GCH

1773–1857, William Pitt Amherst, Governor General of India.

20   *By C. Turner, 1824,* mezzotint (Ath. Fol. I. 8; O'D 2) after the oil by Lawrence painted for the British Factory in Canton, now in Toledo Museum of Art, Ohio (Garlick 24b).
Presented by the publisher, Colnaghi & Co, 1830.

THOMAS AMYOT, FSA

1775–1850, antiquary and a founding member of the Club.

21   *By W. Drummond, 1836,* lithograph after Wageman, published as *Athenaeum Portraits* no.42, reproduced Ward 1926, p. 102.

HENRY ANDREWS

1744–1820, astronomical calculator to the Board of Longitude and author of Moore's Almanack.

22   *By T. Blood,* stipple engraving, private plate (Ports Q.I.23) after a portrait by J. Watson.
Presented by Robert Cole, 1850.

THE MARQUESS OF ANGLESEY, KG, GCB

1768–1864, Field Marshal, who 'lost a leg at Waterloo'.

By Mrs Dawson Turner after Chantrey, 1819, see Appendix I, no. 2.

23   *By C. Turner, 1828,* mezzotint (Ath. Fol. I.11; O'D 8), after the oil by Lawrence at Plas Newydd (Garlick 33).
Presented by the publisher, Colnaghi & Co, 1830.

SIR EDWARD VICTOR APPLETON, FRS

1892–1965, Nobel prize (physics) 1947; elected to the Club in 1933.

24   *Anon.* photograph in the Nobel Prize book, 1947.

25   *After Sir William Hutchison,* 1957, photograph in Ath. Ports. Red 61.

ROLLO APPLEYARD, OBE

1867–1943, consulting engineer, elected to the Club in 1920.

26   *Photograph,* c.1920, in Ath. Ports. Red 52.

ARMSTEAD, ARMITAGE AND GORHAM, *see* Groups No. 957

MATTHEW ARNOLD

1822–88, poet and Professor of Poetry at Oxford; elected to the Club in 1856 and used to sit for hours in the South Library, frequently composing entries for the Question Book. 'This Athenaeum is a place at which I enjoy something resembling beatitude' (Murray op. cit. p. 152).

27   *By Henry Weigall* [Pl. IV (a)]

Canvas, 66 × 51 cm (26 × 20 in) HS to right, light grey coat, black waistcoat, dark green vest, black hair and side-whiskers, blue eyes.

Probably commissioned by James Knowles, editor of *The Nineteenth Century,* who wished to add Arnold to his collection of portraits of contributors. 'There will be as many portraits of me as of Rubens's wife', said Arnold in a letter to his daughter Lucy, 1878 (Murray, p. 328).

Condition: cleaned by William Drown, 1958.

Exhibition: Wordsworth Trust, Grasmere 1988/9.

Literature: Nicholas Murray, *Life of Matthew Arnold* (1996).
Presented by J.W. Weigall Esq. 1926.

HUGH OAKELEY ARNOLD-FORSTER, MP

1855–1909, Secretary of State for War; elected to the Club in 1903.

28 *By Harris Brown, 1907*
Canvas, 110 × 84.5 (43¼ × 33¼ in), signed and dated top left: *H. Harris Brown 1907.* TQL seated facing, black suit, left hand on dispatch-box; blue eyes, dark hair, light brown moustache.

Presented by J.A. Arnold-Forster, OBE, 1952.

LORD ASHBOURNE, PC

1837–1913, Edward Gibson, Lord Chancellor of Ireland; elected to the Club in 1885.

29 *By J. Brown, 1885*, stipple vignette, artists' names only (Wells-Grillion 19; O'D 1), from a drawing by H.T. Wells for Grillion's Club.
Presented by H.T. Wells, 1898.

LORD ASHBURTON (1731–83), WITH LORD SHELBURNE (1737–1805) AND COLONEL ISAAC BARRÉ (1726–1802)

30 *By James Ward, 1788–9*, mezzotint (O'D 1), after the oil by Reynolds painted for Francis Baring in 1787 and hanging for many years in Baring's Bank in the City (Waterhouse 1941, p. 80).
Presented by Barbara (Lady) Freyberg, 1938.

RIGHT HON. ANTHONY EVELYN ASHLEY, PC

1836–1907, land-owner, elected to the Club in 1879.

31 *After H. T. Wells, 1896*, autotype facsimile (Wells-Grillion 34) of a drawing with signature and artist's monogram.
Presented by H.T. Wells, 1898.

HERBERT ASQUITH, 1852–1928, Prime Minister, *see* OXFORD AND ASQUITH, **Satires No. 1041**

HIS ROYAL HIGHNESS PRINCE AUGUSTUS FREDERICK
DUKE OF SUSSEX, EARL OF INVERNESS & BARON OF ARKLOW, K.G.
GRAND MASTER OF THE UNITED ANCIENT
FREE & ACCEPTED MASONS OF ENGLAND,
COLONEL OF THE LOYAL NORTH BRITONS, &c.&c.&c.&c.

34

FRANCIS WILLIAM ASTON, FRS

1877–1945, Nobel Prize (chemistry) 1922; elected to the Club in 1925.

32 *Anon.* photograph in Nobel Prize book, 1922.

AUBREY, JOHN, antiquary, *see* **Appendix I no. 3**

AUGUSTUS

63 B.C.–14 A.D., succeeded his uncle as Caesar Octavius in 45 B.C and received the title of Augustus in 27 B.C He was one of the great creative rulers of the Western world.

33 *By Luigi Clerici, 1881*
Marble bust 54 cm (21½ in) high, incised: *L. Clerici / Roma /*

1881; a nineteenth-century copy of the Roman bust in the Vatican showing Caesar Augustus as a young man.

Literature: O. Brendel, *Ikonographie des Kaisers Augustus* (1931), p 374; Campos & Calvesi, *Treasures of the Vatican* (1962) p.2, repr. a whole length late 1st cent. BC statue of Augustus in the Chiaramonti Museum.
Presented by Humphry Rivers Pollack, 1936.

AUGUSTUS FREDERICK, DUKE OF SUSSEX

1773–1843, 4th son of George III, a founding member of the Club.

34 *By W. Skelton, 1806,* line engraving (Ports I.7; O'D 3), in Highland dress, after an oil by Beechey commissioned by the Freemasons.
Presented by William Skelton, 1831.

35 *By W. Skelton, 1824,* line engr. (O'D 15), after the oil by J. Lonsdale, exh RA 1823 and now at Trinity College, Cambridge.
Presented by Arthur Jaffé, 1932.

LORD AVEBURY, PC, FRS

1834–1913, banker, scientist and inventor of the bank holiday; elected to the Club in 1857.

36 *After H.T. Wells, 1896,* autotype facsimile (Wells-Grillion 37) with signature and artist's monogram, from a drawing for Grillion's Club.
Presented by H.T. Wells, 1898.

SIR GEORGE BACK, FRS

1796–1878, Admiral and Arctic explorer; elected 1836 under Rule II.

37 *By W. Drummond, c.1837,* lithograph after Eddis, published as *Athenaeum Portraits* no.50.

LORD BADEN-POWELL, OM

1857–1941, Robert Baden-Powell, founder of Boy Scouts and Girl Guides.

By Alan Swinton, group photograph at Jesmond Dene, see Groups No. 958.

JOHN CANN BAILEY

1864–1931, critic and essayist; elected to the Club in 1902.

38 *By Lafayette,* photograph (Ath. Ports. Red 41).

39

MATTHEW BAILLIE, MD, FRS

1761–1823, morbid anatomist and physician extraordinary to George III.

39 *By J. Bromley,* engraving (Ports M. I.4, but not a member), after a bust by Nollekens in the Royal College of Surgeons, London.
Presented by Mrs Baillie, 1830.

40 *By C. Turner, 1809,* mezzotint (O'D 1), after an oil by Hoppner.
Presented by Mr Hunter Baillie, 1830.

FRANCIS BAILY, FRS

1774–1844, four times President of the Royal Astronomical Society; a founding member of the Club.

41 *By T. Lupton, 1839,* mezzotint (Ath. Fol. I.28; O'D 1), after the oil by T. Phillips in the Royal Astronomical Society.
Presented by the Revd Richard Sheepshanks, 1846; another copy was presented by A.G. Horton Smith in memory of his father, L.G.H. Horton Smith, 1954.

GEORGE BAKER

1781–1851, historian of Northamptonshire.

42   *By Miss Turner,* lithograph vignette (Ports Q.I.20; O'D 11) after a drawing by N.G. Branwhite, 1838.

SIR HERBERT BAKER, KCIE, FRIBA

1862–1946, architect; elected to the Club in 1919 under Rule II.

43   *After Sir W. Rothenstein,* litho-facsimile of a drawing of 1925 (R698), in the National Portrait Gallery. Presented by Sir William Rothenstein.

SIR SAMUEL WHITE BAKER

1821–93, explorer, traveller and sportsman; elected in 1866 under Rule II.

44   *By Maull & Co,* signed photograph (Ports M. III. 40).

EARL BALDWIN, KG, FRS

1867–1947, Stanley Baldwin, three times Prime Minister between 1923 and 1927; elected in 1913 and a Club trustee 1930–47.

By Sir Max Beerbohm 1924, see **Satires,** No. 1000.

45   *After Sir W. Rothenstein, 1928,* litho-facsimile of a draw-ing (in NPG) made in the cabinet room, 10 Downing Street, as one of the pall bearers at Thomas Hardy's funeral in Westminster Abbey, 1928 (see *Men and Memories* III (1939), p.100).

46   *By Francis Dodd, 1942* [Pl. IX (a)]

Chalk and watercolour on buff paper, 47 × 32.5 cm (18½ × 12¾ in),HS to left, signed under mount: *Francis Dodd,* and inscribed: *Lord Baldwin of Bewdley, June 1942.* A WL chalk ver-sion is in the NPG and a finished oil in Rhodes House, Oxford. None of these portraits is mentioned in Middlemas & Barnes, *Life of Baldwin* (1969).

Presented by the artist, 1942.

EARL OF BALFOUR, KG, OM

1848–1930, Arthur James Balfour, created 1st Earl 1922 Prime Minister 1902–5; elected to the Club in 1886.

47   *After Sir W. Rothenstein,* litho-facsimile of a drawing (R674), made in 1923 for his sister, Alice Balfour (M&M III (1939), p.15).
Presented by the artist in 1937.

48   *After Philip de Laszlo, 1924.* Photograph of a portrait exh

Paris Salon 1924, now at Trinity College Cambridge.

SIR CHARLES BALLANCE, KCMG

1856–1936, surgeon; elected to the Club in 1903.

49   *After W.W. Ouless, 1919,* photograph (Ath. Ports. Red 53) of a presentation portrait in Royal College of Surgeons, London.

SIR SQUIRE BANCROFT

1841–1926, actor manager; elected to the Club in 1909. For the Bancroft Cup see **Memorabilia** No. 1470 where both portrait and cup are illustrated.

50   *By Walter William Ouless, 1881*

Oil on canvas fixed to board, 70 × 60 cm (27½ × 23½), HL profile to left, aged 40, brown coat, white winged collar, red tie. Brown eyes, dark greying hair, brown (dyed) moustache), monocle in right eye.

Exhibition: RA 1884 (190); London Guildhall, 1894 (34) lent by the sitter.

Engraving: photogravure by Goupil & Co. Paris, 1888. Presented by George Pleydel Bancroft, 1938.

SIR JOSEPH BANKS, PRS, *see* **Appendix I, nos. 5 and 6**

CHARLES JOHN BARING (1730–1836), with SIR FRANCIS BARING, MP (1740–1810) and CHARLES WALL (1756–1815), bankers

51   *By James Ward, 1806,* mezzotint (O'D 1), after the oil by Lawrence exh RA 1807, now in a private collection (Garlick 62).
Presented by Barbara (Lady) Freyberg, 1930.

THE HON. MAURICE BARING, OBE

1874–1945, Wing-Commander, poet and man of letters; elected in 1933 under Rule II.

52   *After Sir W. Rothenstein,* litho-facsimile of a drawing, 1925 (R736).
Presented by the artist 1937.

THOMAS BARING, MP

1799–1873, banker; elected to the Club in 1835.

53   *By W. Holl,* stipple vignette (Eng. A.I.39; O'D 1), after a

drawing by G. Richmond for Grillion's Club.
Presented by W.M. Powell, 1910.

SIR THOMAS BARLOW, Bt. KCVO, FRS

1845–1945, physician at University College Hospital, Holme Professor of Clinical Medicine, and centenarian. He was physician extraordinary to Queen Victoria, Edward VII and George V. Elected under Rule II in 1904.

54 *By Catherine Dodgson, 1936*
Red chalk drawing on buff paper, 38.5 × 28.5 cm (15¼ × 11¼ in), signed and dated (under mount): *C. Dodgson 1936.*

Exhibition: RA 1936 (1236)
Presented by the sitter's granddaughter, Mrs Carl Winter, 1969.

54

SIR ALAN BARLOW, Bt. GCB

1881–1968, eldest son of Sir Thomas Barlow above; principal private secretary to the Prime Minister, Ramsay Macdonald; He married Nora, a granddaughter of Charles Darwin. He was elected to the Club in 1915, chairman 1951–55, Trustee 1946–68 and donor of the

Isnik pottery, **Oriental** Nos 1417–24 where both portrait and ceramics are illustrated and discussed in relation to his role as a distinguished collector.

55 *By Peter Garrard, 1971*
Pencil on light cream paper, 46.5 × 35.3 cm (18¼ × 13⅞ in), inset 34 × 30 cm (13¼ × 11¼ in), signed and dated: *PJG 1971,* probably from a photograph by Walter Stoneman.

Presented by his sister, Helen Barlow, 1971.

COLONEL ISAAC BARRÉ PC

1726–1802, MP for Chipping Wycombe and Calne

56 *By J. Holl,* line engraving 1787 (O'D 2), after the oil by G. Stuart, 1785, in Brooklyn Museum, NY (L. Park *Gilbert Stuart* (1926) I, p.131). *and see* **Ashburton**, No. 30.
Presented by Barbara (Lady) Freyberg, 1938, in memory of her grandfather, Joseph Jekyll.

SIR JOHN BARROW, Bt

1764–1848, Secretary of the Admiralty; elected in 1825.

57 *By G.T. Payne,* stipple engraving, proof before letters (Ports II. 34), after an oil attributed to Jackson in the NPG.

SIR JOHN WOLFE-BARRY (1836–1918), see **Satires** No.1014

SIR DUNBAR PLUNKET BARTON, PC

1853–1937, Judge of the High Court of Justice, Ireland; elected in 1900 under Rule II.

58 Photograph, [TQL seated to left, right hand on knee].

ELIZABETH JACOBS BAS

59 *By Charles Waltner,* etching after Rembrandt's portrait, c.1642, in the Rijksmuseum, Amsterdam (KK 1909, p.262; Beraldi XII. 120).
Lucas bequest 1918.

EDMUND POLLEXFEN BASTARD OF KITLEY

1784–1838, MP for Devonshire.

60 *By C. Turner, 1819,* mezzotint (Ath. Fol. I 27; O'D 1), after George Jones.

WILLIAM BATESON, FRS

1861–1926, biologist and 'founder of genetics', a word he coined; elected to the Club in 1910.

61 *After Sir W. Rothenstein, 1925*, litho-facsimile of a drawing (R717). An earlier version, 1917, is in the National Portrait Gallery.
Presented by the artist, 1937.

SALISBURY BAXENDALE

1827–1907, civil engineer; elected to the Club in 1858.

62 *Photograph* in Ath. Ports. Red 9.

SIR ROBERT BAYNE-POWELL, CB

1910–95, Senior Registrar at the High Court of Justice; elected to the Club in 1936 and a trustee from 1986.

63 *By Paddy Curzon-Price, 1986*

Oil on art board, 40.5 × 30.5 cm (16 × 12 in) inset 39 × 29 cm, signed with monogram in red: *CP*, and inscribed on the back: *Paddy Curzon-Price / Robert Bayne-Powell at the Athenaeum, December 1986.*

Presented by the sitter.

EARL OF BEACONSFIELD, KG

1804–81, Benjamin Disraeli, Prime Minister and novelist; elected to the Club in 1866 under Rule II.

64

64 **By G. Pilotell,** drypoint vignette on India paper 35 × 29.5 cm (14 × 11½ in), signed *Pilotell.*
Exhibition: RA 1876 (1115).

SIR GEORGE BEAUMONT, Bt

1753–1827, artist, collector, benefactor of the National Gallery, and present at the Somerset House meeting, 16 Feb 1824.

65 *By J.S. Agar, 1812*, stipple engraving (O'D 2), after the oil by Hoppner 1803, in the National Gallery (Egerton 1998, p.370–5).

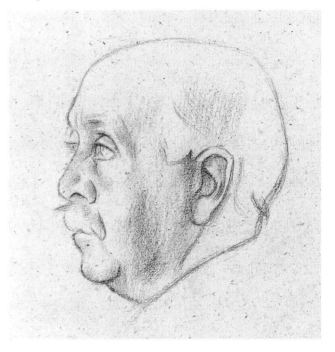

66

SIR MAX BEERBOHM

1872–1956, dramatic critic, broadcaster, cartoonist and author of *Zuleika Dobson* (1911), *Seven Men* (1919), etc. He was elected in 1929 under Rule II.

66 *By Sir William Rothenstein, 1928*

Pencil on coarse grey paper, 27 × 27 cm (10⅝ × 10⅝ in) inset 22 × 20 cm, head only profile to left, uninscribed but has a red chalk scribble on the back. A more finished version, signed and dated 1928, is in the National Portrait Gallery.

Max and Will had been friends since they first met in 1893. Will's first drawing of Max appeared in *Oxford Characters* (1893–96), his last of 1932 is in the Ashmolean Museum. His three volumes of recollection, *Men and Memories*, mention Max throughout, and their letters were edited and published by Mary Lago in 1990 (see Bibliography).

Literature: Men & Memories III (1939) p.50 mentions the NPG version; Lago 1991, pp.129–30.
Bought by the Club from the artist's family, 1993.

67 *After W. Rothenstein, 1928*, litho facsimile of No. 66.

CANON G.C. BELL

c.1845–1913, Master of Marlborough College 1876–1903; elected to the Club in 1881.

68 *By H.W.B. Davis, 1880*

Bronzed plaster medallion, 48 × 41 cm (19 × 16 in), incised: *H.W.B.D.1880.*

Presented by the sculptor's son, H.J. Banks-Davis.

PROFESSOR J.F. BELL, *see* **Satires**, No. 1017

JOHN BELL, KC

1764–1836, senior wrangler, barrister; a founding member of the Club.

69 *By S. Cousins, 1832*, mezzotint (Ports M.I.9; O'D 1) after an oil by T. Stewardson.

THOMAS BELL,

1785–1860, antiquary, elected in 1850 under Rule II.

70 *By Maull & Polyblank, 1860*, signed photograph (Ports M.III.44).

JOHN BENNETT (d.1833), House Steward of the ATHENAEUM, *see* **Memorabilia**, No. 1449–50

REV MR BENNETT

71 *By F. Holl, 1845–50*, stipple engraving in crayon manner, proof before letters (Richmond Coll. II. 26), after a drawing by George Richmond.
Presented by George Richmond, 1865.

MOST REV EDWARD WHITE BENSON

1829–96, Archbishop of Canterbury; elected in 1877.

72 *By C.W. Sherborne, 1890*, etching (Wells-Grillion 28;

O'D 2), from a drawing by H.T. Wells for Grillion's Club.
Presented by H.T. Wells, 1898.

SIR HENRY BENTINCK, KCB

1796–1878, General, Coldstream Guards.

73 *By C.A. Waltner, c.1845–50*, etching, proof before letters, artists' names in pencil (Richmond Coll V. 16) from a drawing by G. Richmond.
Presented by George Richmond, 1865.

REV WILLIAM H. EDWARD BENTINCK

1784–1868, Rector of Sigglesthorne, Hull.

74 *By S. Bellin*, mezzotint, artist's names only and facsimile signature (Richmond Coll. III, 10; O'D 1), after an oil by George Richmond.
Presented by George Richmond, 1865.

SIR ISAIAH BERLIN, OM, CBE

1909–98, Chichele Professor of Social and Political Theory, President of the British Academy; elected to the Club in 1962.

75

75　*By Paul Benney, 1994,* charcoal drawing 51 x 44 cm (20 x 17¼ in) sight size,
signed and dated and one of a series of studies for a group picture, 'The Supreme Court of Israel' 1994 Jerusalem, copy at Waddesdon Manor.
Presented by Lady Berlin, 1999.

SIR WILLIAM BETHAM

1779–1858, Ulster King-of-Arms; elected to the Club 1858.

76　*After Daniel Maclise, 1827,* engraving (Ports M.I.52).

77　*By W. Drummond 1837,* lithograph, published as *Athenaeum Portraits* no.20.

ERNEST BEVIN (1881–1951), *see* **Satires** No. 1025

GEORGE BIDDER, CALCULATING BOY, *see* **Appendix I, no.6**

ELIZABETH BILLINGTON as St Cecilia

1768–1818, singer especially of Handel oratorios.

78　*By J. Ward, 1803,* mezzotint (O'D 5) after the Reynolds, 1789, in the Beaverbrook Art Gallery, New Brunswick (Penny 1986, p. 35).
Presented by James Ward, 1825, but no longer in the Collection.

LAURENCE BINYON, CH

1869–1943, poet, art historian and Keeper of Prints and Drawings at the British Museum; elected to the Club in 1914 under Rule II.

79　*By Francis Dodd, 1920*
Pencil on white paper, 34.3 × 24.9 cm (13½ × 9¾ in), inset 22 × 15 cm), head only slightly to right, signed and dated *Francis Dodd 1920,* and inscribed under the mount: *Dodd 1920 / Binyon / Francis Dodd.*
Presented by the artist in 1944.

80　*By William Strang, 1898,* litho-facsimile of a dry-point (Strang-Binyon 341; Ath.Ports.Red 46).

EDWARD BIRD, artist, *see* **Appendix I, No.7**

PRINCE OTTO VON BISMARCK, 1815–98, *see* **Satires Nos. 988–90**

79

SIR JAMES BLACK, FRS

1924– , Nobel Prize (medicine) 1988; elected to the Club in 1989.

81　*Photograph* in the Nobel Prize book, 1988.

LORD BLACKETT, OM, CH

1897–1974, Nobel Prize (physics) 1948; elected to the Club in 1947.

82　*After William Evans,* photograph in the Nobel Prize book, 1948, of an oil in the Royal Society.

SIR CHARLES BLAGDEN, physician, *see* **Appendix I, no. 8**

ROBERT WILLIS BLENCOWE

a founding member of the Club.

83　*By F. Holl,* stipple engraving, artists' names only and

facsimile signature (Richmond Coll. I. 24) from a drawing by George Richmond.
Presented by George Richmond, 1865.

JOHN BLIGH, *see* DARNLEY, and **Groups** No. 945

RIGHT REV CHARLES JAMES BLOMFIELD

1786–1857, Bishop of London, editor of 'Aeschylus'.

84   *By W. J. Ward, 1827,* mezzotint (O'D 1), as Bishop of Chester, after S. Lane.

85   *By J. Thomson, 1847,* stipple engraving published J. Hogarth 1847 (Richmond Coll. II. 2; O'D 3), as Bishop of London after a drawing by G. Richmond, 1833–46.
Presented by George Richmond, 1865.

SIR REGINALD BLOMFIELD, RA PRIBA, FSA

1856–1942, architect; elected to the Club in 1902.

86   *After Sir W. Rothenstein,* litho-facsimile of a drawing at Burlington House (R662).
Presented by the artist, 1930.

PROFESSOR BARUCH BLUMBERG, FRCP

b. 1925, Master of Balliol, Nobel Prize (physiology of medicine) 1976; elected to the Club in 1984.

87   *Photograph* in the Nobel Prize book, 1976.

SAMUEL BODDINGTON

1767–1848, collector and a founding member of the Club.

88   *By W. Drummond, c.1836,* lithograph published as *Athenaeum Portraits* no. 24.

SIR JOSEPH EDGAR BOEHM, Bt

1834–90. sculptor, elected in 1875 under Rule II.

89   *By G.J. Stodart, 1888,* stipple vignette, proof before letters (Wells-Grillion 21), from a drawing by H.T. Wells for Grillion's Club.
Presented by H.T. Wells, 1898.

89

JEAN-JACQUES DE BOISSIEU

1736–1810, French painter and engraver

90–1   *Self-portraits, 1796,* two etchings, 29 × 23 cm (11⅜ × 9 in), two states of the same etching, one holding a portrait of his wife, the other (a later issue), a reproduction of one of his own oil paintings, "Les Grandes Vaches".
Lucas bequest 1918.

JOHN BOSTOCK, FRS

1773–1846, physician, geologist, vice-president of the Royal Society, and a founding member of the Club.

92   *By W. Drummond, 1836,* lithograph after J. Partridge, published in *Athenaeum Portraits,* no.19.

JACQUES BOUCHER DE PERTHES

1788–1868, French customs officer, antiquary and expositor of pre-history.

93 *By A.L. de Lemercier,* litho-vignette (Ports M.III.6), after a drawing by G. Grevedon, 1831.

REV THOMAS BOURDILLON

Vicar of Fenstanton, Hunts, from 1802–54

94 *By J.H. Lynch,* lithograph with facsimile: 'Yr Truly affectionate Father Thos Bourdillon' (Richmond Coll. III. 15), after a drawing by G. Richmond.
Presented by George Richmond, 1865.

MISS JANE BOWLES

1772–1812, later Mrs Richard Palmer.

95 *By C. Turner, 1817,* mezzotint (Eng.C.I.1), after the oil by Reynolds in the Wallace Collection (P36).

LORD BOYD ORR, MC, DSO, CH

1880–1971, nutritionist, Nobel Prize (peace) 1949; elected to the Club in 1938.

96 *Photograph* in the Nobel Prize book, 1949.

SIR CHARLES VERNON BOYS, FRS

1855–1944, physicist and inventor, elected to the Club in 1905.

97 *After the Hon. J. Collier,* photograph of an oil exh RA 1915 (Ath.Ports.Red 34), and see **Groups** No. 960 and **Satires** No. 1019.

SIR WILLIAM HENRY BRAGG, KBE, OM

1862–1942, physicist, Nobel Prize (physics 1915), President of the Royal Society; elected to the Club in 1921.

By Campbell Swinton, c.1900, group photograph, see **Groups** No. 964.

98 *By Randolph Schwabe, 1932*

Pencil on buff paper, 31.5 × 22 cm (12⅜ × 8⅝ in), signed and dated in ink: *R. Schwabe Aug. 1932.,* and inscribed under the mount: *Sir William Bragg.* A version, also of 1932, is in the NPG.

Presented by the artist, 1947.

99 *After Harold Knight,* photograph of a oil, 1941, in the Royal Society, Nobel Prize book 1915.

SIR WILLIAM LAWRENCE BRAGG, MC, CH

1890–1971, Nobel Prize (physics) 1915 with his father;

98

elected to the Club in 1932

100 *Anon,* two photographs in the Nobel Prize book, 1915.

SIR FREDERICK JOSEPH BRAMWELL, Bt

1818–1903, engineer, elected in 1875 under Rule II.

101 *By Alan Swinton,* group photograph at Jesmond Dene, *see* **Groups** No. 958.

SIR DAVID BREWSTER, FRS

1781–1868, natural philosopher and President of Royal Society of Edinburgh; elected 1852 under Rule II.

102 *By Maull & Polyblank, c.1860,* signed and dated photograph 186? (Ports M.III.37).

SIR BENJAMIN BRODIE, Bt. FRS

1783–1862, chemist; elected to the Club in 1846.

103 *By Maull & Polyblank, c.1860,* photograph (Ports M.III.38).

SIR JAMES BROOKE, KCB

1803–68, Rajah of Sarawak; elected in 1848 under Rule II.

104 *By G.R. Ward, 1849,* engraving (Ports M.II.38; O'D 1), after the oil by Grant in the NPG.
Presented by John Murray, 1908.

LORD BROUGHAM AND VAUX

1778–1868, lord chancellor; elected to the Club in 1825.

105 *By Maull & Polyblank 1860,* signed photograph (Ports M.II.24).

JOHN BROUGHTON

1705–89, prize fighter and 'public bruiser'.

106 *By F. Ross 1842,* lithograph (Ath Fol. I. 19; O'D 1) after a picture by Hogarth, location unknown.
Presented by Henry Ralph Willett, 1842.

HORACE T. BROWN, FRS 1848–1925, Brewer, *see* Groups No. 961.

VEN. ROBERT WILLIAM BROWNE

1809–95, Archdeacon of Bath.

107 *By W. Holl 1853,* stipple engraving in crayon manner, proof before letters, published 1853 (Richmond Coll. II. 10; O'D 1), after a drawing by G. Richmond.
Presented by George Richmond, 1865.

DUKE OF BUCCLEUCH, KG, KT

1806–84, Walter Scott, 5th Duke.

108 *By H. Robinson, 1845–50,* stipple engraving, crayon manner, proof with artists' names only (Richmond Coll. I. 2), after a drawing by G. Richmond.
Presented by George Richmond, 1865.

VERY REVD. WILLIAM BUCKLAND, *see* Satires No. 1007

GEORGE EARLE BUCKLE

1854–1935, editor of *The Times* and author of *Life of Disraeli*; elected in 1887 under Rule II.

109 *After Sir W. Rothenstein, 1934,* litho-facsimile of a draw-ing, mentioned in *Men and Memories* III (1939), p. 299. Photographs in the Club library, inscribed in ink: "To the Athenaeum, a tribute to the sitter by the limner Wm Rothenstein 10.10.34" (Ath. Ports I.25 and Ath.Ports.Red 25).
Presented by G.P. Pirie Gordon, 1989.

JAMES BUCKNALL-ESTCOURT, MP

1802–55, Major-General, died in the Crimea.

110 *By F. Holl, c.1850,* stipple engraving in crayon manner, proof before letters, facsimile of signature, printed by McQueen (Richmond Coll. I. 11), after a drawing by G. Richmond.
Presented by George Richmond, 1865.

JAMES WENTWORTH BULLER, MP

1798–1867, MP for North Devon; a founding member of the Club.

111 *By W. Holl, c.1850,* stipple engraving in crayon manner, proof with artists' names only and facsimile signature (Richmond Coll. I. 25; O'D 1), from a drawing by G. Richmond for Grillion's Club.
Presented by George Richmond, 1865.

SIR REDVERS BULLER, VC, GCB

1839–1908, General; elected in 1894 under Rule II.

112 *By G.J. Stodart, 1889,* stipple vignette, proof before let-ters (Wells-Grillion 25; O'D 1), from a drawing by H.T. Wells for Grillion's Club.
Presented by H.T. Wells, 1898.

CATHERINE BUNBURY AND MARY GWYN

actresses in *The Merry Wives of Windsor*.

113 *By W. Dickinson, 1780,* mezzotint (O'D 1), after an oil by Daniel Gardner in Nottingham Castle.

SIR THOMAS CHARLES BUNBURY Bt. MP

1740–1821, Whig MP for Burton, Suffolk, slave trade abolitionist, head of the Jockey Club, and owner of 'Diomed' which won the first Derby in 1780.

114 *By C Turner, 1819,* mezzotint (Ports II.16; O'D 3), after an oil by Samuel Lane sold at Christies's 25 May 1934 (150).
Presented by Samuel Lane, 1839.

115

BARON VON BUNSEN

1791–1860, Prussian diplomat and Ambassador in London 1841–54.

115 *By H. Robinson,* stipple engraving in crayon manner, proof with artists' names only, published J. Hogarth 1859 (Richmond Coll. I. 18), from a drawing by G. Richmond.
Presented by George Richmond, 1865.

WILLIAM JOHN BURCHELL, explorer, *see* Appendix I, No. 9

SIR FRANCIS BURDETT Bt. MP

1770–1844, reforming MP for Westminster; elected to the Club in 1825.

116 *By W. Sharp, 1811,* line engraving (O'D 6), after J. Northcote's portrait 'painted during his imprisonment in the Tower' 1810 (Walker 1985, p.77).
Presented by Arthur Jaffé, 1930.

EDMUND BURKE, MP

1729–97. Statesman, orator, and author of *On the Sublime and Beautiful* (1756), *Thoughts on the Present Discontents* (1770) and *Reflections on the French Revolution* (1790). He also started *The Annual Register* in 1759.

117 *After John Hickey (Fig. D)*
Glazed plaster cast, 67.5 cm (26½ in) after a bust by John Hickey, incised on the cartouche: BURKE. Hickey's original marble bust, R.A. 1785, cannot now be safely identified. A marble variant is in Trinity College, Dublin, exh. 'Treasures of Trinity College', RA 1961 (74). and see Crookshank & Webb, *Paintings and Sculpture in Trinity College,* Dublin (1990), p.30, no.5). A marble copy by E.H. Baily, RA 1840, is in National Gallery of Ireland, Dublin.

Literature: Gunnis 1953, pp. 199–200.
Presented by Thomas Haviland Burke, 1830.

RICHARD BURKE

d. 1794, Recorder of Bristol and brother of Edmund Burke.

118 *By E. Train,* line engraving 1828 (Ports I.17; O'D 1), with lines from Goldsmith's *Retaliation:* 'Here lies honest Richard …'.
Presented by Thomas Haviland Burke, 1828.

THOMAS HAVILAND BURKE

Elected to the Club in 1825, member of the committee and a donor.

119 *By W. Drummond, 1835,* lithograph after Eddis, published as *Athenaeum Portraits* no.2.

REV CHARLES BURNEY

1757–1817, chaplain to George III and son of the musicologist.

120 *By W. Sharp, 1802,* line engraving (O'D 3), after Lawrence's oil of 1802 (Garlick 145).
Presented by Arthur Jaffé, 1932.

By Mrs Dawson Turner, etching, see Appendix I, no. 10.

SIR ALAN BURNS, GCMG

1887–1980, colonial governor (British Honduras, Gold Coast), author of *Colonial Civil Servant* (1949); Chairman of the General Committee 1966–69.

H.A. Freeth 1969

Sir Alan Burns

121 *By H. Andrew Freeth, 1969*

Watercolour heightened with white on grey-green paper, 45 × 35.5 cm (17¾ × 14 in), HS to right in a grey suit, signed and dated in brown ink: *H.A. Freeth 1969*, and inscribed under the mount: *Sir Alan Burns.*

Bought by private subscription from members of the Club.

SIR JAMES BURROUGH 1750–1839, Judge

122 *By T. Lupton,* mezzotint (O'D 1), after an oil by T. Phillips, 1827
Presented by Barbara (Lady) Freyberg, 1938.

DECIMUS BURTON

1800–81, founding member and architect of the Athenaeum; in April 1824 the Committee resolved that 'Decimus Burton be nominated as the Club's architect'; he was then aged twenty-four and completed the work by May 1830. Other London work includes the screen at Hyde Park Corner, the camel and giraffe houses at the Zoo, and extensive remodelling to Nash's United Services Club opposite the Athenaeum.

123 *By E.U. Eddis, c.1830–35 [Frontispiece]*

Pencil heightened with white chalk on brown paper, 50 × 33 cm (19½ × 13 in), inscribed in pencil: *Decimus Burton Architect.*

Probably presented by the sitter (Ports M.I.34).

124 *By M. Gauci,* engraving in chalk manner (O'D 1) imitating the drawing by Eddis above.

A later photograph of Burton appears in Ward 1926, p. 66, and Cowell 1975, p.20, taken from *The Illustrated London News,* LXXIX (1881), 650.

REV EDWARD BURTON

1794–1836, Regius Professor of Divinity, Oxford; elected to the Club in 1825.

125 *By S. Cousins, 1837,* mezzotint (O'D 1), after Corbet 1836. Presented by Arthur Jaffé, 1930.

JAMES BURTON (HALIBURTON)

1788–1862, Egyptologist and a founding member of the Club.

126 *By W. Drummond, c.1835,* lithograph published as *Athenaeum Portraits* no. 22.

REV GEORGE BUTLER

1774–1853, headmaster of Harrow; a founding member of the Club.

127 *By R.J. Lane, 1854,* lithograph with an autograph letter, 7 July 1854 (Ports M.II.6; O'D 1), after an oil by F.W. Wilkin, 1822,
Presented by C.S. Long, 1854.

SIR EDWARD FOWELL BUXTON, Bt 1812-58

128 *By F. Holl, c.1850,* stipple engraving in crayon manner, proof before letters (Richmond Coll. V. 7; O'D 1) after a drawing by G. Richmond.
Presented by George Richmond, 1884.

SIR THOMAS FOWELL BUXTON, Bt

1786–1854, slavery abolitionist; elected to the Club in 1825.

129 *By H. Robinson, 1850,* stipple engraving in crayon manner with facsimile signature (Richmond Coll. III. 16), from a drawing by G. Richmond.
Presented by George Richmond, 1865.

LORD BYRON

1788–1824, poet ('he awoke and found himself famous') and eponymous Regency rake. Author of *Childe Harold's Pilgrimage* and *Don Juan,* and a great number of brilliant letters.

130 *After Thorwaldsen*

Royal Danish Porcelain Factory biscuit figure, 24.6 cm (9¾in), marked on the base in blue, and in addition impressed on the back: = / Eneret / T. This latter form of mark was first introduced in 1837 but there is uncertainty about the 'T' (perhaps used by the Factory's modeller, Alfred Gade, active 1854–91, see Grandjean pp. 11–12, no. 26p.29). A similar figure is Thorwaldsen's marble statue at Trinity College, Cambridge, originally intended for Westminster Abbey. Its rejection by the Abbey authorities was the occasion for Macaulay's famous quip, 'we know no spectacle so ridiculous as the British public in one of its periodical fits of morality'.

Literature: Bredo Grandjean, *Biscuit efter Thorvaldsen* (Copenhagen 1976); Walker 1985, p. 86; Annette Peach , 'Portraits of Lord Byron', *Walpole Society Journal* LXII, 2000, p. 80 (b)

130

EARL CAIRNS

1819–85, Hugh McCalmont Cairns, Lord Chancellor; elected to the Club in 1868.

131 *By John & Charles Watkins,* signed photograph (Ports M. III. 28).

CHARLES STUART CALVERLEY

1831–84, poet, parodist, barrister.

132 *By G. Stodart,* stipple vignette published by G. Bell & Sons (not in O'D).
Presented by Major E.L. Calverley, 1934.

SIR HARRY CALVERT, Bt GCB. GCH

1763–1812, general; Lieutenant Governor of Chelsea Hospital.

133 *By R. Golding, 1828,* line engraving (O'D 1), after an oil by Thomas Phillips.
Presented by Barbara (Lady) Freyberg, 1938.

RICHARD OWEN CAMBRIDGE, satirist, *See* **Appendix I, no. 11.**

CHARLES HAY CAMERON

1795–1880, jurist and a founding member of the Club.

134 *By W. Drummond, 1836,* lithograph published as *Athenaeum Portraits* no. 35.

JOHN, BARON CAMPBELL, LORD CHANCELLOR, *see* **Satires No.1010**

THOMAS CAMPBELL

1777–1844, poet and friend of Byron, founding member.

135 *By S.W. Reynolds, 1829,* mezzotint (Ports M.II. 17), after an oil by T. Phillips 1818 in the John Murray collection.
Presented by John Murray, 1908.

136 *By W. O. Geller, 1847,* mezzotint (O'D18), after an oil by T.C. Thompson exh RA 1834, as Rector of Glasgow University.
Presented by J.H. Hawkins.

GEORGE CANNING, MP

1770–1827, Foreign Secretary and a founding member of the Club.

137 *By C. Turner, 1829,* mezzotint (Ath. Fol. I.2; O'D 7), after the oil by Lawrence in the Royal Collection, painted for George IV (Millar 887; Garlick 160c).
Presented by the publisher, Colnaghi & Co, 1829.

By Mrs Turner, see Appendix I, no.12.

ALONSO CANO

1601–67, Spanish artist

138 *By Henry Macbeth-Raeburn, 1888,* mezzotint after Cano's self-portrait in the Hermitage, St Petersburg.
Lucas bequest 1918.

CANOVA, sculptor, *see* **Appendix I, no.13.**

VISCOUNT CANTERBURY, PC, GCB, DCL

1780–1845, Charles Manners-Sutton MP, Speaker of the House of Commons; elected to the Club in 1832.

139 *By S. Cousins, 1835,* mezzotint (O'D 3), after an oil by H.W. Pickersgill 1833, in the NPG.

BISHOP OF CAPETOWN
Right Rev Robert Gray, DD 1800–72

140 *By J. Thomson, c.1848,* stipple engraving in crayon manner, proof with artists' names only, published Colnaghi 1848 (Richmond Coll. II. 13), after a drawing by G. Richmond.
Presented by George Richmond, 1865.

REV EDWARD CARDWELL

1787–1861, church historian; elected to the Club in 1825.

141 *By F. Holl,* stipple engaving in crayon manner, proof before letters (Richmond Coll. II. 16; O'D 1), from a drawing by G. Richmond for Grillion's Club.
Presented by George Richmond, 1865.

EARL OF CARLISLE, KG

1802–64, George Howard, 7th Earl, Viceroy of Ireland.

142 *By F. Holl,* stipple engraving in crayon mannner, proof before letters (Richmond Coll. I. 3; O'D 4), after a drawing by G. Richmond.
Presented by George Richmond, 1865.

EARL OF CARLISLE

1843–1911, George James Howard, succeeded as 9th Earl in 1889.

143 *By C.W. Sherborne, 1894,* etching (Wells-Grillion 29; O'D 1), from a drawing by H.T. Wells for Grillion's Club.
Presented by H.T. Wells, 1898.

THOMAS CARLYLE

1794–1881, author and founder of the London Library; elected to the Club in 1853 under Rule II.

144 *By Walter L. Collis,* photogravure after the marble bust by Boehm, c.1875, in the London Library (Ormond 1973, p.90).

144

LADY ALMIRIA CARPENTER

d.1809, daughter of the Earl of Tyrconnell

145 *By J. Watson, 1768,* mezzotint (O'D 2), after an oil by Reynolds 1768–69, whereabouts unknown (Waterhouse 1941, p.86).

SIR CODRINGTON CARRINGTON, MP

1769–1849, Chief Justice of Ceylon; elected to the Club in 1830.

146 *By W. Drummond, 1836,* lithograph published as *Athenaeum Portraits* no.39.

LOUIS-EUGÈNE CAVAIGNAC

1802–57, French general

147 *By M.A. Alophe, c.1845,* litho vignette (Ports Q.I.22).

VISCOUNT CAVE, PC

1856–1928, Home Secretary, Lord Chancellor; elected to the Club in 1911.

148 *After Francis Dodd, 1925*, photogravure of an oil, exh RA 1932, at St John's College, Oxford.

LORD FREDERICK CAVENDISH, MP

1836–83, Chief Secretary for Ireland.

149 *By C. Holl, 1876*, stipple vignette, proof before letters (Wells-Grillion 7), from a drawing by H.T. Wells for Grillion's Club.
Presented by H.T. Wells, 1898.

SIR JAMES CHADWICK, CH, FRS

1891–1974, Nobel Prize (physics) 1935; elected to the Club in 1936.

150 *Photograph* in the Nobel Prize book, 1935.

SIR ERNEST CHAIN, FRS

1906–79, biochemist, Nobel Prize (medicine) 1945; elected to the Club in 1972.

151 *Photograph* in the Nobel Prize book, 1945.

ALEXANDER CHALMERS, FSA

1759–1834, editor of the *General Biographical Dictionary*

152 *By R.J. Lane*, litho vignette (Eng. C.I.27; O'D 2)
Presented by Henry Foss.

SIR EDMUND CHAMBERS, KBE, CB, DLitt. FBA

1866–1954, historian of the theatre; elected to the Club in 1924 under Rule II.

153 *After Sir W. Rothenstein*, litho-facsimile of a drawing, 1924 (R709), in the NPG.
Presented by the artist, 1937.

NICOLAS CHANGARNIER

1793–1877, French general.

154 *By M.A. Alophe, c.1845*, litho vignette (Ports Q.I.22).

SIR FRANCIS CHANTREY, RA, FRS, FSA

1781–1841, celebrated sculptor; present at the Somerset

155

House meeting, 16 Feb. 1824, and a member of the first working sub-committee, contributing frequent suggestions for the decoration and internal arrangements. His large fortune, bequeathed to the Royal Academy (the Chantrey Bequest), exists for the purchase of contemporary works of art.

155 *By C. Turner, 1843*, mezzotint with facsimile of signature and a letter 6 March 1843, (Ports II; O'D 1), after an oil by Raeburn exh RA 1819.
Presented by Charles Stokes, FSA, 1843.

A copy of *Sir Francis Chantrey, RA. Recollections of His Life, Practice and Opinions* (1849) was presented to the Club by the author, George Jones, 1850.

CHARLES X

1757–1836, King of France

156 *By C. Turner, 1829*, mezzotint (Ath. Fol. I.9), after the oil by Lawrence in the Royal Collection, painted for George IV (Millar 890; Garlick 183).
Presented by the publishers, Colnaghi & Co, 1830.

CHARLOTTE AUGUSTA

1766–1828, Princess Royal of England and Queen of Würtemberg.

157   *By W. Skelton, 1828,* stipple engraving (Ports I.19; O'D 4) after a miniature by Paul Fischer in the Royal Collection.
Presented by W. Skelton, 1831.

PRINCESS CHARLOTTE

1797–1817, daughter of George IV.

158   *By R. Golding 1822,* line engraving (Ath. Fol. I.10; O'D 27), after the oil by Lawrence in the Belgian Royal Collection, painted as a birthday present for Prince Leopold (Garlick 187).
Presented by the publishers, Colnaghi & Co, 1830.

JOHN GEORGE CHILDREN, FRS

1777–1852, Secretary of the Royal Society; a founding member of the Club.

159   *After B.R. Faulkner, 1826,* engraving (Ports M. I.53; O'D 3), printed by Graf & Soret.

160   *By W. Drummond, 1835,* lithograph after Eddis, published as *Athenaeum Portraits* no.9.
Presented by Charles Stokes.

SIR JOSEPH CHITTY, QC

1828–99, Lord Justice of Appeal; elected in 1882.

161   *By C.W. Sherborne, 1890,* etching (Wells-Grillion 27; O'D 1), from a drawing by H.T. Wells for Grillion's Club.
Presented by H.T. Wells, 1898.

JAMES CHRISTIE

1773–1831, auctioneer; a founding member of the Club.

162   *After W. Behnes,* line engraving (Ports M. I. 13; O'D 1), printed by Engelmann, Graf & Co. after a marble bust exh RA 1826.
Presented by Dawson Turner, 1830.

SIR WINSTON CHURCHILL, KG, OM

1874–1965, Prime Minister, Nobel Prize (literature) 1953; elected to the Club in 1955.

163   *Anon* photograph in the Nobel Prize book, 1953.

EARL OF CLARE, KP, GCH

1792–1851, Governor of Bombay ; a founding member of the Club.

164   *By E. Finden, 1833,* stipple vignette (O'D 4), after J. Slater.

EARL OF CLARENDON, KG, KP

1800–70, George Villiers, 4th Earl; a founding member of the Club.

165   *By W. Holl,* stipple vignette (Eng. AI. 35; O'D 4), after a drawing by G. Richmond for Grillion's Club.
Presented by W.M. Powell, 1910.

SIR CHARLES MANSFIELD CLARKE, Bt. MD, FRS

1782–1857, physician to Queen Adelaide and accoucheur at St George's Hospital.

166   *By T. Hodgetts, 1833,* mezzotint (Ath. Fol. I. 26; O'D 1) after an oil by Samuel Lane, exh RA 1832, in the Royal College of Physicians, London.
Presented by Samuel Lane, 1839.

EDWARD DANIEL CLARKE, traveller, see Appendix I, no.14

THOMAS CLARKSON, MP

1760–1846, slavery abolitionist and author.

167   *By C. Turner, 1828,* mezzotint (Ath. Fol. I. 14), after a portrait by A.E. Chalon.
Presented by the publishers, Colnaghi & Co.

THOMAS HENRY SHADWELL CLERKE

1792–1849, military journalist; elected to the Club in 1826.

168   *By W. Drummond, 1835,* lithograph after Eddis published as *Athenaeum Portraits* no.11.

169   *By M. Gauci, c.1835,* lithograph (Ath. Fol. I. 3; O'D 1), same picture.
Presented by Major Shadwell Clerke.

RICHARD COBDEN, MP

1804–65, champion of Free Trade and leader of the Anti-Corn Law League; elected to the Club in 1858.

170 *By Lowes Dickinson 1861,* stipple engraving used as illustration in Morley's *Life of Cobden* (jubilee edition 1896).

Lowes Dickinson was commissioned by the Reform Club in 1865 to execute two portraits of Cobden, one for the Club and one for the NPG. They were painted from photographs, a drawing he made from life in 1861, and from a miniature by Bean or Beau (Ormond 1973, p.106).
Presented by Arthur Jaffé, 1931.

SIR JOHN COCKCROFT, OM

1897–1967, Nobel Prize (physics) 1951; elected to the Club in 1941.

171 *Photograph* in the Nobel Prize book, 1951.

ARTHUR C. COFFIN

Director of Education, Bradford; elected to the Club in 1937, proposed by Sir W. Rothenstein.

172 *By Sir William Rothenstein, 1936*
Red and white chalk on coarse buff paper, 38.5 × 29 cm (15⅛ ×11⅜ in) inset 23.5 × 15 cm, signed and dated *W. Rothenstein 1936.*
Presented by the sitter, 1955.

RIGHT REV LORD COGGAN, DD, PC

1909–2000, Archbishop of Canterbury; elected to the Club in 1955 and a trustee.

173 *By the Hon. George Bruce, 1961*

Oil on canvas 61.5 × 50 cm (24¼ × 19⅝ in), signed and dated: *George J.D. Bruce 1961.* HS to right in white surplice, robes of DD, rimless glasses, slight smile.

Presented by the artist, 1975.

ARTHUR COHEN, KC, PC

1830–1914, counsel to the Secretary of State for India; elected to the Club in 1884.

172

173

174   *By Sir Frank Short 1917*, mezzotint after an oil by J.S. Sargent (Short-Hardie II, 96).
Presented by P.A. Cohen, 1935.

THOMAS COKE OF NORFOLK, *see* LEICESTER

EDWARD COLEBROOKE

175   *By T.L. Atkinson*, mezzotint, private plate with facsimile signature (Richmond Coll. V. 5), from an oil by G. Richmond [HL with stick and Newgate fringe].
Presented by George Richmond, 1889.

REV EDWARD COLERIDGE

1800–83, Vicar of Mapledurham.

176   *By H.Robinson, 1847*, stipple engraving in crayon manner, proof with artist' names only published J. Hogarth 1847 (Richmond Coll. II. 25; O'D 2), from a drawing by G. Richmond.
Presented by George Richmond, 1865.

PAUL COLNAGHI

1751–1833, printseller.

177   *By R. Easton*, stipple engraving (Ports II, 6; O'D 1), after a medallion by J.P. Dantan inscr. in ink: *Paul Colnaghi July 30. 1833* and printed: *Drawn & Engraved by R. Easton after a bust by Danlan* [sic] *Ob. Aug. 26 1833. Ae 82.*
Presented by Sir Dominic Colnaghi.

JOHN CAMPBELL COLQUHOUN

1785–1854, writer on psychics and translator from German.

178   *Anon* lithograph, *c.*1850, with German inscription, Colquhoun coat of arms, and British medals (Ports II. 8).

SIR SIDNEY COLVIN, DCL

1845–1927, Keeper of Prints and Drawings, British Museum; elected to the Club in 1879.

179   *By Sir William Rothenstein*, lithograph vignette, 1897 (R55).
Presented by A.M. Hind, 1931.

SPENCER COMPTON, *see* NORTHAMPTON

177

LORD CONWAY OF ALLINGTON, MP (1856–1937), *see* **Satires** NO. 1002

MAJOR A.H.S COOMBE-TENNANT, MC 1909–

180   *Photograph* of a clay model, head only, by Mrs R. Zeitler, 1940.

SIR ASTLEY PASTON COOPER, Bt. FRS

1768–1841, surgeon; a founding member of the Club.

181   *By S. Cousins, 1830*, mezzotint (Ath. Fol. I. 4; O'D 1), after the portrait by Lawrence in Royal College of Surgeons, London (Garlick 208).
Presented by the publishers, Colnaghi & Co, 1830.

BRANSBY BLAKE COOPER, FRS

1792–1853, professor of surgery at Guy's Hospital; elected to the Club in 1826.

182   *By W.H. Simmons*, engraving after an oil by Eddis, exh RA 1842.
Presented by E U Eddis, 1842.

THOMAS COPELAND, FRS

1781–1855, writer on surgery, elected to the Club in 1826.

183 *By W. Drummond, 1836,* lithograph after Stewardson, published as *Athenaeum Portraits* no.26.

184

SIR ALCON CHARLES COPISAROW

b.1920, scientist and public servant; elected in 1963, chairman of the Club 1989–92 and trustee.

184 *By John Ward, 1992*

Chalk and wash on buff paper, 47.4 × 32 cm (18⅝ × 12⅝ in), signed and dated: *John Ward 1992.* HL seated in the Club drawing-room.

Presented in 1992 by artist and sitter.

EDWARD COPLESTON

1776–1849, provost of Oriel College and bishop of Llandaff; a founding member of the Club.

185 *By S.W. Reynolds & S. Cousins, 1822,* mezzotint (Ports M.II.29; O'D 1), after an oil by Phillips in Oriel College, Oxford (Poole II.42).
Presented by John Murray, 1908.

MARQUESS CORNWALLIS, *see* No. 1329

COSTER, DE, Napoleon's guide, *see* Appendix I. no. 16.

JOHN SELL COTMAN, artist, *see* Appendix I. nos. 17–18

LORD COTTESLOE

1798-1890, Thomas Fremantle, 1st baron.

186 *By W. Holl,* stipple vignette (Eng. A.I.34; O'D 1), after a drawing by G. Richmond for Grillion's Club.
Presented by W.M. Powell, 1910.

COURTENA\Y, *see* DEVON

REV GEORGE CRABBE

1754–1832, poet of *The Village, The Borough* etc.; elected to the Club in 1825.

187 *By W. Holl, 1847,* engraving (Ports M. II.32; O'D 1), after an oil by Phillips in the John Murray Collection.
Presented by John Murray, 1908.

EARL OF CRANBROOK

1814–1906, Gathorne Gaythorne-Hardy, 1st Earl; elected in 1866.

188 *By Maull & Co. 1865,* signed photograph (Ports M. III. 34).

LORD CRANWORTH

1790–1868, Robert Monsey Rolfe, Lord Chancellor.

189 *By F. Holl, 1850,* stipple engraving in crayon manner, proof with artists' names only, published J. Hogarth (Richmond Coll. I. 8; O'D 2), from a drawing by G. Richmond of 1847.
Presented by George Richmond, 1865.

JOHN CROKER

1743–1814, father of the Club's founder, JWC, Surveyor General of Customs & Excise, Dublin, and recipient of the silver Croker Cup, No. 1427 where both portrait and cup are illustrated.

190   *By E. Scriven,* line engraving inscribed *John Croker Esq. Late Surveyor General of Dublin,* from a portrait by W. Haines, after 1807.

JOHN WILSON CROKER

1780–1857. Secretary of the Admiralty, politician and essayist, famous for his philistine criticism of Keats's *Endymion.* His idea that 'literary men and artists require a place of rendezvous' is generally considered to be the origin of the Athenaeum, and his energetic mobilisation of a distinguished committee, where Sir Humphry Davy took the chair on 16 February 1824, resulted in the Resolution: 'That the … Club is established this day'.

For the Croker Salver and Dinner Service *see* **Memorabilia** No. 1428–48.

191   *By Sir Francis Chantrey*

Marble bust, including circular socle, 60 cm (23½ in), incised (1857 or after) on the back: *J.W. CROKER / 1780–1857 / F.L. CHANTREY. Sculpt.*

Literature: Ward 1926, p. 64 and repr. p.8; Cowell 1975, p. 17; Walker 1985, p.135. The bust is not mentioned in the Chantrey Ledgers but is listed in the *Walpole Soc. Journal* LVI (1994) p.336, as 'attributed to Chantrey'. The incision on the back was added years after Chantrey's death.

'Discovered' by Lord Rosebery and Mr John Murray at Messrs Graves, Pall Mall, and bought by the Club for twenty guineas in 1901.

192   *Attributed to Thomas Kirk*

Marble bust, including circular socle, 65.5 cm (25½ in), unsigned but incised on the cartouche: *CROKER.*

Formerly ascribed to Chantrey, but there is no mention of a bust of Croker in the Chantrey Ledgers, nor does it resemble the other bust in the Drawing Room, incised *Chantrey* (No. 191). Thomas Kirk, an Irish sculptor, is known to have made a bust of Croker in 1819, formerly in Peel's collection and now missing. Kirk exhibited this (or another) RA 1825.

Literature: Strickland (1913) I, p.589; Gunnis 1953, p. 230; Cowell 1975, there attributed to Chantrey and reproduced on p. 20.

192

Provenance: unknown but acquired after 1902; possibly Sir Robert Peel's collection, sold Peel heirlooms, Robinson & Fisher, 10–11 May 1900 (125).

193   *After William Owen*

Oil on (relined) canvas, 76 × 63.5 cm (20 × 25 in), HS to left, facing, dark coat, brown patterned cravat.

A copy of Owen's portrait (in a green coat), *c.*1812, given by Croker himself to Edward Locker, and by his son, Frederick Locker-Lampson, to the NPG (Walker 1985, pp. 134–5).
Presented by Mackenzie D. Chalmers, 1925

194   *By H. Meyer,* engraving 1812 (Ports M. II.13), after a portrait by J. Jackson.
Presented by John Murray, 1908.

195   *By Samuel Cousins,* mezzotint 1829 (O'D 2), after the oil by Lawrence, 1825, in the National Gallery of Ireland (Garlick 223). Croker was a pall-bearer at Lawrence's funeral.
Presented by Thomas McLean, 1836.

196 *By T.H. Parry*, engraving 1834 (Ports M. III.18; O'D 4), after the oil by Lawrence above acquired in 1901.

197 *By W. Drummond, c.1836*, lithograph after Lawrence, published as *Athenaeum Portraits* no.44.

RICHARD CROSSMAN, *see* Satires No. 1005

SIR WILLIAM CUBITT, FRS

1785–1861, civil engineer; elected in 1832 under Rule II.

198 *After G. Clarke, 1832*, lithograph of a marble bust (Ports Q.2).

REV FRANCIS CUNNINGHAM

199 *By C.E. Wagstaff, c.1850*, stipple engraving, proof before letters (Richmond III. 11), from a drawing by G. Richmond.
Presented by George Richmond, 1865.

BEATRICE DE CUSANCE, PRINCESS DE CANTECROIX

1614–63, a celebrated beauty known as 'La Gentillese de Cusance'.

200 *By F.A. Laguillermie*, etching after an oil by Van Dyck in the Royal Collection (Millar 158).
Lucas bequest, 1918.

SIR HENRY DALE, OM, PRS

1875–1968, physiologist-pharmacologist, Nobel Prize (medicine) 1936; elected to the Club in 1923.

201 *After James Gunn, 1945*, photograph in the Nobel Prize book, 1936, of an oil in the Royal Society.

MARQUESS OF DALHOUSIE, KT

1812–60, Sir James Ramsay, Governor-General of India; elected to the Club in 1857.

202 *By H. Robinson, 1849*, stipple engraving, proof before letters, published J. Hogarth (Richmond I. 13; O'D 1), from a drawing by G. Richmond.
Presented by George Richmond, 1865.

EARL OF DALKEITH

1831–1912, William Montagu-Douglas-Scott, later 6th Duke of Buccleuch, KG, KT.

203 *By J. Brown, c.1850*, stipple engraving in crayon manner, proof before letters (Richmond Coll. I. 5), from a drawing by G. Richmond.
Presented by George Richmond, 1865.

RIGHT REV THOMAS DAMPIER

1748–1812, bishop of Ely and an insatiable collector of books and prints.

204 *By E. Scriven, 1812*, stipple engr. (O'D 3), after an oil by Northcote, 1811 at King's College, Cambridge, with a version at Bishop's House, Ely.
Presented by Arthur Jaffé, 1932.

EARL OF DARNLEY

1767–1831, John Bligh, 4th Earl; a founding member of the Club.

205 *By H.H. Meyer, 1816*, stipple engraving (O'D 1), after an oil by T. Phillips.
Presented by Arthur Jaffé, 1931.

CHARLES ROBERT DARWIN, FRS

1809–82, naturalist who stated the evidence for the theory of evolution in *The Origin of Species* (1859). Elected to the Club, among 'the forty thieves' in 1838.

206 *By the Hon. John Collier, (1881)*

Oil on canvas, 127 × 101.5 cm (50 × 40 in), signed lower left in red paint: *John Collier*. TQL facing in dark brown suit, light brown cloak with black collar, grey hat in left hand, blue eyes, long white beard.

Collier's original portrait was commissioned by the Linnean Society with sittings in August 1881, '… standing facing the observer in the loose cloak so familiar to those who knew him, with his slouch hat in his hands … According to my idea it is not so simple and strong a representation of him as that given by Mr Ouless' [Down House with a replica at Christs College, Cambridge]. Darwin himself preferred Collier's portrait and thought the Ouless made him 'a venerable acute melancholy old dog' (Francis Darwin, op. cit. p.292). The Athenaeum portrait is a replica by Collier of his original in the Linnean Society library: 'I shall be proud some day to see myself suspended at the Linnean Society' (letter to John Collier, Feb 1882). Another replica was presented to NPG in 1896 by Darwin's eldest son, William Edward.

Condition: cleaned by W. Drown, 1957

Literature: Francis Darwin, *Charles Darwin* (1902).

206

Presented by the artist and Sir Frederick Macmillan, 1929.

207 *By E. Flameng, 1883,* etching after Collier published by the Fine Art Society 1883, with a vignette drawing of Darwin's head, signed by Collier and Flameng.
Presented by Sir Godfrey Lushington, 1901.

SIR GEORGE HOWARD DARWIN, KCB, FRS

1845–1912, astronomer, son of Charles Darwin; elected to the Club in 1884.

208 *After Gwendolen Darwin,* photograph by Hollyer.

CHARLES DAUBENY, MD

1795–1867, chemist, botanist and a founding member of the Club.

209 *By W. Drummond, 1836,* lithograph after M. Houghton, published as *Athenaeum Portraits* no. 27.

RIGHT REV LORD DAVIDSON OF LAMBETH

1848–1930, Archbishop of Canterbury; elected to the Club in 1890.

210– *By Alan Swinton,* photographs in Ath. Ports. Red 6 and
211 13b.

SIR JOHN FRANCIS DAVIS, Bt. KCB, FRS

1795–1890, Governor of Hong Kong; elected 1833.

212 *Anon* litho vignette (Ports M. I. 47), proof before letters. Presented by the sitter, 1844.

213 *By W. Drummond, 1836,* lithograph published as *Athenaeum Portraits* no. 38.

SIR HUMPHRY DAVY, Bt. FRS

1778–1829, pioneer of electro chemistry and inventor of the safety lamp (1815). President of the Royal Society 1820–7. An original member, he took the chair at the Somerset House meeting on 16 February 1824 and 'Resolved that the … Club is established this day'.

214 *By S.W. Reynolds, 1822,* mezzotint (Ports M. II. 22; O'D 11), after an oil by Phillips (1821), in the NPG.
Presented by John Murray, 1908.

215 *By W. Walker, 1830,* stipple engraving private plate (O'D 3), 'from the Original Picture in Lady Davy's possession by John Jackson Esq. RA', *c.*1820,
Presented by Dr Stephen Parks of Yale University, 1988.

216 *By R. Newton, 1830 ,* line engraving (O'D 4), after an oil by Lawrence, 1821, in the Royal Society (Garlick 241).

217 *By W.H. Worthington, 1831 ,* line engraving. (O'D 5), after the Lawrence above, framed with a letter from Davy to the Club secretary, 18 May 1825.

218 *By Henry Howard, 1835* [Pl. II]

Oil on canvas: 127 × 101 cm (50 × 40 in), signed and dated lower left in capitals: *H. HOWARD 1835.* Nearly whole length seated in a red upholstered chair at mahogany table, elbow on open book, hand to chin. Brown eyes, reddish brown hair, fresh complexion., aged twenty five.

The portrait is a version by Howard of his slightly smaller oil exhibited at the Royal Academy in 1803 and now in the National Portrait Gallery. It was engraved in mezzotint by S.W. Reynolds in 1804.

Literature: Walker 1985, p.147.
Presented in 1924 the centenary year by Sir Humphry Davy Rolleston Bt. GCVO, KCB, FRCS, etc, whose mother, Grace Davy, was the sitter's niece.

AUGUSTIN PYRAME DE CANDOLLE, botanist, *see* **Appendix I, no.19**

EARL DE GREY OF WREST, KG, PRIBA

1781–1859, Thomas Phillip Robinson (later Wedell and later De Grey); elected to the Club in 1858.

219 *By W. Brett & S. Cousins,* mezzotint 1835 (Ports I.31; O'D 1), after an oil by W. Robinson.

EARL DE GREY AND RIPON, *see* Satires No. 1011

ABBÉ GERVAIS DE LA RUE

1751–1835, professor and author of a *History of Caen.*

220 *By L. Parez, 1814,* lithograph (Ports Q. 9), presented by Dawson Turner.

LT COLONEL DIXON DENHAM, FRS

1786–1828, African traveller and governor of Sierra Leone.

221 *By J. Bromley, 1831,* mezzotint (Ports I. 18, 33; O'D 1), after an oil by Phillips, 1826, in the NPG.

BARON DENON, *see* Appendix I, No.18

EARL OF DERBY, KG

1799–1869, Prime Minister; elected to the Club in 1830.

222 *By F.C. Lewis,* stipple vignette (Eng. A.I.46; O'D 6), when Lord Stanley, after a drawing by J. Slater for Grillion's Club.
Presented by W.M. Powell, 1910.

223 *Photograph,* c. 1860, signed (Ports M.III.33).

EARL OF DEVON

1768–1835, William Courtenay, 19th Earl, when Viscount Courtenay; elected to the Club in 1830.

224 *By C. Turner (pubd J. Murphy, 1809),* mezzotint, margins cut (O'D 1), after a miniature by Richard Cosway 1791, at Powderham Castle (see *British Portraits,* exh RA 1956/57, no. 347).

225 *By W. Drummond, 1836,* lithograph published as *Athenaeum Portraits* no. 30.

EARL OF DEVON

1807–67 William Courtenay, succeeded as 21st Earl in 1859

226 *By G. Zobel,* mezzotint, proof before letters with facsimile signature (Richmond Coll. V. 20), from an oil by G. Richmond at Powderham Castle, wearing Garter star. Presented by George Richmond, 1884.

DUKE OF DEVONSHIRE, KG, FRS

1833–1908, succeeded as 8th Duke in 1891; elected to the Club in 1877.

227 *By C. Holl, 1876,* stipple vignette, proof before letters (Wells-Grillion 6), from a drawing by H.T. Wells for Grillion's Club.
Presented by H.T. Wells, 1898.

DUCHESS OF DEVONSHIRE (1757–1806) with her daughter, GEORGIANA, later Countess of Carlisle (1783–1858)

228 *By P. Lightfoot,* engraving (Ports M. III. 19; O'D 30), after an oil in the Royal Collection from the original by Reynolds, 1784, at Chatsworth (Penny 139).

THOMAS FROGNALL DIBDIN, FRS

1776–1847, bibliographer and a founding member of the Club.

229 *By H.H. Meyer, 1816,* stipple engraving (O'D 1), after a drawing by Henry Edridge.
See also Appendix I. no. 20.

CHARLES DICKENS

1812–70, author of *The Pickwick Papers, Oliver Twist, David Copperfield,* and many other famous works which opened the public conscience to a variety of social evils. Elected to the Club, among 'the forty thieves' in 1838. An 'empty chair' from Gadshill also belongs to the Club and is kept in the south library (*see* **Memorabilia** No. 1452 where it is illustrated).

230 *By T.O. Barlow, 1862,* mezzotint, after the oil by W.P Frith, exh RA 1859 and now in the V&A Museum.

Literature: V&A *Charles Dickens* 1970 (010); Ormond NPG 1973, p.144.

Presented by Percy Fitzgerald, 1906.

LEWIS WESTON DILLWYN

1778–1855, naturalist; a founding member of the Club.

231   *By M. Gauci,* 1833, lithograph (Ports M.I. 39), after a drawing by E.U. Eddis.

BENJAMIN DISRAELI, *see* BEACONSFIELD

ISAAC DISRAELI, DCL

1766–1848, author of *Curiosities of Literature* (1791); a founding member of the Club.

232   *By William Drummond,* 1836, lithograph after Denning, published as *Athenaeum Portraits,* no.49.
Presented by Thomas McLean, 1836.

AUSTIN DOBSON

1840–1921, poet and biographer; elected to the Club in 1891.

233   *By William Strang,* 1894, signed etching (O'D 1; Strang 1962, p. 51).
Presented by B.H. Dobson, 1946.

FRANCIS DODD, R.A.

1874–1949, painter and etcher, specially of portraits; elected to the Club in 1935, and donor.

234   *By Randolph Schwabe,* 1916
Etching on off-white paper 33 × 25 cm (13 × 9⅞ in), signed and dated top left: *R. Schwabe 1916;* TQL seated to left in a black hat.
Presented by Professor Schwabe, 1946.

235   *By D.S. MacColl,* 1939
Pencil on buff paper, 16 × 13 cm (6¼ × 5⅛ in), signed and dated: *DSM The Athenaeum July 1939,* head in profile to left wearing glasses.
Presented by the artist, 1939.

CAMPBELL DODGSON, FBA

1867–1948, Keeper of Prints and Drawings, British Museum 1912–32; elected to the Club in 1913.

236   *By R. Schwabe,* 1932, lithograph of a sketch dated 8 May 1932 (Ath.Ports. Red 45).

EARL OF DORSET, KG

1536–1608, Thomas Sackville, 1st Earl of Dorset. Lord Treasurer.

234

235

237 *By George Vertue,* line engraving, published Knapton (O'D 1), after the prototype oil at Knole (Strong NPG 1969, p.67).

LORD DOVER, FRS, FSA

1797–1833, George Agar Ellis, MP, present at the Somerset House meeting, 16 Feb 1824, and an original member.

238 *By J. Burnet, 1817,* line engr. (Ath. Fol. I.5; O'D 5), as the Hon. George Agar Ellis in fancy dress, after George Sanders.

239 *By W. Brett, 1827,* mezzotint (Ports M. I. 8; O'D 3), after an oil by Lawrence in the Yale Center for British Art (Garlick 13).
Presented by the sitter.

240 *By R.J Lane, 1827,* lithograph (Ports M. I.10; O'D 6), after a drawing by Slater for Grillion's Club.
Presented by the sitter, 1830.

GEORGIANA, LADY DOVER (1804–60), with her son the Hon. HENRY AGAR ELLIS (1825–99)

241 *By S. Cousins,* 1831, mezzotint (Ports I. 29; O'D 7), published by Colnaghi, 1831, after an oil by Lawrence in a private collection (Garlick 14).

SIR HUGH DOW, GCIE

1886–1978. Indian Civil Servant; elected to the Club in 1949, a distinguished occupant of the 'sofa', and donor.

242 *By T.B. Huxley-Jones*
Bronze head, 27 cm (10⅝ in) high, incised below his left ear: *T.B. Huxley-Jones.*

Exhibition: R.A. 1964 (1181)
Presented by the sitter, 1978.

WILLIAM DUDDELL, FRS

1872–1917, civil engineer, *see* **Groups** No.960

MARQUESS OF DUFFERIN & AVA, KP, GCB

1826–1902, Viceroy of India; elected to the Club in 1864 under Rule II.

243 *By C. Holl, 1872,* stipple vignette, proof before letters (Wells-Grillion 3; O'D 5), after a drawing by H.T. Wells for Grillion's Club.
Presented by H.T. Wells, 1898.

244 *By D. Wehrschmidt, 1887,* mezzotint (O'D 3), after an oil by F. Holl formerly in the Royal Colonial Institute, with a copy at the Oriental Club.
Presented by Arthur Jaffé, 1930.

DR RENATO DULBECCO, FRS

1914–, molecular biologist, Nobel Prize (medicine) 1975; elected to the Club in 1976.

245 *Photograph* in Nobel Prize book, 1975.

REV SIR HENRY DUKINFIELD, Bt

1791–1858, vicar of St Martin-in-the-Fields; elected to the Club in 1843.

246 *By C. Jousiffe, 1848,* mezzotint (O'D 1), after an oil by Sir Martin Archer Shee, exh RA 1843.
Presented by Arthur Jaffé, 1930.

PHILIP BURY DUNCAN, DCL

1772–1863, Keeper of the Ashmolean Museum, a founding member of the Club, and donor.

247 *By T.G. Lupton, 1825,* mezzotint (O'D 1), after an oil by T. Kirkby at New College, Oxford (Poole II, 72)
Presented by the sitter, 1843.

248 *By M. Gauci,* lithograph (Ports II. 28; Ports M. II. 39; O'D 2), after a portrait by W. Smith.
Presented by John Murray, 1908.

EARL OF DURHAM, GCB

1792–1840, John Lambton, 1st Earl of Durham, governor general of North America; elected to the Club in 1825.

249 *By H. Robinson,* stipple engraving (O'D 10), after a drawing by J. Stewart.

SIR FRANK WATSON DYSON, KBE, DSC, FRS

1868–1939, Astronomer Royal; elected in 1911.

250 *After Sir W. Rothenstein,* litho-facsimile of a drawing 1920 (R541).
Presented by the artist, 1937.

SIR LEWIS DYVE

1599–1669, royalist.

251 *By P. Audinet,* line engraving (Eng. C.I.6; O'D 1), 'from an original picture…'.
Presented by the Rev J.M. Traherne, 1832

HENRY EARLE, FRS

1789–1838, surgeon; elected to the Club in 1825.

252 *By S. Cousins,* mezzotint, private plate (Ports II. 22; O'D 1), after a marble bust by Behnes, 1817, in the Foundling Hospital.

SIR CHARLES LOCK EASTLAKE , FRS , PRA

1793–1865, painter, writer and a founding member of the Club.

253 *By D.J. Pound,* line engraving (O'D 5), wearing PRA medal, after a John Watkins photograph.

SIR ARTHUR EDDINGTON, OM, DSC, FRS

1882–1944, mathematician and astrophysicist; elected in 1926.

254 *After Sir W. Rothenstein,* litho-facsimile of a drawing, 1928–9, in the NPG.
Presented by the artist, 1937.

EDWARD AUGUSTUS

1767–1820, Duke of Kent and Strathearn, fourth son of George III.

255 *By W. Skelton,* 1815, line engraving (Ports I.5; O'D 3), after the oil by Beechey in the Fishmongers Hall.
Presented by W. Skelton, 1831.

EDWARD VII as Prince of Wales

1841–1910, reigned 1901–10.

256 *By F. Holl, 1859,* stipple engraving in crayon manner, published Colnaghi 1859 (Richmond Coll. I. 1; O'D 5), aged seventeen, from a drawing by G. Richmond. A pastel version, 1858, in NPG.
Presented by George Richmond, 1865.

EDWARD EDWARDS, author, *see* Appendix I, no.21

WILLIAM CAMDEN EDWARDS

1777–1855, engraver.

257 *By Mrs Dawson Turner, 1817 ,* etched vignette, finished by Edwards himself (O'D 1), after a drawing by J.P. Davis.
Presented by Arthur Jaffé, 1933.
See also Appendix I, no.22.

LORD FRANCIS EGERTON, MP, *see* ELLESMERE

EARL OF ELDON, FRS, FSA

1751–1838, John Scott, Lord Chancellor; elected a member in 1825.

258 *By J. Posselwhite, 1835,* litho vignette (Ports M. I.24; O'D 4), after a drawing by E.U. Eddis 'in the possession of Lady Elizabeth Repton'.

THOMAS STEARNS ELIOT, OM

1888–1965, poet, Nobel Prize (literature) 1948; elected to the Club in 1949.

259 *Photograph* in the Nobel Prize book, 1948

ELIZABETH, QUEEN OF THE BELGIANS

260 *Photograph:* 'The sympathetic and brave Queen who has voluntarily shared countless hardships for the sake of her noble husband and deeply wronged nation' (Ports II. 18).

LORD ELLENBOROUGH, PC

1750–1818, Lord Chief Justice of England.

261 *By C. Turner,* 1809, mezzotint (O'D 2), , after an oil by Lawrence 1806, privately owned (Garlick 269).
Presented by Barbara (Lady) Freyberg, 1938.

EARL OF ELLESMERE, KG, DCL

1800–57, as Lord Francis Egerton, created Earl in 1846; a founding member of the Club.

262 *By H. Cousins, 1837,* mezzotint (O'D 1), after an oil by J. Bostock in the Wellcome Institute.
Presented by Arthur Jaffé, 1934.

263 *By F. Holl, 1855,* stipple engraving in crayon manner, proof with artist' names only (Richmond Coll. I. 4), after a drawing by G. Richmond listed in Richmond's account book under 1852, p.56.
Presented by George Richmond, 1865.

264 Another copy presented by Arthur Jaffé, 1934.

SIR HENRY ELLIOTT, KCB

1808–53, Indian civil servant and historian; elected in 1845.

265 Engraving of the memorial tablet in Winchester Cathedral (Ports M. II. 12).

JOHN HUGH ARMSTRONG ELLIOT

barrister; elected to the Club in 1895.

266 *By John Tweed*, photograph of a clay bust, 'never carried further'.

JOHN LETTSOM ELLIOT

1804–98, he joined in 1824 aged 21, and became 'the last surviving original member of the Club'. In 1850 he presented a copy of his comedy, *Three to One,* still in the library.

267

267 *By Richard Cockle Lucas, 1850*
White wax medallion on maroon ground, 47 × 29 cm (18½ x 11⅜ in), profile to left, signed and dated: *J.L. Elliot Esq. / R.C. Lucas scpt 1850.*

Literature: Ward 1926, pp.14, 26; not mentioned in E.J. Pyke's *Dictionary.*
Presented by Lieutenant-Colonel G.B. Croft-Lyons, 1924.

WALTER ELLIOT, MP, *see* **Satires** No. 1024

THE HON. MOUNTSTUART ELPHINSTONE

1779–1859, Governor of Bombay, elected to the Club in 1830.

268 *By C. Turner, 1833*, mezzotint (Ath. Fol. I.7; O 'D 1), after the unfinished oil by Lawrence completed by John Simpson, in Elphinstone College Bombay (Garlick 273). Presented by John Murray, 1908.

R. ELPHINSTONE

269 *By G J Stodart* (Ports M. II.31)

SIR HENRY ENGLEFIELD, Bt. antiquary, *see* **Appendix I, no.23.**

ERASMUS

1466–1536, scholar and humanist, closely associated with Holbein, Colet and Thomas More.

270 *By Felix Bracquemond*, etching after the portrait by Holbein at Longford Castle (Ganz 34). Lucas bequest 1918.

LORD ERSKINE, KT

1750–1823, Lord Chancellor.

271 *By C. Turner, 1806*, mezzotint (O'D 7), after the portrait by Lawrence 1802, at Lincoln's Inn (Garlick 277). Presented by Barbara (Lady) Freyberg, 1938.

THE HON. H. ERSKINE

272 *By F. Holl*, stipple engraving in crayon manner, proof before letters (Richmond I. 17), from a drawing by G. Richmond.
Presented by George Richmond, 1865.

EURIPIDES

5th century BC, Greek dramatist.

273 *By P. Audinet,* stipple engr. private plate (Eng. C.I.14) 'from an Ancient Bust found at Athens, in the possession of Ralph Carr Esq.'
Presented by Henry Smedly, 1830.

GENERAL SIR GEORGE DE LACY EVANS, GCB

1787–1870, MP for Westminster.

274 *By W & J Clerk,* lithograph (Ports II. 27; O'D 2), after a drawing by M. O'Connor.

275 *By M. Gauci, 1834,* lithograph (Ports M. I.30 but not a member), after a portrait by A.E. Chalon.
Presented by A.E. Chalon, RA, 1834

SIR JOHN EVANS, KCB, FRS

1823–1908, archaeologist and numismatist; elected to the Club in 1892.

276 Engraving (Ports M. II. 46) after a portrait by A.S. Cope 1900 in the Royal Society.

VISCOUNT EVERSLEY

1794–1888, Charles Shaw-Lefevre, Speaker of the House of Commons; elected a member of the Club in 1825.

277 *By W. Holl,* stipple vignette (Eng. A.1.37; O'D 1), after a drawing by G. Richmond for Grillion's Club.
Presented by W.M. Powell, 1910.

SIR JAMES ALFRED EWING, KCB, FRS

1855–1935, physicist and engineer, Professor of Applied Mechanics, Cambridge, Principal of Edinburgh University, President of the British Association. Elected in 1901 under Rule II.

278 *By Reginald Henry Campbell, c.1925*

Oil on canvas, 51 × 41 cm (20 × 16 in) HS in dark suit, bow tie, winged collar; white hair, eyebrows, and moustache, aged *c.*70.

Presented by his widow, 1938.

By Campbell Swinton, group photograph, *see* **Groups** No. 968.

MICHAEL FARADAY

1791-1867. Founder of modern physics, discoverer of electro-magnetism and a brilliant lecturer at the Royal Institution. He joined the Athenaeum in 1824 having previously acted as secretary to the founding committee.
For his invalid chair *see* **Memorabilia** No. 1451 where it is illustrated.

279 *After Edward Hodges Baily (1823)*

Plaster cast, 68.5 cm (27 in) of the marble bust by E.H. Baily

1830, in the Royal Institution. Inscribed on the socle: *Michael Faraday FRS 1791–1867 / by E.H. Baily RA / Secretary of the Athenaeum 1824 / Presented by Miss Magrath 1917,* and in ink on the back: *Faraday 1834.*

Baily's original marble bust, of 1823, was at the Crystal Palace Portrait Gallery in 1854. Another, exhibited RA 1830, is in the Royal Institution, and another plaster cast is in the University Museum, Oxford.

Literature: Ward 1926, repr. p 26; Gunnis 1953, p 34; Ormond 1973, p.169.
Presented by Miss Magrath, 1917.

280 *By W. Drummond, 1835,* lithograph after E.H. Baily's bust, published as *Athenaeum Portraits* no. 10.

281 *By S. Cousins, 1830* , mezzotint (O'D 6), after the oil by Pickersgill c.1829, in the Royal Institution, London.
Presented by Colnaghi Son & Co. 1830.

282 *By Miss Turner,* lithograph (Ports Q. 15; O'D 2), after a drawing by Eddis, 1831. (reproduced in reverse, Cowell 1975, p.140–1).
Presented by Dawson Turner.

283 *After Thomas Phillips (1842)*

Oil on canvas 59 × 50.5 cm (23 × 20 in), HS to right, black coat, neckcloth, white shirt; a copy by Edmund Dyer of the portrait by Phillips, 1842, in the NPG (Ormond 1973, p.168).

Presented by Sir Frederick Macmillan, 1925.

284 *By Herbert Watkins,* photograph, whole-length with ledger (Ath. Ports. Red 1a).

285 *By John & Charles Watkins,* photograph, reading newspaper (Ath. Ports. Red 1b).

TREVOR FARQUHAR,

1827–46

286 *By J. Posselwhite,* stipple engraving in crayon manner, published Dixon & Ross (Richmond IV. 6), from a drawing by G. Richmond inscribed: 'Trevor Farquhar / Obiit Alliewal, 31 Jan 1846, Aetatis 19'.
Presented by George Richmond, 1865.

GEORGE FINLAY

1799–1875, author of *A History of Greece.* (7 vols 1877); vol I contains his autobiography. He was a friend of Byron who said to him: 'You are young and enthusiastic and therefore sure to be disappointed when you know the Greeks as well as I do' (*Ward 1926,* p 183). He was elected to the Club in 1860 under Rule II.

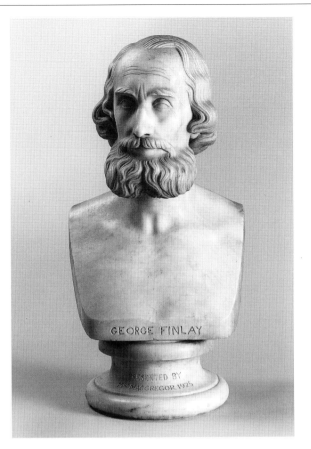

287

287 *By John Kossos, 1857*

Marble bust, 61 cm (24 in) high, incised on the back: CEMM-
MGHEIR JADEV AWTO IX JORRORECOIGR (born 21
December 1799 John Kossos fecit 24 June 1857), and in front:
George Finlay / presented by Mrs MacGregor 1925.

Literature: Richard Garnett in DNB; *Journals and
Letters of George Finlay* (ed. J.M. Hussey 1995).

Finlay mentions the bust in a letter to Professor
Cornelius Felton, Harvard University, 26 Nov. 1861: 'A
Greek sculptor Mr Kossos, who made busts of Sir
Thomas Wyse, Miss Wyse, Lady Young and me, is now
modeling a figure of Greece for the London exhibition'
(Hussey op. cit. II, p. 880).
Presented by his step-daughter-in-law, Mrs MacGregor,
1925.

H.A.L FISHER, OM, FRS, MP

1865–1940, historian and Warden of New College;
elected to the Club in 1908 under Rule II.

288 *After Sir W. Rothenstein, 1920* , litho-facsimile of a drawing at Winchester College (R551).
Presented by the artist, 1937.

SAMUEL FISHER

Clerk to the Merchant Taylors' Company.

289 *By J.R. Jackson,* mezzotint, proof with artists' names
only (Richmond Coll. III. 17; O'D 1), from an oil by G.
Richmond painted for the Hall.
Presented by Geeorge Richmond.

JOHN FLAXMAN, sculptor, *see* Appendix I, no. 24.

SIR PETER HESKETH FLEETWOOD, Bt MP

1801–66, founded Fleetwood, Lancashire in 1836; a
founding member of the Club.

290 *By J.S. Templeton,* lithograph from life (Ports M. I.18;
O'D 2).

SIR ALEXANDER FLEMING, FRS

1881–1955, bacteriologist and discoverer of penicillin,
Nobel Prize (medicine) 1945; elected to the Club in 1948.

291 *Photograph* in the Nobel Prize book, 1945.

LORD FLOREY, OM

1895–1968, pathologist, together with Sir Ernest Chain
isolated and purified penicillin, Nobel Prize (medicine)
1945; elected to the Club in 1944.

292 *After Henry Carr, 1965,* photograph, Nobel Prize book
1945, of an oil in the Royal Society,

JOHN HENRY FOLEY, RA

1818–74, sculptor; elected in 1859 under Rule II.

293 *By George Stodart, 1877* , stipple engraving (not in O'D),
after a bust by Sir Thomas Brock exh RA 1873.

THOMAS FORSTER

1761–1825, botanist.

294 *By Miss Turner,* litho vignette inscr: 'Dr Tho. Forster &
his dog Shargs' (Ports Q.19; O'D 1).

WILLIAM EDWARD FORSTER, MP

1818–86, Chief Secretary for Ireland; elected to the Club
in 1870.

295 *By C. Holl, 1875,* stipple vignette, proof before letters (Wells-Grillion 5; O'D 2), from a drawing by H.T. Wells for Grillion's Club.
Presented by H.T. Wells, 1898.

HUGO FOSCOLO, poet, *see* **Appendix I, no.25**

GEORGE CAREY FOSTER, FRS

1835–1919, Principal of University College, London; elected to the Club in 1888.

296 Photographic reproduction of an oil [TQL seated to left in robes, roll of paper under l hand]

SIR JOHN FRANKLIN, GCH, FRS

1786–1847, arctic explorer; a founding member of the Club.

297 *By L. Haghe,* lithograph (Ports M. I. 48; O'D 1), after a drawing by J.M. Negelen.
Presented by Captain Washington.

COMTE DE FRANQUEVILLE

1840–1919, Amable-Charles Franquet, President of the French Institute, an authority on British institutions (parliament, judiciary, etc); elected an honorary member of the Club in 1864. He was donor of a silver rose bowl (no longer in the Collection) presented 'in grateful remembrance of his honorary membership of the Club, 1864–1914'.

298 *By J.C. Chaplain, 1893,* cast bronze medal. Obverse: a portrait bust in profile to left, uniform and decorations, with inserted inscription: A.C.F. COMTE. DE. FRAN-QUEVILLE. MEMBRE. DE. L' INSTITUT. Reverse: a moated château in wooded landscape, with inserted exergue inscription: BOURBILLY.
Presented by the Count in 1893.

Literature: F. Mazerolle, *J.C. Chaplain, Biographie et Catalogue de son oeuvre* (Paris 1897); Forrer I, p.254.

JAMES BAILLIE FRASER

1783–1856, traveller, author, and founding member of the Club.

299 *By W. Drummond, c.1837,* lithograph published as *Athenaeum Portraits* no.46.

SUSANNA FRASER, *see* **Appendix I, no.26**

298 (obverse)

298 (reverse)

FREDERICK THE GREAT

1712–86, succeeded his father, Frederick William I, in 1740, as Frederick II, King of Prussia.

300 *By Johann Heinrich Christian Francke, c.1775.* Oil on canvas, 127 × 91.5 cm (50 × 36 in), uninscribed. TQL to left in black uniform, hand holding up tricorne hat, left

FREDERICK II. KING OF PRUSSIA
BY FRANCKE OF POTSDAM.
Presented by
The Hon. W. WARREN VERNON ___ 1911

300

hand down holding brown glove, sword, Star of Black Eagle; ruddy face, staring eyes turned to front, short grey wig. Frame with integral crown, is contemporary.

The first volume of Carlyle's *Frederick the Great* was published in 1858. In that year, Warren Vernon, the second son of Lord Vernon, lent him the Francke portrait which Carlyle kept at 5 Cheyne Row for several weeks, 'till I satiate myself with seeing it'. Five effusive letters from Carlyle to Vernon are in the Club library, enclosed in Warren Vernon's own copy of the six volume work. The portrait shows Frederick doffing his hat in greeting the populace, one of 'the fierce King's' favourite gestures – General von Marwitz describes, how riding through the streets of Berlin to visit his sister, he raised his hat at least two hundred times.

Francke painted three versions or copies, and possibly more. Frederick did not give sittings to artists after his accession in 1740; they were compelled to paint from memory or chance glimpses. Carlyle believed that Francke painted the portrait from 'watching' the king at parade. He considered it to be the best likeness ('no other has the least credibility for me') and indeed commissioned an engraving of a Berlin version.

Other versions are, or were formerly, in Berlin (Masons' Lodge and Daun & Splittgerber's Bank). A head and shoulders version is in Schloss Charlottenburg (Mitford op. cit. p.186). A drawing, half-length only, by John Downman, 'in the possession of the Hon. Mr Pelham', was engraved by H. Downman and published 1 Jan. 1791.

Condition: cleaned by M. Braddell, 1953.

Literature: Carlyle, *History of Friedrich II of Prussia, called Frederick the Great* (1858–65), V, *frontispiece*, an engravng dated 1860 after the similar version of Francke's picture in the Schickler Banking-house, Berlin; also, VI, p.661.P. Seidel, *Hohenzollern Jahrbuch* I (1897); Warren Vernon, *Recollections* (1917) where Carlyle's letters about the portrait are published on pages 155–9; Thieme-Becker XII, p.347; Nancy Mitford, *Frederick the Great* (1970).

Provenance: Admiral Sir John Borlase-Warren whose daughter married Lord Vernon; presented by their son, the Hon. William Warren Vernon, 1911.

FREDERICK AUGUSTUS

1763–1827, Duke of York and Albany, second s. of George III; elected to the Club in 1825.

301   *By W. Skelton, 1812,* line engraving (Ports I.4; O'D 4),

after an oil by Beechey c.1812 (Walker 1985, 585a). Presented by W. Skelton, 1831.

SIR FRANCIS FREELING, Bt

1764–1836, secretary to the General Post Office and a founding member of the Club.

302   *By C. Turner, 1834,* mezzotint (Ath. Fol. I.18; O'D 1), after George Jones.

303   *By Miss Turner,* litho vignette (Ports Q.6; O'D 2), probably intended for *The Athenaeum Portraits.*

THOMAS F. FREMANTLE, *see* COTTESLOE

SIR HENRY BARTLE FRERE, Bt. GCB, GSI

1815–84, colonial administrator; elected to the Club in 1858 under Rule II.

304   *By G. J. Stodart,* stipple engraving one of the Grillion's Club series (formerly Ports M. II.40; O'D 2), after an oil by W.E. Mille . Presented by John Murray, 1908.

REV JAMES WILLIAM FRESHFIELD

Elected to the Club in 1843.

305   *By J. Posselwhite, 1850,* line and stipple engraving, private plate with facsimile autograph: 'Very Sincerely yours F W Freshfield, Betchworth 29 Oct 1850' (Richmond III. 17), from an oil by G. Richmond [TQL seated to right]. Presented by George Richmond, 1865.

JAMES FRESHFIELD

306   *By F. Holl,* stipple engraving proof with artists' names only (Richmond III. 19), from an oil by G. Richmond [TQL standing to right]. Presented by George Richmond, 1865.

ELIZABETH FRY

1780–1845, Quaker social reformer and prison visitor.

307   *By S. Cousins, 1850,* mezzotint, proof with artists' names only, published J. Hogarth 1850 (Richmond IV. 12; O'D 6), from a watercolour by G. Richmond, 1843 (private collection and copy at Walsingham Abbey), used as basis for the statue by Vyse in the Old Bailey. Presented by George Richmond, 1865.

HENRY FUSELI, RA

1741–1825, painter, writer and professor of painting at the Royal Academy.

308 *By F.C. Lewis*, stipple engraving (O'D 16), after a drawing by G.S. Newton 1820–25 (Sotheby's 18 Dec. 1963).

DENNIS GABOR, FRS, CBE

1900–79, electrical engineer invented holography and the laser, Nobel Prize (physics) 1971; elected to the Club in 1958.

309 *Photograph* in the Nobel Prize book, 1971

SIR THOMAS GAGE, Bt. See Appendix I, no. 31

JOHN GALSWORTHY , OM, LLD

1867–1933, writer, Nobel Prize (literature) 1932; elected in 1920 under Rule II.

310 *After Sir W. Rothenstein, 1928*, litho-facsimile of a drawing at New College, Oxford. The drawing was one of a series made of the pall bearers at Thomas Hardy's funeral in Westminster Abbey. They were Baldwin, Ramsay Macdonald, J.M. Barrie, Bernard Shaw, Kipling, Housman, Gosse, Galsworthy, the Master of Magdalene, and the Provost of Queen's College, Oxford (*Men & Memories* III 1939, p. 100)
Presented by the artist, 1937.

311 *Photograph* in the Nobel Prize book, 1932

LEON MICHEL GAMBETTA

1838–82, French statesman.

312 *By Alphonse Legros*, etching 48 × 34 cm (19 × 13½ in), (Legros-Bliss nos. 156–165).
Lucas bequest 1918.

DAVID GARRICK

1717–79, actor, playwright and theatre manager.

313 *After John van Nost the Younger, 1779*
Painted plaster bust, 60 cm (23½ in) high, from a marble bust by John van Nost, of which 'copies were in every barber's shop-window, as a place for wigs' (*Smith 1920*, II p 207).

Literature: small black basalt copies were produced by Wedgwood in 1779 (see *Garrick 1997*, S11-12)

315

GAYTHORNE-HARDY, *see* Cranbrook, No. 188

GEORGE III

1738–1820, reigned 1760–1820

314 *By W. Skelton, 1810*, line engraving (Ports I.1; O'D 25), after an oil by Beechey in the Royal Collection (Millar 658).
Presented by W. Skelton, 1831.

315 *By F.H. Hardenberg, 1820*

Biscuit statuette, 28.5cm (11¼in) high, wearing morning coat, breeches, heavy boots, Garter star, holding staff and ear-trumpet, indistinctly incised on the square stand: *May 8th 1820 … Hardenberg …[Grosvenor] Square, London.*

A polychrome version, also dated 1820, is in the NPG (Report 1964–65, p 22). Similar figures were 'published' by L. Gahagan in 1811 and 1814. They all stem from Henry Edridge's pencil and wash drawing of 1803, in the Royal Collection (Oppé 1950, no.197 and plate 11).

Literature: Gunnis 1953, p. 187.

After J. Ward, engraving presented by Colnaghi, 1829, no longer in the Collection.

318

GEORGE IV

1762–1830, reigned 1820–30

316 *By William Skelton, 1819,* line engraving (Ports I. 2; O'D 14), after an oil by Phillips, 1806, in hussar uniform.
Presented by W. Skelton, 1831.

317 *By W. Holl, 1829,* stipple engraving (Ports M.I.1; Ports I.11; O'D 124).
Presented by the publisher, W. Sams, 1831.

318 *By Sir Thomas Lawrence, 1829-30*
Oil on canvas, c. 141 × 155 cm (95 × 61 in), one of the many copies of the state portrait (Millar 919), painted by Lawrence shortly before his death (1830) specially for the Athenaeum (Minutes 19 Jan 1830, pp. 82–7) and disposed of to the Corporation of Brighton in 1857 (Minutes 14 Oct 1856 – 5 June

1857), and to be returned (on loan) to the Club after cleaning in 2001 (see pp xiii–xv). No photograph of a better quality could obtained before cleaning.

GEORGE VI 1895–1952, reigned 1936–52, *see* Groups No. 969.

CHARLES MARCH GERE, RA

1869–1957, artist; elected to the Club in 1933.

319 *By Francis Dodd, 1927,* dry point etching, 30 × 26 cm (11¼ × 10¾ in), TQL seated to right, holding paintbrush, signed in pencil lower right, and inscribed along the top: *Francis Dodd 1927 / C.M. Gere.*
Presented by W.E.F.Macmillan, 1939.

EDWARD GIBBON

1737–94, historian.

320 *By J. Hall, 1780,* line engraving (O'D 7), frontispiece to his *Decline and Fall,* pubd Strahan & Cadell 1780, after the oil by Reynolds exh RA 1780, in Lord Rosebery's collection (Waterhouse 1941, p. 71).

FREDERICK WAYMOUTH GIBBS, CB

Elected to the Club in 1848.

321 *By Morris & Co.,* proof lithograph from a drawing (Ports M.III.14).

SIR VICARY GIBBS, MP

1751–1820, Chief Justice of Common Pleas, known as 'Vinegar Gibbs'.

322 *By S.W. Reynolds and T.G. Lupton,* mezzotint (O'D 1), after an oil by W. Owen.
Presented by Barbara (Lady) Freyberg, 1938, in memory of her grandfather, Joseph Jekyll.

WILLIAM GIFFORD

1756–1826, first editor of the *Quarterly Review.*

323 *By R.H. Cromek,* line engraving (Ports M.II.16 but not a member; O'D 1), used as frontispiece to Gifford's *Juvenal* (1802), after an oil by Hoppner in the John Murray Collection.
Presented by John Murray, 1908.,

319

DAVIES GILBERT, DCL, FSA, MP

1767–1839, President of the Royal Society; an original member of the Club and present at the Somerset House meeting, 16 Feb 1824.

324 *By S. Cousins, 1828,* mezzotint (O'D 1), after an oil by Henry Howard, exh RA 1827, formerly at Gawdy Hall, Suffolk.

325 *By W. Drummond, 1835,* lithograph of a marble bust by Westmacott at Pembroke College Oxford, published as *Athenaeum Portraits,* no.13.

SAMUEL GILES

326 *By ? F. Holl, c. 1850,* stipple engraving in crayon manner, proof before letters (Richmond Coll. III. 22), from a drawing by G. Richmond.
Presented by George Richmond, 1865.

JOHN GILLIES, LLD, FRS, FSA

1747–1836, historiographer of Scotland; a founding member of the Club.

327 *By C. Picart, 1813,* stipple engraving (O'D 3), after an oil by Opie in the Scottish NPG.
Presented by Arthur Jaffé, 1931.

WILLIAM GILPIN

Treasurer of Christ's Hospital.

328 *By J.R. Jackson,* mezzotint, proof before letters (Richmond Coll. III. 21; O'D 1), after an oil by G. Richmond, 1854, at Christ's Hospital
Presented by George Richmond, 1865.

GIORGIONE (called)

1477–1510, Venetian artist.

329 *By Cornelius van Dalen,* engraving proof before letters, after an oil now called 'Portrait of a Bearded Man, *c.*1508' and attributed to Lorenzo Lotto, in the Royal Collection, Hampton Court (Shearman 142, plate 25)

Literature: Hollstein V. p.107; Berenson, *Lorenzo Lotto* (1956), p.44.

JOHN HALL GLADSTONE, FRS

1827–1902, Fullerian Professor of Chemistry at the Royal Institution; elected to the Club in 1865.

330 *By F. Holl,* stipple engraving in crayon manner, proof with artists' names only and facsimile of signature (Richmond Coll. I. 20), from a drawing by G. Richmond.
Presented by George Richmond, 1865.

SIR RICHARD GLAZEBROOKE, FRS, KCB

1854–1935, physicist; elected 1898 under Rule II.

By Campbell Swinton, group photograph, see **Groups,** No. 964.

REGINALD MORIER YORKE GLEADOWE, CVO

1888–1944, Slade professor, Oxford, member of the Court of Assistants, Goldsmiths Company, designed the Stalingrad sword (see **Memorabilia** 'Coronation Bowl', No. 1460); elected a member of the Club in 1939.

331 *By Randolph Schwabe, 1944*

Pencil on buff paper, 9.5 × 6.25 cm (3¾ × 2½ in), signed and dated: *R. Schwabe 1944 / Gleadowe.*

Presented by the artist, 1945.

331

GEORGE ROBERT GLEIG

1796–1888, chaplain-general to the forces 1844–75, elected to the Club in 1829.

332 *By W. Drummond, 1836*, lithograph after Eddis, published as *Athenaeum Portraits* no. 31.

SIR WILLIAM GOLDING, CBE

1911–93, author of *Lord of the Flies*, etc. Nobel Prize (literature) 1982; elected to the Club in 1976.

333 *Photograph* in the Nobel Prize book, 1982.

T.S. GOOCH, MP, *See* **Appendix I, no. 27**

REV JOSEPH GOODALL

1760–1840, provost of Eton and a founding member of the Club. He is mentioned in Disraeli's *Coningsby* as 'the courtly Provost, the benignant Goodall'.

334 *By C. Turner, 1828*, mezzotint (O'D 2), after an oil by J. Jackson at Eton College.

RIGHT REV HARVEY GOODWIN

1818–91, Bishop of Carlisle, elected to the Club in 1870.

335 *By T.L. Atkinson*, mezzotint, proof before letters, engraver's name in pencil (Richmond Coll. V. 19; O'D 2), from an oil by G. Richmond [HL hands on book] Presented by George Richmond, 1884.

FRANCIS GORE

Governor of Upper Canada; elected to the Club in 1825.

336 *By W. Drummond, 1835*, lithograph after Eddis, published as *Athenaeum Portraits* no.1.

GORE-BROWN, *see* **SELBOURNE, No. 764**

GORHAM, *see* **Groups No. 950**

EARL OF GOSFORD

1776–1849, Archibald Acheson; a founding member of the Club.

337 *By R.J. Lane, 1828*, lithograph (Ports M. I.21; O'D 1), after an oil, 1826, by Phillips.

EARL OF GOSFORD

1806–64, when Lord Acheson; elected to the Club in 1827 as an undergraduate at Oxford.

338 *By R.J. Lane*, lithograph (Ports M. I. 20; O'D 1), as a boy in Highland dress, after T. Phillips.

HENRY GOULBURN, MP

1784–1856, Chancellor of the Exchequer.

339 *By ? F. Holl*, stipple engraving, proof before letters (Richmond Coll. III. 20), from an oil by G. Richmond. Presented by George Richmond, 1865.

MARIA GRAHAM, LADY CALLCOTT, *see* **Appendix I, no. 28**

THOMAS GRAHAM, FRS

1805–69, Master of the Mint; elected 1846 under Rule II.

340 *By Maull & Polyblank,* photograph (Ports Q. 26).

LE GRAND ESPAGNOL

341 *By Alphonse Legros,* etching, 29 × 23.5 cm (11½ × 9¼ in), (Legros-Bliss no.95).

Exhibition: Le Gros Memorial Exh. Tate Gallery 1912. Lucas bequest 1918.

COLONEL THE HON. FRANCIS GRANT, MP

1778–1853, later Earl of Seafield; elected to the Club in 1825.

342 *By E Scriven 1825,* engr. (Ports M. I.28; O'D 1), after an oil by Phillips exh RA 1819.

SIR WILLIAM GRANT, DCL, MP

1752–1832, Master of the Rolls and a founding member of the Club.

343 *By S.W. Reynolds, 1820 ,* mezzotint (O'D 2), after an oil by G. H. Harlow in Lincolns Inn.
Presented by Barbara (Lady) Freyberg, 1938.

SIR MOUNTSTUART GRANT-DUFF, GCSI, FRS

1829–1906, Governor of Madras; elected to the Club in 1858.

344 *By G.J. Stodart, 1889,* stipple vignette, proof before letters (Wells-Grillion 26), from a drawing by H.T. Wells for Grillion's Club.
Presented by H.T. Wells, 1898.

EARL GRANVILLE, KG

1815–91, when Rt Hon George Leveson-Gower, MP for Lichfield; elected to the Club in 1852.

345 *By W. Walker, 1853,* mezzotint (O'D 2), after R. Lehmann, exh RA 1851.
Presented by Rudolf Lehmann, 1900.

346 *By T.L. Atkinson,* mezzotint, with arms and facsimile signature (Richmond Coll. V. 8; O'D 2), from an oil by G. Richmond.
Presented by George Richmond, 1884.

CHARLES L. GRAVES, *see* **Satires**, No. 1026-7

347

GEORGE BELLAS GREENOUGH, FRS

1778–1855, first president of Geographical Society; a founding member of the Club.

347 *By M. Gauci,* lithograph (Ports M. I.37; O'D 1), after a drawing by Eddis.
Presented by Decimus Burton who built his villa in Regent's Park (see Nos 1298–9)

GREGORY XVI

1765–1846, Bartolomeo Cappellari, Pope from 1831

348 *By C. Motte, 1831* (Ports I.13), published and presented by Colnaghi & Son, 1831.

THOMAS GRENVILLE, PC

1755–1846, First Lord of the Admiralty; book collector, the Grenville Library was his magnificent bequest to the British Museum

349 *By J. Posselwhite,* stipple engraving in crayon manner, proof before letters (Richmond Coll. IV. 7; O'D 5), from

SIR GEORGE GROVE
By HERBERT A. OLIVIER
Presented by the Artist, 1937

a drawing by G. Richmond, 1845, at Inverary Castle, the sitter aged 90.
Presented by George Richmond, 1865.

VISCOUNT GREY OF FALLODON, *see* **Satires**, No. 998

SIR PHILIP DE MALPAS GREY-EGERTON, Bt, MP, FRS

1806–81, palaeontologist, elected in 1831.

350 *By J.R. Jackson,* mezzotint, proof with artists' names only (Richmond Coll. V. 4; O'D 2), from an oil by G. Richmond [HL seated to right].
Presented by George Richmond, 1884.

ELIZABETH, COUNTESS GROSVENOR

1797–1891, later Marchioness of Westminster.

351 *By S. Cousins, 1833,* mezzotint (Ports I.24 and II.4; O'D 1), after the oil by Lawrence (as Lady Elizabeth Leveson-Gower) exh RA 1818, the Countess of Sutherland's collection (Garlick 490).

SIR GEORGE GROVE, CB, DCL, DD

1820–1900, Director of the Royal College of Music, editor of *Grove's Dictionary of Music;* elected to the Club in 1871.

352 *By Herbert Olivier, 1895*
Oil on canvas, 125 × 89 cm (49¼ × 35 in), signed and dated top left: *Olivier 95.* TQL standing in black morning coat, leaning on a desk with papers inscribed: *Franz Schubert;* grey hair, mutton-chop whiskers.

Condition: cleaned by Reeves, 1955.

Exhibition: RSP 1896.
Presented by the artist, 1937.

REV WILLIAM GUNN, *see* **Appendix I,** no. 28

DR ALBERT GÜNTHER, FRS

1830–1914, zoologist; elected 1879 under Rule II.

353 *By G.T. Harcourt Powell,* photograph (Ath. Ports. Red 11b).
Presented by his son, R.W.T. Gunther.

HUDSON GURNEY, MP, *see* **Appendix I,** no. 30

HON SIR JOHN GURNEY, KC

1768–1845, judge, Baron of the Exchequer; elected 1832.

354 *By W. Holl, 1821,* stipple engraving (Ports M. I. 49; O'D 1), from an oil by G.H. Harlow,

355 *By J. Posselwhite,* stipple engraving in crayon manner, proof with artists' names only and facsimile signature (Richmond Coll. IV. 5; O'D 2), from an oil by G. Richmond.

REV JOSEPH JOHN GURNEY

1788–1847, Quaker minister and philanthropist..

356 *By C.E. Wagstaff,* mezzotint, proof with artists' names only (Richmond Coll. III. 23; O'D 2), from an oil by G. Richmond.
Presented by George Richmond, 1865.

357 *Anon* lithograph (Ports Q. 35a).

RIGHT HON RUSSELL GURNEY, QC, FRS

1804–78, Recorder of Windsor.

358 *By C. Holl, 1877,* stipple vignette, proof before letters (Wells–Grillion 9), from a drawing by H.T. Wells for Grillion's Club.
Presented by H.T. Wells, 1898.

MARY GWYN, actress, *see* **Bunbury,** No. 113

SIR FRANCIS SEYMOUR HADEN, FRCS, PRE

1818–1910, surgeon, etcher, and Whistler's brother-in-law; elected to the Club in 1881.

359 *By Sir Hubert von Herkomer, 1892*
Etching, 15.5 × 20.5 cm (6 × 8 in), inscribed top right: *Hubert Herkomer 92* and along bottom edge in pencil: *H.H. Imp / Hubert Herkomer.*

Presented by Marion Spielmann, 1947.

JOHN HALES, *see* **Appendix I,** no. 32

THOMAS CHANDLER HALIBURTON, MP

1796–1865, author of *Sam Slick;* Judge of Supreme

359

Court, Nova Scotia, MP for Launceston; elected to the Club in 1839 under Rule II.

360 *By D.J. Pound, 1839,* engraving after a Mayall photograph.

VISCOUNT HALIFAX, GCB

1800–85, Sir Charles Wood, Secretary of State for India; elected to the Club in 1854.

361 *By J.D. Miller,* mezzotint, proof with artists' names only and facsimile signature (Richmond Coll. V. 3), from an oil by G. Richmond, 1873 (copy in NPG). Presented by George Richmond, 1884.

SIR DANIEL HALL, KCB, FRS

1864–1942, Director of the John Innes Horticultural

Institute; elected in 1920 under Rule II.

362 *By Sir Richard Paget Bt. 1933*

Black chalk heightened with white on blue-grey paper, 22.75 × 14.25 cm (9 × 5⅝ in) , inscribed: *SIR DANIEL HALL 1933 (Drawn on the train between Dover &Victoria) R.A.S.P.* HS in glasses, reading.

Presented by the artist, 1944.

JOHN HALL, Engraver, *see* **Appendix I., no. 33**

HENRY HALLAM

1777–1859, historian and a founding member of the Club.

363 *After T. Phillips, 1834,* litho vignette (Ports Q. 8, repr.

362

Ward 1926, p. 100), from an oil in the John Murray Collection.
Presented by John Murray, 1908.

364 *By W. Holl*, stipple engraving in crayon manner, proof with artists' names only and facsimile signature (Richmond Coll. I. 26), from a drawing by G. Richmond, 1843, in NPG.
Presented by George Richmond, 1865.

HENRY FITZMAURICE HALLAM

1824–50, son of HH above and also a historian.

365 *By (F. Holl)*, stipple engraving in crayon manner, proof before letters (Richmond Coll. I. 27; O'D 1), from a drawing by G. Richmond.
Presented by George Richmond, 1865.

WILLIAM AND ELIZABETH HALLET

366 *By Arman Mathey*, etching, 66 × 49 cm (26 × 19¼ in), published 1903 by Dowdeswell & Dowdeswells … and Thomas Agnew & Sons, after 'The Morning Walk' by Gainsborough in the National Gallery.
Lucas bequest 1918.

EARL OF HALSBURY

1823–1921, Lord Chancellor; elected to the Club in 1885.

367 *Photograph* (Ports M. III. 30).

EDMUND STORR HALSWELL

a founding member of the Club and donor.

368 *By M. Gauci*, lithograph (Ports M. I. 36; O'D 1), after a portrait by Eddis.
Presented by the sitter.

LORD GEORGE HAMILTON, MP

1845–1927, Secretary of State for India; elected to the Club in 1885.

369 *After H. T. Wells, 1897*, autotype facsimile of a drawing, with signature and artist's monogram (Wells-Grillion 39).
Presented by H. T. Wells, 1898.

GENERAL SIR IAN HAMILTON, GCB, GCMG, DSO

1853–1947, colonel of Gordon Highlanders, commanded at Gallipoli; elected to the Club in 1902.

370 *After Sir W. Rothenstein, 1916*, litho-facsimile of a drawing in the NPG, one of three, made in 1916 (R.377–9).
Presented by the artist, 1937.

RIGHT REV WALTER HAMILTON

1808–69, Bishop of Salisbury; elected to the Club in 1860.

371 *By F. Holl, 1862*, stipple engraving in crayon manner, proof before letters, published Colnaghi 1862 (Richmond Coll. II. 4; O'D 1), from a drawing by G. Richmond.
Presented by George Richmond, 1865.

376

THOMAS HAMMERSLEY

1748–1812, banker.

372 *By R. Golding, 1822* , line and stipple engraving (O'D 1),
after an oil by H.D. Hamilton, *c.*1810, at Claydon House.
[Christie's 13.5.83 (162)]
Presented by Barbara (Lady) Freyberg, 1938.

LUKE HANSARD

1752–1828, parliamentary printer.

373 *By F.C. Lewis,* lithograph vignette (Ports II. 13),
inscribed: *Your affectionate and loving Father Luke
Hansard / ob. Oct. 29. 1828 AE 77,* after an oil by S. Lane in
the House of Commons.
Presented by Samuel Lane, 1839.

VISCOUNT HARDINGE OF LAHORE, GCB

1785–1856, Governor-General of India; elected to the
Club in 1825.

374 *By E. Dalton, 1846,* lithograph (Ath. Fol. I.29; O'D 5)
after Sir William Ross.
Presented by the publisher, Thomas McLean, 1846.

375 *By C. Turner, 1833,* mezzotint (Ports M. I. 29; O'D 1),
after a portrait by E.U. Eddis.
Presented by Charles Turner, 1833.

THOMAS HARDY, OM

1840–1928, poet and novelist; elected to the Club in 1891
under Rule II.

376 *By Sir William Rothenstein, 1916.*

Black chalk on coarse buff paper, 28 × 21 cm (11 × 8¼ in),
signed and dated: *W.R 1916,* head only, facing, wearing collar
and tie, straggly moustache. One of nine drawings made at
Max Gate in 1916, described in *Men and Memories* (R362–70).

Presented in 1939 by a group of members of the Club
(Mr St John Hornby, Hugh (Lord) Molson, Sir Hugh
Walpole, Sir Saxton Noble, Mr D.R.H. Williams,
Mr G.H. Baillie).

377 *After Sir W. Rothenstein,* litho-facsimile of No. 376
Presented by the artist 1937.

378 *By Sir William Rothenstein, 1916*

Black chalk on coarse buff paper, 30 × 25 cm (11¾ × 9⅞ in),
signed and dated: W.R. 1916, head only, profile to left (R.368).

Formerly in Charles Rutherston's collection; presented
by Major Michael Salaman, 1945.

VEN JULIUS CHARLES HARE

1795–1855, Archdeacon of Lewes; elected to the Club in
1825.

379 *By H. Robinson, 1862,* stipple engraving in crayon manner, proof with artists' names only (Richmond Coll. II.
27; OD 1), from a drawing by G. Richmond.
Presented by George Richmond, 1865.

COUNTESS OF HAREWOOD

d. 1859, Lady Louisa Thynne, married 3rd Earl 1823.

380 *By F. Holl,* line engraving, proof before artists' names
(Richmond Coll. IV. 11; O'D 2), from a drawing by G.
Richmond.
Presented by George Richmond, 1865.

JAMES HARRINGTON, author of Oceana, *see*
Appendix I, no. 34

ARTHUR LISTER HARRISON, JP

elected to the Club in 1928

381 *Photograph,* probably 1930s [HS to right, filmstar-ish]

BENJAMIN HARRISON

1771–1856, Treasurer of Guy's Hospital.

382 *By J. Posselwhite,* stipple engraving in crayon manner (Richmond Coll. III. 24), from a drawing by G. Richmond.
Presented by George Richmond, 1865.

EARL OF HARROWBY, PC

1762–1847, Dudley Ryder, 1st Earl; conservative statesman and a founding member of the Club.

383 *By H.B. Hall, 1837,* stipple and line engraving (O'D 1), plate to *Eminent Conservative Statesmen* (1837) after a painting by Mme Meunier.

EARL OF HARROWBY, KG, FRS

1798–1882, 2nd Earl; elected to the Club in 1865.

384 *By F.C. Lewis,* stipple vignette (Eng. A.I. 45; O'D 1), as Viscount Sandon, after a drawing by J. Slater for Grillion's Club.
Presented by W.M. Powell, 1910.

EARL OF HARROWBY, PC

1831–1900, 3rd Earl, educationalist.

385 *By H. Cousins,* mezzotint (Richmond Coll. III. 1), from a drawing by G. Richmond, 1860, in NPG.
Presented by George Richmond, 1865.

WILLIAM HARVEY

1578–1657, physician to St Bartholomew's Hospital,, famous for his discovery of the circulation of the blood, first propounded at a Lumleian lecture, 1616.

386 *After Peter Scheemakers (c.1739)*
Plaster bust, 61cm (24 in) high, cast from the marble bust of *c.*1739 by Peter Scheemakers, then belonging to Dr Richard Mead and presented by him to the Royal College of Physicians, where there are also two plaster casts, one by L. Bruggiotti.

Literature: Keynes 1949, plates 27–30; Gunnis 1953, p.331 (there attributed to Roubiliac); Piper 1963, p.160; Wolstenholme & Piper 1964, p 210).

CHARLES HATCHET, FRS

1765?–1847, chemist, vice-president of the Royal Society; an original member of the Club and present at the Somerset House meeting, 16 Feb 1824.

387 *By W. Drummond, 1836 ,* lithograph vignette (O'D 1) after Phillips exh RA 1816, published as *Athenaeum Portraits* no.15.

LORD HATHERLEY

1801–81, William Page Wood, Lord Chancellor.

388 *By F. Holl,* stipple engraving in crayon manner, proof before letters (Richmond Coll. I. 10; O'D 2), from a drawing by G. Richmond for Grillion's Club.
Presented by George Richmond, 1865.

EDWARD HAWKINS, FRS, FSA

1780–1867, numismatist; a founding member of the Club.

389 *By M. Gauci, 1833 ,* lithograph (Ports M. I.42; O'D 1), after a drawing by Eddis,
Presented by Colnaghi & Son,

390 *By W. Drummond, 1835,* lithograph after Eddis, published as *Athenaeum Portraits* no.5.

SIR WALTER HAWORTH, FRS

1883–1950, Nobel Prize (chemistry) 1937; elected to the Club in 1943.

391 *Photograph* in the Nobel Prize book, 1937

B.R. HAYDON, artist, *see* Appendix I, no. 35

SIR GEORGE HAYTER, RA

1792–1871, portrait and history painter; a founding member.

392 *Self-portrait,* lithograph (Ports M.I.3; O'D 2), the head only similar to the oil of 1820 in the NPG. In a spirit of self-mockery the drawing shows the young artist in 17th century costume, with palette attached to a 'spear'.
Presented by the artist, 1826.

SIR FRANCIS BOND HEAD, Bt. KCH

1793–1875, Lieutenant Governor of Upper Canada; elected to the Club in 1830.

392

393 *By C. Turner, 1837,* mezzotint (Ports M. II.14; O'D 1),
after an oil by Nelson Cook.
Presented by the publisher, Colnaghi & Son.

CHARLES HEATH, engraver, *see* **Appendix I,** no. 37

JAMES HEATH, engraver, *see* **Appendix I,** no. 36

SIR WILLIAM HEATHCOTE, Bt. MP

1801–81, MP for Oxford and a founding member of the
Club.

394 *Anon* mezzotint, first proof with Latin title (Richmond
Coll. V. 2), from an oil by G. Richmond.
Presented by George Richmond, 1884.

RIGHT REV REGINALD HEBER

1783–1826, Bishop of Calcutta and hymn writer; his

half-brother, Richard Heber, famous bibliographer and book-collector, was an original member of the Club.

395   *By F.C. Lewis,* stipple vignette (Eng. A.I. 47; O'D 6), after a drawing by J. Slater for Grillion's Club.
Presented by W.M. Powell, 1910.

By Miss Turner after Phillips, see Appendix I, no. 39.

SIR ROBERT GEORGE WYNDHAM HERBERT, GCB

1831–1905, Permanent Under Secretary of State, elected to the Club in 1866.

396   *After H.T. Wells, 1897,* autotype facsimile of a drawing for Grillion's Club, with signature and artist's monogram (Wells-Grillion 38).
Presented by H.T. Wells, 1898.

SIR HUBERT VON HERKOMER, RA, CVO, DCL

1849–1914, artist; elected in 1889 under Rule II.

397   *Self-portrait, 1909,* lithograph vignette, s/d *H.H. 1909.* A smaller pencil version, signed/dated 1910, belonged to Mrs B.P. Lockett.
Presented by Marion Spielmann, FSA, 1947.

SIR JOHN CHARLES HERRIES, MP

1778–1855, Chancellor of the Exchequer; a founding member of the Club.

398   *By S. Freeman,* stipple engraving, plate to *Portraits of Conservative Statesmen,* II (1844).

SIR JOHN HERSCHEL, FRS

1792–1871, astronomer; elected to the Club in 1825.

399   *By W.J. Ward, 1835,* mezzotint (O'D 1), after an oil by Pickersgill in St John's College, Cambridge.

LORD HERSCHELL

1837–99, Sir Farrer Herschell, Lord Chancellor; elected to the Club in 1881.

400   *By London Stereoscopic Co.,* photograph (Ports M. III. 29), inscribed on verso: *Sir Farrer Herschell.*

401   *By G.J. Stodart, 1887,* stipple engraving, proof before

397

letters (Wells-Grillion 20; O'D 2), from a drawing by H.T. Wells for Grillion's Club.
Presented by H.T. Wells, 1898.

MARQUESS OF HERTFORD, GCB

1812–84, Francis Seymour, 5th Marquess, a cousin of the founder of the Wallace Collection.

402   *By J.R. Jackson,* mezzotint, proof with artists' names only (Richmond Coll. V. 12; O'D 1), from an oil by G. Richmond.
Presented by George Richmond, 1884.

JOHN PEMBERTON HEYWOOD

1803–77, Liverpool merchant.

403   *By S. Cousins,* mezzotint, private plate (Richmond Coll. V. 13; O'D 1), from an oil by G. Richmond.
Presented by George Richmond, 1884.

ROBERT HICHENS

404   *By W. Holl,* stipple engraving in crayon manner, proof before letters (Richmond Coll. I. 28; O'D 1), from a drawing by G. Richmond.
Presented by George Richmond, 1865.

SIR JOHN HICKS, FBA

1904–89, Nobel Prize (economics) 1972; elected to the Club in 1975.

405   *Photograph* in the Nobel Prize book, 1972.

SIR MICHAEL HICKS-BEACH, *see* ST ALDWYN

JOHN SOMERVILLE HIGHFIELD 1871–1945, electrical engineer, *see* **Groups** No. 956

ARCHIBALD VIVIAN HILL, CH, FRS

1886–1977, physiologist, Nobel Prize (medicine) 1922; elected to the Club in 1922.

406   *Photograph* in the Nobel Prize book, 1922.

SIR GEORGE HILL, KCB, FBA

1867-1948, numismatist, Director of the British Museum; elected to the Club in 1920.

407   *By Roderic Hill*, photograph of an etching.

SIR ROWLAND HILL, KCB, FRS

1795–1869, originator of penny postage; elected to the Club in 1860.

408   *By W.O. Geller, 1848* , mezzotint, proof before letters (O'D 2), after a drawing by Abraham Wivell.

THOMAS WILLIAM HILL

Assistant Secretary to the Club, 1890–after 1925 (*see* Ward 1926, pp.vii, 83).

409   *Photograph* in Ath. Ports. Red 60.

RIGHT REV GEORGE HILLS

1826–95, Bishop of British Columbia (Vancouver).

410   *By F. Holl*, stipple engraving in crayon manner, proof with artists' names only (Richmond Coll. II. 15; O'D 1 photograph), from a drawing by G. Richmond.
Presented by George Richmond, 1865.

ARTHUR MAYGER HIND, OBE

1880–1957, historian of engraving, Keeper of Prints and Drawings, British Museum; elected to the Club in 1929.

411   *Photograph*, c.1930, in Ath. Ports. Red 47.

417

REV ROGER HINES

c.1825–c.1915, Vicar of Royston, Herts

412   *By J.R. Jackson*, mezzotint, proof with artists' names only (Richmond Coll. III. 12), from an oil by G. Richmond.
Presented by George Richmond, 1865.

SIR CYRIL HINSHELWOOD, OM

1897–1967, bio-chemist, Nobel Prize (chemistry) 1956; elected to the Club in 1943.

413   *After Sir Gerald Kelly, 1960* , photograph in Nobel Prize book, 1956, of an oil in the Royal Society.

JOSEPH HODGSON, FRS

1788–1869, surgeon; elected to the Club in 1851.

414   *By S. Cousins, 1849*, mezzotint (Ath. Fol. I. 32; O'D 1), after a portrait by J. Partridge.

ARTHUR HOLDSWORTH, MP

1780–1860, Governor of Dartmouth Castle; elected to the Club in 1830.

420

415 *By M. Gauci, 1832,* lithograph (Ports M. I. 33; O'D 1) after an oil by Eddis. (An oil by S. Hodges, exh RA 1857, was painted for the Town Hall, Dartmouth).
Presented by the sitter, 1832.

CHARLES H. HOLDSWORTH

Governor of Portsmouth Castle

416 *By Walter F. Tiffin,* lithograph after a portrait by Sydney Hodges, probably painted for the Town Hall, Portsmouth.

SIR THOMAS ERSKINE HOLLAND, KC, FBA

1835–1926, Chichele professor of international law and diplomacy, Oxford; author of *The Elements of Jurisprudence* (1880); elected in 1883 under Rule II.

417 *By Hugh G. Riviere, 1914*

Oil on canvas, 102 × 79 cm (40 × 31 in), signed and dated in black paint: *HRiviere 1914.*

'The portrait had been presented to Sir Thomas 'by friends at home and abroad in 1914' *(DNB);* it was presented to the Club by his son, Sir Robert Holland, 1960.

418 A photogravure copy by *Swan Electric Engraving,* signed by artist and sitter, was presented by Arthur Jaffé in 1948.

WILLIAM HOLMES, MP

d.1851, Tory whip for thirty years; elected to the Club in 1830.

419 *By S. Freeman, 1837,* stipple engraving (O'D 1), plate to *Eminent Conservative Statesmen,* after a portrait by J. Moore .
Presented by Arthur Jaffé, 1932.

SIR CHARLES HOLROYD

1861–1917, painter, etcher, Director of the National Gallery and first Keeper of the Tate Gallery; elected to the Club in 1914.

420 *By Alphonse Legros,* etching 27.5 × 18 cm (10¾ × 7 in), signed twice in pencil and ink (Legros-Bliss no. 283).
Presented by Mervyn O'Gorman, 1940.

EARL OF HOME

1799–1841, Cospatrick Home, 11th Earl, diplomat.

421 *By H. Cousins,* mezzotint, proof with artists' names only and facsimile signature Richmond Coll. III. 2; O'D 1), from an oil by G. Richmond.
Presented by George Richmond, 1865.

COUNTESS OF HOME

1805–77, Lucy Elizabeth Scott-Montagu, m. 11th Earl 1832.

422 *By J.R. Jackson,* mezzotint, (Richmond Coll. III. 4), after an oil by G. Richmond.
Presented by George Richmond, 1865.

VERY REV WALTER HOOK, DD

1798–1875, Dean of Chichester; elected in 1865 under Rule II.

423 *By C.E. Wagstaff, 1838,* mezzotint (O'D 1) after a portrait by F. Rosenberg.
Presented by Arthur Jaffé, 1932.

428

Nobel Prize (medicine) 1929, President of the Royal Society; elected in 1922 under Rule II.

426 *After Meredith Frampton, 1838,* photogravure, copy
-7   published Belcolor Gravure, Slough, of the oil in the Royal Society. Another is in the Nobel Prize book, 1929. Presented by Colonel Sir Henry Lyons, 1940.

JOHN HOPKINSON, FRS, DSC

1849–98, Professor of Electrical Engineering, King's College, London; elected in 1887 under Rule II.

428 *By R.H. Campbell,*

Oil on canvas, 51 × 41 cm (20 × 16 in), signed lower right: *R.H. Campbell.* HS nearly profile to left, fawn coat and waistcoat, grey shirt, purplish tie; light brown hair and beard, grey eyes,

Presented by his widow and other members of his family, 1913.

DR LEONARD HORNER, FRS

1785–1864, President of the Geological Society; elected to the Club in 1830.

429 *By Maull & Polyblank,* photograph (Ports M. III.43).

LORD HOUGHTON, FRS

1809–95, Richard Monckton Milnes, MP, President of the London Library.

430 *By F. Holl, c.1850,* stipple engraving in crayon manner, proof before letters (Richmond Coll. II. 24; O'D 1), from a drawing by G. Richmond.
Presented by George Richmond, 1865.

SIR GODFREY HOUNSFIELD, FRS

b. 1919, engineer, inventor of Computer Assisted Tomography (CAT) Scanning, Nobel Prize (medicine) 1979, elected to the Club in 1980.

431 *Photograph* in the Nobel Prize book, 1979.

SIR WILLIAM HUGGINS, KCB, OM

1824–1910, astronomer, President of the Royal Society; elected in 1879 under Rule II.

432 *After John Collier, 1906,* photogravure reproduction from the oil by John Collier in the Royal Society (with replica in the Royal Astronomical Society and preliminary sketch in NPG).

424 *By ? W. Holl, 1849,* stipple engraving in crayon manner, proof before letters published J. Hogarth (Richmond II. 17; O'D 2), from a drawing by G. Richmond. Presented by George Richmond, 1865.

MARIA, LADY HOOKER, NÉE MISS TURNER, *see* **Appendix I, no. 40**

SIR WILLIAM JACKSON HOOKER, FRS, FLS

1785–1865, Director of Kew Gardens and a founding member of the Club.

By Miss Turner after Cotman, 1813, see Appendix I, no. 39

425 *By W. Drummond, 1837,* lithograph after Eddis published as *Athenaeum Portraits* no. 51.

JOHN HOOLE, translator, *see* **Appendix I, no. 41**

SIR FREDERICK GOWLAND HOPKINS, OM

1861–1947, biochemist and discoverer of vitamins,

436

SIR SAMUEL HULSE, Bt. GCH

1747–1837, Field Marshal.

433 *By R.J. Lane, 1830*, line engr, proof (Ports II. 12; O'D 1), after a portrait by S. Lane exh RA 1830.
Presented by Samuel Lane, 1839.

ALEXANDER VON HUMBOLDT, traveller, *see* **Appendix I, no. 42**

SIR ABRAHAM HUME, Bt. FRS, MP

1749–1838, a Director of the British Institution, pioneer art historian, and a founding member of the Club.

434 *By T. Lupton, 1814,* , mezzotint (O'D 4), after the oil by Reynolds, 1783, at Belton House (National Trust).
Presented by Arthur Jaffé, 1934.

435 *By J. Jenkins, 1832*, stipple engraving (O'D2), plate to Jerdan's *National Portrait Gallery,* after a drawing by Henry Edridge exh RA 1815.

ALFRED WILLIAM HUNT

1830–96, landscape painter, follower of Turner and praised by Ruskin; elected in 1883 under Rule II.

436 *By D.S. MacColl, 1890*
Pencil on off-white paper, 19.5 × 16 cm (7¼ × 6½ in), inscribed: *Alfred Hunt / Whitby / 1890 / DSM.* See No. 1236 for a related drawing by Hunt himself.
Presented by the artist, 1940.

CECIL A. HUNT, RWS

1873–1965, barrister, landscape painter, elected in 1910, donor and a long-serving member of the Art Committee set up to advise on our collection of pictures.

437 *By G.W. Lambert, 1906*
Pencil, 28 × 23.5 cm (11 × 9¼ in) sight size, signed and dated: *GW Lambert 1906,* and inscribed: *Cecil A. Hunt by G.W. Lambert ARA.*
Presented by the sitter, 1933.

438 *After Sir William Russell Flint, 1948,* , photo-reproduction of a pencil drawing.
Presented by the sitter, 1954.

442

WILLIAM HOLMAN HUNT, O.M.

1827–1910, one of the founders of the Pre-Raphaelite Brotherhood; painter of many famous pictures such as 'The Light of the World' and 'The Scapegoat'; elected in 1868 under Rule II.

439 *Self-portrait, c.1880* [Pl. III]

Oil on canvas, 105 × 75 cm (41⅛ × 29½ in), inscribed on backing-board: *copy by* [erased] *of W. Holman-Hunt OM.* TQL facing, in a dark green studio coat with light green sash and red cuffs, palette in right hand, brushes under left. Framed in an idiosyncratic contemporary frame with wedge-shaped indentations, corner rosettes and ivory inlay.

The portrait is a copy by himself (or perhaps by his close friend and assistant, Edward Robert Hughes) of his self-portrait, signed and dated 1875, presented to the Uffizi Gallery, Florence, in 1907.

Condition: cleaned by W. Drown, 1958.
Presented by Mrs Holman Hunt, 1926

440 *By the London Stereoscopic Company,* a chromolithograph vignette copy of the head, with facsimile of signature (a pair to that of Tennyson).

JOHN HUNTER, FRS

1728–93, surgeon and anatomist in whose honour the Hunterian Lectures of the Royal College of Surgeons are named.

441 *By T.H. Maguire, 1849,* lithograph (Ports M. III.20; O'D 1), after a drawing by Nathaniel Dance in the Royal College of Surgeons, London.

LORD HURCOMBE, GCB

1883–1975, Cyril William Hurcombe, civil servant, president of the Society for the Promotion of Nature Reserves; elected to the Club in 1940 and a trustee.

442 *By John Ward, 1970*

Ink and wash on buff paper, 55.5 × 40 cm (21⅞ × 15¾in), signed and dated: *John Ward 1970 / 1st July;* HL seated to right, hands crossed.

Bought by private subscription from members of the Club, 1970.

WILLIAM HUSKISSON, MP

1770–1830, elected to the Club in 1825 and the first railway casualty.

443 *By W. Finden, 1831,* line and stipple engraving (Ports

447

M.II.18; O'D 3), frontispiece to his *Speeches* (1831), after a portrait by Lawrence at Harewood House (Garlick 425).
Presented by John Murray, 1908.

WILLIAM HUSTLER

d.1832, registrar to Cambridge University; elected to the Club in 1825.

444 *By Miss Turner,* litho vignette (Ports Q.10; O'D 1).

ALDOUS HUXLEY

1894–1963, author of *Brave New World,* etc; elected to the Club in 1922.

445 *By Sir W. Rothenstein, 1922,* litho-facsimile of a drawing (R619). A variant, in profile to left, is in Manchester City Art Gallery (R616).
Presented by the artist, 1937.

By Low, 1933, see **Satires**, No. 1022.

SIR ANDREW HUXLEY, OM, PRS

b.1917, physiologist, Master of Trinity College, Cambridge; Nobel Prize (medicine) 1963; elected in 1963.

446 *After Michael Noakes, 1985*, photograph of an oil in the Royal Society.

451

THOMAS HENRY HUXLEY, PC, FRS.

1825–95, scientist, friend of Darwin ('Darwin's Bulldog'), coined the word 'agnostic', President of the the Royal Society, author of *Collected Essays* (9 vols 1893–4); elected to the Club in 1858 under Rule II, and a frequent contributor to the Suggestion Book.

447 *By the Hon. John Collier (1883)*

Oil on Windsor & Newton canvas, 127 × 102 cm (50 × 40 in), signed in red paint: *John Collier;* TQL seated holding a skull, books on table to right. A version by Collier (his son-in-law) of his portrait of 1883 in the NPG.

Condition: cleaned by M. Braddell, 1953.
Presented by the Hon John Collier and Sir Frederick Macmillan, 1924.

A photograph of 1857 is repr. in Ward 1926, p. 176 and Adrian Drummond, *Huxley: The Devil's Disciple* (1994), pl. 18.

MOHAMMED MEERZA IBRAHEEM

compiler of a Persian Grammar; elected to the Club in 1830.

448 *By W. Drummond, c.1837*, lithograph after Partridge, published as *Athenaeum Portraits* no. 48.

VERY REV WILLIAM RALPH INGE, KCVO

1860–1954, Dean of St Paul's, known, from his pessimistic articles in *The Evening Standard*, as 'the gloomy dean'; elected in 1919 under Rule II.

449 *After Sir W. Rothenstein, 1920*, litho-facsimile of a drawing at King's College, Cambridge (R504).
Presented by the artist, 1937.

456

SIR ROBERT INGLIS, Bt, FRS

1786–1855, MP for Dundelk, Ripon and Oxford University 1824–54.

450 *By J. Faed,* mezzotint, proof before letters (Richmond Coll. IV. 8; O'D 5), from an oil by G. Richmond (chalk drawing, 1845, in NPG).
Presented by George Richmond, 1865.

SIR HENRY IRVING

1838–1905, the first actor to be knighted. He was elected in 1882 under Rule II.

451 *By Mortimer Menpes, 1898*

Pencil on white card, 22.5 × 16 cm (8⅞ × 6¼ in), inset 19.5 × 14 cm, signed and dated: *M.M. 1898.* A variant is in the Garrick Club, no.322. A large collection of Menpes etchings, including one of Irving, was sold at Sotheby's 2 Dec. 1977 (162).

Literature: Mag. of Art (1899), pp. 98–100; Mortimer Menpes, *Henry Irving* (1906), pp. 1–25 illustrating twelve watercolour portraits of Irving.

463

Exhibition: 'Modern Illustration', V&A Museum 1900 (3120).
Presented by Marion H. Spielmann through his son, Dr Percy Spielmann, 1947.

452 *By T.O. Barlow,* mezzotint after an oil by Millais, 1883 (Garrick Club no.323) 'All the world's a stage' logo and facsimile signature.
Presented by Mrs John Harris, 1939.

WASHINGTON IRVING

1783–1859, American writer; elected in 1825.

453 *By M.I. Danforth,* engraving (Ports M. II. 21), after C.R. Leslie.
Presented by John Murray, 1908.

PRINCESS ISABELLA

1566–1633, Infanta of Spain, m. Archduke Albert of Austria.

454 *By J. Muller, 1615,* line engraving (Singer 82589) after an oil by Rubens, location unknown presumed lost (Burchard *Corpus Rubensianum,* XIX. 62).
Lucas bequest 1918.

HENRY JACKSON, OM

1839–1921, Regius Professor of Greek, Cambridge; elected in 1897.

455 *By William Strang,* mezzotint (O'D 1), after an oil by C.W. Furse, 1890, in Trinity College, Cambridge.

456 *By Henry Lamb, 1906*

Black chalk and pencil on off-white paper, 37.5 × 29 cm (14¾ × 11⅜ in), signed and dated: *Henry Lamb 1906;* HS nearly in profile to left, repr. in *Supplement to the Cambridge Review,* 22 Feb 1906.

Presented by General Sir Henry C. Jackson, KCB, DSO.

JOHN JACKSON, RA

1778–1831, portrait painter; elected to the Club in 1825.

457 *Self-portrait,* c.1823 [Pl VII (a)]

Pencil and watercolour on white paper, 28 × 22.5 cm (11 × 8⅞ in); HS to left , turned facing, uninscribed. Under the paper is a copy of Thompson's stipple engraving of 1823 and a note by Spielmann identifying the watercolour as Jackson. This is a sketch for the third and latest type of Jackson self-portraits, showing the artist at half length holding a palette (NPG no.443).

Exhibition: 'Victorian Exhibition', New Gallery 1891–92, no.251–3.
Presented by Marion H. Spielmann, 1947.

RIGHT REV JOHN JACKSON

1811–85, Bishop of Lincoln and London; elected to the Club in 1853.

458 *By C.W. Sharpe, 1854,* stipple engraving in crayon manner, proof with artists' names only (Richmond Coll. II. 6; O'D 2), from a drawing by G. Richmond.
Presented by George Richmond, 1865.

WILLIAM JACOB, FRS

1762?–1851, statistical writer.

459 *By M. Gauci, c.1844,* lithograph (Ports II. 31; O'D 1), after a drawing by Eddis.
Presented by E.U. Eddis, 1844.

RIGHT REV WILLIAM JACOBSON

1803–84, Bishop of Chester, Regius Professor of Divinity, Oxford; elected to the Club in 1866.

460 *By F. Holl,* stipple engraving in crayon manner, proof before letters (Richmond Coll. II. 18), from a drawing by G. Richmond.
Presented by George Richmond, 1865.

ARTHUR JAFFÉ

1880–1954, civil engineer, barrister, connoisseur; elected in 1918, and donor of a large collection of engravings.

461 *Photograph* in Ath. Ports Red 48.

WALTER JAMES, *see* NORTHBOURNE

SIR JAMES JEANS, FRS

1877–1946, astronomer and author of *The Mysterious Universe* (1930) etc.

By Campbell Swinton, group photograph, *see* **Groups** No. 964

RIGHT REV JOHN JEBB, DD, FRS

1775–1833, Bishop of Limerick; elected to the Club in 1825.

462 *By T. Lupton, 1830,* unpublished mezzotint (Ports M.I.7;

465

O'D 1), after a portrait by Lawrence, c.1826, whereabouts unknown (Garlick no.437).
Presented by the bishop himself.

JOSEPH JEKYLL, FRS, FSA, MP

1754–1837, Master in Chancery and an original member of the Club.

463 *By W. Say, 1818,* mezzotint (O'D 1), after an oil by Lawrence exh RA 1817 (Garlick 438). A portrait by George Dance, 1796, in the NPG, is reproduced in Ward 1926, p. 16.
Presented by Miss E. Magrath, 1918.

SIR FRANCIS JEUNE, *see* ST HELIER

THOMAS WILLIAM JEX-BLAKE

1832–1915, headmaster of Rugby and dean of Wells Cathedral; elected to the Club in 1867.

464 *By J. C. Webb, 1890,* mezzotint, published Agnew 1892, after an oil by Herkomer at Rugby School.
Presented by A.J. Buxton, 1929.

AUGUSTUS JOHN, OM, *see* Satires, No. 1121

CHARLES JOHNSON, CBE, FBA

1870–1961, Public Records Officer and author of *The Care of Documents and Management of Archives* (1919), etc. elected to the Club in 1929 and donor.

465 *By Laurence Binyon, 1891*

Pencil drawing on white paper, 17 × 13.5 cm (6¾ × 5¼ in), inscribed in pencil: *Original drawing by Laurence Binyon 1891.*

Presented by Charles Johnson, 1947.

CHARLES PLUMTRE JOHNSON, JP

1853–1938, writer on Dickens and Thackeray, elected to the Club in 1904.

466 *After F.M. Bennett,* photogravure by Emery Walker of an oil by Bennett.
Presented by the sitter, 1933.

SIR GEORGE JOHNSON, FRS, FRCP

1818–96, Physician-Extraordinary to Queen Victoria; elected in 1885 under Rule II.

467 *By Sir Frank Short,* mezzotint after an oil by Frank Holl., 1888, in the Royal College of Physicians, London. (Short-Hardie III, 322).
Presented by C.P. Johnson the sitter's son, 1933.

DR SAMUEL JOHNSON, LLD

1709–84, poet, biographer, essayist, sage, and author of the *Dictionary of the English Language.* A facsimile of Dr Johnson's letter of thanks to the vice-chancellor of Oxford, 4 March 1755, is in the Club library (Eng. C. I. 21).

By Miss Turner after Ozias Humphry, 1773, see Appendix I, no. 43.

468 *After Nollekens (1777)*

Painted plaster bust, 54.5 cm (21½ in) high, after the original marble bust by Nollekens in Westminster Abbey. Chantrey

475

thought that this was Nollekens's finest bust, but Dr Johnson himself was displeased at the heavy crop of hair which made him look like an ancient poet. The hair actually belonged to George White, one of Sir Joshua Reynolds's favourite models, 'a sturdy Irish beggar, originally a street paviour'. A marble replica is at Pembroke College, Oxford, a marble copy by E.H. Baily is NPG no.996, and a lead cast is in the V&A Museum.

Literature: Boswell IV, pp. 554–5; Smith 1920, I p 47.

469 *By A.L. Vago*

Terracotta bust 61 cm (24 in), damaged and repaired, by A.L. Vago after Nollekens, incised on the back: *Dr Johnson / By Nollikens / A.L. Vago Fecit.*

Vago was probably a member of a Hungarian family practising in the late 19th as architects, sculptors and portrait-painters *(Thieme-Becker).*
Presented by Percy Fitzgerald Esq.

470 *By John Opie, 1783*

Oil on canvas, 76 × 61 cm (30 × 24 in), uninscribed. HL to left, brown coat and waistcoat, slight smile, heavy grey wig.

Opie had sittings from Johnson in 1783: 'On Monday the 16th I sat for my picture and walked a considerable way with little inconvenience'. Soon afterwards he suffered 'a paralytic stroke and my speech was taken from me but I had no pain' (letter to Hester Thrale 19 June 1783). Opie produced at least three versions, the prime being either that in the collection of Lord Crawford and Balcarres in Scotland, or in the Houghton Library, Harvard University (repr. Letters op. cit. III). Copies are in the NPG and Dr Johnson's House, Gough Square. The Athenaeum version was spurned by Dr Hill in his magnificent edition of Boswell's *Life*: '... but the face has lost all vigour and is hardly recognisable as Johnson's; the painting is of moderate quality and lacks the brilliance of the original' (Hill IV pp. 455–7). A line engraving by J. Heath was published as frontispiece to *The Dictionary* (1786). A superb mezzotint by Charles Turner was published in 1792.

Literature: Letters of Samuel Johnson, III (ed Bruce Redford 1992); James Boswell, *Life of Samuel Johnson* (ed G.B. Hill 1934); J.J. Rogers, *Opie and His Works* (1878) pp.115–7; Ada Earland, *John Opie and His Circle* (1911), pp.288–9.

Condition: damaged in 1961, relined and repaired by Herbert Lank, 1962.
Presented by Thomas Humphry Ward, 1889.

HENRY BENCE JONES, FRS

1814–73, physician, friend and biographer of Faraday, secretary to the Royal Institution; elected in 1854 under Rule II.

471 *By C. Holl,* stipple engraving 1873 (Ports M. III. 47; O'D 1), after a drawing by G. Richmond.

REV HERBERT WALSINGHAM JONES

1826–89, elected to the Club in 1851.

472 *Photograph* presented by Sir Lawrence Jones (Ath. Ports. Red 4b).

SIR JOHN THOMAS JONES, Bt. KCB

1783–1843, major-general and engineer; elected to the Club in 1830.

473 *By Edward Morton,* lithograph (first fifty proof, Ath. Fol. I.30; O'D 1) from a drawing by E.H. Corbould of the statue by W. Behnes in St Paul's Catheral.
Presented by Sir Willoughby Jones, Bt. 1848.

SIR LAWRENCE JONES, Bt

1857–1954, elected to the Club in 1891.

474 *Photograph, c.1920,* in Ath. Ports Red. 35.

475 *By Sir Richard Paget, 1929*
Pencil sketch on Club writing paper, 10 × 15 cm (4 × 5⅝ in), inscr: *10. 6. 29 / Sir Lawrence Jones,* head in profile to left, holding forth, among a group of drawings made by Paget in the Club.
Presented by the artist.

REV RICHARD JONES

1790–1855, Professor of Political Economy at King's College, London; elected to the Club in 1830.

476 *By M. Gauci,* lithograph (Ports M.I.43; O'D 1), after an oil by Eddis.

477 *By J. Posselwhite, 1855,* engraving (Ports M. II. 8), after J. Carpenter.

WALLACE JONES, 1846–1924, engineer, *see* Groups, No. 962

SIR WILLOUGHBY JONES, Bt.

1820–84, elected to the Club in 1848.

478 *Anon* photograph in Ath. Ports, Red 4a.
Presented by Sir Lawrence Jones, Bt.

REV BENJAMIN JOWETT

1817–93, Master of Balliol and Regius Professor of Greek, Oxford.

479 *By F. Holl,* stipple engraving in crayon manner, proof with artists' names only (Richmond Coll. II. 23), from a drawing by G. Richmond at Balliol College.
Presented by George Richmond, 1865.

CHARLES JOHN KEAN, AS 'MACBETH', *see* Theatre Designs No. 1390

REV JOHN KEBLE

1792–1866, founder of the Oxford Movement, author of *Tracts for the Times* and *The Christian Year.*

480 *By S. Cousins, 1845,* mezzotint (Richmond III. 13; O'D 1), from a watercolour by G. Richmond, 1844, at Keble College, Oxford.
Presented by George Richmond, 1865.

481 *By W. Holl, 1864,* stipple vignette, first proof published J. Chance 3 Dec 1863 (Richmond Coll. III. 14; O'D 2), from

a chalk drawing by G. Richmond, 1863, in NPG.
Presented by George Richmond, 1865.

SIR ARTHUR KEITH, FRS, 1866–1955,
anthropologist, *see* **Groups** No. 961

SAMUEL KEKEWICH, MP

482 *By J. Bellin,* mezzotint, proof before letters (Richmond
Coll. III. 25), after an oil by G. Richmond.
Presented by George Richmond, 1865.

LORD KELVIN, GCVO, OM

1824–1907, William Thomson, physicist, inventor and
President of the Royal Society; elected in 1870 under
Rule II.

483 *After W.W. Ouless,* photogravure of an oil, 1902, in the
Clothmakers Company, London.

By Alan Swinton, group photograph at Jesmond Dene,
see **Groups** No. 958

His portrait by his sister, Elizabeth King, 1887 in NPG,
reproduced Ward 1926, p. 228.

SIR JOHN KENDREW, FRS

b.1917, Nobel Prize (chemistry) 1962; elected to the Club
in 1963.

484 *Photograph* in the Nobel Prize book, 1962.

SIR FREDERICK KENYON, KCB, GBE, FBA

1863–1952, Director of the British Museum, elected to
the Club in 1908.

485 *By Burchett of Emery Walker Ltd,* photograph of a bust
by J.A. Stevenson in the BM(Ath. Ports Red 40).

WILLIAM PATON KER, FBA

1855–1923, Professor of Poetry, Oxford; elected to the
Club in 1905 under Rule II.

486 *After John Tweed,* photograph of a bronze bust at All
Souls College, Oxford.

SIR EDWARD KERRISON, Bt, MP

1774–1853, General.

487 *By G. Sanders,* mezzotint, proof with artists' names only

(Richmond Coll. IV. 9), from a drawing by G. Richmond, 1858, 'presented to him by neighbours and
tenants'.
Presented by George Richmond, 1865.

LORD KEYNES, see **Satires** No. 1114

LORD KILLANIN OF GALWAY

1826–1901, Sir Michael Morris, Bt., Lord of Appeal;
elected to the Club in 1867.

488 *After H.T. Wells, 1895,* autotype facsimile of a drawing
for Grillion's Club, with signature and artist's monogram (Wells-Grillion 30).
Presented by H.T. Wells, 1898.

THOMAS M. KILLOPE

489 *By F. Holl,* stipple engraving in crayon manner, proof
before letters (Richmond Coll. I. 29), from a drawing by
G. Richmond.
Presented by George Richmond, 1865.

LORD KING OF OCKHAM

1776–1833, author of *Life of John Locke;* a founding
member of the Club.

490 *By M. Gauci, 1833,* lithograph (Ports M. I.39; Ports Q.5;
O'D 1), after a drawing by Eddis.

RIGHT REV EDWARD KING

1829–1910, Principal of Cuddesdon College and Bishop
of Lincoln.

491 *By T.L. Atkinson, 1877,* mezzotint, private plate
(Richmond Coll. V. 10), from an oil by G. Richmond.
Presented by George Richmond, 1884.

ALEXANDER WILLIAM KINGLAKE, MP

1809–91, author of *Eothen, History of The Crimean War;*
elected in 1853 under Rule II.

492 *By C. Kiddell,* engraving from a photograph by [? Elliott
& Fry – TQL to right holding book].
Presented by his great-niece, Miss Harford, 1957.

By Spy, see **Satires** No. 1012.

494

RUDYARD KIPLING

1865–1936, masterly writer of stories (*Kim, Jungle Books,* etc); he was elected in 1897 under Rule II, but said 'it feels like entering a cathedral between services'. Kipling refused to become poet laureate and was offered the OM three times. Nobel Prize (literature) 1907.

By Burne-Jones, 1897, see **Satires**, No. 1013

493 *By William Strang, 1898,* etching signed in ink: *Rudyard Kipling* (Strang 1912, no.345; collotype facsimile in Ath. Ports. Red 42).
Presented by the sitter, 1929.

494 *By W. Cushing Loring, 1901*

Pencil on greyish paper, 38.5 × 15 cm (15⅛ × 6 in), signed and dated: *W. Cushing Loring / Jany 6th 1901 / Boston U.S.A.* , and scrawled below is the indistinct signature: (?) *Rudyard.*

There is a mystery over the precise date. Kipling was not in Boston in 1901 but Loring was in London, though there is no record of a meeting. There is a possibility that the drawing was *ad vivum,* but more likely that it was done from memory or a photograph.

Literature: Kipling Society Journal, December 1988 and March 1989, where doubt was cast on the identity and Sir Edmund Gosse put forward as the sitter. But the drawing was hanging in the Billiard Room, during Kipling's lifetime and no protest is recorded.

Presented by Percy Fitzgerald, 1905.

495 *By Sir William Nicholson, 1899*

Woodcut, 28 × 22 cm (11 × 8⅛ in), inscribed top left: *William Nicholson.* Coloured impressions were also printed.

Presented by M. O'Gorman, 1937.

496 *Photograph* in the Nobel Prize book, 1907.

THOMAS ANDREW KNIGHT, FRS, FLS

1759–1838, horticulturist and a founding member of the Club.

497 *By Miss Turner,* litho vignette (Ports Q.7; O'D 2), after a drawing by S. Cole 1834.

SIR JAMES KNIGHT-BRUCE, MP

1797–1866, Lord Justice of Appeal; elected in 1830.

498 *Anon, 1845–50,* stipple engraving in crayon manner, proof before letters (Richmond Coll. I. 6), from a drawing by G. Richmond.
Presented by George Richmond, 1865.

JOHN KNOWLES

1781–1841, authority on Fuseli and a founding member of the Club.

499 *By W. Drummond, c.1836,* lithograph after C. Landseer, published as *Athenaeum Portraits,* no.25.

VISCOUNT KNUTSFORD, GCMG

1825–1914, Henry Thurston Holland, Secretary of State for Colonies; elected to the Club in 1880.

500 *By J. Brown, 1882,* stipple vignette, artists' names only (Wells-Grillion 16; O'D 1), from a drawing by H.T. Wells for Grillion's Club.
Presented by H.T. Wells, 1898.

CHARLES KÖNIG

1774–1851, Keeper of Minerals in the British Museum; elected to the Club in 1825.

501 *By Miss Turner,* litho vignette (Ports Q.13; O'D 1) after a drawing by Eddis.

CHARLES CARMICHAEL LACAITA, MP

1853–1933, MP for Dundee; elected to the Club in 1880.

502 *Photograph* from *Naturel Paris,* signed and dated: *Charles Lacaita 1930 aet.77.*

SIR JAMES LACAITA, KCMG

1813–95, Italian scholar, completed the Vernon edition of Dante in the Club library; elected to the Club in 1867.

503 *Anon* photograph in Ath. Ports. Red 23a.

RT HON WILLIAM LAMB, *see* MELBOURNE, No. 592

LORD CHARLES WILLIAM LAMBTON

1818–31, eldest son of the Earl of Durham.

504 *By S. Cousins, 1827,* mezzotint (Ports I. 26; O'D 1), published 27 March 1827, after the oil by Lawrence, 1825, still in the family collection (Garlick 463).

505 *By C.A. Waltner, 1882–3,* etching after Lawrence, based on the Cousins mezzotint above, published Dec 1882 by Obach & Co, with small vignette of Lawrence's head (Beraldi 111).
Lucas bequest, 1918.

506

SIR EDWIN LANDSEER, RA

1802–73, portrait painter, immensely popular as animal painter ('Dignity and Impudence', 'Monarch of the Glen'); designed bronze lions in Trafalgar Square; elected to the Club in 1830, but denounced its food: 'they say there's nothing like leather; this beefsteak is!'

506 *By Sir Francis Grant, PRA*

Ink and sepia wash on blue RA voting paper, 17.5 × 21.55 cm. inscribed: *Reminiscence of Sir Edwin Landseer sketched on an election evening at the Royal Academy by – Grant RA & given by him to E.M.Ward Novr 2nd 1857 / on the reverse of a voting paper.*

Literature: Ward, *Memories,* p.4; Ormond 1973, p.254.
Presented by Iolo Williams, 1950.

RICHARD JAMES LANE

1800–72, engraver.

507 *By McLean, Melhuish & Napper & Co,* photograph (Ports M.II.10).

MOST REV LORD LANG OF LAMBETH

1864–1945, Archbishop of Canterbury; elected to the Club in 1909 under Rule XII.

508 *By Francis Dodd, 1944*

Pencil on pink paper, 42 × 31 cm (16½ × 12¼ in), inscribed: *Lord Lang of Lambeth,* and signed and dated: *Francis Dodd 1944.*

Presented by the artist, 1946.

508

LORD LANGDALE

1783–1851, Henry Bickersteth, Master of the Rolls; elected Club in 1825.

509 *By H. Robinson,* stipple engraving in crayon manner, proof with artists' names only (Richmond Coll. I. 9), from a drawing by G. Richmond.
Presented by George Richmond, 1865.

SIR JOSEPH LARMOR, 1857–1942, mathematician, *see* **Groups** Nos. 959, 963

PETER MERE LATHAM

1789–1875, Physician-Extraordinary to Queen Victoria.

510 *By F. Holl,* stipple engraving in crayon manner, proof before letters (Richmond Coll. I, 22), from a drawing by G. Richmond.
Presented by George Richmond, 1865.

ELIZABETH LATOUCHE

b. 1758, wife of Peter Latouche, MP for co. Leitrim.

511 *By W.J. Ward, 1831,* mezzotint (Ath. Fol. I.15; O'D 1), aged 73, after A.E. Chalon.

SIR THOMAS LAWRENCE, PRA

1769–1830, Regency portrait painter, an original member, and present at the Somerset House meeting, 16 Feb. 1824. When Lawrence died in January 1830, of 'ossification of the heart', the Club minutes recorded that 'his memory be
thanked for assiduous attendance and guidance … in all points connected with decoration and the Fine Arts' (7 May 1830, p. 156). He designed the Club Seal (see No. 1278).

512 *By R.J. Lane, 1830,* lithograph (Ports II.5; O'D 23), 'from a Plaster-cast taken at the age of thirty-four in the Possession of an attached Friend' (i.e. Mrs Denham; *see* Walker 1985, p.312).
Presented by J.C. Denham, 1830.

513 *By M. Gauci, 1830,* lithograph (Ports M.I.15; O'D 1), after a sketch from memory by A.E. Chalon, 1828.
Presented by A.E. Chalon, 1830.

LORD LAWRENCE OF INDIA

1811–79, Governor-General of India; elected to the Club in 1850 under Rule II.

514 *By Maull & Polyblank,* signed photograph dated indistinctly, 13 June 186? (Ports M. III.36).

SIR AUSTEN LAYARD, GCB, MP

1817–94, excavator of Nineveh; elected in 1848 under Rule II.

515 *By Maull & Polyblank,* signed photograph dated 4 May 1861 (Ports M.III.41).

WILLIAM EDWARD LECKY, MP, OM

1838–1903, historian; elected in 1867 under Rule II.

516-7 *By G.J. Stodart, 1888,* stipple vignette, proof before letters (Wells-Grillion 23) after a drawing by H.T. Wells for Grillion's Club. Two copies.
Presented by H.T. Wells, 1898, and Mrs Lecky.

523

SYDNEY LEE, RA

1866–1949, treasurer of the Royal Academy; elected in 1931 under Rule II.

518 *Photograph;* HS slightly to left, tweed jacket and waist-coat, c.60.

THE HON HENEAGE LEGGE

1788–1844, s. of George, Earl of Dartmouth; a founding member of the Club.

519 *By F.C. Lewis, 1832,* stipple vignette (Eng. A.I 42; O'D 1), after a drawing by J. Slater for Grillion's Club.
Presented by W.M. Powell, 1910.

EARL OF LEICESTER

1752–1842, Thomas Coke of Holkham, MP ('Coke of Norfolk'), 1st Earl, agricultural improver; elected to the Club in 1825.

By Miss Turner after Cotman, 1817, see Appendix I, no. 15.

520 *By M. Gauci, 1834,* lithograph (Ports M. II.14), after an oil by S. Lane at Holkham.
Presented by Samuel Lane, 1839.

EARL OF LEICESTER, KG

1822–1909, 2nd Earl, agricultural adviser to the Prince of Wales at Sandringham.

521 *By F. Joubert,* mixed engraving printed by T. Brooker, (Richmond IV. 1; O'D 1), after an oil by G. Richmond at Holkham.
Presented by George Richmond, 1865.

LORD LEIGHTON, PRA

1830–96, sculptor and the leading Victorian classical painter; elected to the Club in 1866.

522 *By J. Brown,* stipple vignette, proof before letters (Wells-Grillion 12; O'D 5), from a drawing by H.T. Wells for Grillion's Club.
Presented by H.T. Wells, 1898.

523 *By Sir Thomas Brock, 1892*
Bronze bust, 82.5 cm (32½ in), incised: *Thomas Brock Sculptor 1892,* and standing on a marble pillar incised: *LEIGHTON.* A plaster cast, also 1892, is in the NPG. Brock made Lord Leighton's memorial tomb in St Paul's Cathedral.

Exhibition: a bronze version, exhibited RA 1893, was presented to the Royal Academy as Brock's diploma work and is still at Burlington House.

Literature: Frederick Leighton 1830–1896, RA exhibition catalogue (1996), 85–6.
Presented by Sir Thomas Brock.

PRINCE LEOPOLD OF SAXE-COBURG, KG

1790–1865, later King of the Belgians; a founding member of the Club.

524 *By F.C. Lewis, 1820,* engr. imitating a drawing, (Ports II.7), after a drawing by Lawrence (*see* Garlick 484).

EARL OF LEVEN AND MELVILLE

1786–1876, John Leslie-Melville, 11th Earl, banker.

525 *By J.D. Miller,* mezzotint, private plate with facsimile signature (Richmond Coll. V. 6; O'D 1 as J.R Jackson engraving), after an oil by G. Richmond.
Presented by George Richmond, 1884.

EARL OF LEVEN AND MELVILLE

1817–89, Alexander Leslie-Melville, 12th Earl, banker.

526 *By J.D. Miller,* mezzotint, private plate proof with artists' names only (Richmond V. 21), from an oil by G. Richmond.
Presented by George Richmond, 1884.

HON. FREDERICK LEVESON-GOWER, MP

1819–1907, s. of Earl Granville, Liberal MP, author of *Bygone Years* (1905).

527 *By C. Holl, 1871,* stipple vignette, proof before letters (Wells-Grillion 1; O'D 1), from a drawing by H.T. Wells for Grillion's Club.
Presented by H.T. Wells, 1898.

HON. GEORGE LEVESON-GOWER, MP. *see* GRANVILLE, No. 345

SIR GEORGE HENRY LEWIS, Bt. CVO

1833–1911, solicitor and friend of Edward VII.

528 *By Marion Son & Co.,* photograph inscr: 'Herbert Spencer from his friend G.H. Lewis, May 1868' (Ath. Ports Red 2).

VERY REV HENRY GEORGE LIDDELL

1811–98, Dean of Christ Church and author, with Robert Scott, of the *Greek-English Lexicon* (1843); elected to the the Club in 1849.

529 *By F. Holl,* stipple engraving in crayon manner, proof before letters (Richmond Coll. II. 20; O'D 2), from a drawing by G. Richmond.
Presented by George Richmond, 1865.

RIGHT REV JOSEPH BARBER LIGHTFOOT

1828–89, Bishop of Durham, elected to the Club in 1873 under Rule II.

530 *By F. Holl,* stipple engraving in crayon manner, proof before letters (Richmond Coll. II.21; O'D 1), from a drawing by G. Richmond.
Presented by George Richmond, 1865.

JOHN LINDLEY, MD, FRS

1799–1865, botanist and a founding member of the Club.

531 *By Miss Turner,* litho vignette (Ports Q. 16; O'D 1) after a drawing by Eddis, 1832.
Presented by Dawson Turner.

JOHN LISTON

1776–1846, actor.

532 *By W. Ward, 1821,* mezzotint (Ports I.27; O'D 7), after an oil by John Jackson exh RA 1820.

GRANVILLE GOWER LOCH, CB

1813–53, Captain Royal Navy.

533 *Anon,* mezzotint, proof before letters (Richmond Coll. III. 26), from an oil by G. Richmond. [TQL standing in uniform, hands on sword]
Presented by George Richmond, 1865.

JAMES LOCH

1780–1855, economist, barrister; elected to the Club in 1825.

534 *By J. Posselwhite,* stipple engraving in crayon manner, proof before letters (Richmond Coll. I. 30; O'D 1), from a drawing by G. Richmond, 1845.
Presented by George Richmond, 1865.

JOHN LOCKE

1632–1704, philosopher, author of *An Essay Concerning Human Understanding* (1690).

535 *after Roubiliac*
Painted plaster bust, 73 cm high, no inscription, after a lost posthumous marble by Roubiliac, probably taken from a copy by E.H. Baily at Magdalen College, Oxford. A statue, said to be by Rysbrack (1757), is at Christ Church, Oxford.

Literature: Poole 1912, II, p 221; Esdaile 1928, p 53; Piper NPG 1963, pp 207–10;

EDMUND LODGE, FSA

1756–1839, biographer (Lodge's *Portraits* 1821–34), herald and a founding member of the Club.

536 *By W. Drummond, 1836,* lithograph after D. Maclise, published as *Athenaeum Portraits,* no. 40.

SIR OLIVER LODGE, DSC, FRS

1851–1940, physicist and pioneer of psychical research; elected to the Club in 1902.

537 *After Sir W. Rothenstein, 1916*, litho-facsimile reproduction of a drawing (R342) in the NPG.
Presented by the artist, 1937.

538 *By Alan Swinton, 1920*, photograph (Ath. Ports. Red 13a).

LORD LONDONDERRY, By A.W. LLOYD, *see* **Satires, No. 996**

SIR CHARLES LONG, KB, PC

c.1761–1838, later Lord Farnborough; benefactor of the National Gallery; an original member, present at the Somerset House meeting, 16 Feb 1824, and a donor.

539 *By C. Picart*, lithograph (Ports M.II.9), proof before letters, for Cadell's *Contemporary Portraits* after a drawing by H. Edridge.

EDWARD LONG

1734–1813, author of *History of Jamaica* (1774).

540 *By W. Sharp*, engr. (Ports M.I.6; O'D 2), after an oil by Opie.
Presented by his grandson, C.E. Long, 1830.

HENRY WADSWORTH LONGFELLOW

1807–82, American poet, dined at the Club in 1868.

541 *By W.H. Mote, 1851*, line and stipple vignette with facsimile of signature: *Yours truly Henry W. Longfellow*, published by D. Baur London, Kirkman, Reid & Field, Boston March 1 1851.

MOST REV CHARLES THOMAS LONGLEY

1794–1868, Archbishop of Canterbury, elected to the Club in 1857.

542 *By T. L. Atkinson, 1887*, mezzotint, proof before letters, artists' names in pencil (Richmond Coll. V.22), from an oil by G. Richmond, (chalk drawing c.1862, in NPG).
Presented by George Richmond, 1887.

RIGHT REV JOHN LONSDALE

1788–1867, Bishop of Lichfield, elected to the Club in 1838.

543 *By J. D. Miller*, mezzotint, private plate with arms and

541

facsimile signature (Richmond Coll. V. 1) from an oil by G. Richmond.
Presented by George Richmond, 1884.

EARL LOREBURN, GCMG, DCL

1846–1923, Lord Chancellor; elected to the Club in 1906.

544 *By Leopold Goetze*, mezzotint after an oil by Fiddes Watt, 1912, at Balliol College, Oxford (Poole II. 80)

LOUIS PHILIPPE

1773–1850, when duc d'Orléans (Philippe Egalité); later King of the French, 1830–48.

545 *By C. Motte*, lithograph (Ports II.12), after an oil by J-B Mauzaisse, 1824.
Presented by Captain Christopher Clarke, c.1831.

SIR BERNARD LOVELL, OBE, FRS

b. 1913, astronomer and founder of Jodrell Bank Experimental Station; elected to the Club in 1963.

546

546 *By John Ward, 1978*

Ink and wash drawing, 48.5 × 32 cm (19 × 12½ in), signed and dated: *Decr 1978*.

Presented by the artist in 1988.

PAMELA LOVIBOND

assistant librarian at the Club 1930–39. She prepared the index for Sir W. Rothenstein's *Men and Memories*, III (1939).

547 *By Sir William Rothenstein, c.1939* [Pl. VIII (b)]

Red and black chalk on coarse off-white paper, 39 × 29 cm (15¼ × 11½ in).

Bequeathed by Sir Stephen Gaselee, KCMG, 1943.

WILSON LOWRY, engraver, *see* **Appendix I, no. 44**

SIR JOHN LUBBOCK, *see* AVEBURY, No. 36

COLONEL FRANCIS ALFRED LUCAS, JP, VD, MP

1850–1918, deputy-chairman of Alliance Insurance,

served 41 years in Reserve Forces; elected in 1883 and a generous benefactor to the Club.

548 *By James Bacon & Sons,* photograph (Ports M. II.45).

HORATIO JOSEPH LUCAS

exh RA 1870–73, etcher.

549 *Self-portrait, 1876,* etching 19.5 × 14 cm (7⅝ × 5½ in), signed and dated with monogram.

ROBERT LUTWIDGE

b. 1802, barrister; elected to the Club in 1825.

550 *By W. Drummond, 1835,* lithograph after Eddis, published as *Athenaeum Portraits,* no.7.

SIR CHARLES LYELL, BT. FRS, PGS

1797–1875, geologist, his work discrediting the 'catastrophe' theories; a founding member of the Club.

551 *By W. Drummond, 1836,* lithograph after Eddis, published as *Athenaeum Portraits,* no. 7.

552 *By J.E. Mayall, 1846,* daguerrotype (Ports M.II.2; O'D 5), of a lithograph by Albert Newsam, published by Mayall of Philadephia.
Presented by the sitter in 1848.

LORD LYNDHURST

1772–1863, John Singleton Copley, Lord Chancellor; a founding member of the Club.

553 *By R.A. Artlett, 1836,* stipple engraving (Ports II.29; O'D 1), after a portrait by A.E. Chalon, exh. RA 1836.
Presented by John Murray, 1908.

554 *By W. Walker, 1845,* stipple engraving (O'D 6), after a miniature by Sir William Ross (photograph in Ports M.III.25).

555 *By W. Holl,* stipple engraving in crayon manner, facsimile of signature and artists' names only (Richmond Coll. I. 7), from a chalk drawing by G. Richmond, 1851, in NPG.
Presented by George Richmond, 1865.

SIR HENRY LYONS, FRS

1864–1944, geographer, treasurer of the Royal Society; elected to the Club in 1916.

556 *Photograph, c.1920,* in Ath. Ports Red 51b.

LORD LYTTELTON, KCMG, DCL, FRS

1817–76, 4th baron; elected to the Club in 1838, among 'the forty thieves'.

557
-8   *By F.C. Lewis,* stipple vignette for Grillion's Club (O'D 1), after a chalk drawing by George Richmond, 1844, at Hagley Hall.
Presented by Arthur Jaffé, 1934. Another copy in ENG.A.I.38.

LORD LYTTON

1803–73, Edward Bulwer-Lytton, novelist; elected to the Club in 1825.

559   *By G. Cook, 1848,* stipple engraving pubd by Richard Bentley from a drawing by R.J. Lane, also engraved by H. Robinson (O'D 4).

LORD MACAULAY, MP

1800–59, historian and poet; elected to the Club in 1830.

560   *By J. Brown,* photograph of a drawing by Eddis, 1850, for B*entley's Miscellany* (1852).

561   *By W. Holl, 1861,* stipple engraving (Richmond Coll. III. 27; O'D 6), from a drawing by G. Richmond, 1850, in Trevelyan Collection (Ormond NPG, p. 290).
Presented by George Richmond, 1865.

ANDRÉ MacCOLL

c.1870–1945, married D.S. MacColl in 1897, see No. 563

562   *By Philip Wilson Steer*
Pencil and dark grey wash on light grey paper, 27.5 × 20.5 cm (10¾ × 8 in).
Presented by Mrs Bodkin in memory of her husband, Professor Thomas Bodkin, 1961.

DUGALD SUTHERLAND MacCOLL, DLitt, LLD

1859–1948, painter and Keeper of the Tate Gallery 1906–11 and the Wallace Collection 1911–24; elected to the Club in 1924 and donor.

563   *By Philip Wilson Steer, 1903* [Pl. VII (b)]
Sepia and watercolour on grey primed paper, 28 × 37.5 cm (11 × 14¾ in), signed and dated: *P.W. Steer 1903.* TQL seated to left sketching.

Literature: D.S. MacColl, 'A Batch of Memories', *Week End Review* 20 Dec. 1930.

561

Bequeathed by D.S. MacColl to Professor Thomas Bodkin and presented by Mrs Bodkin in 1961.
By Powys Evans, 1922, see **Satires**, No. 1018.

564   *By Ronald Gray, 1927,* photograph of an oil 'now in possession of A.D. MacColl, Brisbane'.

JAMES RAMSAY MACDONALD, DCL, FRS

1866–1937, labour Prime Minister; elected to the Club in 1924.

565   *After Sir W. Rothenstein, 1823,* litho-facsimile of a drawing, (R673), in the Manchester City Art Gallery, one of many drawings of the PM by Rothenstein who loved visiting 10 Downing Street.
Presented by the artist, 1937.

JOHN WILLIAM MACKAIL, OM

1859–1945, poet and translator, President of the British Academy; Burne-Jones's son-in-law and biographer of William Morris; elected to the Club in 1900.

566   *By ? Elliot & Fry,* photograph.

SIR THOMAS MACKENZIE, GCMG

1854–1930, High Commissioner for New Zealand, *see* **Groups** No. 969.

SIR HENRY MCMAHON, GCMG, 1862–1949, SPY cartoon, *see* Satires No. 1020

SIR PERCY MCMAHON, FRS 1854–1929, mathematician, elected to the Club in 1903 under Rule II, *see* Groups No. 957

LORD MACMILLAN, GCVO, PC

1873–1952, Hugh Pattison Macmillan, judge, created Baron Macmillan 1930; elected to the Club in 1922 and chairman of trustees 1936–45; his autobiography *A Man of Law's Tale*, published in 1952.

567   *By Sir William Rothenstein, 1937*

Chalk drawing on coarse buff paper, 38 × 32 cm (15 × 12½ in), signed and dated: *Wm Rothenstein 1937*.

Presented by the artist, 1937.

GEORGE AUGUSTIN MACMILLAN

1855–1936, publisher, secretary of the Society of Dilettanti from 1911; elected to the Club in 1894.

568   *After J.S. Sargent* 1925, Emery Walker photograph, signed *GAM,* of an oil in the Society of Dilettanti collection, Brooks's Club, London.

By Linley Sambourne, see **Satires**, No. 1037.

TELFORD MACNEILL

1834–1934, elected to the Club in 1876.

569   *By Walter Davey of Harrogate,* photograph (Ath. Ports. Red 8a).

WILLIAM CHARLES MACREADY

1793–1873, actor specially remembered for his 'Macbeth' and 'Lear'; elected to the Club in 1838.

570   *By C. Picart, 1820,* stipple vignette (Ports I.20; O'D 6), from a drawing by J. Jackson.

SIR FREDERIC MADDEN

1801–73, palaeographer; elected to the Club in 1839.

571   *By W. Drummond, 1837,* lithograph published as *Athenaeum Portraits,* no.53. (Ports M.II.1; O'D 6).

LAURIE MAGNUS

1872–1933, publisher; elected to the Club in 1911.

572   *By Whitlock, 1931,* photograph in Ath. Ports. Red 29.

EDWARD MAGRATH

1790–1856, succeeded Faraday as secretary of the Club 1824–55. His resignation letter, after thirty years, was pinned up in the hall and appears in the Minute Book, 27 Feb 1855.

573   *By Edward Upton Eddis, 1832*

Oil on canvas, 66 × 56 cm (26 × 22 in), signed and dated: *E.U. Eddis 1832.* HL to left, black coat and bow tie, white shirt and upturned collar; grey eyes, dark hair.

Presented by his niece, Miss Eleanor Magrath, 1918.

574   *By M. Gauci,* lithograph of an earlier copy, lettered: *E W Eddis del. 1831,* printed by M. Johnson, Norwich.

575   *By M. Gauci,* lithograph of the head only (Ports M.I.11; O'D 2), after Eddis.

576   *By William Drummond, 1836,* lithograph after Eddis, published as *Athenaeum Portraits* no.17, repr. Ward 1926, p. 62.

SIR HENRY MAINE, KCSI

1822–88. jurist, Master of Trinity Hall, Cambridge; elected 1862 under Rule II.

577   *By C.W. Walton,* proof lithograph (Ports M. III.15), published by Walton & Co.

SIR GEORGE MAKINS, GCMG, CB, PRCS

1853–1933, surgeon; elected to the Club in 1903.

578   *After J.S. Sleator,* photogravure of an oil. Presented by the sitter, 1932.

SIR JOHN MALCOLM, GCB

1769–1833, author of *History of Persia, History of India,* etc. and a founding member of the Club.

579   *By R.J. Lane, 1832,* lithograph (Ports M.I.31; O'D 2), after an oil by G.Hayter 1815.
Presented by Thomas Cornish, 1833.

573

NEIL MALCOLM

580 *By W. Holl,* mixed engraving, proof before letters (Richmond Coll. IV. 10), from an oil by G. Richmond, exh RA 1845.
Presented by George Richmond, 1865.

ADMIRAL SIR PULTENEY MALCOLM, GCB

1768–1838, C in C Mediterranean.

581 *By W.J. Ward, 1836,* mezzotint (Ports II.26; O'D 1), after an oil by S. Lane.
Presented by Samuel Lane, 1839.

HENRY REGINALD MALLOCK, FRS, d.1933, engineer, *see* Groups No. 953

GEORGE MANBY, inventor, *see* **Appendix I**, no.45

BISHOP OF MANCHESTER
Right Rev James Prince Lee, 1804–69

582 *By H. Robinson, c.1850,* stipple engraving in crayon

584

manner, proof before letters (Richmond Coll. II. 8), from a drawing by G. Richmond.
Presented by George Richmond, 1865.

MANNERS-SUTTON, *see* CANTERBURY, No. 139

CARDINAL MANNING

1808–92, Henry Edward Manning, became a Roman Catholic in 1851 and cardinal in 1873; elected to the Club in 1870 under Rule II; 'his favourite haunt was the Athenaeum' (Strachey, *Eminent Victorians;* Ward 1926, p. 226).

583 *By F. Holl, 1851,* stipple engraving in crayon manner, proof before letters (Richmond Coll. II. 11; O'D 3), from a drawing by G. Richmond.
Presented by George Richmond, 1865.

584 *By G.F. Watts, 1886*

Pencil on grey paper, 25 × 17 cm (9¾ × 6¾ in), inscribed under the mount: *H.E. Cardinal Manning / G.F. Watts, R.A. / 1886.* The drawing seems to be a copy from the oil of 1882 in the NPG, possibly made for an engraving.

Literature: Wilfred Meynell, 'Portraits of Cardinal Manning', *Mag. of Art* (Sept 1893) pp. 361–6.
Presented by Marion H. Spielmann FSA, through his son, Dr Percy Spielmann, 1947.

585 *By Alphonse Legros, 1877*

Etching inscribed: *à mon ami F. Burton / A. Legros.*

Literature: Legros-Bliss no. 322 illustrated; Legros-Wright, p. 16.
Presented by the artist to Sir Frederick Burton, director of the National Gallery, and by him to the Athenaeum .

WILLIAM MANSEL, Bishop of Bristol, *see* **Appendix I, No. 46**

EARL OF MANSFIELD

1705–93, William Murray, Lord Chief Justice.

586 *After Nollekens,* plaster bust 60 cm (23½ in) high, incised: *Mansfield.* A cast from a marble by Nollekens at Trinity College, Cambridge. Nollekens's original marble bust, dated 1779, is at Kenwood.

Literature: 'The True Resemblance of Lord Mansfield', Kenwood exhibition 1971.

GIDEON ALGERNON MANTELL, LLD, FRS

1790–1852, geologist, elected in 1840 under Rule II.

587 *By S. Stepney, 1837,* stipple engr. (Ports II.25; O'D 1), after an oil by Masquerier.
Presented by the sitter, 1840.

MARGARITA, INFANTA OF SPAIN

1651–73, d. of Philip IV and Mariana of Austria, *m.* the Emperor Leopold I, 1666.

588 *By Luderitz of Berlin, 1832,* line engr (Eng. I. 10) after the portrait by Velasquez in Vienna (version in Wallace Collection). The Infanta is also the central figure of *Las Meniñas* in the Prado.

WILLIAM MARSDEN, orientalist, *see* **Appendix I, no. 47**

MASKELYNE, *see* STORY-MASKELYNE

SIR THOMAS BYAM MARTIN, GCB

1773–1854, Admiral of the Fleet, MP for Plymouth.

589 *By H. Robinson,* stipple engraving in crayon manner, artists' names only (Richmond Coll. I. 12), from a drawing by G. Richmond.
Presented by George Richmond, 1865.

THOMAS JAMES MATHIAS

1754? –1835, satirist and Italian scholar.

590 *Anon.* litho vignette (Ports Q. 35b).
Presented by Dawson Turner, 1845.

SIR ROBERT HENRY MEADE, GCB

1835–98, Permanent Under Secretary of State; elected to the Club in 1894.

591 *After H.T. Wells, 1896,* autotype facsimile of a drawing for Grillion's Club, with signature and artist's monogram (Wells-Grillion 32).
Presented by H.T. Wells, 1898.

LORD MELBOURNE

1779–1848, Prime Minister.

592 *By S. Freeman, 1846,* stipple engr. 1846, after an oil by Lawrence in the NPG (Garlick 459c).

REV HENRY MELVILLE

1798–1871, Canon of St Paul's Cathedral; elected in 1845 under Rule II.

593 *By C. Turner,* 1835, mezzotint (O'D 1), after J. Rand .

LORD MENUHIN, OM, KBE

1916–99, Yehudi Menuhin, violinist; elected to the Club in 1969.

594 *Photograph*
Presented by his son-in-law, Jonathan C. Benthall, 1988.

LIONEL WALTER MIDDLETON

1908–75, hall porter of the Athenaeum, 1926–73, affectionately known as George.

595 *By John Ward, 1974*

Ink and watercolour on buff paper, 32.5 × 23.8 cm

595

(12¾ × 9⅜ in), signed and dated: *John Ward July 3rd 1974*. TQL standing at entrance to the Coffee Room

Presented by the artist, 1974.

SIR JOHN EVERETT MILLAIS, *see* **Satires**, Nos. 1008-9, 1036

WILLIAM MILLER

1769–1845, publisher.

By Miss Turner after Phillips, 1814, see Appendix I, no. 48

596 *By J.C.D. Engleheart, 1826*, lithograph vignette (O'D 1) after a miniature by Engleheart.

ARTHUR MILLS

1816–98, MP for Taunton and Exeter, elected to the Club in 1870.

597 *By J.D. Miller,* mezzotint, private plate with facsimile signature (Richmond Coll. V. 18), from an oil by G. Richmond.
Presented by George Richmond, 1889.

HENRY HART MILMAN

1791–1868, Dean of St Paul's

598 *After G.F. Watts's portrait in the NPG*, engraving (Ports M.II.42)
Presented by Dr. Arthur Milman, 1908-9.

ALEXANDER MILNE,

a founding member of the Club.

599 *By M. Gauci,* lithograph (Ports M.I.35; O'D 1).
Presented by E. Halswell.

JOHN MILTON

1608–74, poet

600 *After Matthew Noble*

Marble bust, 68.5 cm (27 in) high, no inscription on the back but incised *MILTON* on the circular socle, and standing on an imitation porphyry scagliola column.

A studio copy from Matthew Noble's marble bust (1866), St Paul's School, London, deriving remotely from the monument by Rysbrack (1731) in Westminster Abbey and a marble bust at Stourhead (National Trust).

Literature: Marsh 1859–60, p. 40; Katharine Eustace, *Michael Rysbrack* (Bristol 1982), no. 76.
Presented by Mrs Trollope by desire of her late husband, Anthony Trollope, 1883.

601 *After Matthew Noble*

Painted plaster bust, 60 cm high, with no inscription but probably by G. Graziani, after the bust by Matthew Noble (see above).

PETER DENNIS MITCHELL, FRS

b. 1920, Nobel Prize (chemistry) 1978; elected to the Club in 1989.

602 *Photograph* in Nobel Prize book, 1978.

WILLIAM MITFORD, MP

1744–1827, author of *History of Greece* (1784–1810); elected to the Club in 1825.

603 *By C. Picart, 1811,* stipple engraving (O'D 1), after a drawing by Henry Edridge in the NPG.

SIR WILLIAM MOLESWORTH, Bt. MP

1810–55, Commissioner of Works; elected to the Club in 1853.

600

607

604 *By W. Walker, 1856,* mezzotint (not in O'D)
Presented by Arthur Jaffé in 1931.

THEODORE MOMMSEN

1817–1903, German historian and an honorary member
of the Club.

605 *After Sir William Richmond,* reproduction of a drawing
made in Berlin 15 May 1890 (see A M W, Stirling, *The
Richmond Papers* (1926), pp. 359–62).

BASIL MONTAGU, KC

1770–1851, Commissioner in Bankruptcy and an intimate friend of both Coleridge and Wordsworth; elected
to the Club in 1825.

606 *By H. W. B. Davis, 1849*
Painted plaster medallion, 46 × 40 cm (18 × 15¾ in), uninscribed. The original was exhibited RA 1850, and then in the
library of the National Gallery of which he was an early
trustee.

SIR MOSES MONTEFIORE, Bt. *see* **Satires No. 1039**

THOMAS MOORE

1779–1852, poet, destroyed Byron's memoirs but edited
his works. He was an early supporter of Croker's plan
for the proposed Club and was among the original
members present at the Somerset House meeting, 16
Feb 1824.

607 *By Gilbert Stuart Newton, 1819*
Black, red and white chalk on grey paper, inset 10.7 × 9.8 cm
(4¼ × 3⅞ in), annotated in pencil under the mount: *Tom
Moore (at 40 years of age) by G.S. Newton RA (Drake
Collection).* The drawing was engraved by W.H. Watt in 1828
(O'D 10).

Formerly in the Drake collection, and presented by
Marion H. Spielmann, 1947.

608 *By J. Burnet, 1820.* engr. 'from a picture in the possession
of Richard Power' by M.A.Shee 1819 (Ports M. II. 24).
Presented by John Murray, 1908.

THE REV ROBERT MORRISON, FRS

1782–1834, missionary in China.

609 *By C. Turner, 1830,* mezzotint (Ath. Fol. I.12; O'D 1),
translating the Bible with two Chinese assistants, after a
picture by Chinnery exh RA 1830, now in a private

collection, USA (Patrick Conner, *George Chinnery 1774–1852* (1993), p.231).
Presented by Sir George Staunton, Bt. 1830.

THOMAS MORTON

1764?–1838, dramatist.

610 *By T.W. Hunt, 1854,* line and stipple engraving (O'D 1), after an oil by M A Shee in the NPG.

SIR NEVILL MOTT, CH, FRS

1905–1996 , Cavendish Professor of Physics, Cambridge, Nobel Prize (physics) 1977; elected to the Club in 1948.

611 *Photograph* in Nobel Prize book, 1977.

THE EARL OF MULGRAVE, GCB

1755–1831, Henry Phipps, 1st Earl of, General, Secretary of State, and a founding member of the Club.

612 *By W. Skelton, 1808,* line engraving (Ports I.9; O'D 1), after an oil by Beechey in the NPG.
Presented by W. Skelton, 1831.

613 *By H. Meyer, 1811,* stipple engraving plate to *Contemporary Portraits* (1811), after an oil by J. Jackson, Sotheby's 5 May 1976 (37).
Presented by Arthur Jaffé, 1932.

SIR ALFRED MUNNINGS, PRA, KCVO

1878–1954, painter especially of equestrian subjects; elected in 1944 under Rule IV. *By A.R. Thomson, see* **Satires** No. 1029.

THE EARL OF MUNSTER, FRS

1794–1842, George Fitzclarence, son of William IV and Mrs Jordan; a founding member of the Club.

614 *By R.A. Artlett,* stipple engraving plate to *Eminent Conservative Statesmen* (1839), after an oil by Thomas Phillips exh RA 1834.
Presented by Arthur Jaffé, 1934.

SIR RODERICK MURCHISON, Bt. KCB, FRS, DCL, LLD

1792–1871, geologist, President of the Royal Geographical Society and a founding member of the Club.

619

615 *By W. Walker, 1851,* mezzotint (O'D 4), after an oil by Pickersgill at Edinburgh University.
Presented by Arthur Jaffé in 1931.

616 *By William Drummond, 1836,* lithograph published as *Athenaeum Portraits* no.41.

THOMAS MURDOCH, FRS

b. 1758, a founding member of the Club.

617 *By R.J. Lane,* lithograph (Portrs M. I.25; O'D 2), aged 58, after an oil by Phillips, 1816, sold Sotheby's 30 Oct 1985 (257).
Presented by the sitter.

GILBERT MURRAY, OM, FBA

1866–1957, Regius Professor of Greek, Oxford, and founder of the League of Nations; elected in 1917 under Rule II.

618 *After Francis Dodd, 1937,* photographic reproduction of a charcoal drawing at St John's College, Oxford.

JOHN MURRAY

1778–1843, publisher, an originator of the idea of the Club, and a founding member.

619 *Anon* stipple engr. with facsimile autograph (Ports M. II. 34; O'D 2), after a portrait by Pickersgill exh RA 1834. Presented by John Murray, 1908.

MOST REV THOMAS MUSGRAVE

1788–1860, Archbishop of York; elected to the Club in 1825.

620 *By S. Bellin,* mezzotint, proof with artists' names only (Richmond Coll. III. 9), from an oil by G. Richmond. [TQL seated in library, open book to right] Presented by George Richmond, 1865.

SIR CHARLES NAPIER, GCB

1782–1853, Lieutenant-General, conqueror of Sind.

621 *'From an original sketch by Major-General William Napier',* litho (Ports M.III.1 though not a member).

NAPOLEON BONAPARTE

1769–1821, Emperor of France.

622 *Sèvres* biscuit medallion, modern copy by the Sèvres Porcelain Manufactory from a marble bust by A-D Chaudet, frequently produced as medallions in marble and porcelain, eg Louvre 1811, Versailles, Chartwell (National Trust). Presented by George Touzenis-Bendeck, 1995.

NAPOLEON III

1808–73, Emperor of the French.

623 *By A. Collette,* litho vignette (Ports Q. 21).

SIR HENRY NEWBOLT, CH, DLitt

1862–1938, poet and historian; elected in 1912 under Rule II.

624 *By William Strang,* 1898

etching signed W. Strang (O'D 1; Strang-Binyon no. 344; collotype facsimile in Ath. Ports. Red 42)

Presented by Mervyn O'Gorman, 1929.

625 *After Sir W. Rothenstein, 1920,* litho-facsimile of a drawing (R538). Presented by the artist, 1937.

627

DUKE OF NEWCASTLE, KG

1785–1851, elected to the Club in 1825.

626 *By W.H. Mote, 1836,* stipple engraving plate to *Eminent Conservative Statesmen* (1837), after an oil by Pickersgill, exhibited RA 1835.

CARDINAL JOHN HENRY NEWMAN

1801–90, leader of the Oxford tractarian movement, author of *Apologia pro Vita sua* and the hymn *Lead Kindly Light.* He became Cardinal in 1879.

627 *By H. Robinson, 1856,* stipple engraving in crayon manner, proof before letters (Richmond Coll. IV.4; O'D 1), from a drawing by G. Richmond, 1844, in NPG. Presented by George Richmond, 1865.

SIR ISAAC NEWMAN,

1642–1727, mathematical scientist.

628 *After Roubiliac (1751)*

Painted plaster bust, 76 cm (30 in), from the original marble bust by Roubiliac (1751) at Trinity College, Cambridge. A marble variation by E.H. Baily (1828) is in the National Portrait Gallery.

Literature: Esdaile 1924, p. 20; Piper NPG 1963, p.250.

629 *After Sir James Thornhill (1710)*

Oil on canvas, 76 × 61 CM (30 × 24 in), HS to right, head to left, light brown cloak lined with blue silk, white shirt open at the neck, hazel eyes, grey hair. A replica (HS only) of Thornhill's TQL portrait in the Master's Lodge at Trinity College, Cambridge, painted in 1710 for Richard Bentley.

Condition: cleaned by Lionel Freeman, Brighton, 1954.
Presented by T. Humphry, 1905.

630 *By John Faber, 1725,* mezzotint (O'D 25), after Vanderbank's portrait, 1725, in the Royal Society.
Presented by A.M. Hind, 1931.

631 *By G.E. Madeley, 1837,* lithograph (Ath. Fol. I.2 & II.2; O'D 16), after a drawing by J.H. Baldrey of Roubiliac's statue at Trinity College, Cambridge.

JOHN NICHOLS, FSA

1745–1826, printer and antiquary.

632 *By H. Meyer,* mezzotint 1811 (formerly in Ports M.II.28; O'D 5), plate to his *History of Leicestershire* (1795), after J. Jackson.
Presented by John Murray, 1908.

JOHN BOWYER NICHOLS, FSA

1779–1863, printer, antiquary, and a founding member of the Club.

633 *By J.H. Lynch, 1850,* lithograph (Ports M.II.7; O'D 1), after Samuel Laurence.
Presented by J.B. Nichols, 1854.

RIGHT REV. FRANCIS RUSSELL NIXON

1803–79, Bishop of Tasmania.

634 *By H. Robinson, 1850,* stipple engraving in crayon manner, artists' names only and facsimile signature (Richmond Coll. II. 12; O'D 1), from a drawing by G. Richmond.
Presented by George Richmond, 1865.

SIR ANDREW NOBLE, Bt. KCB, FRS

1831–1915, physicist and chairman of Armstrong-Whitworth; elected to the Club as Captain Noble, Royal Artillery, in 1873.

635 -6 *By Alan Swinton,* photographs (Ath. Ports. Red 7 and 11g), and see **Groups** No. 951.

EARL OF NORMANTON, PC

1736–1809, Charles Agar, Archbishop of Dublin.

637 *By William Daniell,* soft ground etching 1809 (O'D 1), after a chalk drawing by George Dance.
Presented by Arthur Jaffé, 1932.

MARQUESS OF NORTHAMPTON, DCL, FRS

1790–1851, Spencer Compton, 3rd Marquess; President of the Royal Society; elected among 'the forty thieves' in 1838.

638 *By W. Walker,* mezzotint private plate (O'D 1), after T. and H.W. Phillips.

LORD NORTHBOURNE

1869–1932, Walter John James, succeeded his father as 3rd Lord Northbourne in 1923; a talented etcher, elected to the Club in 1903.

639 *By Sir Charles Holroyd,*

Chalk on buff paper, 41.5 × 26.5 cm (16⅜ × 10½ in), signed in pencil: *Walter James / Charles Holroyd.* HS to left, red tie.

Presented by Michael Holroyd, 1939.

639

EARL OF NORTHBROOK, GCSI

1826–1904, Thomas George Baring, Viceroy of India; elected to the Club in 1881.

640 *By C. Holl, 1872,* stipple vignette, proof before letters (Wells-Grillion 2; O'D 1), from a drawing by H.T. Wells for Grillion's Club.
Presented by H.T. Wells, 1898.

JAMES NORTHCOTE, RA

1746–1831, portrait-painter and author.

641 *By F.C. Lewis, 1824,* stipple engraving (O'D 6), after an oil by George Harlow used as an illustration in Stephen Gwynn's *Memorials of an Eighteenth Century Painter* (1898).
Presented by Arthur Jaffé, 1934, to replace a copy presented by Henry Smedley, 1830.

THE DUKE OF NORTHUMBERLAND, KG, FRS, FSA

1785–1847, Hugh Percy, 3rd Duke; a founding member of the Club.

642 *By S.W. Reynolds, 1844,* mezzotint (O'D 1), after R. Ansdell.

GEORGE, LORD NUGENT, GCMG

1789–1848, lord high commissioner of the Ionian Islands; a founding member of the Club.

643 *By B.P. Gibbon, 1830,* engraving (Ports M. I.32; O'D 3), after a miniature by S-J Rochard who also exhibited a miniature of Lady Nugent, RA 1830,

BENJAMIN OAKLEY

Engraver and collector; elected to the Club in 1825.

644 *By B. Oakley,* lithograph (Ports M. I. 14; O'D 1), from a painting by A. Callcott.
Presented by the sitter, 1830

AGNES O'DONNELL

housekeeper to the Athenaeum, 1972–99, when she retired.

645 *By John Ward* [Pl. VIII(a)]
Chalk on coarse yellowish paper, 48.5 × 32.2 cm, signed in pencil: *John Ward.*
Presented by the artist, 1991.

647

MERVYN O'GORMAN, CB

1871–1958, lieut-colonel in the Royal Flying Corps, artist; elected to the Club in 1917 and an early member of the Art Committee.

646 *By C.J. B, 1917,* litho-facsimile of a sketch, wearing hat, smoking pipe (Ath. Ports. Red 50)

647 *By Edward le Bas, RA. 1930*
Red chalk on grey paper, 39.5 × 29 cm (15½ × 11⅜ in), signed and dated: *E. le Bas. '30.* HS to left smoking a pipe. Collotype facsimile in Ath. Ports. Red 49.
Presented by Mervyn O'Gorman, 1931.

ARTHUR ONSLOW, MP

1759–1833, Sergeant at Law; elected to the Club in 1825.

648 *By M. Gauci,* lithograph (Ports M. I.46; O'D 1), after a drawing by E. Eyre.

AMELIA OPIE, novelist, *see* **Appendix I,** no. 49

EARL OF ORFORD

1752–1822, Horatio Walpole, MP, succeeded as 2nd Earl in 1809.

649 *By H. Dawe*, mezzotint private plate (Ports II.20; O'D 1), after an oil by Samuel Lane.
Presented by Samuel Lane, 1839.

DUKE OF ORLÉANS, *see* LOUIS PHILIPPE, No. 545

COUNT ALEXIS ORLOFF

1787–1862, distinguished general in the Napoleonic wars, created prince in 1856.

650 *By C. Turner, 1841,* mezzotint, octagon 39.5 × 29.5 cm (15½ × 11½ in), after an oil by A E Chalon, as 'Duke's Preceptor'.
Presented by A E Chalon, 1850.

GEORGE ORMEROD, FRS

1785–1873, author of *History of Chester* (1819) and a founding member of the Club.

651 *By W. Drummond, 1836,* lithograph after J. Jackson, published as *Athenaeum Portraits* no. 29.

SIR WILLIAM ORPEN, *see* Satires, No. 1029

LORD OXFORD AND ASQUITH, *see* Satires No. 1041

SIR JAMES PAGET, Bt. DCL, FRS, FRCS

1814–99, President of the Royal College of Surgeons.

652 *By T.O. Barlow, 1873,* mixed engraving (O'D1), after an oil by Millais, 1872, in St Bartholomew's Hospital.
Lucas bequest 1918.

ELIZABETH, LADY PALGRAVE, née TURNER, *see* Appendix I, No. 51

SIR FRANCIS PALGRAVE, KH

1788–1861, medieval historian and a founding member of the Club.

653 *By Thomas Woolner, 1861*
White plaster medallion, 28 cm (11 in) diameter, incised: *T.*

Woolner sc / Sir Francis Palgrave. 1861. Thomas Woolner exhibited a medallion of Palgrave RA 1861, and a cast is in the National Portrait Gallery, incised: *T. WOOLNER Sc. 1861*

Palgrave was among the group of 'individuals known for their scientific or literary attainments' (including Thomas Campbell, T.R. Malthus and the Duke of Wellington) specially invited to join the Club under the Resolution of 1 March 1824.

Literature: Amy Woolner, *Thomas Woolner* (1917), p.338; Cowell 1975, p. 11; Ormond NPG 1973, p.354.
Presented by G.P. Barker Esq, 1946.

FRANCIS TURNER PALGRAVE

1824–97 (son of Sir Francis Palgrave), Professor of Poetry at Oxford and editor of *The Golden Treasury* (1896); elected to the Club in 1854. In 1855 he presented his *Essay on the First Century of Italian Engraving.*

654 *By George Howard, 9th Earl of Carlisle, 1895*
Pencil drawing 39 × 29.5 cm (15⅜ × 11⅝ in), inscr: *FRANCIS TURNER PALGRAVE 1895* (Carlisle monogram).

Presented by the Rev Francis Palgrave, 1941

WILLIAM PALGRAVE, father of Mrs Dawson Turner, *see* Appendix I, no. 50

SIR ROUNDELL PALMER, *see* SELBORNE, No. 764

LORD PALMERSTON, KG, DCL, LLD

1784–1865, Henry Temple, 3rd Viscount, Prime Minister and one of the original members, but is reputed to have dined here only once when he bribed the chef home by offering him an extra £15.

655 *By H. Cook, 1832,* stipple engraving (O'D 4), plate to Jerdan's *National Portrait Gallery,* after a portrait by J. Lucas, exh RA 1829.

656 *By F. Holl, 1855,* stipple engraving in crayon manner, proof before letters (Richmond Coll. I. 6; O'D 8), from a drawing by G. Richmond, 1852 (Ormond NPG p. 360).
Presented by George Richmond, 1865.

SIR WOODBINE PARISH, KCH

1796–1852, diplomat; elected to the Club in 1848.

657 *By J.W. Slater,* lithograph (Ports M. I. 12; O'D 1), after an oil by Phillips.

658 *By Maull & Polyblank, c.1850* signed photograph (Ports M.III.42)

654

LORD PARMOOR, *see* **Satires, No. 1001**

SAMUEL PARR, LLD

1747–1825, scholar, critic and Whig politician.

659 *By W. Skelton,* etching 1823 (O'D 11), after a portrait by J.S. Lonsdale in the Fitzwilliam Museum, Cambridge.

660 *By A. Chisholm,* lithograph (Ports I.14; O'D 2), 'From an Original Drawing in the possession of the Revd Robert Fellowes'.

SIR CHARLES PARSONS, KCB, OM

1854–1931, chairman of Parsons Steam Turbine Company; elected to the Club in 1894.

661 *After Sir William Orpen,* photogravure (formerly Ports M.II.47).
Presented by the Hon. Charles A Parsons, 1933.

By Campbell Swinton, group photographs, *see* **Groups** Nos. 959, 963–6.

RICHARD PARTRIDGE, FRS, FRCS

1805–73, surgeon; elected to the Club in 1839.

662 *By F. Holl,* stipple engraving in crayon manner, private plate with facsimile signature, printed by McQueen (Richmond Coll. I. 31), from a drawing by G. Richmond.
Presented by George Richmond, 1865.

LORD PASSFIELD, *see* **Satires, No. 1001**

JOHN WILSON PATTEN, PC

1801–92, Lieut-General, Chief Secretary for Ireland, later Baron Winmarleigh; elected to the Club in 1830.

663 *By S. Cousins,* mezzotint, artists' names only (Richmond Coll. III. 28), from an oil by G. Richmond. [TQL in uniform]
Presented by George Richmond, 1865.

WILLIAM AND JACOB PATTISSON

1801–32 and 1803–74, sons of W.H. Pattisson of Witham, Essex.

664 *By J. Bromley, 1834,* mezzotint (Ports I.21; O'D 1), after the oil by Lawrence, 1811–17, at Polesden Lacey, National Trust (Garlick 634).
Presented by Colnaghi & Son, c.1834.

PAVLOVA, *see* **Theatre Designs, Nos. 1392–3**

SIR JOSEPH PAXTON, FLS

1801–65, gardener and architect, designed the glass pavilion for the Great Exhibition, 1851.

665 *By J. & C. Watkins, 1863,* signed photograph (Ports M.III.39 though not a member).

SIR ROBERT PEEL, Bt. MP

1788–1850, Prime Minister; a founding member.

666 *By A.R. Freebairn, 1837,* engraving (Ports M.II.36; O'D 1) from a double sided intaglio gem by J.S. De Veaux after a marble bust by Chantrey, both made for William IV 1835–7; the gem is now in the British Museum (see Tait 1984, p. 127, no 847, with illustration 111.).
Presented by John Murray, 1908.

WILLIAM YATES PEEL, MP

1789–1858, brother of the Prime Minister; elected to the Club in 1827.

667 *By J.H. Lynch, 1859,* lithograph published by Colnaghi (Ports M. III. 4).

REV SAMUEL PEGGE, LLD, FSA

1704–96, prebendary of Lincoln Cathedral.

668 *By P. Audinet, 1818,* stipple and line engraving (Eng. C.I.26; O'D 2), plate to Nichol's *Literary Illustrations* (1822), from an oil by Elias Needham.

HENRY FRANCIS PELHAM, FSA

1846–1907, Bodley's Librarian and President of Trinity College, Oxford; elected in 1892 under Rule II.

669 *After Sir Hubert von Herkomer, 1893,* photogravure of an oil at Trinity College, Oxford (Poole, III, p. 142).

RIGHT REV JOHN THOMAS PELHAM

1811–94, Bishop of Norwich.

670 *By F. Holl,* stipple engraving in crayon manner, proof before letters (Richmond Coll. II. 5), from a drawing by G. Richmond.
Presented by George Richmond, 1865.

EDWARD HENRY PEMBER, QC

1833–1911, barrister, secretary to the Society of Dilettanti; elected to the Club in 1889.

671　*By Emery Walker,* engraving after MA Shee (Ports M. II. 44).

EARL OF PEMBROKE, PC, GCVO

1853–1913, succeeded as 14th Earl 1895.

672　*After H.T. Wells, 1897,* autotype facsimile of a drawing for Grillion's Club, with signature and artist's monogram (Wells-Grillion 40).
Presented by H.T. Wells, 1898.

RICHARD PENN, FRS

1784–1863, humorist and a founding member of the Club.

673　*By M. Gauci, 1834,* lithograph after Eddis (Ports M. I. 40; O'D 1).

SIR GEORGE LIONEL PEPLER, KBE, CB

1882–1959, planning consultant; elected to the Club in 1934.

674　*Anon. photograph, c.1930* (Ath. Ports. Red 57).

WILLIAM HASLEDINE PEPYS

1775–1856, inventor and a founding member of the Club.

675　*By W. Drummond, 1836,* lithograph after Walter, published as *Athenaeum Portraits,* no.34.

SPENCER PERCEVAL, PC

1762–1812, the only Prime Minister to be assassinated.

676　*By W. Skelton, 1813,* line engraving (Ports. I. 10; O'D 1) after an oil by Beechey in University College Hospital.
Presented by W. Skelton, 1831.

JACOB PERKINS, American inventor, *see* Appendix I, no. 52

JOHN PERRY, FRS, 1850–1920, electrical engineer, *see* Groups No.962

R.H.K. PETO

1877–1931, elected in 1930, died in the Himalyas.

677　*By Haines,* photograph (Ath. Ports. Red 54).

LOUIS HAYES PETIT, FRS, MP

1774–1849, book collector and a founding member .

678　*By F.C. Lewis, 1822,* stipple engraving (Ports. M. II. 3) from a drawing by G. Lewis.

THOMAS JOSEPH PETTIGREW, FRS, FSA

1791–1865, surgeon; elected to the Club in 1830.

679　*By Miss Turner, 1831,* litho vignette after Eddis (Ports Q. 14; O'D 1).

PHILIPPA

daughter of Henry IV; later became Queen of Denmark

680　*By E.T.,* engraving (Eng. C.I.23), from her brass tomb in Wadstena, Sweden (Transactions of the Antiquarian Society, Newcastle upon Tyne).
Presented by W.C. Trevelyan.

SAMUEL MARCH PHILLIPS, PC

1780–1862, under secretary of state, elected to the the Club in 1825.

681　*By F.C. Lewis,* stipple vignette (Eng. A.I. 43; O'D 1), after a drawing by J. Slater for Grillion's Club.
Presented by W.M. Powell, 1910.

THOMAS PHILLIPS AND FAMILY, *see* Appendix I, nos. 53–5

REV WILLIAM SPENCER PHILLIPS

1795–1868, Vicar of Newchurch and Rye, Isle of Wight; a founding member of the Club.

682　*By J.H. Lynch, c.1830,* lithograph (Ports M. II. 8), after a miniature by Alfred Tidey.
Presented by the sitter, 1851.

HENRY PHIPPS, 1755–1831, *see* MULGRAVE

SIR ARTHUR WING PINERO, 1855–1934, playwright; *see* Satires, No. 1016

ANN PITT, Lord Chatham's sister, *see* **Appendix I,**
no. 56

WILLIAM PITT, PC

1759–1806, Prime Minister.

683 *By F.H. Hardenberg, 1820*

Biscuit statuette, 33cm (13 in) high, WL standing, holding a
book, inscribed: *Published July 10th 1820 / by F.H. Hardenberg,
Mount [Street], Grosvr Squre London.* The figure is based on
Westmacott's marble statue (1813) in Pembroke College,
Cambridge.

684 *By G. Keating, 1794,* mezzotint (O'D 11), after a drawing
by S. De Koster.

Literature: Sir George Scharf, *The Portraits of William
Pitt* (1886).

683

JOSEPH PLANTA, MP

1787–1847, son of the BM librarian and diplomat; a
founding member of the Club.

685 *By S.W. Reynolds, 1865,* mezzotint (Ports. I. 32; O'D 1),
after an oil by T. Phillips.

SIR FREDERICK RICHARD POLLOCK, KCSI

1827–99, major-general Bengal staff corps; elected to the
Club in 1879.

686 *By C.W. Walton,* proof lithograph (Ports M. III. 16) of a
drawing by Walton himself.

SIR FREDERICK POLLOCK, Bt. PC

1845–1937, jurist; elected to the Club in 1879.

687 *By Maull & Polyblank,* photograph (Ports M. III. 31).

ALEXANDER POPE

1688–1744, poet and satirist

688 *After Michael Rysbrack*

Marble bust, 49.5 cm (19½ in) high, a copy by Messrs Plowden
& Smith (c.1985), made from an original marble bust by
Rysbrack.

Rysbrack's original marble, incised: *ALEX: POPE Poeta
/ M- - R-S- 1730,* was made in 1730, probably from a terracotta model mentioned in *The Weekly Journ. of the
British Gazetter,* 29 March 1729: 'Reisbrank, no longer let
thy Art be shown / in forming Monsters from the *Parian
Stone* …' Pope himself disliked it and told Lord Oxford,
'Tis granted Sir: the Busto's a damn'd head. / Pope is a
little Elf. / All he can say for't, is, He neither made / the
Busto, nor himself'. Vertue mentions it in 1732 among a
list of thirty-nine mainly marble Rysbrack busts 'mod-
elld from the life' (Notebooks III, p.56). Pope returned it
without payment. We then lose sight of it till about 1800
when it was acquired by Sir William Garrow, baron of
the exchequer (1760–1840), whose executor, Edward
Badeley, bequeathed it to the Club in 1868.

In 1985, after a spate of burglaries, the Club decided
the bust was too vulnerable in our collection and it was
sold, with Treasury approval for a price agreable to all
parties, to the National Portrait Gallery, where it now
adorns the room devoted to Pope's fellow Augustans.
The Club mourns the loss of the Rysbrack original, but
Plowden & Smith's faithful copy is a practical solution
to a difficult problem.

Literature (for Rysbrack's original): M.I. Webb, *Michael Rydbrack (1954)*, 1954, p. 77, plate 12; W.K. Wimsatt, *The Portraits of Alexander Pope* (1965), pp. 100–06; Kerslake 1977, p 221, plates 641–2.

Commissioned by the Trustees in 1985.

LORD PORTAL OF LUDDENHAM, OM, PRS

1920–71, Nobel Prize (chemistry) 1967; elected to the Club in 1966.

689 *photograph* in Nobel Prize book, 1967.

REV ROBERT POTTER, translator, see Appendix I, no. 57

WINTHROP MACKWORTH PRAED, MP

1802–39, poet, elected to the Club in 1825.

690 *By W. Drummond, 1837*, lithograph after A. Mayer, published as *Athenaeum Portraits* no.41.

W.H. PRESCOTT

691 *By F. Holl*, stipple engraving in crayon manner, artists' names only (Richmond Coll. I. 32), from a drawing by G. Richmond.
Presented by George Richmond, 1865.

SIR JAMES PRIOR, FSA

1790–1869, naval surgeon, author of *Life of Burke;* elected to the Club in 1830.

692 *By W. Drummond, 1835*, lithograph after Eddis, published as *Athenaeum Portraits* no.8.
(Another copy (Ports. Q. 4) presented by Dawson Turner).

MAJOR G.H. PUTNAM

693 *After Sir William Orpen, 1926*, photograph of a drawing inscr: 'To the major with admiration William Orpen, Savile Club London 1926, (after port)' (Ports. M. III.45).
Presented 15 May 1927.

EARL OF RADNOR

1815–89, Jacob Pleydell-Bouverie, 4th Earl.

694 *By J.R. Jackson, 1874*, mezzotint, artists' names only and facsimile signature, (Richmond Coll. V. 15; O'D 1), from an oil by G. Richmond at Longford Castle.
Presented by George Richmond, 1884.

LORD RADSTOCK, CB

1786–1857, George Waldegrave, Vice-Admiral of the White, and an avid collector of pictures.

695 *By (F. Holl)*, stipple engraving (Richmond Coll. III. 3; O'D 1), from a drawing by G. Richmond.
Presented by George Richmond, 1865.

SIR WALTER RALEGH

1552?–1618, naval commander, navigator, explorer and author.

696 *By R. Bell*, engraving (Ports. M.III. 5; O'D 36) 'from an original picture in the possession of James T. Gibson Craig Esq.' now in National Gallery of Ireland. (see L. Cust, 'The Portraits of Sir Walter Ralegh', *Walpole Soc. Journ.* VIII (1920), p. 8)

697 The Bell engraving is accompanied by another of Elizabeth Throgmorton, Lady Ralegh, also from the Gibson Craig collection.

SIR WILLIAM RAMSAY, FRS, KCB

1852–1916, discoverer of argon, Professor of General Chemistry, University College, London, Nobel Prize (chemistry) 1904; elected to the Club in 1905.

698 *By Campbell Swinton, c.1905*, photograph (Ath. Ports. Red 19).

699 *Photograph* in Nobel Prize book, 1904.

REV RICHARD RAMSDEN

1761–1831, Deputy Regius Professor of Divinity, Cambridge.

700 *By W. Say, 1811*, mezzotint (Ports. II.19; O'D 1), after an oil by S. Lane at Trinity College, Cambridge.
Presented by Samuel Lane, 1839.

LORD RAYLEIGH, OM, PC, PRS

1842–1919, J.W. Strutt, discoverer, with Ramsay, of argon, Nobel Prize (physics) 1904; elected to the Club in 1878.

701 *After Sir George Reid, 1903*, photograph of an oil in the Royal Society.

By Campbell Swinton, group photograph, *see* **Groups,** No. 960.

LORD RAYMOND

1673–1733, Lord Chief Justice.

702 *By George Vertue, 1724/5,* line engraving (O'D 2) after an oil by J. Richardson.
Presented by Barbara (Lady) Freyberg, 1938.

SIR CHARLES HERCULES READ, FBA

1857–1929, Keeper of Medieval Antiqities, British Museum, and President of the Society of Antiquaries; elected to the Club in 1899.

703 *By Seymour Lucas, 1912,* litho-facsimile of a chalk head (Ath. Ports. Red 39).

704 *By Augustus John, OM, 1921* [Pl. V (a)]

Oil on canvas, 86.5 × 61 cm (34 × 24 in), signed *John*. HL seated to left, black suit, brown tie, holding walking stick.

Condition: cleaned by William Drown, 1957 (photograph in Ath. Ports. Red 39).

Exhibition: Leeds Art Gallery, Lockett Thomson collection 1931.
Presented by Denys Roger Hesketh Williams, 1932.

LORD REDESDALE, FRS, FSA

1748–1830, John Freeman-Mitford, Speaker of the House of Commons, Lord Chancellor of Ireland; a founding member of the Club.

705 *By G. Clint, 1804,* mezzotint (O'D 1), a variant after Lawrence's portrait in the Palace of Westminster (Garlick 671a).
Presented by Barbara (Lady) Freyberg, 1938.

SIR CHARLES REILLY, OBE, LLD. FRIBA

1874–1948, Roscoe Professor of Architecture, Liverpool; elected to the Club in 1931.

706 *After Augustus John,* photograph of an oil in University of Liverpool.

LORD REITH, *see* **Satires, No. 1023**

REMBRANDT

1606–69, Dutch artist.

707 *By Charles Waltner,* 44.5 x 36 cm (17½ x 14 in), etching after Rembrandt's self-portrait, aged 63, in the National Gallery (Beraldi XII. 112).
Lucas bequest 1918.

708 *By William Unger,* etching after Rembrandt's self-portrait in the Liechtenstein Gallery, Vienna.
Lucas bequest 1918.

JOHN RENNIE

1761–1821, civil engineer, builder of Waterloo Bridge opened by the Prince Regent in 1817.

709 *By Sir Francis Chantrey, c. 1818*

Buff-coloured plaster bust, 77 cm (30½ in) high, painted on the socle: *JOHN RENNIE / 1761–1821 / Original Cast by Chantrey / Presented by John A. Rennie Esq 1925.*

A cast from Chantrey's marble bust of 1818, in the NPG, was commissioned by Rennie himself, probably to mark the completion of Waterloo Bridge.

Literature: Chantrey Ledger 66b; Walker NPG 1983, p.410.
Presented by his great-grandson, John Mackworth Rennie, in 1925

SIR JOSHUA REYNOLDS, PRA

1723–92, painter and first President of the Royal Academy.

710 *After Joseph Ceracchi (Fig. C)*

Painted plaster bust, 63.5 cm (25 in) high, no inscription but a cast from the marble bust by Ceracchi (1778) at Burlington House. The cast was made 'for the drawing room by Mr Sarte together with another of Sir Christopher Wren' (Minutes 23 Feb. 1830, p. 106).

Literature: Gunnis 1953, p.90.

PROFESSOR OSBORNE REYNOLDS, FRS

1842–1912. engineer and physicist.

By Alan Swinton, see **Groups** No 958

REV JOSEPH LOSCOMBE RICHARDS

1798–1854, Rector of Exeter College, Oxford; elected to the Club in 1827.

711 *By F. Holl,* stipple engraving in crayon manner, proof before letters (Richmond Coll. II. 22), from a drawing by G. Richmond (Poole II, pp. 75–6).
Presented by George Richmond, 1865.

SIR OWEN RICHARDSON, FRS

1879–1959, researcher in electron physics, Nobel Prize (physics) 1929; elected to the Club in 1930.

712   *Photograph* in the Nobel Prize book, 1929.

VISCOUNT RIDLEY, PC

1842–1904, Sir Matthew White Ridley, Bt, cabinet minister; elected to the Club in 1892.

713   *By J. Brown, 1882*, stipple vignette, artists' names only (Wells-Grillion 17; O'D 2), from a drawing by H.T. Wells for Grillion's Club.
Presented by H.T. Wells, 1898.

EDWARD RIGBY, physician, *see* **Appendix I, no. 58**

LORD RITCHIE OF DUNDEE

1838–1906, C. T. Ritchie, MP 1874–1905; elected to the Club in 1887.

714   *By Arman & Swan, 1886*, photogravure of a drawing by John Pettie, published by the Fine Art Society 1886 (Ports. M. III. 17).

LORD ROBARTES

1808–82, Thomas James Agar Robartes, MP. elected to the Club in 1830.

715   *By R. Jackson*, mezzotint, private plate, artists' names only (Richmond Coll. V. 9), from an oil by G. Richmond. HL to right, hat and stick.
Presented by George Richmond, 1884.

EARL ROBERTS, KG, VC

1832–1914, Field Marshal; elected in 1881 under Rule II and a trustee 1906–14.

716   *By Sir Hubert von Herkomer, 1895*, herkomergravure signed by the artist, reproduced in A.L. Baldry, *Hubert von Herkomer* (1901).
Presented by the artist, 1901.

717   *By Sir William Nicholson, 1900*, woodcut (see Colin Campbell, *W. Nicholson, The Graphic Work* (1992), p. 104).

718   *By John Tweed, 1926*, photograph (Ath. Ports. Red 5) of the marble bust in St Paul's Cathedral.
Presented by the sculptor.

719

DAVID ROBERTS, RA

1796–1864, artist; elected to the Club in 1845 under Rule II.

719   *By C. Baugniet, 1844*, lithograph vignette 'drawn on stone from life' (O'D 1).
Presented by Arthur Jaffé, 1934.

RICHARD ROBERTS (JONES) of Liverpool, *see* **Appendix I, no. 59**

SIR ROBERT ROBINSON, FRS, OM

1886–1975, organic chemist, Nobel Prize (chemistry) 1947; elected to the Club in 1933.

720   *Photograph* in the Nobel Prize book, 1947.

SAMUEL ROGERS

1763–1855, poet, banker, and an original member of the Club present at the Somerset House meeting, 16 Feb. 1824.

721 *By H. Meyer, 1822,* engraving (Ports. M. II. 25), from a drawing by Lawrence in the British Museum (Garlick 687).
Presented by John Murray, 1908.

722 *By H. Robinson, 1850,* stipple engraving in crayon manner, proof before letters (Richmond Coll. IV. 13; O'D 14), from a drawing by G. Richmond, 1848, in NPG.
Presented by George Richmond, 1865.

REV WILLIAM ROGERS,

1819–96, Chaplain to Queen Victoria and Rector of St Botolph's, Bishopsgate; elected in 1883 under Rule II.

723 *After A.S. Cope 1894,* photographic reproduction, by R W Artlett, of an oil by Cope in the Corporation of London collection.

PETER MARK ROGET, MD

1799–1869, author of *Thesaurus,* Secretary of Royal Society, and a founding member of the Club.

724 *By W. Drummond, c.1836,* lithograph after Eddis, published as *Athenaeum Portraits,* no. 43 (Ports. M. I. 51). Another copy presented by the sitter in 1846.

SIR HUMPHRY ROLLESTON, Bt. GCVO

1862–1944, physician; elected to the Club in 1900.

725 *Anon* photograph in Ath. Ports. Red 32.

WILLIAM ROSCOE

1753–1831, banker, botanist, collector, historian and a member of the Liverpool Athenaeum. The Walker Art Gallery, Liverpool, has a special Roscoe Room.

By Miss Turner after Gibson, 1813, see Appendix I, no. 60

726 *By William Spence,* c.1813

Marble bust, 21.5 cm (8½ in), lettered in high relief on the socle: *ROSCOE.*

Spence exhibited a bust of Roscoe at the Liverpool Academy in 1813. Several versions exist, in both marble and bronze.

Literature: Walker NPG 1985, p.425.
Presented by T. R. Blakesley, 1919.

EARL ROSEBERY, KG

1847–1929, Archibald Primrose, liberal Prime Minister,

three times a Derby winner, insomniac; elected to the Club in 1885.

727 *Clapperton / Selkirk,* photograph (Ports. M. II. 43).

SIR EDWARD DENISON ROSS, CIE, PhD

1871–1940, orientalist, Director School of Oriental Studies and Professor of Persian, London University; elected to the Club in 1914.

728 *By Sir Richard Paget, Bt. 1929*

Pencil sketch on Club writing paper, 10 × 15 cm (4 × 5⅝ in), inscribed: *Sir Arnold Wilson / Sir D. Ross 10.6.29.* profile to right, among a group of drawings made in the Club.

Presented by the artist,

729 *Anon. photograph, c. 1930* (Ath. Ports. Red 44).

SIR JAMES CLARK ROSS, FRS

1800–62, Rear-Admiral, Arctic explorer, elected in 1834 under Rule II.

730 *By A. Fox, 1831,* engraving (Ports. M. II.4; O'D 2) after an oil by Pickersgill at Greenwich.
Presented by Lady Ross, 1850.

JOHN ROSS, CBE, *see* Groups, No. 971

COLONEL SIR RONALD ROSS, KCB, FRS

1857–1932, discoverer of the moquito cycle in malaria, Nobel Prize (medicine) 1902; elected in 1922 under Rule II.

731 *Photograph* in the Nobel Prize book, 1902.

SIR JOSEPH ROTBLAT, KCMG, CBE, FRS

b. 1908, Nobel Prize (peace) 1995; elected to the Club in 1964.

732 *Photograph* in the Nobel Prize book.

SIR JOHN ROTHENSTEIN, *see* Satires, Nos. 1004, 1015

SIR WILLIAM ROTHENSTEIN

1872–1945, painter and Principal of the Royal College of Art 1920–35; elected in 1925 under Rule II and donor of

733

several of his portrait drawings and a large collection of lithographic facsimiles; author of *Men and Memories* (3 vols 1933–39).

By Henry Tonks, 1903, see **Satires** No. 1015

733 *By A.K. Lawrence, RA*

Charcoal and pencil, 44.3 × 34.3 (17½ × 13½ in) inscribed under mount in pencil: *Sir William Rothenstein.*

Presented by his son, Sir John Rothenstein, CBE, PhD, 1959.

WILLIAM HENRY DENHAM ROUSE

1863–1950, headmaster of Perse School, Cambridge; elected to the Club in 1918.

734 Photograph of an oil at the Perse School (Ath. Ports. Red 56).

RUNCIMAN, *see* **Satires, No. 1003**

JOHN RUSKIN

1819–1900, author, artist and social reformer; elected in 1849 under Rule II. Ruskin liked to write in the south library, looking out of the window and thinking of the

735

Athenaeum as 'my cottage in the country' (information from Sir Richard Body, MP).

735 *By F. Holl, c.1843,* stipple engraving in crayon manner, facsimile of signature (Richmond Coll. I. 33; O'D 8), from a drawing by G. Richmond reproduced as frontispiece to *Selections from the Writings of John Ruskin* (1861)

Presented by George Richmond, 1865.

736 *By George Richmond, 1853,* coloured litho-facsimile (Ports. M. II. 41) of a watercolour, half length seated facing, left arm across walking stick, signed *Geo Richmond 1853.* The drawing is not listed as Ruskin in Richmond's Account Book, nor mentioned in 'Bibliography – Portraits', Cook & Wedderburn XXXVIII, p. 207, and its identity as Ruskin is doubtful.

By Sir John Millais, 1853, see **Satires** No. 1036.

LORD ARTHUR RUSSELL, MP

1825–92, brother of Francis, 9th Duke of Bedford; collector of engraved portraits of scientists bequeathed to the Linnean Society, London; elected to the Club in 1858.

737 *By G.J. Stodart, 1888*, stipple vignette (Wells-Grillion 22), from a drawing by H.T. Wells for Grillion's Club. Presented by H.T. Wells, 1898.

EARL RUSSELL, KG

1792–1878, Lord John Russell, Prime Minister; a founding member of the Club.

738 *Anon* photograph, *c. 1870*, (Ports M. III. 32), standing on a balcony, left arm on marble pillar.

EARL RUSSELL, OM

1872–1970, Bertrand Russell, mathematician and philosopher; elected to the Club in 1909, expelled 1916, re-elected under Rule 2 in 1952.

739 *Photograph* in Nobel Prize book, 1950.

LORD RUTHERFORD OF NELSON, OM, FRS

1871–1937, physicist, Nobel prize winner (chemistry) 1908; elected in 1917 under Rule II.

740 *By W.H. Hayles, c.1920*, signed photograph (Ath. Ports. Red 51a).

741 *After Sir W. Rothenstein, 1925*, litho-facsimile of a drawing in the NPG.

742 *By Randolph Schwabe, 1928* [Pl. IX (b)]

Pencil on beige paper, 34 × 28 cm (13⅛ × 11 in), signed and dated in pencil: *R. Schwabe Aug. 1928*.

Presented by the artist, 1938.

743 *Photograph* in Nobel Prize book, 1908.

LORD RUTHERFURD

1791–1854, judge; elected to the Club in 1838.

744 *By Thomas Lupton, 1848*, mezzotint, after the portrait by Sir John Watson-Gordon in the Scottish NPG. Presented by Arthur Jaffé, 1930.

DUKE OF RUTLAND, KG, GCB

1818–1906, known as Lord John Manners until he succeeded as 7th Duke in 1888.

745 *By C. Holl, 1892*, stipple vignette (Wells-Grillion 4; O'D 3), from a drawing by H.T. Wells for Grillion's Club. Presented by H.T. Wells, 1898.

MARTIN RYCKAERT

1587–1631, one-armed Flemish landscape painter, an intimate friend of Van Dyck.

746 *By Charles Waltner*, etching after a portrait by Van Dyck in the Prado (KK.332, Larsen 609; Beraldi 23). Lucas bequest, 1918.

JOSEPH SABINE, FRS, FLS

1770–1837, horticulturist and a founding member of the Club.

747 *By Miss Turner, 1834*, litho vignette (Ports. Q. 12; O'D 3), from a drawing by Elizabeth Rigby.

748 *By W. Drummond, 1837*, litho vignette after Eddis, published as *Athenaeum Portraits,* no. 6.

THOMAS SACKVILLE, *see* DORSET, No. 237

EARL ST ALDWYN, PC

1837–1916, Sir Michael Hicks Beach, cabinet minister.

749 *After H.T. Wells, 1896*, autotype facsimile of a drawing for Grillion's Club (Wells-Grillion 35). Presented by H.T. Wells, 1898.

LORD ST HELIER, GCB

1843–1905, Sir Francis Jeune, judge; elected to the Club in 1888.

750 *After H.T. Wells, 1896*, facsimile of a drawing for Grillion's Club, with signature and printed Autotype Company name. Presented by H.T. Wells, 1898.

ST JOHN, SIR OLIVER, LCJ, *see* **Appendix I, no. 71**

MARQUESS OF SALISBURY, KG

1830–1903, Derby winner and three times Prime Minister; elected to the Club in 1858.

751 *By John Tweed, 1875*

Bronze seated figure by John Tweed, on a verde antique marble and mahogany base, 33 cm (13 in) high; a reduced version of a marble statue at Hatfield.

Literature: Auerbach & Adams, *Painting & Sculpture at Hatfield House* (1971), p.241.
Presented in memory of the artist, July 1934, by the subscription of sixteen members.

751

756

752   *By J. Phillips studio,* Belfast, photograph.
Presented by P.N.G. Gilbert, 1989.

EDWIN LINLEY SAMBOURNE, cartoonist, *see*
Satires No. 1137

LORD SANDERSON, KCMG, GCB

1841–1923, Permanent Under Secretary; elected to the
Club in 1904.

753   *After H.T. Wells, 1896,* autotype facsimile of a drawing
for Grillion's Club.
Presented by H.T. Wells, 1898.

SANDON, VISCOUNT, *see* HARROWBY, No. 384

SIR GEORGE SCHARF, KCB, FSA

1820–95, first Director of the National Portrait Gallery;
elected to the Club in 1855.

754   *By Maull & Polyblank, 1861,* photograph (Ports. M. II. 11)

CHEVALIER B. SCHLICK

c.1818–59, son of an Austrian general, Franz, Graf von
Weisskirchen (1789–1862).

755   *By F.C. Lewis, c.1835,* litho vignette, proof before title
(Ports I. 16), after a portrait by G.S. Newton.

RANDOLPH SCHWABE, RWS

1885–1948, Slade Professor of Fine Art, University
College, London; elected to the Club in 1934 and donor.

756   *By Francis Dodd, 1916*

Etching on off-white paper, 28 × 24.5 (11 × 9⅝ in), signed:
Dodd 1916 seated to right holding palette and brush.

Bought by the Club in 1996.

SIR GEORGE GILBERT SCOTT, RA, PRIBA

1811–78, architect, leading exponent of the Gothic
Revival (Albert Memorial, St Pancras Station and
Hotel); elected in 1860 under Rule II.

757   *By J.D. Miller, 1880,* mezzotint (O'D 5), after the portrait
by George Richmond in the RIBA.

JOHN SCOTT OF BUNGAY, d. 1838

758 *By W.C. Edwards, 1838,* line engraving (Ports II. 24) after an oil by R. Mendham 1836.
Presented by J.B. Scott Esq, 1838.

LORD JOHN SCOTT

759 *By H. Robinson,* stipple engraving in crayon manner, proof before letters Richmond Coll. I. 14), from a drawing by G. Richmond.
Presented by George Richmond, 1865.

SIR WALTER SCOTT, Bt.

1771–1832, novelist, poet, historian, present at the Somerset House meeting, 16 Feb 1824, and a member of the original Management Committee.

760 *After Sir Francis Chantrey*

Plaster bust 68 cm high (26¾ in), no inscription.

One of many casts from the marble bust (without the plaid squaring) made by Sir Francis Chantrey (1820), at Abbotsford, 'presented by the Sculptor to the Poet, as a token of esteem, in 1828'. Chantrey said that about forty-five casts were made for Scott's most ardent admirers, but they were ruthlessly pirated and Cunningham remembered 1500 such casts ordered in a single year.

Literature: Chantrey Ledger 117b; Walker 1985, pp 441–2; Francis Russell, *Portraits of Sir Walter Scott* (1987), pp.33–4.

761 *By S.W. Reynolds, 1822,* proof mezzotint (Ports. M. II. 15; O'D 49), after an oil by Phillips formerly in the John Murray collection (see Francis Russell, *op. cit.* no, 157).
Presented by John Murray, 1908.

762 *By Sir Edwin Landseer, RA. c.1824*

Pen and ink on white paper, 14.5 × 10 cm (5¾ × 4 in), uninscribed; head in profile to left.

763 Sketches of horse and eagle show through from the back of the paper. This is one of a number of sketches preparatory for the unfinished oil in the National Portrait Gallery, usually dated to Landseer's first visit to Abbotsford in 1824 – 'Mr Landseer, who has drawn every dog in the house but myself, is now at work upon me'.
Literature: Ormond 1981, pp.61–2; Walker 1985, p.440; Russell 1987, p.56.
Presented by Percy Fitzgerald, 1905.

762

763

SCOTT, SIR WILLIAM, see STOWELL

G. POULETT SCROPE, FRS

1797–1876, MP for Stroud 1833–68; a founding member of the Club.

764 *By J.S. Templeton, 1848,* lithograph (Ath. Fol. I. 31; O'D 1), after a painting by E.U. Eddis.
Presented by the sitter., 1850.

REV ADAM SEDGWICK, FRS

1785–1856, geologist; a founding member of the Club.

765 *By S. Cousins, 1833,* mezzotint (Ports. M. II. 23; O'D 3) after an oil by T. Phillips in the Sedgwick Museum, Cambridge.
Presented by John Murray, 1908.

EARL OF SELBORNE, QC

1812–95, Sir Roundell Palmer, Lord Chancellor; elected in 1865 under Rule II.

766 *By Maull & Polyblank,* photograph (Ports. M. III. 27).

EARL OF SELBORNE AND BISHOP GORE-BROWNE

William Waldegrave Palmer (1859–1942), 2nd Earl of Selborne, KG, DCL, High Commissioner in South Africa; elected to the Club in 1901 under Rule XII. Right Rev Wilfred Gore-Browne (1860–1928), Bishop of Kimberley 1912 to 1925.

767 *By Herbert Olivier, 1901* [Pl. V (b)]

Oil on canvas, 102 × 127.5 cm (40 × 45 in), signed and dated: *H.A. Olivier 1901.* Conversation piece of two seated figures, the bishop to left in black, Selborne to right in brown coat; table with two vases of flowers, window in background.

Condition: cleaned by Reeves of Bond St. at Sir Alfred Munnings's expense, 1955.
Presented by the artist, 1937.

VISCOUNT SELBY

1835–1909, William Court Gully, Speaker of the House of Commons.

768 *By Dickinson & Foster, 1899,* photogravure (Richmond Coll. IV, 14), of an oil by G. Richmond.
Presented by G. Richmond's executors.

RIGHT REV GEORGE AUGUSTUS SELWYN

1809–78, Bishop of Lichfield.

769 *By S. Cousins, 1842,* mezzotint, artists' names only (Richmond Coll. III.8; O'D 1), 'Pubd for the Proprietor, the Rev. Edward Coleridge, 1842', from an oil by G. Richmond.
Presented by George Richmond, 1865.

SENECA

4BC–AD65, Roman Stoic philosopher and political adviser to Nero.

770 *By P. Audinet,* stipple engraving private plate (Eng. C.I.13), after a drawing by Harriet Cheney 'from an Ancient Bust in the possession of Ralph Carr Esq.', now in the Ashmolean Museum and known as Pseudo-Seneca.
Presented by Henry Smedley, 1830.

NASSAU WILLIAM SENIOR

1790–1864, economist and a founding member of the Club.

771 *By W. Drummond, 1836,* lithograph after a bust by Behnes published as *Athenaeum Portraits* no. 28.

DOMINIC SERRES, RA, marine painter, *see* Appendix I, no.62

EARL OF SHAFTESBURY

1801–85, Anthony Ashley Cooper, 3rd Earl; philanthropist, elected to the Club in 1830.

772 *By Maull & Polyblank, c.1860,* photograph (Ports. M. III. 35).

WILLIAM SHAKESPEARE

1564–1616, dramatist and poet.

773 *After Peter Scheemakers (1735)*

Plaster bust 62 cm (24½ in) high, no inscription but deriving remotely from the Scheemakers statue in Westminster Abbey.

Bust versions are at Windsor Castle, Trinity College, Dublin, and several are recorded as early as 1749 (Roscoe, op. cit. p. 203). Plaster library busts were produced by Benjamin and Robert Shout, c. 1806 (see *Garrick 1997,* no. S30), and a marble copy by E.H. Baily was sold by Sotheby's (Shadwell Park, Norfolk) 21–22 October 1992 (466).

Literature: Piper 1964, p 18; Strong 1969, pp 283–4; Ingrid Roscoe, *Walpole Soc. Journ.* LXI (1999), p. 203).

774 *By J. Vitalba, 1792,* line engraving lettered: 'BAS RELIEF IN THE FRONT OF THE SHAKESPEARE GALLERY / PALL MALL', from the alto-relievo executed by T. Banks, 1789, for Alderman Boydell's new gallery in Pall Mall. It shows the bard between the 'Dramatic Muse and the Genius of Painting', and is now at Stratford-on-Avon.

775 *By S. Cousins, 1849,* mezzotint (Ports. M. III. 2; O'D 69) from the Chandos portrait in NPG.

776 *By George Scharf, Nov. 1863,* lithograph 55 × 43 cm (21¾ × 17 in), 'traced from the original picture by George Scharf Esq FSA'. The Chandos Skakespeare, listed as number one in the National Portrait Gallery (Strong NPG 1969, pp. 279–83), was presented to the Gallery by Lord Ellesmere in 1856. The tracing was made by Sir George Scharf, the NPG's first director.

THOMAS SHARP OF COVENTRY, *see* Appendix I. no. 63

SHAW-LEFEVRE, *see* EVERSLEY, No. 277

LORD SHELBURNE, *see* ASHBURTON, No. 30

PERCY BYSSHE SHELLEY

1792–1822, poet.

777 *By M & N Hanhart,* oval lithograph (Ath. Fol. II. 22), from a drawing by Edwin Beyerhaus, based on the oil by Amelia Curran, 1819, in the NPG.

SIR CHARLES SHERRINGTON, OM, PRS

1857–1952, physiologist of the central nervous system, Nobel Prize (medicine) 1932; elected to the Club in 1921.

778 *After R.G. Eves, 1927,* photograph of an oil in the Royal Society, Nobel Prize book, 1932.

RIGHT REV AUGUSTUS SHORT

1802–83, Bishop of Adelaide.

779 *By J. Thomson, 1849,* stipple engraving in crayon manner, artists' names only (Richmond Coll. II. 7, O'D 1), from a drawing by G. Richmond.
Presented by George Richmond, 1865.

MRS SIDDONS, actress, *See* Appendix I, nos. 64-5

REV EDWIN SIDNEY

d.1872, author of *Life of Revd Roland Hill*.

780 *By E.U. Eddis, 1839,* litho vignette (Eng. C. I. 28; O'D 1). Presented by Dawson Turner, 1841.

JOHN SIMS, physician, *see* Appendix I, no. 66

EDWARD SKEGG

781 c.1820–30, not a member of the Club.
By R.G., stipple vignette (Ports. M. III. 10).

WILLIAM SLADE

d.1858, Lt. Colonel Commandant of Loyal Lambeth and Christchurch Volunteers.

782 *By J. Wallis, 1807,* stipple engraving (Ports Q. 24), presented by his younger brother, Felix Slade, 1852 (see page xxiii).

REV WILLIAM BOULTBEE SLEATH

1763–1842, High Master of St Paul's School; elected to the Club in 1825.

783 *By C. Turner, 1810,* mezzotint (O'D 1) after T. Barber Presented by Arthur Jaffé, 1930.

ADAM SMITH

1723–90, political economist, author of *The Wealth of Nations* (1776).

784 *By James Tassie, 1787*
Wedgwood medallion, oval 8.9 × 6.4 cm (3½ × 2½ in), signed and dated 1787, but no longer in the Collection.

Similar Tassie profiles of Adam Smith are in the NPG and Wedgwood Museum, Barlaston (Reilly & Savage 1973, p. 309).

RIGHT REV GEORGE SMITH

1815–71, Bishop of Victoria (Hong Kong).

785 *By F. Holl,* stipple engraving in crayon manner, with arms (Richmond Coll. II. 14, O'D 1), from a drawing by G. Richmond.
Presented by George Richmond, 1865.

SIR JAMES EDWARD SMITH, botanist, *see* **Appendix I, no. 67**

JAMES SMITH

1775–1839, co-author of *Rejected Addresses* and a founding member of the Club.

786 *By H. Cousins, 1835*, mezzotint (Ports. II. 1; O'D 1), after J. Lonsdale.

REV SYDNEY SMITH

1771–1843, essayist, wit, and canon of St Paul's Cathedral; elected in 1832 under Rule II.

787 *By William Drummond, 1836*, litho vignette published as *Athenaeum Portraits* no. 14, from a bust by Westmacott in St Paul's. His portrait by Briggs, exh RA 1833, repr. Ward 1926, p. 228.

WILLIAM SMITH

d.1835, print seller in Lisle Street.

788 *By S. Freeman, 1836*, engraving (Ports. M. III.9; O'D 1), from a picture by W. Fisk.

WILLIAM SMITH, FSA

1808–76, printseller and a powerful force in establishment of the National Portrait Gallery; elected in 1825.

789 *By W. Carpenter, 1858*, etching (Ports M. III. 8; O'D 2), with artist's signature and title.

WILLIAM HENRY SMITH, MP

1825–91, news agent and bookstall monopolist; elected to the Club in 1877.

790 *By J.D Miller, 1882*, mezzotint, signed artists' proof (Richmond Coll. V. 11; O'D 1), from an oil by G. Richmond.
Presented by George Richmond, 1884.

WILLIAM HENRY SMYTH, RN, FRS

1788–1865, Admiral, founder of the Royal Geographical Society; elected in 1835 under Rule II.

791 *By Day & Haghe*, coloured lithograph as 'Captain Smyth' (Ports. Q. 3).
Presented by Dawson Turner, 1841.

LORD SNELL, PC, CH

1865–1944, Henry Snell, Labour MP, chairman of London County Council; elected in 1939 under Rule II.

792 *By Francis Dodd, 1934*
Charcoal on buff paper, 38 × 27.9 cm (18 × 11 in), inscribed in pencil along top edge: *Lord Snell / F. Dodd 1934*, and again under the mount.
Presented by the artist, 1945.

SIR JOHN SNELL 1869–1938, civil engineer, *see* **Groups No. 962**

THOMAS SOPWITH, FRS

1803–79, mining engineer and geologist; elected to the Club in 1852.

793 Anon, lithograph (not in O'D).
Presented by Arthur Jaffé, 1932.

WILLIAM SOTHEBY

1757–1833, translator of Homer and Virgil; a founding member of the Club.

794 *By F.C. Lewis*, chalk manner engraving (Ports. M. II.27; O'D 1), from a drawing by Lawrence, 1807, in the NPG (Walker 1985, p. 467).
Presented by John Murray, 1908.

ROBERT SOUTHEY

1774–1843, poet laureate and author of *The Life of Nelson* (1813).

By Miss Turner after Phillips, 1815, see Appendix I, no.68

795 *By H. Dawe, 1826*, mezzotint (not in O'D), after an oil by S. Lane at Balliol College, Oxford (Poole II. 30).
Presented by Samuel Lane, 1839.

JAMES SOWERBY, botanist, *see* **Appendix I, No. 70**

EARL SPENCER

1758–1834, George John Spencer, 2nd Earl, book collector, naval administrator; an original member present at the Somerset House meeting, 16 Feb. 1824.

796 *By H. Meyer, 1809*, mezzotint (Ports. M. II. 26; O'D 4), from a drawing by J. Wright after an oil by Hoppner at

798

Althorp (Garlick, *Walpole Soc. Journ. XLV* (1976), no. 285)
Presented by John Murray, 1908.

EARL SPENCER, KG

1835–1910, John Poyntz, 5th Earl, Viceroy of Ireland; elected to the Club in 1880.

797 *By J. Brown, 1881*, stipple vignette (Wells-Grillion 15; O'D 4), from a drawing by H.T. Wells for Grillion's Club.
Presented by H.T. Wells, 1898.

HERBERT SPENCER

1820–1903, philosopher; elected in 1868 under Rule II and became a frequent player in the Club billiard-room where he is said to have remarked, on defeat that 'proficiency in billiards was proof of a misspent life'.

798 *By Alice Grant, 1904*

Oil on canvas, 94 × 72 cm, signed and dated lower left in black paint: *Alice Grant 1904*. HL seated to right, head to left, crimson coat, brown waistcoat, watch and chain in right hand; hazel eyes, grey hair and whiskers, quizzical expression.

Painted mainly from a photograph taken for Sargent in 1898. Spencer preferred this portrait to the oil by Herkomer in the Scottish National Portrait Gallery. His diaries and letters, bequeathed to the Club in 1903, are now on loan to the University of London library.

Condition: cleaned by Lionel Freeman, 1956.

Literature: David Duncan, *Life and Letters* (1908), p.394; Ward 1926, p.219, repr. p. 222.
Presented by Miss Meinertzhagen, 1916

799 *By E. Gulland,* herkomertype 1899 (Ports. M.III.11; O'D 1), after the oil by Herkomer in the Scottish NPG.

REV THOMAS SPENCER

1796–1853, uncle of the philosopher, Herbert Spencer.

800 *By Herbert Spencer, 1842*

Clay bust, 54.5 cm (21½ in), made by his nephew, Herbert Spencer, during a visit to Hinton in 1842 "without any display of artistic faculty".

Literature: (*Autobiography* (1904), I. pp.205–7); Cowell 1975, p 85.
Presented by the Herbert Spencer Trustees, 1922.

MARION HARRY SPIELMANN, FSA

1858–1948, editor of the *Magazine on Art* and historian of *Punch;* elected to the Club in 1916 and donor.

801 *By Emile Wauters, 1890* [Pl. VI (b)]

Chalk on paper on canvas, 50 × 38.5 cm (19⅝ × 15⅛ in), inscribed top left: *à l' ami Spielman / Emile Wauters.* HL profile to right, head turned facing, black coat, white shirt and winged collar, yellow waistcoat.

802 *By Frank Bowcher, 1922*

Silvered metal plaquette, rectangular with arched top, 48 × 33 mm (1⅞ × 1¼ in), head in profile to right in an oval; obverse in relief: *Marion H. Spielmann / author art-critic / aetatis suae LXIV;* reverse in relief: *To M.H. Spielmann FSA FRSL in grateful recognition of his judgment in the Fine Arts eminently in the medallic arts / from Frank Bowcher RBS London 1922.*

Literature: Forrer VII, p. 109.
Presented by the sitter.

PERCY EDWIN SPIELMANN

1881–1964, physician, arranged most of the many gifts to the Collection from his father, Marion H. Spielmann; elected to the Club in 1922.

803　*By Frank Bowcher, 1828*
Silvered metal plaquette, rectangular 48 × 33 mm (1⅞ × 1), HS profile to right; obverse lettered in relief: *Percy Edwin Spielmann Ph.d., B.Sc. / Aetatis Suae XLVII 1928 / F. Bowcher. F.*
Presented by the sitter.

REV WILLIAM ARCHIBALD SPOONER

1844–1930, Warden of New College, Oxford, and celebrated for his transposition of initial letters, hence 'Spoonerism'; elected to the Club in 1893.

804　*By J.C. Webb,* mezzotint proof before title(O'D 1) after the portrait by H.G. Riviere, 1913, at New College (Poole II. 80).

SIR JOHN COLLINS SQUIRE, FSA

1884–1958, poet and man of letters; elected to the Club in 1924.

805　*After Sir W. Rothenstein, 1920,* litho-facsimile of a drawing in the NPG.
Presented by the artist, 1937.

MADAME DE STAËL, novelist, *see* **Appendix I, no. 69**

EARL STANHOPE

1738–1905, Arthur Philip, 6th Earl, First Church Estates Commissioner.

806　*By J. Brown 1880,* stipple vignette (Wells-Grillion 13), from a drawing by H.T. Wells for Grillion's Club.
Presented by H.T. Wells, 1898.

HON EDWARD STANHOPE

1840–93, second s. of 5th Earl, cabinet minister; elected to the Club in 1873.

807　*By J. Brown, 1880,* stipple vignette (Wells-Grillion 14; O'D 1), from a drawing by H.T. Wells for Grillion's Club.
Presented by H.T. Wells, 1898.

EDWARD STANHOPE, *see* **Satires, No. 1033**

RIGHT REV EDWARD STANLEY

1779–1849, Bishop of Norwich; elected to the Club in 1838, among 'the forty thieves'.

808　*By T.H. Maguire, 1849,* lithograph (O'D 1).
Presented by Arthur Jaffé, 1934.

HON EDWARD GEORGE STANLEY, *see* DERBY

SIR HARRY LUSHINGTON STEPHEN, Bt.

1860–1945, Judge of the High Court, Calcutta; elected to the Club in 1904.

809　*By William Strang, 1906,* reproduction of a drawing (Strang 1962,).
Presented by the sitter.

SIR LESLIE STEPHEN, KCB

1832–1904, philosopher, mountaineer, and first editor of the *Dictionary of National Biography;* elected in 1877 under Rule II.

810　*After G.F. Watts,* photogravure with facsimile of signature, from an oil by Watts in a private collection, Norwich.
Presented by the Memorial Committee, 1945.

GEORGE STEPHENSON

1781–1848, railway engineer, designer of 'The Rocket', the first successful locomotive.

811　*By W. Lucas, 1857,* mezzotint (Ports. M. III. 3), after a marble bust by C. Moore in Newcastle.

ROBERT STEVENSON

1772–1850, civil engineer and lighthouse designer.

812　*By F. Holl, 1860,* stipple engraving in crayon manner, presentation copy printed by McQueen (Richmond Coll. 1. 34), from a drawing by G. Richmond, 1849.
Presented by George Richmond, 1865.

THOMAS STEWARDSON

1781–1859, portrait painter; elected to the Club in 1845.

813　*By W.W. Barney,* mezzotint (Ports. II.33; O'D 1) after an oil by J. Opie, c.1804.
Presented by the Rev T.R. Robinson, 1846.

CHARLES STOKES, geologist, *see* **Appendix I, 72**

REV G.S. GRIFFIN STONESTREET, FSA

Prebendary of Lincoln; elected to the Club in 1838.

814 *By M. Gauci, 1831,* lithograph (Ports. II.32) after a drawing by J. Slater.

HENRY STORKS

fl. 1800–36, Serjeant-at-Law and a founding member of the Club.

815 *By W. Drummond. 1837,* lithograph after Eddis, published as *Athenaeum Portraits* no.23.

MERVYN HERBERT NEVIL STORY-MASKELYNE, FRS, MP

1823–1911, mineralogist; elected to the Club in 1854

816 *By the Hon. John Collier, 1896* [Pl. IV (b)]

Oil on canvas 71.5 × 36 cm (28 × 14¼in), HL seated to right holding a crystal and a measuring instrument, signed and dated: *John Collier 1896.*

Presented by J. Arnold Foster, 1953.

LORD STOWELL, DCL

1745–1836, maritime and international lawyer, and Judge of the High Court of Admiralty; MP for Oxford University; a founding member of the Club.

*By Mrs Turner after Phillips, 1816, s*ee Appendix I, no. 61.

817 *By C Turner, 1828,* mezzotint (O'D 6), after the portrait by T. Phillips in the Middle Temple.
Presented by Barbara (Lady) Freyberg, 1938.

RIGHT REV THOMAS BANKS STRONG, DD, CBE

1861–1944, Bishop of Oxford; elected in 1916 under Rule II.

818 *By John Wheatley*

Chalk and watercolour, 47.4 × 35.5 cm (18¼ × 14 in) HS to right in clerical garb, inscribed on reverse: *John Wheatley / The Rt Rev Thomas Banks Strong C.B.E., DD / sometime Bishop of Oxford.*

Presented by the artist, 1943.

LORD JOHN AND LORD BERNARD STUART

Sons of the Duke of Lennox though this traditional identification has now been rejected and the subjects are described as 'Two Young Englishmen'.

818

819 *By J. McArdell,* mezzotint after Van Dyck's picture in the National Gallery.
Lucas bequest 1918.

HON JAMES STUART-WORTLEY, MP

1805–81, Solicitor General.

820 *By F.C. Lewis,* stipple vignette ((Eng, A. I.48; O'D 1) after a drawing by J. Slater for Grillion's Club.
Presented by W.M. Powell, 1910.

MOST REV JOHN BIRD SUMNER

1780–1862, Archbishop of Canterbury; a founding member of the Club.

821 *By F. Holl, 1849,* stipple engraving in crayon manner, proof before letters (Richmond Coll. II. 1; O'D 3), from a drawing by G. Richmond in the NPG.
Presented by George Richmond, 1865.

822 *By Maull & Polyblank,* signed photograph (Ports. M. III. 21).

SUSSEX, DUKE OF, *see* AUGUSTUS FREDERICK, No. 34

ALAN ARCHIBALD CAMPBELL SWINTON

1863–1930, electrical engineer, photographer; elected to the Club in 1901.

823   *Photograph* (Ath. Ports. Red 12, 14a).

PROFESSOR SYMES

824   *By F. Holl,* stipple engraving in crayon manner, proof before letters (Richmond Coll. I. 21), from a drawing by G. Richmond.
Presented by George Richmond, 1865.

MARIE TAGLIONI

1809–84, 'romantic' ballerina for whom 'La Sylphide' was created by her father.

825   *Attrib. to R.J. Lane, c.1830s,* lithograph (Ath. Fol. I. 16), from a watercolour drawing by A.E. Chalon (Ormond NPG 1973, p.443). Chalon presented six lithographs of her in 1831.

MOST REV ARCHIBALD CAMPBELL TAIT

1811–82, Archbishop of Canterbury; elected to the Club in 1856.

826   *By H. Cousins, 1850,* mezzotint published Ryman 1850, (Richmond Coll. III. 7; O'D 1), from an oil by G. Richmond, when headmaster of Rugby.
Presented by George Richmond, 1865.

827   *By Maull & Polyblank,* photograph (Ports. M. III. 22), when Bishop of London, 1856–69.

HON JOHN CHETWYND TALBOT, QC

1806–52, Recorder of Windsor.

828   *By W. Holl,* stipple vignette (Eng. A.I. 40) after a drawing by G. Richmond for Grillion's Club.
Presented by W.M. Powell, 1910.

TALLEYRAND, *see* Satires, No. 1006

TALMA, French actor, *see* Appendix I, no. 73

MARIE-LOUISE DE TASSIS

1611–38, daughter of the connoisseur and collector, Antonio de Tassis.

829   *By J.F. Vogel,* line engraving after an oil by Van Dyck in the Liechtenstein Collection, Vienna.
Lucas bequest 1918.

REV JAMES TATE, MA

1771–1843, Master of Richmond Grammar School; elected in 1833 under Rule II.

830   *By S. Cousins,* mezzotint private plate (Ports II. 23; O'D 1), after Pickersgill.

DR EDGAR TAYLOR, FSA

1793–1839, solicitor and author.

831   *By C. Turner, 1841,* mezzotint (Ports II. 21; O'D 1), after Eddis.
Presented by E.U. Eddis (Minutes 5 April 1842).

EDWARD TAYLOR, JP

d.1851, of Kirkham Abbey.

832   *By F.C. Lewis,* stipple vignette (Eng. A. I, 44; O'D 1) after a drawing by J. Slater for Grillion's Club.
Presented by W.M. Powell, 1910.

JOHN TAYLOR, FRS

1779–1863, mining engineer; elected to the Club in 1825.

833   *By C. Turner, 1831,* mezzotint (Ports M.I.19; O'D 1), after an oil by Lawrence, destroyed by fire in 1870 (Garlick 758).
Presented by Mrs Taylor, 1831.

834   *By W. Drummond, 1837,* lithograph after Lawrence, published as *Athenaeum Portraits,* no.45.

JOHN LOWTHER DU PLAT TAYLOR, CB

835   d.1904. lithograph, published 19 August 1875.

HENRY RICHARD TEDDER, FSA

1850–1924, librarian to Lord Acton, librarian and secretary of the Athenaeum, 1874–1922, and an honorary life member. His *History of the Club* was finished after his death by Humphry Ward.

PLATE I: (a) 1279: Athena, design for the Club seal, by Sir Thomas Lawrence, 1824 (enlarged).
(b) 1279: Relief and frame, for the Athena miniature, signed by E.F. Watson, 1827–8 (reduced).

PLATE II: 218: Sir Humphry Davy, by Henry Howard, 1803–1835.

WILLIAM HOLMAN-HUNT, O.M.

COPY OF THE PORTRAIT PAINTED BY HIMSELF FOR THE UFFIZI GALLERY.

PLATE III: 439: William Holman Hunt, self-portrait, *c.* 1880.

PLATE IV: (a) 27: Matthew Arnold, by Henry Weigall, c. 1870–78.

(b) 816: Nevil Storey-Maskelyne, by the Hon. John Collier, 1896.

PLATE VI: (a) 896: G.F. Watts,
by Cecil Schott, 1889.

(b) 801: Marion Spielmann, by Emile Wauters, 1890.

(b) 563: D.S. MacColl, by Philip Wilson Steer, 1903.

PLATE VIII: (a) 645: Agnes O'Donnell,
by John Ward, *c.*1990.

(b): 547 Pamela Lovibond,
by Sir William Rothenstein, *c.*1939.

PLATE IX: (a) 46: Stanley Baldwin, by Francis Dodd, 1942.

(b) 742: Lord Rutherford, by Randolph Schwabe, 1928.

(b) 1014: Sir John Wolfe-Barry by SPY, 1905.

"Silence that dreadful Bell"
Othello..Act ii. Sc.3.

(b) 1391: Pavlova as 'An Amazon', by Albert Rutherston, 1914.

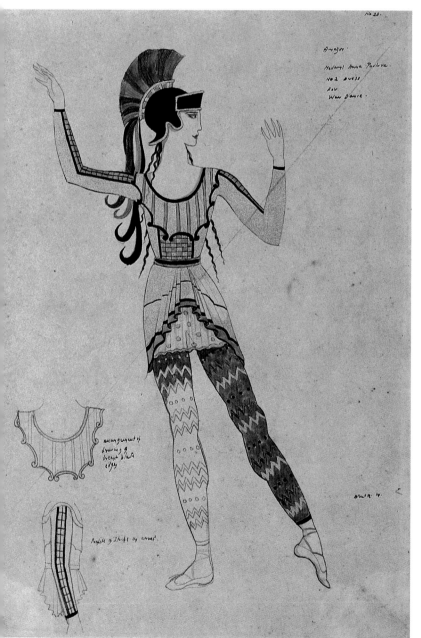

PLATE XIII: (a) 1393: 'Prince Florizel'
(*Winter's Tale*), by Charles Ricketts.

(b) 1390: Charles Kean as 'Macbeth',
by A.E. Chalon, 1840.

PLATE XIV: 1270: The Coffee Room, by Sir Albert Richardson, 1935.

PLATE XV: 1271: Coffee Room Window (Dickens's Table) by A. M. Hind, 1939.

PLATE XVI: 979: The Three Clubs, by Sir Osbert Lancaster, 1953.

836 *By G. Hall Neale*

Oil on canvas, 138 × 94 cm (54½ × 37 in), signed in capitals lower left: *G. Hall Neale*. TQL standing in the library, black frockcoat, white winged collar, white goatee beard, glasses.

Although a professional librarian, playing an enormous part in the formation of the Club library, Mr Tedder is shown in his portrait clearly extracting a book improperly. An Emery Walker photograph of the portrait is reproduced in Humphry Ward (1926), p. 84.

Condition: cleaned by Lionel Freeman, Brighton, 1955.

Exhibition: RA 1915
Presented to Mr Tedder by the Club in 1914, and presented by Tedder himself in 1924, the Club's centenary year.

837 *By Campbell Swinton, c.1900,* photograph (Ath. Ports. Red 20b).

THOMAS TELFORD

1757–1834, civil engineer (Caledonian Canal, Menai Suspension Bridge) and a founding member of the Club.

838 *By H. Macbeth Raeburn,* mezzotint (exh RA 1936) after the portrait by Sir Henry Raeburn at Port Sunlight. Presented by Sir Alexander Gibb, 1936.

DAVID TENIERS, Flemish painter, *see* **Appendix I, no. 74**

LORD TENNYSON

1809–92, poet laureate; elected to the Club in 1887.

839 *By the London Stereoscopic Co.,* 1864, chromolithograph vignette(O'D 37), with facsimile of signature, published in Cassell's *Modern Portrait Gallery* (1874–8).

WILLIAM MAKEPEACE THACKERAY

1811–63, novelist; he was blackballed in 1850 but immediately elected under Rule II. He was also blackballed from the Travellers: 'we don't want any writing fellows here'. His letter sympathising with the blackballer is reproduced in Waugh 1890, pp. 34–6. His billiard cue is in the Collection (*see* **Memorabilia** No. 1453 where it is illustrated).

840 *Self-portrait, c. 1835*

Ink and wash on grey paper, 21.2 × 16.5 cm (8⅜ × 6½ in), uninscribed; nearly WL facing holding drawing-board.

840

A letter is framed with the drawing: '109 St George's Square / This sketch must have been made about 1835 by my Father - W.M.T. of himself. He was then studying in an atelier in Paris. The drawing has been ever since in an old album of my mother's, and now goes to a good friend . Anne Thackeray Ritchie, March 17 1908'. On the back is an envelope stamped one penny and addressed to C.P. Johnson Esq, 14 Cavendish Place W. Photo facsimiles of the drawing were made for members in 1931 (Ath. Ports. Red 3).

Exhibition: 'Huit siècles de la vie Britannique', Musée Gallière, Paris, 1948, no. 543.
Presented by Charles Plumptre Johnson, 1930.

841 *By L. Poyet, 1842–5,* photograph (Ports. M. III. 12) of a portrait painted in Paris, repr. Ward 1926, p. 152.

842 *By W.J. Alais,* stipple vignette, HS profile to left, with facsimile of signature.

843 *By Sir Joseph Boehm, 1864,* a terracotta statuette of Thackeray appears in a photograph of the north library, in *The Antique Collector,* Dec. 1972, p. 291, but is no longer in the Collection (see Ormond NPG 1973, p. 462 , and Waugh 1899, p.29).

844 *By George Richmond, RA*

Red and black chalk 37.5 c 35.5 cm (14¾ × 14 in)(sight size), with provenance labels on back of frame.

This drawing by George Richmond RA was left by him to his daughter, Mrs Laura Buchanan – and given by her to Sir James Crichton-Browne; it is believed to be a recollection of W.M.Thackeray. There is no mention of it in the Richmond Account Book and the identity is uncertain.

Presented by Lady Crichton-Browne in memory of Sir James, 1938.

SIR GEORGE D. THANE, FRCS

1850–1930, Professor of Anatomy, University College; elected to the Club in 1897.

845 *After Sir W. Rothenstein,* photograph of an oil (Ath. Ports. Red 36).

RIGHT REV CONNOR THIRLWALL, DD

1797–1875, historian and Bishop of St David's; a founding member of the Club.

846 *By F. Holl,* line and stipple engraving after an oil by S. Laurence.

SIR DARCY THOMPSON, FRS

1860–1948, zoologist, classical scholar, and author of *On Growth and Form*; elected to the Club in 1908.

847 *By G. Coleridge, 1938,* photograph of a sculptured profile.

SIR HENRY THOMSON, Bt

1820–1904, surgeon.

848 *Photograph, May 1899,* signed and dated (Ath. Ports. Red 22).

SYLVANUS THOMPSON, FRS

1851–1916, physicist; elected in 1907 under Rule II.

849 *By Campbell Swinton, c.1890,* group photograph, see **Groups** No. 967.

SIR ALEXANDER THOMSON

1744–1817, Chief Baron of the Exchequer.

849 *By H. Meyer, 1812,* mezzotint (O'D 1) after an oil by William Owen exh RA 1812.

Presented by Barbara, (Lady) Freyberg, 1938.

ALLEN THOMSON, FRS

1809–84, biologist; elected in 1878 under Rule II.

850 *Photograph,* Ath. Ports. Red 10.

SIR BASIL THOMSON, KCB

1861–1939, Assissant Commissioner of Metropolitan Police; elected to the Club in 1895.

851 *By Vandyke,* photograph (Ath. Ports. Red 27).

Presented by his brother, Sir W.F.H. Thomson, Bt.

SIR GEORGE THOMSON, FRS

1892–1972, only son of Sir Joseph (see below), discoverer of electron diffraction by crystals, Nobel Prize (physics) 1937, Master of Corpus Christi College, Cambridge; elected to the Club in 1935.

852 *Photograph* in the Nobel Prize book, 1937.

SIR JOSEPH THOMSON, OM, PRS

1846–1940, physicist, discoverer of the electron, Nobel Prize (physics) 1906, Master of Trinity College, Cambridge; elected to the Club in 1901.

853 *By Francis Dodd,* etching signed and dated 1925

Presented by W.E.F. Macmillan, 1939.

854 *After Sir W. Rothenstein, 1920,* litho–facsimile of a drawing in the NPG.

Presented by the artist, 1937.

855 *After G. Fiddes Watt, 1922,* photograph of an oil in the Royal Society.

THOMAS THOMSON

1768–1852, lawyer and literary critic; elected to the Club in 1825.

856 *By G. Baird Shaw,* line and stipple engraving (Ports M. III. 7; O'D 1) dedicated by the artist to the members of the Bannatyne Club, after an oil by R.S. Lauder in the Scottish NPG.

SIR WILFRED FORBES HOME THOMSON, Bt

1858–1939, banker; elected to the Club in 1892.

853

857 *By Vandyck, 1931*, signed photograph dated 18 May 1931 (Ath. Ports. Red 28).

SIR EDWARD THORNBOROUGH, GCB

1754–1834, Admiral.

858 *By H. Dawe*, mezzotint, private plate (Ath. Fol. I. 25; O'D 1), after an oil by S. Lane at Greenwich. Presented by Samuel Lane, 1839.

ELIZABETH THROGMORTON, LADY RALEGH, *see* RALEGH No. 694

LORD THURLOW, KC, MP

1731–1806. Lord Chancellor.

859 *By F. Bartolozzi, 1782*, line and stipple engraving (O'D 19), after an oil by Reynolds at Longleat. Presented by Barbara (Lady) Freyberg, 1938.

REV GEORGE AUGUSTUS THURSBY

1771–1836, Rector of Abington and a founding member of the Club.

860 *By W. Drummond, 1835*, lithograph after Eddis published as *Athenaeum Portraits* no. 12.

HENRY GEORGE THURSFIELD

1882–1963, Rear-Admiral; elected to the Club in 1919 as Commander.

861 *Photograph*

LORD TODD OF TRUMPINGTON, OM, PRS

1907–1997, Nobel Prize (chemistry) 1957, Master of Christ's College, Cambridge; elected to the Club in 1941.

862 *After W.E. Narraway, 1979*, photograph of an oil in the Royal Society, Nobel Prize book, 1957

WILLIAM TOOKE, MP

1777–1863, President of the Society of Arts; a founding member of the Club and, with William Rose, 'actual Founder of the Library' (Ward 1926, p. 100).

863 *By C. Turner, 1836*, mezzotint (Ports. M. I. 49; O'D 1), after a portrait by J. White.

CHARLES TOWNELEY, 1735–1805, collector, *see* Groups No. 953

REV GEORGE TOWNSEND

1788–1857, Prebendary of Durham, author of chronological arrangements of the Bible; elected to the Club in 1825.

864 *By W. Drummond, 1836*, lithograph published as *Athenaeum Portraits* no. 36.

BENJAMIN TRAVERS, FRS

1783–1858, eye surgeon to Queen Victoria; elected to the Club in 1827.

865 *By R.J. Lane, 1834*, lithograph (Ports. M. I. 44; O'D 1), after a drawing by the sculptor, W. Behnes. Presented by the sitter, 1835.

MOST REV RICHARD CHENEVIX TRENCH

1807–86, Archbishop of Dublin; elected in 1858 under Rule II.

866 *By J.R. Jackson, 1863*, mezzotint (Richmond Coll. III. 5, O'D 1), from an oil by G. Richmond [HL facing r. hand on papers]
Presented by George Richmond, 1865.

HENRY TRESHAM, RA, artist, *see* Appendix I, no. 75

SIR CHARLES EDWARD TREVELYAN, BT. KCB

1807–86, Governor of Madras; elected in 1861 under Rule II.

867 *By F. Joubert,* mezzotint after an oil by E.U. Eddis exh RA 1850.
Presented by Arthur Jaffé, 1934.

GEORGE MACAULAY TREVELYAN, OM

1876–1962, historian, Master of Trinity College, Cambridge; elected to the Club in 1910.

868 *After Sir W. Rothenstein, 1913,* litho-facsimile of a drawing at Trinity College, Cambridge.
Presented by the artist, 1937.

MARMADUKE T. TUDSBERY, CBE

1892–1983, the Club's honorary consultant engineer, elected in 1924 and served as chairman of the General Committee 1962–65.

869 *By Francis T. Tudsbery, c. 1920,* photograph (Ath. Ports. Red 59).

870 *By T.B. Huxley Jones, 1960*
Bronze head, 34.5cm (13½ in) high, incised: *H.J. 1960.*

871

Exhibition: RA 1962 (1081).

Literature: Cowell 1975, p 87.
Presented by fellow members in 1976, 'in gratitude for long years of assiduous service to the best interests of the Club'.

871 *By P. Phillips, 1969*
Dark grey wash highlighted with white chalk on light grey paper, 37.75 × 27 cm (14⅞ × 10⅝ in), signed: *P. Phillips 1969,* and inscribed: *M.T. Tudsbery Esq. C.B.E.*

Bought with private subscriptions from members of the Club, 1970.

DAWSON TURNER

1775–1858, botanist, Norfolk antiquary MSS collector; a founding member of the Club and donor.

872 *By W. Drummond, 1837,* lithograph after Eddis published as *Athenaeum Portraits,* no.52.
An etching by Mrs Dawson Turner, after a drawing by T. Phillips 1816, is reproduced in A.N.L. Munby, *The Cult of the Autograph Letter in England* (1962), p. 34. Dawson Turner presented the Club with a copy of his *Outlines of Lithography* in 1842.

ELIZABETH TURNER, LADY PALGRAVE, *see* Appendix I, no. 51

SIR GEORGE TURNER

1798–1867, Lord Justice of Appeal in Chancery.
By F. Holl, stipple engraving in crayon manner, proof before letters (Richmond I. 15; O'D 1), from a drawing by G. Richmond.
Presented by George Richmond, 1865.

HANNAH SARAH TURNER, *see* Appendix I, no. 77

JOSEPH TURNER, Dean of Norwich, *see* Appendix I, no. 76

MARIA TURNER, LADY HOOKER, *see* Appendix I, no.40

REV CHARLES TURNOUR

elected to the Club in 1846. He presented a number of sumptuosly bound books on the fine arts.

874 *By G.E. Madeley,* 1839, lithograph (Ports. M. I.2 and Ports Q.27), after an oil by J. Wood.

RICHARD TWISS, FLS, traveller, *see* **Appendix I, no. 78**

SAMUEL TWYFORD

elected to the Club in 1830.

875 *By Day & Haghe, c.1837,* lithograph published as *Athenaeum Portraits,* no. 54.

PATRICK FRASER TYTLER

1791–1849, Scottish historian; elected in 1834 under Rule II.

876 *By W. Drummond,* 1836, lithograph published as *Athenaeum Portraits,* no. 33.

THOMAS USBORNE, JP

1840–1915, MP for Chelmsford 1892–1902.

877 Photogravure of an oil signed *Thomas Usborne, May 30. 1901.*

WILLIAM WARREN VERNON

1834–1919, second s. of 5th Baron Vernon; elected to the Club in 1886 and presented the portrait of Frederick the Great in the hall (No. 300). Carlyle's letters about the portrait are in the Club library, and published in Vernon's *Recollections* (1917). He also presented a large collection of books and papers relating to the study of Dante.

878 *By Eden Upton Eddis, c.1860*

Chalk on brownish oval paper, 51 × 40 cm (20 × 16 in), uninscribed, HS facing, black bow tie, brown eyes, dark hair.

Presented by Mrs Frank Vernon-Walker, 1934.

A photograph of him, *c.*1900, repr. Ward 1926, p. 108.

MOST REV EDWARD VERNON-HARCOURT

1757–1847, Archbishop of Canterbury.

879 *By G. Brown,* 1847, stipple engraving in crayon manner (Richmond Coll. IV. 2; O'D 5), from a drawing, 'in the 90th year of his age Sept. 11th 1847', by G. Richmond. Presented by George Richmond, 1865.

878

QUEEN VICTORIA

1819-1901, reigned 1837–1901.

880 *By A.R. Freebairn,* 1837, anaglyptograph (Ports II. 3; O'D 240).
Presented by W. Brockedon, *c.*1837.

881 *By F. Forster , Paris 1846,* line engraving 46 × 33 cm (18 × 13 in), pubd 1 May 1847 by F.G. Moon, from the oil by Winterhalter 1842 in the Royal Collection, Windsor Castle (Millar 809).

882 *By S. Cousins 1838,* mezzotint, proof before letters (O'D 105–6), after a portrait by A.E. Chalon in the Belgian Royal Collection. This head was used for several early stamps including the 'penny black'.
Presented by A.E. Chalon, 1848. The librarian ordered a special portfolio to contain this print (Minutes 8 Aug 1848, p. 87).

QUEEN VICTORIA (called)

883 *By William Calder Marshall, 1849*

Marble bust, 70 cm (27½ in) high, incised: *W.C. Marshall ARA sc / 1849,* on a circular marble base and pink scagliola column to match that of Milton.

The identity of this bust as Queen Victoria is doubtful.

Calder Marshall is not recorded as having made a bust of her, it does not appear in the usual reference books, and it bears very little resemblance to the Queen as she is portrayed in 1849. Calder Marshall left no sitter-book, and his name is not mentioned in the Queen's voluminous diaries and letters.

Literature: Cowell 1975, p 86.
Presented by Hector Bolitho Esq. 1946.

GEORGE VILLIERS, *see* CLARENDON, No. 165

RIGHT REV HENRY MONTAGU VILLIERS

1813–61, Bishop of Carlisle and Durham; elected to the Club in 1841.

884 *By F. Holl,* stipple engraving in crayon manner, proof before letters (Richmond Coll. II.3), from a drawing by G. Richmond.
Presented by George Richmond, 1865.

REV EDWARD WALFORD (identity uncertain)

1823–97, editor of biographical, genealogical and topographical works.

.885 *By F. Holl,* stipple engraving in crayon manner (Richmond Coll. I. 35), from a drawing by G. Richmond
Presented by George Richmond, 1865.

ARTHUR BINGHAM WALKLEY

1855–1926, dramatic and literary critic; elected to the Club in 1923.

886 *After Sir W. Rothenstein,* litho-facsimile of a drawing 1925 (R724).
Presented by the artist, 1937.

CHARLES WALL

1756–1815, son-in-law of Sir Francis Baring, *see* Baring, No. 51

NATHANIEL WALLICH, MD, FRS

2786–2854, Danish botanist, elected in 1847 under Rule II.

887 *By M. Gauci,* lithograph (Ports M. I. 26; O'D 1) after a drawing by A. Robertson.

888 *By E.U. Eddis,* lithograph (Ports Q. 1), presented by Dawson Turner, 1831.

ROBERT WALPOLE

1781–1856, classical scholar; elected in 1825.

889 *By W.J. Ward,* mezzotint (Ath. Fol. I. 20; O'D 1) after J. Jackson.

REV RICHARD WARD

Rector of St James's, Piccadilly; elected in 1825.

890 *By M. Gauci, 1834,* lithograph (Ports II. 15) after S. Lane.
Presented by Samuel Lane, 1839.

SIR FABIAN WARE, KCVO

1869–1949, originator of Imperial War Graves Commission; elected to the Club in 1926.

891 *Anon.* photograph, *c.* 1930, in Ath. Ports. Red 55.

CHARLES WARREN

1767–1823, line engraver and a founding member of the Club.

892 *By S.W. Reynolds, 1824,* mezzotint (Ports M. II. 30; O'D 1), after a marble bust by W. Behnes.
Presented by John Murray, 1908.

LORD WARRINGTON OF CLYFFE, PC

1851–1937, Lord Justice of Appeal; elected to the Club in 1904 under Rule XII, a trustee and chairman of the General Committee.

893 *By Sir William Rothenstein, 1932*
Chalk on grey-blue cartridge paper, 51.3 × 35.5 cm (20¼ × 14 in), signed and dated: *W. Rothenstein 1932.*
Presented by the artist, 1932.

JOHN FORBES WATSON

1827–92, Director of the India Museum, London; elected to the Club in 1866.

894 *Anon* stipple engraving in crayon manner, proof before letters (Richmond Coll. I. 23; O'D 2), from a drawing by G. Richmond.
Presented by George Richmond, 1865.

893

SIR THOMAS WATSON, Bt. FRS, FRCP

1792–1882, physician.

895 *By S. Cousins,* mezzotint, private plate, artists' names only (Richmond Coll. V. 17: O'D 1), from an oil by G. Richmond in Royal College of Physicians, London.
Presented by George Richmond, 1884.

GEORGE FREDERICK WATTS, OM, RA

1820–1904, Victorian artist; elected in 1873 under Rule II.

896 *By C. Schott, 1889* [Pl.VI (a)]

Oil on canvas on card, 26.5 × 13 cm (10½ × 5⅛ in), inscribed: *Sketch of my master G.F. Watts in the garden of Little Holland House 1889 Cecil E. Schott.* WL to right in white painting coat, straw hat, red tie, starved appearance.

Presented by Dr Marion Spielmann.

897 *By Alphonse Legros*
Etching, 31 × 20 cm (12¼ × 8 in), signed in pencil: A. Legros (Legros-Bliss nos. 172, 323)
Lucas bequest 1918.

SIR PHILIP WATTS, KCB, FRS

1846–1926, naval architect; elected to the Club in 1908 under Rule II.

By Campbell Swinton, group photograph, *see* **Groups** No. 959

JAMES CLAUDE WEBSTER

Club secretary 1855–89.

898 *Photograph.*

LORD WELBY, GCB

1832–1915, Chairman of London County Council; elected to the Club in 1866.

899 *After H.T. Wells, 1896,* autotype facsimile of a drawing by H.T. Wells for Grillion's Club.
Presented by H.T. Wells, 1898.

REV HENRY WELLESLEY

1791–1866, scholar, antiquary, and a founding member of the Club.

900 *By W. Holl,* stipple vignette (Eng. A. I. 41; O'D 1) after a drawing by G. Richmond for Grillion's Club.
Presented by W.M. Powell, 1910.

DUKE OF WELLINGTON, KG

1769–1852, Field Marshal, Prime Minister, and a founding member of the Club, with his personal mounting-block outside the front door.

By Mrs Dawson Turner after Chantrey, 1822, see Appendix I, no. 79.

901 *By Joseph Pitts 1852,* parian ware statuette 42.5 cm (16¾ in) high, incised: *Jos^h. Pitts. S^c. London 1852.*

Literature: Atterbury 1909, p 244; Steegmann 1935, plate 48, as 'by Abbott after Crowquill'.
Presented by Lady Butt, 1933, appeared in an illustration of the north library, *Antique Collector,* Dec 1972, p.296, but no longer in the Collection.

902 *By A. Freebairn, 1838,* anaglyptograph (Ports I. 2; O'D 128) after an oval medallion by H. Weigall.

Engraved portraits of the Duke were presented by Henry Moseley 1838, and by Colnaghi 1848, neither in the Collection now.

LORD WESTBURY

1800–73, Richard Bethel, Lord Chancellor; elected to the Club in 1825.

903 *Anon* signed photograph, *c.* 1860 (Ports M. III.26).

MOST REV RICHARD WHATELEY, DD

1787–1863, Archbishop of Dublin.

904 *By Miss Turner, 1830,* litho vignette (Ports Q. 17; O'D 2) 'from a Phrenological bust by R. Childs, 1830'.

REV WILLIAM WHEWELL, DD, FRS

1794–1866, Master of Trinity College, Cambridge; a founding member of the Club.

905 *By W. Walker,* mezzotint, proof before title 1853 (O'D 1), after an oil by Samuel Laurence at Trinity College. Presented by Arthur Jaffé, 1930.

906 *By William Drummond, 1835,* lithograph (Ports M.I 54) after Eddis, published as *Athenaeum Portraits* no. 7.

SAMUEL WHITBREAD, MP

1830–1915 a Lord of the Admiralty; elected to the Club in 1882.

907 *By J.R. Jackson,* mezzotint (Richmond Coll. III.29), from an oil by G. Richmond, 1862. Presented by George Richmond, 1865.

908 *By C. Holl, 1877,* stipple vignette (Wells-Grillion 10), from a drawing by H.T. Wells for Grillion's Club. Presented by H.T. Wells, 1898.

SIR WILLIAM HENRY WHITE, KCB

1845–1913, naval architect, elected to the Club in 1895.

By Campbell Swinton, photograph, *see* **Groups** No. 965.

REV WALTER WHITER

1758–1832, philologist, author of *Etymologicon Magnum.*

909 *By Mrs Dawson Turner 1825,* litho vignette (Ports Q. 11;) from a bust by Mazocchi. [? Mazzotti]

JOHN HENRY WHITLEY, PC

1866–1935, Speaker of the House of Commons; elected in 1932 under Rule II.

910 *After Sir W. Rothenstein,* litho facsimile of a drawing, signed but undated. Presented by the artist, 1937.

SIR JAMES WIGRAM, KC, MP

1793–1866, Vice-Chancellor; elected to the Club in 1842.

911 *By W. Walker, 1849,* mezzotint (O'D 1), after an oil by Sir J. Watson Gordon Presented by Arthur Jaffé, 1934.

RIGHT REV SAMUEL WILBERFORCE

1805–73, Bishop of Oxford and Winchester, known as 'Soapy Sam', opposed T.H. Huxley, at Oxford in 1860, in a celebrated exchange on man's ancestry; elected to the Club in 1840.

912 *By H. Robinson, 1845,* stipple engraving in crayon manner (Richmond Coll. II. 9; O'D 4), from a drawing by G. Richmond. Presented by George Richmond, 1865.

913 *By S. Bellin,* mezzotint, private plate, proof before letters (Richmond, III.6; O'D 1), from an oil by G. Richmond, c.1864, in NPG. Presented by George Richmond, 1865.

914 *By J.R. Jackson, 1871,* mezzotint, proof before letters (Richmond Coll. V. 14; O'D 3), from an oil by G. Richmond. [HL leaning forward, hand on book] Presented by George Richmond, 1884.

915 *By D.J. Pound,* mixed engraving (Ports M. II.35 and III, 13; O'D 5) from a photograph by Mayall. Presented by John Murray, 1908.

916 *By Maull & Polyblank,* signed photograph (Ports M. III. 23) nearly WL seated to left reading a book, when Bishop of Oxford.

WILLIAM WILBERFORCE

1759–1833, evangelical, philanthropist and slavery abolitionist; elected to the Club in 1825.

917 *By S. Cousins, 1834,* mezzotint (Richmond Coll. III. 30; O'D 7), from a watercolour drawing by G. Richmond, 1833, in NPG. Presented by George Richmond, 1865.

ROGER WILBRAHAM, FRS, MP

1743–1829, collector and a founding member of the Club.

918 *By Miss Turner, 1828,* litho vignette (Ports Q. 18; O'D 1) after a drawing by C. Smith.

DAVID WILKIE, RA, artist, *see* **Appendix I**, no. 80

HIRAM PARKES WILKINSON, KC

1866–1935, judge; elected to the Club in 1917.

919 *Anon. photograph* (Ath. Ports. Red 33a).

WILLIAM IV

1765–1837, reigned 1830–37; elected to the Club in 1828.

920 *By W. Skelton, 1821*, line engraving (Ports I. 3; O'D 44). Published and presented by William Skelton, 1831.

921 *By W. Holl, 1830*, stipple engraving (Ports M. I. 1; O'D 49), from a drawing by A. Wivell
Presented by the publisher W. Sams, 1831.

922 *By F.C. Lewis, 1831*, chalk imitation engraving (Ath. Fol. I. 1; O'D 32), after a drawing by Lawrence at Goodwood (Garlick 823b). The finished WL portrait is in the Royal Collection (Millar 877).
Published and presented by Colnaghi Son & Co. 1829.

SIR ARNOLD TALBOT WILSON, DSO, MP

1884–1940, Lieutenant-Colonel, explorer, linguist; elected in 1929 under Rule II.

923 *By Sir Richard Paget, Bt. 1929*

Pencil sketch on Club writing-paper, 10 × 15 cm, inscribed: *Sir Arnold Wilson / Sir D. Ross 10.6.29*, profile to right among a group of drawings made in the Club, framed together.

Presented by the artist,

CLAUDE WILSON

924 *After Sir W. Rothenstein, 1930*, photograph of a drawing, signed and dated 1933 (Ath. Ports. Red 33b).

RIGHT REV DANIEL WILSON, DD

1788–1855, Bishop of Calcutta; elected to the Club in 1825.

925 *By J. Bromley, 1833*, mezzotint (O'D 4), after an oil by Thomas Phillips.
Presented by Arthur Jaffé, 1930.

JOHN WILSON

1785–1854, 'Christopher North' of Blackwoods; elected to the Club in 1825.

926 *By H. Dawe, 1833*, mezzotint (Ports I. 28; O'D 3) after an oil by J. Watson Gordon in the NPG.

EARL OF WILTON, GCH, PC, DCL

1799–1882, diplomat, 'the beau ideal of a dandy'; elected in 1825.

927 *By C. Turner, 1835*, mezzotint (O'D 1), after J. Bostock
Presented by Arthur Jaffé, 1930.

SIR ANTHONY WINGFIELD, Comptroller, *see* Appendix I, no. 81

EDMOND WODEHOUSE

1784–1855, MP for Norfolk.

928 *By H. Dawe, 1826*, mezzotint on steel (Ath. Fol. I. 24; O'D 1) after S. Lane.
Presented by Samuel Lane, 1839.

JOHN GORDON WODEHOUSE

1826–1902, later Earl Wodehouse of Kimberley, KG; elected to the Club in 1869.

929 *By W. Holl*, lithograph (Eng. A. I. 36; O'D 1), after a drawing by G. Richmond for Grillion's Club.
Presented by W.M. Powell, 1910.

HUMBERT WOLFE

1886–1940, poet; elected to the Club in 1929.

930 *After Sir W. Rothenstein, 1931*, photograph of a drawing inscribed: "Humbert from Will. Jan 1931" (Ath. Ports. Red 58).

SIR JOHN WOLFE-BARRY, *see* Satires No 1014.

ISABELLA ANNE WOLFF

?1771–1829, close friend of Sir Thomas Lawrence.

931 *By S. Cousins, 1831*, mezzotint (Ports I. 23; O'D 1) after an oil by Lawrence in Chicago, with a version at Croft Castle, National Trust (Garlick 838).

WILLIAM HYDE WOLLASTON, MD, FRS

1766–1828, physician, natural philosopher, and inventor of the camera lucida used by Sir Francis Chantrey; elected to the Club in 1825.

932

932   *By W.J. Ward,* mezzotint (O'D 2), after an oil by J. Jackson, c.1820.
Presented by Frederick L. Wollaston, 1827.

933   *By R.J. Lane, 1829,* litho vignette (Ports II. 30; O'D 1) after a drawing by Chantrey.

934   *By W. Skelton, 1830,* proof engraving (Ports M. I. 22; O'D 3), after an oil by J. Jackson presented to the Royal Society by Wollaston's family.
Presented by William Skelton, 1831.

The Club minutes also record the gift from Mr Charles Stokes of "A Portrait of the late Dr Wollaston from a sketch made with the camera lucida by Chantrey" (Minutes 1 Aug. 1843, p. 20 , probably No. 933). Similar sketches are in the NPG, and Chantrey's marble bust is in the Royal Institution, London.

VISCOUNT WOLSELEY, KP, OM

1833–1913, Sir Garnet Wolseley, Field Marshal, elected to the Club in 1876 under Rule II.

935   *By J. Brown, 1884,* stipple vignette, artists' names only (Wells-Grillion 18), from a drawing by H.T. Wells for Grillion's Club.
Presented by H.T. Wells, 1898.

RIGHT REV CHRISTOPHER WORDSWORTH

1807–85, Bishop of Lincoln.

936   *By W. Skelton, 1854,* stipple engraving in crayon manner (Richmond, Coll. IV. 3), as Archdeacon of Westminster, from a drawing by G. Richmond, 1853.
Presented by George Richmond, 1865.

WILLIAM WORDSWORTH

1770–1850, poet laureate; not a member of the Club.

937   *By William Wyon, 1835,* medallion published as *Athenaeum Portraits no.5.*

938   *By Thomas Woolner, 1851*

Plaster medallion 34 cm (13⅜) (inset 26 cm), incised: *Woolner Sc. 1851,* cast from the memorial tablet by Woolner in Grasmere Church, which was based on Chantrey's bust lent by Henry Crabbe Robinson.

Literature: Art Journal 1 December 1851, p.327; Woolner 1917, pp 12–13; Blanshard 1959, pp 180–81.
Presented by W. Reeve Wallace, 1940.

REV THOMAS WORSLEY

1777–1885, Master of Downing College, Cambridge; a founding member of the Club.

939   *By (W. Holl),* stipple engraving in crayon manner, proof before letters (Richmond Coll. II. 19), from a drawing by G. Richmond (oil 1869 at Downing College).
Presented by George Richmond, 1865.

SIR CHRISTOPHER WREN, PRS

1632–1723, architect, mathematician, scientist and one of the originators of the Royal Society.

940   *By Mr Sarte, c.1830,* cast from the bust in St Paul's Catheral (Minutes 23 Feb. 1830, p. 106), but no longer in the Club Collection.

WILLIAM WYON, RA

1795–1851, medallist; elected to the Club in 1830.

941   *By W. Drummond, 1835,* lithograph after Eddis, published as *Athenaeum Portraits* no.3.

WILLIAM BUTLER YEATS

1865–1939, poet and dramatist, Nobel Prize (literature) 1923; elected in 1937 under Rule II.

942 *Photograph* in the Nobel Prize book, 1923.

CHARLES MAYNE YOUNG

1777–1856, actor and a founding member of the Club.

943 –5 *By M. Gauci, 1835,* litho vignette (Port M. I. 27 and M. II. 20) after E.U. Eddis.
Presented by George Young, 1833. Another copy was presented by John Murray, 1908.

THOMAS YOUNG, MD, FRS

1773–1829, physicist and Egyptologist; an original member present at the Somerset House meeting, 16 Feb 1824.

By Mrs Dawson Turner after Andrew Dunn, 1813, see **Appendix I**, no. 82

946 –8 *By C. Turner, 1830,* mezzotint (Ports M. I. 17; O'D 1), after the portrait by Lawrence still in the family collection (Garlick 861).
Presented by Hudson Gurney, MP, *c.1830.* Other copies were presented by John Murray 1908, and Miss E. Magrath, 1918.

1 (b) GROUPS

OFFICERS OF THE SHOOTING COMPANY OF ST GEORGE, BY FRANS HALS, 1633

949 *By A.C. Cramer, 1871,* engraving, 43 × 72 cm (16¾ × 36 in), signed and dated lower right, after the picture in the Rijksmuseum, Amsterdam, begun by Frans Hals in 1633 and completed by Pieter Codde in 1637.
Lucas bequest, 1918.

GOVERNORS OF THE ST ELIZABETH HOSPITAL, HAARLEM, BY FRANS HALS, 1641

950 *By Henri J. Zimmerman, 1866,* engraving, 43 × 72 cm (17 × 28½ in), signed and dated lower right, after the picture by Frans Hals, 1641, at Haarlem.
Lucas bequest, 1918.

THE ARREST OF CHARLES I

951 *By Charles Waltner,, 1887,* photogravure published by Boussod Valadon & Co.

CHARLES II AND QUEEN CATHERINE, 1683, *see* **Landscapes No. 1171**

TRIAL OF LORD WILLIAM RUSSELL, 1683

952 *By Sir George Hayter, inv. pinx. sculp. 1825,* line engraving after the picture by Hayter at Woburn Abbey.
Presented by the artist, 1826.

LONDON: THE TOWNELEY GALLERY, PARK STREET, WESTMINSTER

Charles Towneley sitting in his gallery with Thomas Ashe, Charles Greville, and M. D'Hancarville.

953 *By W.H. Worthington,* line engraving 83 × 61 cm (32⅝ × 24 in), (Ath. Fol. III. 15; O'D Groups p. 57), after the oil by Zoffany then in possession of Peregrine Townley Esq (Manners & Williamson, p. 21).
Presented probably by Charles Towneley's nephew who also gave the Club, in 1830, five quarto vols. of *Engravings … of Ancient Marbles in the British Museum* (Minutes 30 March 1830, p. 130).

DEATH OF THE STAG IN GLEN TILT, 1824-30

954 *By J. Bromley, 1833,* mezzotint (Ath. Folio III. 12), after the picture by Landseer, exh RA 1830, in the collection of the Duke of Atholl. It shows portraits of the Duke of Atholl, the Hon George Murray, and the celebrated foresters, John Crerar, Macintyre and Charles Crerar.

Literature: Richard Ormond, *Sir Edwin Landseer* (1982), p. 74.

QUEEN VICTORIA AND PRINCE ALBERT attacked by the Villain, EDWARD OXFORD, 1840

955 *By T.C. Wilson,* lithograph published as Star No. 24.

THE ATHENAEUM CLUB, BALLOT DAY 1892

956 *By J. Walter Wilson, RA*
Grey wash drawing heightened with white and buff body colour (43 × 75 cm (17 × 29½ in) sight size, signed and dated

958

lower left 1892, with a key numbered 1 to 59. The drawing, of an imaginary scene in the drawing room, was reproduced in a Clubland article in *The Illustrated London News*, and the Collection also has off-prints of cuts by J.W. Wilson, from the same article, of Athena and the Club seal, the front entrance with the Liverpool Street station omnibus, the morning room with C.P. Villiers and the last surviving original member, John Lettsom Elliot, the hall and main staircase, the coffee room, a memorable game of whist between Trollope, W.E. Forster, Abraham Hayward and Sir George Jessel, a general view of the south library showing the Rysbrack bust of Pope (see No. 685), and finally of Macaulay's corner, also in the south library.

Literature: *The Illustrated London News*, 11 March 1893, pp. 305-10, where a cut of the drawing was inserted separately as a full-page spread (key p. 309); and see Waugh 1899, p. 28 and Cowell 1975, 140
Presented by the Proprietors of *The Illustrated London News*, 1892.

ARMSTEAD, ARMITAGE AND GORHAM, 1893

Probably Henry Hugh Armstead, sculptor (1828–1905), elected to the Club in 1874, Edward Armitage RA

(1817–96), elected in 1885, and Mr Gorham, aboard the paddle-steamer 'Abruna'.

957 *By Walter William Ouless, 1893*

Pencil sketch, 8.5 × 15 cm (4¾ × 6 in), inscribed: *Armstead, Armitage, Gorham, Abruna 18 August '93.*

Presented by Miss Catherine Ouless, 1934.

CORONATION OF EDWARD VII, 1902, *see* No. 1169

JESMOND DENE, NEWCASTLE-UPON-TYNE

958 *By Campbell Swinton, c.1910*, photograph of an FRS group at Jesmond Dene, the home of Sir Andrew Noble, Bt. Present were, top row: Professor Osborne Reynolds, Captain Casella (Italian Roy. Navy), Lord Kelvin, Sir Frederick Bramwell Bt, Sir Robert Baden-Powell OM; bottom row: Sir Andrew Noble himself, Sir Frederick Abel, Bt, and Sir William Abney (Ath. Ports Red 11a).
Presented by Sir Squire Bancroft, 1917.

GROUP

959 *By Campbell Swinton, c.1910*, photograph with: C.A. Parsons, Swinton?, Philip Watts and Sir Joseph Larmor (Ath Ports. Red 14a).

GROUP

960 *By Campbell Swinton, c.1910,* photograph with: W. Duddell, C. Boys, Swinton?, H.R. Mallock, Wood (USA) and A.J. Strutt, later Lord Rayleigh (Ath. Ports. Red 14b).

GROUP

961 *By Campbell Swinton, c.1910,* photograph with: Jackson, Kennedy, Keith, Swinton(?), Horace Brown, J.M. Thomson (Ath. Ports. Red 15a).

GROUP

962 *By Campbell Swinton, c.1910,* photograph with: Swinton, Snell, J.B. Elphinstone, Wallace Jones, Walter, John Perry, Kingsbury (Ath. Ports. Red 15b).

GROUP

963 *By Campbell Swinton, c.1910,* photograph with: Edwin Houston, Jake, J.S. Highfield, Colonel Smith, AC. Swinton, J.C. Mclaren, Sir Joseph Larmor, Sir Charles Parsons (Ath. Ports. Red 16a).

GROUP

964 *By Campbell Swinton, c.1910,* photograph with: Sir William Bragg, Retorvel, Sir Joseph Larmor, Sir D. Clarke, Sir James Jeans, Sir Charles Parsons, P.A. McMahon, Sir Richard Glazebrook (Ath. Ports. Red 16b).

GROUP

965 *By Campbell Swinton, c.1910,* photograph with: Sir Philip Watts, FRS, Sir Charles Parsons, OM, and Sir William Henry White (Ath. Ports. Red 17a).

GROUP

966 *By Cambell Swinton, c.1910,* photograph with: Campbell Swinton, J.S. Highfield, John Monday, Sir Charles Parsons, and J.B. Elphinstone (Ath. Ports. Red 17b)

GROUP

967 *By Campbell Swinton, c.1910,* photograph with Trotter (?), Ramsay, Sylvanus Thompson (Ath. Ports. Red 18a).

GROUP

968 *By Campbell Swinton, c.1910,* photograph with: A. Parsons, J.A. Ewing and an unknown (Ath. Ports. Red 18b).

RETIREMENT DINNER, 1920

969 Group photograph (Ath. Ports. Red 21) of a farewell dinner given by Lord Blyth to Sir Thomas Mackenzie upon his retirement as High Commissioner for New Zealand, at the Athenaeum 13 July 1920. A pencilled key names 28 diners including the Duke of York, later George VI.

THE ATHENAEUM CLUB, BALLOT DAY DINNER, 1992

970 *Photograph.*
Members, gathered on the main staircase, present at the dinner held on Wednesday 29 April 1992 to celebrate the centenary of 'Ballot Day at the Athenaeum', 'drawn by Sir John Gilbert' for *The Illustrated London News* of 11 March 1893. The drawing was actually by J.W. Wilson (see No. 944).

JOHN ROSS CBE, GIVES A LIBRARY TALK ON ERASMUS, 1992

Polymath, elected to the Club in 1963 and a frequent contributor to the Question Book.

971 *By Creswick Cottingham, 1992*

Pencil drawing on white paper, 32 × 29 cm (12½ × 15¼ in), signed and dated; *Creswick Cottingham 8.11.92,* and inscribed: *Athenaeum library / lecture on Erasmus.* The talk took place in the Ladies' Annexe, recently re-named the Garden Room. Calder Marshal's bust called 'Queen Victoria', No. 874, is seen in the corner. Among the audience were Keith Davey (chairman of the library committee) and Sarah Dodgson (librarian).

Presented by G.P. Dews, 1993.

II SATIRES AND CARTOONS

arranged in subjects and then chronologically:

(i) THE ATHENAEUM

THE BOILED OWL

972 *By George Morrow, c.1910*

Ink on thin paper, 23.7 × 36.1 cm, (9⅜ × 14¼ in), signed: *Geo. M.* and inscribed: *Entertainments at which we have never assisted. Bringing on the BOILED OWL at the Christmas dinner at the Athenaeum Club.*

Presented by W.E.F. Macmillan, 1925.

972

THE SIEGE OF THE ATHENAEUM

973 *By George Morrow, c.1910*

Ink drawing, 14.5 × 22.5 cm (5⅝ × 8⅞ in), signed *Geo. Morrow*. Police grapple with unruly members, mainly clerical, 'by an untrustworthy artist in London'.

Presented by Mr Justice Cusack, 1969.

BUT, MY DEAR BOY ...

974 *By Fougasse, c.1934*

Ink drawing, 35 × 25.5 cm (13¾ × 10 in), signed *Fougasse* and inscribed:*" But, my dear boy, I can't walk on those things!" – an* elderly lady hesitates at a pedestrian crossing, introduced by a Traffic Act in 1934, when Leslie Hore-Belisha, Minister of Transport, invented 'Belisha Beacons' and pedestrian crossings.

Presented by the artist,

THE COMIC STRIP

975 *By Joe Lee, 1936*

Ink drawing, 53 × 37 cm (21 × 14½ in), from 'London Laughs, Atheneum (sic) Club', *Evening Standard* 18 June 1936. An American visitor in co-respondent shoes and cigar admires the Henning frieze(*I said I like the comic strip round the top*) to a deeply shocked member.

THE BEST CLUBS

976 *By Fougasse, 1944*

An off-print from *Punch* 29 March 1944, 24 × 18 cm (9½ × 7 in) sight, signed *Fougasse* in ink and inscribed: *The best clubs have always been rather difficult to get into – now they've become well-nigh impossible – even if you're a member* (signed in ink: 'with respectful greetings from Fougasse').

Literature: Bevis Hillier, *Fougasse* (ed. 1977).

975

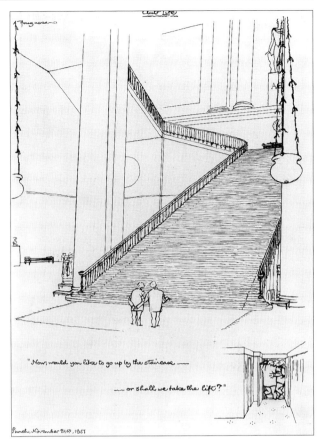

977

CLUB LIFE

977 *By Fougasse, 1951*

Black ink on Windsor & Newton card, 38.5 × 31.7 cm (15⅛ × 12½ in), signed *Fougasse* and inscribed: *Club Life / "Now, would you like to go up by the staircase – or shall we take the lift?"* Two members hesitate at the foot of the huge Club staircase while others scramble into a minute lift (*Punch*, 21 Nov 1951).

HAVE A CARE, FONTWATER ...

978 *By Sir Osbert Lancaster, 1951*

Black ink, wash and blue chalk cartoon, 39.5 × 13.5 cm (15½ × 5¼ in) inscribed: *"Have a care Fontwater – we're not in Whites'!" Osbert Lancaster.*

The cartoon refers to an assault on Nye Bevan by Lord Fox-Strangeways at Whites Club, reported in the *Sunday Express* 1951.

A colleague restrains a ferocious bishop who threatens a mildly smiling cleric, Dr Hewlett Johnson, the Red

Dean of Canterbury, who descends the front steps of the Athenaeum.

Presented by the artist, *c.*1955.

VIEW OF THE ATHENAEUM, TRAVELLERS AND REFORM CLUBS

979 *By Sir Osbert Lancaster, 1953* {Pl. XVI.]

Ink and colour wash cartoon, 33 × 51 cm (13 × 20 in), sight size. Two clubmen stroll past the Athenaeum; one is Sir Osbert himself, heavily moustached and dressed in flashy tweed.

Bought by the Club, 1996.

GRAVE NEWS FONTWATER ...

980 *By Sir Osbert Lancaster, 1961*

Ink and black wash cartoon, 25.5 × 15.5 cm (10 × 6 in), signed in ink and with typed label: *"Grave news Fontwater! It appears that it is not St Paul's Mr Clore is taking over – it's the*

980

Athenaeum!" Evening News, 13 January 1961, referring to Sir Charles Clore's business activities.

Presented by the artist, 1961.

PON MY WORD, BARNSTAPLE ...

981   *By Sir Osbert Lancaster, 1962*

Black ink and wash cartoon, 23.5 × 16 cm (9⅛ × 6¼ in), signed and with typed inscription: *"Pon my word Barnstaple, it must have been worse than the Athenaeum on boat race night"*. Two bishops reading a *Daily Express* headline: '3000 Bishops in Rome' (13 October 1962) reporting on the Vatican Council.

Presented by the artist.

I'M TELLING YOU, PLAINSONG ...

982   *By Sir Osbert Lancaster, 1969*

Black ink, wash and blue chalk cartoon, 25 × 16 cm (10 × 6½ in), inscribed: *"I'm telling you Plainsong, it's the thin end of the wedge. Before you can say 'Apostolic succession' they'll be letting*

983

Jehovah's Witnesses into the Athenaeum". Two bishops read a *Church Times* headline: REUNION (Daily Express 7 Feb. 1969).

Presented by the artist, 1969.

'LES FOLIES'

983   *By JAK, 1973*

Ink and wash, 43 × 54 cm (17 × 21¼ in), signed JAK and inscribed: *"This will teach you bounders to pay your bills at 'Les Folies' in future !"*, dated 1 January 1973, the day of Britain's entry into Europe.

Presented by Lord Stamp, 1973.

TELL ME BISHOP ...

984   *By Sir Osbert Lancaster, 1975*

Black ink, wash and blue chalk cartoon, 25.5 × 16 cm (10 × 6¼ in), signed *Osbert Lancaster* and with typed inscription: *"Tell me Bishop, is it true that even the Athenaeum's thinking of going bi-sexual?"* (Daily Express, 18 Feb. 1975); a nice use of a malapropism.

Presented anonymously, 1975.

JIM FIXED IT ...

985   *By JAK, 1984*

Off-print from *The Standard*, 23 Feb 1984, signed JAK and inscribed: "Jim Fixed it for him!". An aged bishop stumbles down the front steps of the Athenaeum supported by two chorus girls. Sir Jimmy Savile, elected in 1984 and an indefatigable philanthropist and supporter of the disabled, was the hero of a television programme, 'Jim'll Fix It'.

AIDS

986 *By JAK, 1986*

Ink and wash, 47 × 56 cm (18½ × 22 in), signed JAK and inscribed: *"This AIDS thing must be a lot more serious than we thought, bishop!"* A group of clergy in the 'Athenaeum Club Gentlemen's' inspect the newly installed Durex dispenser (*The London Standard*, 19 Nov. 1986).

I SAY LANE! ...

987 *By JAK, 1990*

Ink and blue wash on CS6 Abraded Board Frisk, 43 × 55 cm (17 × 21½ in), signed *JAK* and inscribed: *"I say Lane! what else did Pickles call you before he was hung drawn and quarterd?'* (Evening Standard, 22 January 1990). A glum-looking judge sits in the Club library reading the Standard headline, 'A Dinosaur living in the wrong age' – a stab at the judiciary's imagined isolation from everyday life.

THE DARLING BUDS OF MAY

988 *By JAK, 1991*

Ink and blue wash on CS6 Abraded Board Frisk, signed *JAK* and inscribed:*" What's the Darling Buds of May?"* Evening Standard, 14 May 1991, referring not to Shakespeare's sonnet nor the H.E. Bates novel, but a new television soap opera.

Bought by the Club, May 1991.

ATHENAEUM CLUB HAPPY HOUR

989 *By JAK, 1992*

Black ink and blue wash on CS6 Abraded Board Frisk, 52 × 60 cm (20½ × 23⅝ in), signed *JAK* and inscribed in pencil: *"I'd be careful how you shake up the Judiciary, Peter, some of them have'nt even been stirred for years!"* Archbishop to Lord Chancellor, referring to Lord Lane's resignation, 27 February 1992.

TARTS AND BISHOPS

990 *By JAK, 1995*

Ink and blue wash, 51 × 49 cm (20 × 19¼ in), signed *JAK* and inscribed in pencil: *"I don't know how to break this to you, Bertie ! but Baywatch Pam has just got married!"* 22 Feb.y 1995. / *Athenaeum: Party Monday 27 February: Tarts and Bishops* Members in the Club read with concern *The Evening Standard,* 'Pam marries in white bikini'.

Presented by Malcolm Bishop, 1995.

(ii) POLITICAL

THE PROCESSION OF THE FLITCH OF BACON

991 *By HB, 1841 (John Doyle),* coloured lithograph (Ath. Folio II.7), HB Sketch 669 & 670 parodying Stothard's 'Admired Picture – Somewhat Metamorphosed', the 'Procession' in the Tate Gallery and showing Queen Victoria, Prince Albert, preceded by the Lord Chancellor, and accompanied by Wellington and other notables. Brougham ahead plays the bagpipes.

NEW VERSION OF JOHN GILPIN AFTER STOTHARD

992 *By HB, 1846 (John Doyle),* coloured lithograph (Eng I. 15), HB Sketches Nos. 858 & 859, showing Peel, Wellington and other Conservatives in full cry after John Bull and Protection, based on Stothard's picture in the Tate gallery.

THE SELF-SUPPORTING INSTITUTION PROPOSED BY MR J.M. MORGAN IN "RELIGION AND CRIME, OR THE DISTRESSES OF THE PEOPLE AND THE REMEDIES", 1842.

993 *By G.F. Bragg,* lithograph (Ath. Folio II. 18), published by Longman & Co. John Minter Morgan (1782–1854), philanthropist and reformer, founded a National Orphan Home and tried to form a self-supporting village in 1850.

SIEGE OF PARIS, 1870-71, *see* **Appendix V**

THE RAKE'S PROGRESS

994 *By Tom Merry, 1884,* coloured lithograph after Hogarth, showing Edward Prince of Wales handing Mr Gladstone (the Rake) a 'Writ for General Election'. Presentation Cartoon for *St Stephen's Review*, 26 July 1884, based on Hogarth's pictures in the Soane Museum.

BISMARCK – HERCULES FURENS

995 *By Edwin Linley Sambourne, 1889*

Ink and wash, 28 × 23 cm (11 × 9 in), signed and dated: *Linley Sambourne Feb. 8. 1889*, standing on a lionskin hurling GEFECKEN over his shoulder, his club marked *Policy*, his tunic *Opposition*. Published in *Punch* 16 Feb. 1889

Lucas bequest, 1918.

BISMARCK – A RETIRING YOUNG MAN

996 *By Edwin Linley Sambourne, 1890*

Ink and wash on white card, 24 × 18.5cm (9½ × 7¼ in), signed and dated: *Linley Sambourne March 7. 1890.* Published in *Punch* 15 March 1890 as: *A Retiring Young Man (Positively his last Appearance)*with three stanzas beginning, *'I linger on the same old stage … Teutons, once again! greet me once again, etc.*

Lucas bequest, 1918.

BISMARCK – OUT IN THE COLD

997 *By Edwin Linley Sambourne, 1892*

Ink and wash on card, 24 × 18.5 cm (9½ × 7¼ in), signed and dated: *Linley Sambourne January 29 1892,* Published in *Punch* 6 Feb. 1892 as "Out in the Cold! I am like a Traveller lost in the Snow who begins to get stiff while the Snowflakes cover him" Speech by Prince von Bismarck at Friedriksruhe.

Lucas bequest, 1918.

BOER WAR, 1899–1902, *see* Appendix V

LORD GREY OF FALLODON

1862–1933, Foreign Secretary, President of the League of Nations, and author of *Fallodon Papers* (1926) and *The Charm of Birds* (1927).

998 *By Sir Bernard Partridge, 1906*

Ink on white paper, 35 × 27 cm (13¾ × 10⅝ in), signed: *Bernard Partridge*. Lord Grey in armour, mounted on a Foreign Office charger, threads his way through a thorny wilderness. A modified version of a cartoon for *Punch*, 18 July

998

1906, appearing in *Punch* 13 September 1933, shortly after Lord Grey's death on 7 September.

Presented by the artist, 1934.

A DULCIFIED AUTOCRACY

999 *By Sir Max Beerbohm, 1913*

Watercolour on grey paper, 33 × 27.5 (13 × 10⅞ in) signed and dated *Max 1913*, and inscribed: *"A Dulcified Autocracy. Mr G S Street (To the Tsar): "Aha! Wouldn't you like to have a colleague, and all responsibilty taken by a nice Lord Chamberlain?"*
The Tsar Nicholas II (1868–1918), is gently twitted by the Lord Chamberlain, G.S. Street (1867–1936).
Literature: Beerbohm-Davies 1972.
Presented by the artist, 1937.

THE OLD AND THE YOUNG SELF

1000 *By Sir Max Beerbohm, 1924* [Pl. XI (a)]

Pencil and watercolour on grey-green paper, 33.2 × 20.5 (13 × 8 in), signed and dated: *Max 1924*, and inscribed: *The Old and the Young Self. Young Self: "Prime Minister? You? Good Lord!!"*

999

1004

Stanley Baldwin (1867–1947), three times prime minister, expresses astonishment at his own success. See Nos. 45–6.

Literature: Beerbohm-Observations 1923, p.48.
Presented by a group of members, 1936.

THE BABES IN THE WOOD

(Lord Parmoor and Lord Passfield)

1001 *By A. W. Lloyd, 1929*

Ink and wash, 17.5 × 19 cm (5⅞ × 7½ in), signed: *A. W. Ll.*

Published in P*unch*, 13 November 1929, illustrating an article, 'The Essence of Parliament', about the Simon Commission on giving Dominion status to India.
Presented by the artist, 1934.

THE CHAMPION OF LONDON

1002 *By A. W. Lloyd, 1933*

Ink and wash, 15 × 15 cm (6 × 6 in), signed: *A. W. Ll.* inscribed: *Lord Conway enters the Lists in defence of Home and Beauty,* published in *Punch,* 28 June 1933, in an 'Essence of Parliament'

article defending the Adelphi as one of the great beauty spots of London.

Presented by the artist, 1934.

A PILOT BALLOON

1003 *By A. W. Lloyd, 1934*

chalk, ink and wash, 19 × 14.5 cm (7½ × 5¾ in), signed *A. W. Ll.* and inscribed: *A Pilot Balloon (Petroleum Bill) Lord Londonderry: "Quite a harmless stunt this – mainly in the air – what?" Mr Runciman: "Yes, but that's just what some of our friends dislike about it, it shows which way the wind is blowing." Punch,* 27 June 1934.

Presented by the artist, 1934.

FURTHER OUTRAGE AT THE TATE

1004 *By Norman Mansbridge, 1956*

Ink and wash, 24 × 18.5 cm (9½ × 7¼ in), signed: *Norman Mansbridge.*

Published in *Punch,* 25 April 1956, based on a press photograph of a burglar walking down the front steps of the

1005

Tate Gallery with *Jour d'été* by Berthe Morisot under his arm. Sir John Rothenstein has been substituted for the picture. The incident was the slightly ludicrous climax to a series of 'outrages' involving the Tate administration and the Lane Bequest of Impressionist pictures. On the morning of 12 April 1956, a Fleet Street photographic agency, Planet News Ltd., received an anonymous telephone call stating that there was to be an Irish demonstration outside the Tate Gallery. A photographer was sent and, failing to find a more interesting subject, took this photograph of a young man walking down the steps of the Gallery carrying a framed painting. The negative was not even considered worth developing until, in the afternoon, the news of the daring removal of Berthe Morisot's *Jour d'été* was published. Planet News immediately developed their photograph and submitted it to Scotland Yard. The man carrying the picture is stated to have been identified by the police as Paul Hogan – indeed the picture is covered with a piece of board bearing his name and address – and his accomplice, just emerging from the revolving door, as William P. Fogarty. This photograph was withheld from

publication while inquiries were made by the police. On Monday, 16 April, the day after the photograph was released to the Press, an "unknown caller" delivered a parcel, addressed to the Ambassador, at the Irish Embassy in London. This was found to contain the *Jour d'été*. The painting was handed over to the Director of the Tate Gallery, who stated that it was in 'perfect condition'.

The picture was part of the disputed Lane Bequest, now happily resolved, and hangs in the Lane Art Gallery, Dublin.
Presented by the artist, 1956.

RICHARD CROSSMAN, PC, OBE AND THE ROBBINS REPORT

1907–74, journalist, politician and diarist.

1005 *By Vicky (V. Weisz), 1964*

Ink and wash cut-out, 34.5 × 23 cm (13½ × 9 in) sight size. He wears gown and mortar board and holds the 'Robbins Report on Higher Education'. Published in *The Evening Standard*, 1964.

Presented by K.A.T. Davey, 1990.

(iii) PERSONAL

TALLEYRAND

1754–1838, Prince Charles Maurice de Talleyrand-Périgord, bishop of Autun, minister for foreign affairs and a moderating influence behind Napoleon. His share in the French Revolution was heavily satirised by Thomas Carlyle. Talleyrand was not a member of the Club but frequented the Travellers.

1006 *By Count D'Orsay, c.1830.*

Ink on white paper, 18 × 12.2 cm (7¼ × 4¾ in) sight size inscribed in another hand: *Pce Talleyrand sketched by D'Orsay*. Whole-length elderly figure in frock coat, holding top hat and walking stick.

Presented by Sir Arthur Elton, Bt. 1958.

REV WILLIAM BUCKLAND

1784–1856, President of the Geological Society; a founding member of the Club. He is the subject of a startling poem by William Plomer, "The Heart of a King".

1007 *By T. Sopwith, 1840*, etching (Ports M. II.33) from

1006

1007

Costume of the Glaciers, showing the great geologist heavily clothed for glacial exploration. In the background is a signpost to Alston, to left are two identical stones, one scratched by a glacier thirty three thousand years before the creation, the other scratched by a cartwheel on Waterloo Bridge the day before yesterday.

SIR JOHN EVERETT MILLAIS, Bt. PRA

1829–96, with Holman Hunt a founding member of the Pre-Raphaelite Brotherhood. He later became a fashionable portrait painter, specially successful with children; elected to the Club in 1866.

1008 *Self-portrait, 1853*

Brown ink on white paper, 17.5 × 11.5 cm (6⅞ × 4½ in), signed and dated in pencil: *JEM 1853*. Two elongated whole-lengths, 'a specimen of a living paper-knife', one in a dressing-gown, the other in tight trousers, a helmeted head in profile top left. A similar drawing, spread-eagled measuring the size of his bedroom at Brig o' Turk, 'not much larger than a snuffbox', was exhibited 'Millais Portraits' NPG 1999, no. 26.

Literature: Millais 1899, II p.490; Lutyens and Warner 1983, p.13, no.1.
Presented by Marion H. Spielmann, FSA, 1947.

MILLAIS – THE NIGHTMARE

1009 *By Frederick Sandys, 1857*

Lithograph, 45 × 49 cm (17¾ × 19½ in), published by Smith ye E. Bere … 1857. A parody of Millais's picture, 'Sir Isumbras at the Ford', exh RA 1857. Millais himself rides a donkey inscribed *J.R. Oxon*. The figure of Rossetti sits in front of the knight instead of the little girl, and Holman Hunt clings to his waist. In the background, disguised as nuns, are Raphael, Michael Angelo and Titian. As a result of this print Sandys was invited to join the Pre-Raphaelites.

1008

LORD CHANCELLOR CAMPBELL

1779–1861, Lord Chancellor; a founding member of the Club.

1010   *By George Richmond, 1860*

Pencil drawing on faded white paper, 11 × 6 cm (4¼ × 2⅜ in), back view drawn at the Athenaeum, inscribed: *Ld Chancellor Campbell,*

MARQUESS OF RIPON, KG, FRS, 1869

1827–1909, Lord President of the Council, elected to the Club in 1862.

1011   *By Ape*, Spy cartoon no. 29, 22 May 1869, 'Qualis ab Inepto'.

ALEXANDER WILLIAM KINGLAKE, 1872
(see No. 490)

1012   *By Cecione*, Spy cartoon, no. 174, 2 March 1872, 'Not an M.P.'

KIPLING JOINS THE CLUB, 1897

1013   *By Sir Edward Burne-Jones, 1897*

Ink on white paper, 17.5 × 22.3 (6⅞ × 8¾ in), inscribed: … *its offices – the latter will amaze you – & you will know more of the inner life of bishops than in a hundred biographies.*

The drawing is part of a letter to Rudyard Kipling congratulating him on his election to the Club and illustrated with drawings of bishops deep in armchairs reading books and newspapers, *'and so on'*. A copy of the letter written from The Grange, North End Road, begins: *Ruddy my dear*, and ends: *Love to you both – nay, all your aff EB-J.*

Exhibition: 'Edward Burne-Jones', Arts Council 1975
Presented by Sir Alfred Webb-Johnson, 1940.

KIPLING in 1901, By W. Cushing Loring, 1901, see No. 492

SIR JOHN WOLFE-BARRY, KCB, FRS

1836–1918, civil engineer; elected to the Club in 1876.

1014   *By Spy (Sir Leslie Ward), 1905* [Pl. X (b)]

Watercolour on bluish paper, 36 × 26.1 cm (14 × 10¼ in), signed SPY, WL to right in frock coat and cigar; original drawing for a *Vanity Fair* cartoon no. 948, published 26 January 1905, 'He has engineered nothing better than his own fortunes'.

Literature: Matthews & Mellini, *Vanity Fair* (1982), p. 244.
Sold Sotheby's 29 Oct 1912 (440); presented by the Hon. Reginald Fremantle, 1930.

SIR WILLIAM ROTHENSTEIN

1872–1945, painter, Principal of the Royal College of Art, and author of 3 vol memoirs, *Men and Memories* (1933–9); elected in 1925 under Rule II.

1015   *By Henry Tonks, 1903* [Pl. XI (b)]

Watercolour on light brown paper, 20 × 27.75 cm (7⅝ × 11 in), uninscribed; three WL figures: William seated in glasses, his wife Alice in enormous skirt and orange hair, his son John throwing himself at Papa.

1013

Presented by D.S. MacColl in memory of Henry Tonks, 1938.

SIR ARTHUR WING PINERO

(1855–1934), playwright, author of *The Second Mrs Tanqueray* (1893), etc; elected to the Club in 1916.

1016 *By Sir Max Beerbohm, c.1920*

Chalk on buff paper, 33 × 27.5 cm (13 × 10¾ in), signed *Max*, and inscribed: *Le Sourciliste*. Max makes fun of his magnificent eyebrows – 'like the skins of some small mammal … just not large enough to be used as mats'.

Literature: Beerbohm 1972, p.; Hall 1997, p.80. Presented by the artist, 1937.

PROFESSOR FRANCIS JEFFREY BELL

c.1855–1924, eccentric natural scientist, elected to the Club in 1900.

1017 *By Frederick Thomas Dalton, c.1920* [Pl. X (a)]

Watercolour, 17.3 × 10.5 cm (6¾ × 4⅛ in), signed: *F.T. Dalton*, and inscribed below: *"Silence that dreadful Bell"* Othello Act ii Sc 3. Small whole-length figure in grey suit and blue bow tie. A pencil caricature of Bell's head is on the back.

Presented by W. Reeve Wallace 1947

D.S. MacCOLL, (see Nos. 563-4)

1018 *By Powys Evans ('Quiz'), 1922*

Ink on white paper, 34.8 × 25 cm (13¾ × 9⅞ in), inscribed at

1016

1018

top in ink: *To R.A. Walker from the culprit / The Victim D.S. MacColl,* and signed: *Powys Evans 1922.* This splendid caricature shows the great art oracle seated amid clouds of optimism. A variant, head and serpent neck only, reproduced in Evans, *Eighty-Eight Cartoons* (1926), no. 1).

Presented by R.A. Walker, 1938.

SIR CHARLES VERNON BOYS, FRS,

1855–1944, physicist and a prolific inventor.

1019 *By Sir Richard Paget, Bt. 1929*

Pen and ink on Athenaeum writing-paper, 20.5 × 12.5 cm (8 × 5 in), signed and dated: *R.A.S.P. 10/4/29,* and inscribed: *C.V. Boys, FRS,* TQL in armchair reading a paper.

Presented by the artist.

LIEUT-COLONEL SIR HENRY McMAHON, GCMG

1862–1949, president of the YMCA 1923–47.

1020 *By Cire,* Spy cartoon.

LORD KEYNES

1883–1946, John Maynard Keynes, economist, member of the Bloomsbury Group; elected to the Club in 1942.

1021 *By Low,* 1933, litho off-print of a cartoon, *The New Statesman & Nation,* 28 Oct 1933.

ALDOUS HUXLEY

1894–1963, polymath and author of *Brave New World,* etc; elected to the Club in 1922.

1022 *By Low, 1933,* litho off-print of a cartoon, *The New Statesman & Nation,* 25 Nov 1933.

A STORY OF THREE
ROYAL
ACADEMICIANS

1028

LORD REITH

1889–1971, Sir John Reith, creator of the BBC; elected in 1927 under Rule II.

1023 *By Low, 1933,* litho off-print of a cartoon, *The New Statesman & Nation,* 11 Nov 1933.

WALTER ELLIOT, PC, MP

1888–1958, politician, elected to the Club in 1924.

1024 *By Low, 1933,* litho off-print of a cartoon, *The New Stateman & Nation,* 18 Nov 1933.

ERNEST BEVIN, PC, MP

1881–1951, trade union leader, Foreign Secretary 1945–51.

1025 *By Low, 1933,* litho off-print of a cartoon, *The New Statesman & Nation,* 30 Dec 1933.

CHARLES L. GRAVES

1856–1944, assistant editor and contributor to *Punch;* elected to the Club in 1902.

1026 *By Sir Bernard Partridge, 1944*

Ink and wash, 18.5 × 13 cm (7⅛ × 5⅛in), signed in ink: *B.P.* Cartoon for *Punch,* 26 April 1944, accompanying an obituary by E.V. Knox, describing the Athenaeum as almost Graves's home.

Presented by the artist, 1944.

1027 *Photograph,* with his brother, Sir Robert Graves KCMG (Ath. Ports. Red 37).

A STORY OF THREE ROYAL ACADEMICIANS

1028 *By A.R. Thomson, c.1950*

Pen and ink on white paper, 26 × 29.5 cm (10¼ × 11⅝ in),

Ancient Military Dandies of 1450 —
Sketch'd by permission from the Originals in the
Grand Armory at the GOTHIC HALL *Pall-Mall*

Modern Military Dandies – of 1819
— Sketch'd without permission from the Life —

1032

showing Augustus John, Sir William Orpen and Sir Alfred Munnings, and their drinking habits. A R Thomson shrinks nervously beside them.

From the collection of Sir William Orpen and presented by Mrs Bodkin in memory of Professor Thomas Bodkin, 1961.

(iv) SCIENCES

VELOCIPEDES

1029 Anon. lithograph 1818: *Draisiennes dites velocipedes. Chevaux portraits et économiques inventés hors de France.*
Presented by Sir David Salomons Bt. 1906.

THE PROGRESS OF STEAM – A VIEW IN WHITE CHAPEL ROAD

1030 *By Henry Alken, 1830*
Coloured aquatint, 21.5 × 27 cm (8½ × 10⅝in), published by S

& J Fuller in *Illustrations of Modern Prophesy.*
Presented by Sir David Salomons, 1906.

VENUS ANADYOMENE AND THE HYGIENIC BAGMAN

1031 *By Henry Tonks, 1912*

Watercolour on folded paper, 23 × 17.5 cm (9 × 6⅞ in), inscribed:*Primordial slime / The Modern Birth of Venus or Oh What a Surprise.* On the back is a letter: *Vale Shades B / Val Ancrum / Chelsea SW / Feb 6 1912 / My dear MacColl / Are you back? I am, I am glad to say. Half a watercolour, £50 expenses and 3 and a half weeks' time. I send you what came to me after reading the paper yesterday / Yours ever Henry Tonks.* Under the mount is a pencilled explanation: *Satire on Professor Schäfer's presidential address to the British Association, 1912 / see leader and report in 'The Times', 5 February 1912. Schäfer contended that there was no essential difference between animate and inanimate matter. 'The chemical constituents of protoplasm are simple enough' he said, 'and he had little doubt of eventual success in building up protoplasm in the laboratory … in short there is no mystery in life at all'.*

Presented by D.S. MacColl, 1938, in memory of Henry Tonks

(v) THE SERVICES

ANCIENT MILITARY DANDIES

1032 *George Cruikshank, 1835*

Coloured etching, 26 × 36 cm (10¼ × 14⅛ in), published by McLean 1835, lettered: *Ancient Military Dandies of 1450, sketched by permission of the Originals in the Grand Armory at the Gothic Hall, Pall Mall. Modern Military Dandies of 1819, sketched <u>without</u> permission from the life.*

Literature: *George Cruikshank,* Arts Council exhibition catalogue, V&A Museum 1974; L. Patten, *George Cruikshank* (1992), 48.

DIVIDED DUTY

1033 *By Edwin Linley Sambourne, 1890*

Ink on white paper, 23 × 19.5 cm (9 × 7⅝in), signed and dated: *Sambourne March 11 1890,* published in *Punch* 19 March 1892:

Right Hon the Minister for War: "Surely, my Lord Chancellor, you can exempt him from Juries 'The Regulars …"

Lord Chancellor: "Well no, Mr Stanhope, I think not" (Aside) "We must make <u>some</u> use of him".

This exchange was a comment on a statement in The Times: "The root of Volunteer inefficiency is to be ascribed to the Volunteer officer. The men are such as their officers make them … The force is 1,100 officers short of its proper complement". The cartoon is accompanied in *Punch* by some doggerel verses by a Volunteer officer defending himself.

1036

MORE KICKS THAN HALFPENCE

1034 *By Edwin Linley Sambourne, 1891*

Ink on white paper, 24 × 15.5 cm (9½ × 6 in) sight size, signed and dated: *Linley Sambourne del. April 1891.* inscribed: *General Red Tape (of the Intelligence Department W.O.): "What! going to resign"* Volunteer Officer: *"Yes. Why should I only get your kicks for my half-pence!"*

Published in *Punch* 11 April 1891.
Lucas bequest 1918.

(vi) SPORT

BILLIARDS

1035 *By Henry William Bunbury, 1824*

Line engraving, 25.5 × 37 cm (10 × 14½ in), published by Watson & Dickinson, 'The Original Plate re-published May 28th 1824 by Z. Sweet …' A drawing of the same subject, by W.H. Pyne, was etched by Williams (Mrs George 15010).

Presented by Arthur Hind, 1945.

A WET DAY'S PASTIME, 1853

1036 *By Sir John Millais*

Pen and sepia wash on paper: 18.3 × 23.2 cm (7¼ × 9⅛ in), inscribed at top: *A wet days pastime,* and signed lower right with the Millais monogram and date 1853.

The scene is Brig o' Turk, Glenfinlas. John Ruskin and Millais's brother, William, energetically play battledore and shuttlecock on the laundry table. In the doorway are Alexander Stewart (the local schoolmaster) and Effie Gray, then married to Ruskin. In back view is the artist himself, who was to marry Effie in 1855.

'The rain is dreadful; we are obliged to play Battledore and Shuttlecock in a barn place redolent of Peat reek and where a school of Gaelic bairns is held every morning' (letter from Effie to Rawdon Brown, 27 July 1853).

Literature: Millais 1899, I, p.203, II, p. 490; Lutyens 1967, p.72; Lutyens and Warner 1983, p.39, no.16.

Exhibitions: RA and Walker Art Gallery, Liverpool, 1967; Arts Council touring exhibition 1979; Fine Arts Society, Edinburgh and London 1983.
Presented by W.E.F. Macmillan, 1937.

LETTER TO GEORGE MACMILLAN, 1895

1855–1936, publisher, see No. 568

1037 *By Edwin Linley Sambourne, 1895*

Ink on writing-paper, 17 × 10.5 cm (6¾ × 4⅛ in), inscribed: *… I have now been at Christchurch since early in August – with many regards always yours sincerely Linley Sambourn / George Macmillan Esq;* at the bottom of the page a small stocky figure of a 'sportsman' with gun over shoulder and dressed in highland clothes (Sambourne himself), 'quite the genuine article' (letter from Ayton Castle, 2 Sept 1895).

Presented by W.E.F. Macmillan, 1953.

(vii) MONEY

MR COHEN

1038 *By Richard Dighton, 1823*

Coloured etching, published by McLean, October 1823, WL profile to right.

Lucas bequest, 1918.

SIR MOSES HAIN MONTEFIORE

1039 *By Richard Dighton, 1824*

Coloured etching, published by McLean, June 1824, WL profile to left.

Lucas bequest, 1918.

WILL YOU LET ME A LOAN, MR GOLDSMITH?

1040 *By Richard Dighton, 1824*

Coloured etching, published by McLean, August 1824, WL profile to right.

Lucas bequest, 1918.

Literature: Thomas McLean, *City Characters drawn and etched by Richard Dighton* (1824); D. Patton, 'Richard and Joshua Dighton', *Antique Collector* (March 1983), pp. 85-7.

1041

(viii) MISCELLANEOUS

DOVE IL 'WAIT AND SEE'? MR ASQUITH AT UDINE STATION.

1041 *By Henry Tonks, 1916*

Watercolour, 19.5 × 25 cm (7⅝ × 9⅞ in), inscribed top left: *PER UOMINI*, and in balloon: *scuse la sue Maesta ma dove il wait and see?*, and below: *(stopped by the censor) The force of habit. The above incident took place at – it was only the*

admirable tact of a certain exalted personage which prevented widespread complications. On the reverse is a faint pencil letter to MacColl from ? Tonks, 16 April 1916, from Aldershot. Tonks had joined a British Ambulance unit, organised by G.M. Trevelyan, and worked at Udine, N. Italy, in September 1915. The scene is clearly imaginary and is a play on Mr Asquith's nickname, 'Old Wait and See', who in a moment of urgency, has mistaken the King of Italy for the station master.

Literature: Joseph Hone, *Life of Tonks* (1939), pp. 122–5.

Presented by D.S. MacColl, 1938.

III LANDSCAPES AND VIEWS

AMSTERDAM: CANAL AND HOUSE

1042 *By T.F. Simon*, coloured etching no.12, 33 × 38.5 cm (12 × 15 in), stamped with monogram: *TFS imp*, and signed in pencil: *TF Simon 12*.
Lucas bequest, 1918.

THE ATHENAEUM CLUB, *see* Nos. 1239-75

ATHENS

View from the north-east.

1043 *By J.H. Schilbach, c.1822, engraving* (Eng. I. 5), after a drawing by Heger.

ATHENS

View from the west.

1044 *By Schilbach, 1822*, line engraving (Eng. I. 2), after a drawing by Hübsch, 1819.

ATHENS: ACROPOLIS

View from the south-east

1045 *By Schilbach 1822*, line engraving (Eng. I. 3) after a drawing by Hübsch.

ATHENS: ACROPOLIS

View from the west.

1046 *By Schilbach, 1823*, line engraving (Eng. I. 4) after a drawing by Hübsch, 1819.

ATHENS: ACROPOLIS

1047 *By W. Curtis Green* [Pl. XVIII (b)]

Watercolour on Roberson's Creswick Card, 27 × 36.75 cm (10⅝ × 14½ in), signed in pencil: *Acropolis W. Curtis Green*.

Exhibition: Green, Lloyd & Adams, Architects, St James's St. 1978.
Presented by W.A.S. Lloyd and Christopher Green, 1960.

BEACON HILL, *see* Witham, Nos. 1237-8

BERRY POMEROY CASTLE

1048a *By J M W Turner, 1816*

Mezzotint, 21.5 × 29.5 cm (8½ × 11⅝in), marked EP (for Epic). A plate from the *Liber Studiorum*, part XII (1816).

Literature: Luke Herrmann, *Turner Prints* (1990), pp.62-4.
Presented by Mrs Arthur Acland Allen, 1940

BEXHILL MARTELLO TOWERS

1048b *By W. Say, 1811*, after J.M.W. Turner

Mezzotint, 20.5 × 29 cm (8 × 11⅜in), marked M (for Marine). A plate from the *Liber Studiorum*, part VII (1811).

Literature: Luke Herrmann, *Turner Prints* (1990), p.51.
Presented by Mrs Arthur Acland Allen, 1940

BORGHESE GARDENS, 1924, *see* Rome, No. 1200

BRIGHTON

1049 *By F. Smith, 1829*, steel engraving (Eng. I. 8), after an oil by Constable in the Tate Gallery.

Literature: G. Reynolds, *Later Paintings and Drawings by John Constable* (2 vols Yale 1984), no. 27.1, colour plate 633.

BRIGHTON PIER

1050 *By Robert Goff*, etching, 12.5 × 22.5 cm (4⅞ × 8⅞ in), signed artist's proof.

1048a

BROOKHILL, *see* Dartmouth, Nos. 1286–7

CALAIS PIER

1051 *By Sir Francis Haden, 1865,* etching with drypoint and mezzotint, 59.5 × 83.5 cm (23⅞ × 32½ in), inscribed *11. Etched by Francis Seymour Haden after a Picture by JMW Turner,* after an oil by Turner in the National Gallery (no. 472).

Literature: Haden-Harrington, no. 145; Haden-Schneiderman, no. 141.
Lucas bequest, 1918.

CARLTON HOUSE, *see* London, Nos. 1103–22, 1145, 1166.

CARROS, VAR

1052 *By Augustus Hare* [Pl. XXVI]
Watercolour, 25 × 37 cm (9⅞ × 14½ in), inscribed: *Carros, Var.*
Presented by Sir Theodore Chambers, KBE, 1934

CASSIS: THE HARBOUR

1053 *By D.S. MacColl*
Pencil, 17 × 26.5 cm (6⅞ × 10½ in), signed lower left: *DSM.*
Presented by the artist, 1934.

'CASTLE IN THE AIR'

1054 *By O-G de Rochebrune, 1870,* etching, 50.5 × 75 cm (19⅜ × 29½ in), inscribed in ink: *Oᴿᵉ de Rochebrune del*

1058

et fec à terre neuve – dediée à Alix^{dre} Rochebrune Jan. 1870.
From the Collection de Terre-Neuve (Beraldi XI. 220).

CEYLON

1055 *By H.W. Burgess, 1830,* lithograph (Eng. A. I. 4–5), from drawings by C.H. Cameron (Bo Tree and Bo-Mallooa at Anhradapoora, and the Malwatté Wharé at Kandy).

CHALONS-SUR-MARNE: CHURCH OF NÓTRE-DAME

1056 *By J-C Maillet,* engraving (Eng. I. 27), two saintly statues in a niche after a drawing by Barbat père.

CHARLOIS, NEAR ROTTERDAM

1057 *By H.J. Lucas, 1870,* etching, 13.5 × 23 cm (5⅜ × 9 in), signed and dated: *HJL / 1870 / Charlois.*
Exhibition: RA 1871 (859).

CHELSEA HOSPITAL, SEE LONDON, NO. 1123

CHEVIOTS FROM THE OTTERCOPS

1058 *By Walter James (Lord Northbourne),* etching, 24.8 × 35 cm (9¾ × 12¾ in), signed *Walter James.*
Presented by the artist, 1930.

1070

CHILL OCTOBER

1059 *By A. Brunet-Desbaines, 1883*, etching, after an oil by Millais, exh RA 1871, also etched by C. Waltner (Millais 1899, II pp. 474, 495).

CHILLON, 1873

1060 *By Sir John Everett Millais*

Pencil, 19.5 × 31.75 cm (7⅝ × 12⅜ in), signed and dated with monogram: *JEM 1873*, and inscribed: *Chillon*. View of the Château de Chillon, Lac Leman, and the Dents du Midi in the background, probably worked up from a drawing made on his tour through Switzerland and Italy in 1865 (Millais 1899, I p. 390).

Presented by A.M Hind, 1937.

CINTRA

1061 *By W.H. Burnett*, lithographs (Eng. A.I. 11–17), seven
-7 views of Cintra: the town, the market place, the entrance from Lisbon, convent of S^{na} S^{ra} da Penna, the church, and an old chapel in the castle.

CLAUDIAN LANDSCAPE

1068 *After Claude*

Oil on canvas, 51 × 79 cm (20 × 31¼ in) sight, uninscribed, derives (in reverse) from a picture at Holkham Hall (*Claude*, Classici dell'Arte, 1975, no.149).

Bequeathed by T. Stirling Boyd, 1974

CLAUDIAN LANDSCAPE

1069 *After Claude*

Oil on canvas, 51 × 79.5 cm (20 × 31¼ in) sight, uninscribed, derives (in reverse) from a picture in the Barber Inst. Birmingham (ibid. no.157).

Bequeathed by T. Stirling Boyd, 1974.

THE CUILLINS, SKYE

1070 *By Cecil Arthur Hunt*

Watercolour and chalk on card, 31.5 × 45 cm (12⅜ × 17¾ in), signed in pencil: *CA Hunt.*

Presented by the artist, 1932.

DIEPPE: ANCIENT BUILDINGS

1071 *By C.G. Lewis, 1831,* etching (Eng. A.I.3), after a water-colour by R.P. Bonington.
Presented by the publisher, Colnaghi & Son.

DURHAM CATHEDRAL

1072 *By Sydney Lee,* etching and aquatint, 56 × 40.5 cm   . (22 × 16 in).
Presented by the artist, 1932.

ELGIN CATHEDRAL: *see* No. 1290

THE "EVENING STAR" IN HER LAST BERTH

1073 *By Sir Frank Short, 1930,* aquatint 17.5 × 28 cm (7 × 11 in), stamped S and signed *Frank Short* (Short-Hardie II, 168).

FEN COUNTRY BRIDGE

1074 *By Sir Frank Short 1903,* etching, 18.5 × 28 cm (7¼ × 11 in), signed in pencil: *Frank Short* (Short-Hardie II, 322).
Lucas bequest, 1918.

FONTAINEBLEAU: TREE

1075 *By Frederick, Lord Leighton, 1855*

Pencil and and grey wash, 32 × 24.75 cm (12½ × 9¾ in), inscribed: *Fontainebleau 18FL55* (monogram bisecting date).

Formerly in the collections of Edwouard von Steinle and Sir Henry S. Theobald, bought by the Club in 1933.

FOREST SCENE

1076 *By Horatio Joseph Lucas, 1871,* etching, Lucas bequest, 1918.

FRINGE OF THE WOOD

1077 *By Walter James (Lord Northbourne)* etching, 15 × 21 cm (5⅞ × 8¼ in), signed in pencil: *Walter James imp* and with monogram *WJ.*
Presented by the artist, 1932.

GREENWICH HOSPITAL, see No. 1124

GRIM SPAIN

1078 *By Sir Francis Haden, 1877,* etching, 15 × 22 cm (6 × 8⅝ in), drawn during a visit to Spain and Portugal with Sir Charles Robinson (Haden-Schneiderman no. 173).
 Lucas bequest, 1918.

HARVEST MOON

1079 *By Robert Walker Macbeth,* etching 33 × 86 cm (13 × 34 in), published 17 Feb 1883 by Robert Dunthorne, after a picture by G. H. Mason, exh RA 1872.
Lucas bequest, 1918.

HEXWORTHY BRIDGE

1080 *By Sir Francis Newbolt, 1936,* etching, 21 × 30 cm (8½ × 11¾ in), signed and dated: *RA 1931 / F. Newbolt.*
Presented by the artist, 1938.

ICELAND: VIEW OF THE GEYSER

1081 *By F. Chesham, 1796,* lithograph (Ath. Folio II. 12), 'from a Drawing made on the Spot in 1789', pubd Dec 1796 by N. Pocock (see Roy. Soc. Edinburgh, *Phil. Trans.* vol III). Presented by Albert Way, 1850 (with accompanying letter).

ICELAND: VIEW OF THE BOILING SPRING, THE NEW GEYSER

1082 *By J. Baynes,* lithograph (Ath. Folio II. 13), 'from a Drawing by Sir John Stanley Bt. 1789'.

ICELAND: VIEW OF THE GREAT GEYSER

1083 *By J. Baynes,* lithograph (Ath. Folio II.14), 'from a Drawing by Sir John Stanley Bt. 1789'.

ICELAND: VIEW OF THE MOUND & OF THE PIPE OR CYLINDER ... AFTER ERUPTION

1084 *By F. Chesham, 1797,* lithograph (Ath. Folio II. 15), 'from a Drawing taken on the spot, 1789'.

ICELAND: VIEW OF THE GEYSER AT THE COMMENCEMENT OF AN ERUPTION

1085 *By F. Chesham, 1797,* lithograph (Ath. Folio II. 16), 'from a Drawing taken on the spot, 1789'.

INDIA: PEACE

1086 *By Day & Son, 1853,* chromo-lithograph (Ath. Folio II. 20)

INDIA: WAR

1087 *By Day & Son, 1858,* chromo-lithograph (Ath. Folio II, 21 Two magnificent chromo-lithographs showing articulated barges driven by steam paddle engines, in peace time and war, for 'Bourne's New System of Indian River Navigation, steam trains of the Oriental Inland Steam Company Limited'.

INVERLOCHY CASTLE, ARGYLL

1088 *By Cecil Arthur Hunt, 1949*

Ink and wash heightened with body colour on card, 56 × 81 cm (22 × 31⅞ in), inscribed: *C.A. Hunt / Inverlochy Castle – near Fort William / Painted 1949 – Cecil A. Hunt R.W.S. / Marked D. RA. 1949 Exh Blackpool 1949 / repainted partly 1951.*

KEW: ROYAL GARDENS, *see* No. 1302

LAKE SCENE

1089 *By A. Brunet-Debaines,* photogravure 44 × 60.5 cm (17¾ × 23¼ in), published by Thomas Agnew, 1 January 1883, after an oil by Millais.

LANDSCAPE WITH CLASSICAL TEMPLE

1090 *By Friedrich von Schennis, 1881,* etching 29.5 × 45 cm (11½ × 17¾ in), signed: *Schennis / Paris 81.* Lucas bequest, 1918.

LANDSCAPE WITH MOONLIT FIGURES

1091 *By Friedrich von Schennis, 1881,* etching 29 × 45 cm (11½ × 17¾ in), signed and dated: *Schennis / Paris 81.* Lucas bequest, 1918.

LANDSCAPE BY CORNELIUS VARLEY

1092 *By J.H. Kernot, 1825,* etching (Eng. C.I.3), after a view in north Wales (camel crossing a suspension bridge), by Cornelius Varley; probably Beddgelert Bridge, a recognised beauty spot much painted by his brother, John Varley (C.M. Kauffmann, *John Varley 1778–1842,* V & A Museum 1989, pp. 111–2).

LANDSCAPE WITH WINDMILL AND BRIDGE, 1870

1093 *By Sir Hubert von Herkomer,* herkomertype after a picture by Collier. Presented by the artist, 1901.

LILY COLUMNS, ST MARK'S, *see* No. 1230

LIMBURG AM ZAHN

1094 *By Axel Herman Haig, 1886,* etching, 87 x 62 cm (34¼ x 24⅛ in), signed and dated: *AH 86.* Lucas bequest, 1918.

LIMESTONE ROCK

1095 *By Sydney Lee, 1904–5,* etching, inscribed *Sydney Lee / 1904–1905 / inven et sculp.* Presented by the artist, 1932.

LOCHES, HÔTEL DE VILLE

1096 *By Sir Aston Webb*

Watercolour, 33.25 × 20.75 cm (13 × 8⅛ in), inscribed in pencil: *Hotel L...*

Presented by Mrs Maurice Webb, 1940.

1096

LONDON 1842

1097 *By W. Little*

12 woodcuts, 79 × 123 cm (31 × 48½ in), from the Illustrated London News, lettered: *LONDON 1842 from the summit of the Duke of York's Column / The Picture of the Metropolis of the British Empire / ILLUSTRATED LONDON NEWS / by the Proprietors supplement January 7 1843 Published by W. Little / Printed by Palmer & Clayton.*

LONDON: ARRIVAL OF PRINCESS ALEXANDRA OF DENMARK FOR HER MARRIAGE TO THE PRINCE OF WALES, 1863, *see* Athenaeum exterior, No. 1245

LONDON: BANK OF ENGLAND, *see* Nos. 1295-6

LONDON BRIDGE

1098 *Unknown artist, c.1900*, etching, 27 × 51 cm (10½ × 20 in), uninscribed.
Lucas bequest, 1918

LONDON: BRITISH INSTITUTION, PALL MALL

1099 *By J. Bluck, 1808*, aquatint after a drawing by Rowlandson & Pugin, published as Plate 13 in *Ackermann's Repository,* 1 April 1808.

LONDON: BUCKINGHAM HOUSE IN ST JAMES'S PARK

1100 *By Sutton Nicholls, c.1720*, line engraving, 33 × 46 cm (13 × 18 in), 'sold by John Bowles at ye black Horse in Cornhill', plate in *Prospects of the Most Considerable Buildings about London* (1725).

LONDON: BUCKINGHAM HOUSE

1101 *By J. Maurer, 1753*, line engraving, plate to Stow's *Survey* (1754-5).

LONDON: BURLINGTON ARCADE, NORTH ENTRANCE

1102 *By J. Stiven*, line engraving after a painting by H. Perry, exhibited RA 1820.

LONDON: CARLTON GARDENS, No. 6 *by Sir Henry Rushbury, 1961, see* No. 1294

LONDON: CARLTON HOUSE AREA, 1894

1103 *Land Registry map*, revised in 1894, showing the area from the Mall northwards to Pall Mall and St James's Square, including the Athenaeum, Travellers', Reform. Carlton, and Royal Automobile Clubs, (Fig.B).

LONDON: CARLTON HOUSE, EXTERIOR

1104 *By W. Woollett*, etching, 38 × 54 cm (15 x 21¼in), lettered: 'Carlton House, Pall Mall / A View of the Garden &c at Carlton House in Pall Mall, a Palace of Her Royal

1106

Highness the Princess Dowager of Wales … To whom it is most humbly inscribed by … John Tinney. Printed for Henry Parker in Cornhil. &c.'

1105 *By Dubois, c.1820,* line engraving 24 × 40 cm (9½ × 15¾ in), after Courvoisier, lettered: 'Vue du Palais du Prince de Galles Régent dans la Grande Rue de Pall=Mall'.

1106 *Unknown artist, c.1820,* coloured aquatint, 12 × 19 cm (4¾ × 7½ in), lettered: 'Carleton House', colonnaded front, four sentry boxes, St Martin-in-the-Fields extreme left. Trade label on back of W.M. Power, Picture Frame Specialist, Victoria St. Westminster.

1107 *By W.P.* steel engraving, 14 × 21 cm (5½ × 8 in), signed left: WP monogram, and right in white: JC monogram. Porticoed entrance right with carriage and pair, two ladies left, two beadles centre, imposing classical entrance left with six corinthian columns. Trade label as above.

See also NOS. 1145, 1166.

LONDON: CARLTON HOUSE, INTERIOR

(see *Carlton House, The Past Glories of George IV's Palace,* exhibition catalogue, The Queen's Gallery, Buckingham Palace, 1991 (abbreviated here to CH 1991), reproducing the original etched watercolours by Charles Wild drawn for W.H. Pyne's *Royal Residences,* vol III, 1819)

ALCOVE, GOLDEN DRAWING ROOM

1108 *By W.J. Bennett, 1 June 1817,* aquatint after C. Wild (Pyne III, p.60).

BLUE VELVET ROOM

1109 *By D. Havell, 1 Oct 1816,* aquatint after C. Wild (Pyne III, p.45).

1166

CONSERVATORY

1110 *By T. Sutherland, 1 August 1817,* aquatint after C. Wild (Pyne III, p. 84; CH 1991, no. 200, detail reproduced in colour on back cover).

CONSERVATORY (SECOND VIEW)

1111 *By R. Reeve, 1 March 1819,* aquatint after C. Wild (Pyne III, p.88).

CONSERVATORY

1112 *By T. Sutherland, 1 April 1817,* aquatint after C. Wild (Pyne III, p.84) and published as Plate 13 in Ackermann's *Repository*, vol 6.

DINING ROOM

1113 *By T. Sutherland, 1 Oct 1819,* aquatint after C. Wild (Pyne III, p.80)

GALLERY OF THE STAIRCASE

1114 *By T. Sutherland, 1 May 1819,* aquatint after C. Wild (Pyne III, p. 18; CH 1991, no.188).

GOLDEN DRAWING ROOM

1115 *By W.J. Bennett, c.1817,* aquatint after C. Wild (CH 1991, no. 189, reproduced in colour on front cover).

GOLDEN DRAWING ROOM

1116 *By T. Sutherland, 1 June 1817,* aquatint after C. Wild (Pyne III, p. 58).

HALL OF ENTRANCE

1117 *By R. Reeve, 1 Nov 1819,* aquatint after C. Wild (Pyne III. p. 13; CH 1991, no. 187)

HALL

1118 *By J. Bluck, c.1819,* aquatint after Rowlandson & Pugin (Plate 15 in Ackermann's *Repository;* cf Great Hall in CH 1991, no. 187)

LOWER VESTIBULE

1119 *By R. Reeve, 1 April 1819,* aquatint after C. Wild (Pyne III, p. 52).

ROSE SATIN DRAWING ROOM

1120 *By D. Havell, 1 Dec 1817,* aquatint after C. Wild (Pyne III, p. 31; CH 1991, no. 191).

ROSE SATIN DRAWING ROOM (SECOND VIEW)

1121 *By R. Reeve, 1 Dec 1818,* aquatint after C. Wild (Pyne III, p. 32; CH 1919, no. 192).

VESTIBULE

1122 *By R. Reeve, 1 April 1819,* aquatint after C. Wild (Pyne III, p. 15).

LONDON: CHELSEA ROYAL HOSPITAL

1123 *Style of Samuel Scott, c.1740*

Oil on canvas, 59 × 109 cm (23 × 43 in), uninscribed, south aspect with river in foreground.

Condition: cleaned by W.R. Drown, Dover St. 1957, and again by Paul Mitchell, 1998.
Presented by Sir Squire Bancroft, 1916.

LONDON: GREENWICH HOSPITAL

1124 *Style of Samuel Scott, c.1740*

Oil on canvas, 58.5 × 99 cm (23½ × 39 in) uninscribed; north aspect with river in foreground.

Scott ran busy studios in Covent Garden and Twickenham; Sawrey Gilpin, William Marlow and Arthur Nelson were registered apprentices, and Joli, Catton and Inigo Richards painted Thames views in a similar style. The two Athenaeum pictures are best classified as 'Style of Scott' (see Richard Kingzett, 'A Catalogue of the Works of Samuel Scott', *Walpole Soc.*

Journ. 48 (1982) p. 1).
Presented by Sir Squire Bancroft, 1916.

LONDON: DOCKSIDE SCENE

1125 *By Edward Edwards, 1972,* woodcut / linocut.

LONDON: DUKE OF YORK'S COLUMN

1126 *By Landells & Gray,* woodcut in *Saturday Magazine,* 2 Feb 1833, as 'View of the York Column, as seen from St James's Park', showing a glimpse of the Athenaeum behind the Column, completed by George Wyatt in 1834.

1127 *By J. Woods, ,* stipple engraving after L. Salmon, published by W.S. Orr & Co.

1128 *By D. Cox, ? Junior*

Watercolour 9.2 × 12.1 cm (3⅜ × 4¾ in), signed lower left*: D. Cox.* View from the north, Duke of York Column in centre, Athenaeum to right, Senior to left.

Presented by his friends in memory of Iolo Williams.

LONDON: FUNERAL OF THE DUKE OF WELLINGTON, *see* No. 1242

LONDON: HORSE GUARDS AND TREASURY

1129 *By G. Cooke, 1810,* line engraving from a drawing by J.R. Thompson for *The Beauties of England and Wales* (1810).

LONDON: HORSE GUARDS

1130 *By W.M. Fellows, 1809,* aquatint 23.5 × 29 cm (9¼ × 11 in), 'South West View of the Horse-Guards, Engraved from a Drawing by Canaletti', from the collection of George Hibbert Esq. FSA, pubd 1 Feb 1809 in J.T. Smith, *Antiquities of Westminster* (W.G Constable, *Canaletto* (1962) II, no. 734).

LONDON: HYDE PARK CORNER BEFORE 1827

**1131
-2** *By J. Holland,* watercolour 18 × 27.5 cm (7¼ × 11 in), 'from an oil painting in the possession of Dec^s Burton'. The watercolour is accompanied by a photograph of a picture, 'Hyde Park Corner 1827', stamped *Athenaeum Library 1871* and annotated: 'From an Oil painting by the late James Holland'.

LONDON: ISLINGTON, see No. 1301

LONDON: ITALIAN OPERA HOUSE (HER MAJESTY'S THEATRE) HAYMARKET

1133 *By R. Ackermann, 1822*, aquatint published as no. 81 of Ackermann's *Repository of Arts &c*, vol. 14, plate 13, 1 August 1822

1134 *By M. Fox, 1828*, steel engraving published in Shepherd & Elmes, *Metropolitan Improvements* (1827-9), p. 148.

1135 *By W.E. Albutt, c.1854*, line engraving after a drawing by Read for *Mighty London*.

LONDON: THE MALL, CORONATION PRO-CESSION OF GEORGE VI

1136 *By Charles Cundall, 1937*

Watercolour on coarse woven paper, 38 × 53.5 cm (15 × 21 in), signed and dated lower left: *C. Cundall 1937*; view of the Mall from the Admiralty looking towards Marlborough House and Carlton House Terrace, the coronation procession driving towards Buckingham Palace to left.

Presented by D.R.H. Williams.

LONDON: PALL MALL

1137 *By W. Birch, 1789*, stipple engraving after W. Hodges & R. Cosway, published Feb 1789 by W. Birch enamel painter, 'A View from Mr Cosway's Breakfast-Room, Pall Mall'. (see Foskett 1987, p. 493a)

1138 *By M. Barrenger, 1828*, steel engraving published in Shepherd & Elmes, I, p. 155. as 'London: Pall Mall East, New Buildings, University Club House'.

1139 *By H.W. Bond, 1829*, steel engraving published *ibid* p. 123. as 'London: Pall Mall East, Suffolk Street'.

1140 *By T. Shotter Boys, c.1840*, lithograph, plate to *Original Views of London* (1842), as 'The Club Houses &c Pall Mall', showing Carlton Gardens between the Carlton and Reform Clubs.

1141 *By Francis Dodd, 1919*

Etching, signed proof, 1919.

View of Pall Mall looking east from the corner of the Athenaeum.
Presented by Professor W.S. Elliott, 1990.

LONDON: PICCADILLY FROM COVENTRY STREET

1142 *Unknown artist, c.1820-25*, line engraving.

LONDON: REGENT CIRCUS, OXFORD STREET

1143 *By L. Tallis, c.1840*, line engraving, plate to John Tallis *London Street Views*, 1838–1840, (1847)

LONDON: REGENT STREET, THE QUADRANT

1144 *Unknown artist, c.1820–25*. The Quadrant was built by John Nash, 1818–20. The colonnade appears in this print but was demolished in 1848. The whole area was rebuilt by Norman Shaw in 1906-23.

LONDON: REGENT STREET FROM THE CIRCUS, PICCADILLY, PREVIOUS TO TAK-ING DOWN CARLTON PALACE

1145 *By Robert Wallis, 1828*, steel engraving published Shepherd & Elmes, I. p. 99.

LONDON: ROYAL THEATRE AND ATHENAEUM

1146 *By J. Thomas*, line engraving published Fisher & Co. London, 1829, including a conjectural view of the Athenaeum.

LONDON: ST JAMES'S PALACE

1147 *By Johannes Kip, 1708*, line engraving, 35 × 48 cm (13¼ × 19 in), lettered: 'St James's House', after a drawing by Leonard Knyff, plate to *Britannia Illustrata* (1708).

1148 *By W.I. Bennett, 1816*, aquatint after C. Wild, lettered: 'Queen's Levée Room, St James's', 1 August 1816, plate in Pyne's *Royal Residences* (1819) III, p. 15.

1149 *By R. Reeve, 1818*, aquatint after C. Wild, lettered: 'Guard Chamber of St James's, 1 June 1818', plate in Pyne's *Royal Residences* (1819) III, p. 9.

1150 *By D.L. Havell, 1816*, aquatint after C. Wild, lettered: 'The German Chapel St James's Palace', 1 August 1816, plate in Pyne's *Royal Residences* (1819), III, p. 39.

1151 *By Wise, 1816*, aquatint after R. Wilkinson, lettered: 'Chapel Royal St. James's Palace Formerly belonging to a House of female Lepers founded by the Citizens of London' plate in Wilkinson's *Londina Illustrata* (1808-15) II pl 65.

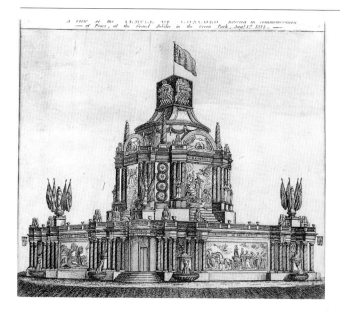

1160

LONDON: ST JAMES'S PARK, THE PROMENADE

1152 *By Edwards, c.1804,* aquatint after E. Pugh, plate from *Modern London* (1804).

LONDON: ST JAMES'S PARK, ENTRANCE FROM CARLTON HOUSE STREET

1153 *By Engelmann & Co.* lithograph (Eng. C.I.8), after J.L. Higgins.

LONDON: ST JAMES'S PARK SHOWING ROSAMOND'S POND

1154 *By F. Rose, 1840,* lithograph (Ath Folio II. 6), after a picture by Hogarth then in collection of H.R. Willett of Merly House, Dorset.

LONDON: ST JAMES'S SQUARE

1155 *By Sutton Nicholls, 1754,* line engraving 33 × 45 cm (13 × 17¾ in), published according to Act of Parliament 1754 for Stowe's *Survey.*

1156 *By David Cox,* [Pl. XXIV (a)]

Watercolour mounted on gold paper, 9.4 × 12.75 cm (3⅝ × 5 in), signed lower right: *D. Cox.* View showing the equestrian statue of William III in the garden.

Given by his friends in memory of Iolo Williams.

LONDON: ST JAMES'S STREET, ENGLISH'S ST JAMES'S ROYAL HOTEL

1157 *By L. Tallis, c.1825,* line engraving.

LONDON: ST JAMES'S BAZAAR

1158 *By L. Tallis, c.1825,* line engraving.

LONDON: ST MARTIN'S CHURCH, NEW OPENING

1159 *By H.W. Bond, 1829,* steel engraving, published 10 Jan 1829 in Shepherd & Elmes I, p. 123. after a drawing by T.H. Shepherd.

LONDON: THE TEMPLE OF CONCORD, GREEN PARK

1160 *By Sands, 1814,* steel engraving after a drawing by J.P. Neale (for *The Beauties of England & Wales*) to celebrate the Treaty of Paris.

LONDON: TOTHILL FIELDS

1161 *By Wenceslaus Hollar,* reproduction of a wood engraving, 9 × 16.5 cm (3½ × 6½ in), lettered: *Totehill fields / S. Peter in westminster / S. Paul in London,* published by the London Topographical Society (Hind, *Hollar* (1922), no. 106).

LONDON: TRAFALGAR SQUARE, MORLEY'S HOTEL

1162 *By L. Tallis, c.1825,* line engraving.

LONDON: TRAFALGAR SQUARE, NATIONAL GALLERY

1163 *By T. Turner,* lithograph 13 × 19 cm (5 × 7⅜ in), 'Drawn and Lithographed by T. Turner / Crane Court Fleet Street, London, Published by R. Reynold, Strand. View from south, St Martins right, two fountains, equestrian Geo IV, carriage and pair left, omnibus right.

1164 *Unkown artist,* steel engraving, 9 × 14 cm (3½ × 5½ in), 'The National Gallery and Nelson's Monument, Trafalgar Square. View from SW, fountains, no statues.

LONDON: TRAFALGAR SQUARE: NELSON'S COLUMN

'Nelson's Column, Trafalgar Square &c / Place de Trafalgar / Die Nelson Saulä'.

1165 *By J. Stury,* steel engraving 14 × 20 cm (5½ × 8 in) sight size. View from SW, two fountains, statue of riderless horse NE, carriage and pair in foreground.

LONDON: WATERLOO PLACE LOOKING TOWARDS CARLTON PALACE

1166 *By Rudolph Ackermann, 1822,* coloured lithograph, from Ackermann's *Repository*.
Presented by the Hon. Arnold Palmer. (Illustrated on p. 137)

LONDON: WATERLOO PLACE AND PALL MALL

1167 *By Rudolph Ackermann, 1822,* coloured lithograph, No. 82 of Ackermann's *Repository*, 1 October 1822.
Presented by the Hon. Arnold Palmer.

LONDON: WATERLOO PLACE, by DAVID COX, *see* Nos. 1128

LONDON: WATERLOO PLACE, 1860, see No. 1244

LONDON: WATERLOO PLACE, 1856 PEACE OF PARIS, 1856.

1168 Cut from *The Illustrated London News*, 31st May 1856, lettered: 'The Peace Illuminations – Waterloo Place'. View looking north, the Athenaeum to left with a fashionable crowd admiring the statue of Athena illuminated with crowned and wreathed VRs, and Garter Stars on surrounding buildings.
Presented by Professor W.I.N. Kessel, MD.

LONDON: WESTMINSTER ABBEY: CORONATION OF EDWARD VII, 1902

1169 *By F.A. Laguillermie, 1902,* etching 57 × 93 cm (22½ × 36½ in), copyright by Thomas Agnew & Sons, after an oil by Edwin Abbey in the Royal Collection.

LONDON: WESTMINSTER ABBEY: DOORWAY

1170 *By J. Keeling, ? 1902,* etching, 37 × 25.5 cm (14¾ × 10 in), signed in pencil: *J. Keeling del & imp*. Main entrance with peers and peeresses in gallery above.

LONDON: WHITEHALL PALACE, 1683

'King Charles II and his Consort witnessing the Lord Mayor's procession to Westminster, 29 October 1683'.

1171 *By Sir Emery Walker, 1909,* photogravure reproduced by the London Topographical Society from a picture, probably by a Dutch artist, in the Royal Collection (Millar 441).

LONDON, ROYAL PALACE OF WHITEHALL FROM THE WATER, c.1690

1172 *By Sawyer junior, 1807,* outline engraving in J.T. Smith, *Ancient Topography of London* (1810-15), from a picture then in the collection of John Charles Crowle, FSA.

LONDON: THE PROSPECT OF WHITEHALL FROM THE PARK OF ST. JAMES.

1173 *By J. Kip,* line engraving, plate from *Britannia Illustrata* (1709).

LONDON: YORK COLUMN, *see* Nos. 1126-8, 1244

LUDLOW CASTLE

1174 *By Cecil Arthur Hunt*
Ink and sepia wash, on cartridge paper, 29 × 39.5 cm (11⅜ × 15½ in), inscribed on the fence: *Ludlow*, and signed lower left: *C.A. Hunt*. An erased watercolour sketch of mountains on reverse.

LYDD, STROLLING PLAYERS

1175 *By Sir Frank Short, 1907,* etching, 17.5 × 25 cm (6⅜ × 9½ in), signed: *Frank Short*. (Short-Hardie III, 335).

MALINES CATHEDRAL, INTERIOR

1176 *By F.H. Shepherd*
Watercolour, 38 × 28 cm (15 × 11 in), signed in pencil: *FHS*.
Presented by the artist, 1934.

MALVERNS TO COTSWOLDS

1177 *By Arthur Hind, 1933*

Watercolour on Newton Z paper, 27.75 × 33.5 cm (11 × 13⅛ in), signed and dated: *A.M. Hind 1933*, and inscribed: *514. From Swinyard Hill looking towards the Cotswolds, Aug. 29 1933, From the Malverns to the Cotswolds: Evening.*

Presented by the artist, 1938.

MEDWAY: THE ENTRANCE

1178 *By Sir Frank Short*, mezzotint, after an oil by Turner at Petworth (Butlin & Joll, *The Paintings of JMW Turner* (1984) 75; A. Wilton, *Turner in his Time* (1987) 735; Short-Hardie, I, 43–44).
Presented by the engraver, 1931.

MIDSUMMER HILL

1179 *By Arthur Hind, 1931*

Sepia wash drawing, 22.5 × 31.5 cm (8⅞ × 12⅞ in) sight size, signed and dated: *A.M. Hind. 1931.*

Presented by the artist, 1938.

MONT ST MICHEL

1180 *By Axel Herman Haig, 1882*, etching, 86.5 × 63 cm (34 × 24¾ in), signed and dated: *AH 1882*.
Lucas bequest, 1918.

MOORLAND SCENE

1181 *By A. Brunet-Debaines, 1888*

Photogravure, 41.5 × 57 cm (16⅜ × 22⅜ in), published by Thomas Agnew, 1 Nov. 1888, after an oil by Millais.

THE MOUNTAIN TORRENT

1182 *By John Cousen, c.1870*, steel engraving. plate to Dafforne, *Pictures by Edwin Landseer* (1873), from Landseer's oil 'The Mountain Torrent and the Hunted Stag', 1833, in the Tate Gallery.

NEW ZEALAND: PART OF LAMBTON HARBOUR IN PORT NICHOLAS ... WATER FRONTAGE OF THE TOWN OF WELLINGTON

1183 *By T. Allom*, coloured lithograph (Ath. Folio II. 10), from a drawing by Charles Heaphy, April 1841.

Presented by John Ward, secretary of the New Zealand Company, 1841.

NEW ZEALAND: PART OF NEW PLYMOUTH SETTLEMENT IN THE DISTRICT OF TARANAKE – MOUNT EGMONT 30 MILES DISTANT.

1184 *By T. Allom*, coloured lithograph (Ath. Folio II. 11), from a Drawing taken on board the Ship Brougham by George Duppa Esq.
Presented by John Ward, secretary of the New Zealand Company, 1841.

'NYMPHS SURPRISED'

1185 *By Henry Tonks, 1934 (FIG.G)*

Oil on canvas, 49.5 × 60 cm (19½ × 23½ in), sight size.

Exhibited at The Tate Gallery, 1936 (No. 10)

Literature: J. Hone, *Life of Henry Tonks* (1939), p.365
Bequeathed by D.R.H. Williams, 1963.

OXFORD: ASHMOLEAN MUSEUM

1186 *By J. Coney, 1816*, line engr. (Eng. C.I.4), 'From a Drawing in the possession of Thos. Dunbar Esq'.
Presented by Thomas Dunbar, 1827.

PARIS: CHAMBER OF DEPUTIES, see No 1307

PARIS: VIEWS, c. 1650

By Reynier Nooms, called Zeeman, etchings:

1187 Louvre and Tuileries, insc: *R. Zeeman fecit / Het hof van Madamoiselle en een stuck Loener tat Parys / F. de Wit Excudit. Amstelodami*, and signed on the boat: *R. Zeeman. 1.*

1188 Château de Conflans, insc: *Conflans tussehen Parys en Cirranton 2.* signed on a stone, *Zeeman*, (Fig. E).

1189 St Denis, inscr: *Een water Molen buyten S. de Nys : 3*

1190 Faubourg St Marceau, insc: *De Tuin van Monsieur de Nue buitent vorburch S. Marsiou tot Parys. 4.* Signed on wall left: *R. Zeeman.*

1191 Chaillot, inscr: *Ciatrou aen de landtsi buyten Parys. 5.*

1192 Faubourg St Marceau, inscr: *Het in Komen vant voorburch S. Marsiou tot Parys. 6*

1195

1193 View of the Seine, inscr: *De Rivier de Cyne en de hoeck van de Malie baen tot Parys. 7*

1194 Porte St Bernard, inscr: *De poort S. Barnaert to Parys. 8.*

The etchings by Charles Meryon, formerly in the Collection, were inspired by these prints by Zeeman.

Literature: M.E. Dutuit, *Manuel de l'Amateur d'Estampes* (1885) III, pp.645-7; Deltail, III, 58-62.

Rumpf Collection, Potsdam (1908); Lucas bequest 1918.

PORDOI PASS

1195 *By Mervyn O'Gorman*

Chalk and watercolour on Windsor & Newton paper, 21.75 × 35.5 cm (8½ × 14 in), inscribed lower right: *Towards Pordoi Pass (S. Marmolata)*, and signed vertically; *MOG*

Presented by the artist, 1934.

PONT AUDEMER, CHURCH INTERIOR

1196 *By A. Brunet-Debaines*

Watercolour, 34.5 × 18.5 cm (13½ × 7¼ in), signed lower left: *A. Brunet-Debaines.*

PORTUGAL, *see* Cintra, Nos. 1061–7

PROVENCE, LANDSCAPE

1197 *By Albert Rutherston, 1934*

Watercolour, 35.5 × 28 cm (14 × 11 in), signed and dated lower right: *Albert R. 1914,* and inscribed indistinctly lower left: *To … April 1934.*

Presented by the artist, 1934.

REMBRANDT LANDSCAPE

1198 *By F.C. Lewis,* 1830, aquatint, private plate by Robert V.R. (Eng. C.I.9), inscr: 'By Frederick C. Lewis after an Origina. Drawing by Rembrandt formerly in the Collection of Richard Cosway R.A. now in possession of H.S.' [Henry Smedley]. Rembrandt's original is now in the Ashmolean Museum.

Literature: K.T. Parker, *Catalogue of Drawings in the Ashmolean Museum* (vol I. 1938), no. 188; Otto Benesch, *Drawings of Rembrandt* (vol IV 1973), no. 840, fig. 1041.

Presented by Henry Smedley, 1830, together with a Rembrandt drawing no longer in the Collection.

1205

RIVER LANDSCAPE WITH BOY FISHING

1199 *By Sir Hubert von Herkomer,* etching, signed in pencil. Presented by the artist, 1901.

ROME: VIEW by VASI, *see* No. 1310

ROME: BORGHESE GARDENS

1200 *By Sir Reginald Blomfield, 1924*

Pencil drawing, 19 × 25.5 cm (7½ × 10 in), inscribed in pencil: *Borghese Gardens, Reginald Blomfield Oct. 1924.*

Presented by the artist, 1933.

ROME: FORUM, *see* No. 1309

ROME: PIAZZA DEL POPOLO

1201 *By H.C. Bradshaw*

Watercolour on cartridge paper, 23 × 33 cm (9 × 13 in), inscribed: *Piazza del Popolo – H.C.B.*

Presented by the artist's widow, 1943.

ROME: PIRANESI VIEWS

Giovanni Battista Piranesi (1720–78), Venetian architect and engraver famous for his *Vedute,* etchings of ancient and modern Rome.

ROME: VEDUTA DELLA BASILICA E PIAZZA DI S. PIETRO IN VATICANO

1202 *By G.B. Piranesi, 1748,* etching (Hind no.3, I; Bacou 137; Wilton-Ely 136).

ROME: VEDUTA DELL' AMFITEATRO FLAVIO DETTO IL COLOSSEO

1203 *By G.B. Piranesi, 1757,* etching (Hind no. 57; Bacou 183); Wilton-Ely 259).

ROME: VEDUTA DELL PIAZZA DI MONTE CAVALLO

1204 *By G.B. Piranesi, 1750*, etching (Hind no. 15; Bacou 140; Wilton-Ely 236).

VEDUTA DEL TEMPIO DI CIBELE A PIAZZA DELLA BOCCA DELLA VERITÀ

1205 *By G.B. Piranesi, 1758*, etching (Hind no. 47; Wilton-Ely 183).

VUE AU COLLEGE SUPPOSE DES ANFICTIONS

1206 *By G.B. Piranesi*, etching from *Views of Paestum* (Wilton-Ely 724).

VUE DES RESSTES DE LA CELLA DU TEMPLE DE NEPTUNE

1207 *By G.B. Piranesi*, etching from *Views of Paestum* (see Hind plate LXXIVb; Wilton-Ely 734).

Literature: A.M. Hind, *Piranesi* (1922), pp. 38–73; Rosaline Bacou, *Piranesi Etchings & Drawings* (1975); J. Wilton-Ely, *The Complete Etchings of Piranesi* (2 vols, San Francisco 1994).

Six Piranesi engravings presented by W. Reeve Wallace, CBE, 1962. Four folio vols of Piranesi's *Antichità Romane* (1756) were also presented, by Charles Romilly in 1846 (Minutes 11 May 1846, p. 69).

ROME: ST PETER'S

1208 *By Sir Henry Rushbury, 1928*

Ink and sepia wash on coarse white paper, 41 × 31 cm (16⅛ × 12¼ in), signed and dated: *Henry Rushbury 1928*, and inscribed under the mount: *Piazza del circo neroniano.*

Literature: Rushbury, *Rome* (1930)
Presented by Francis Dodd,

ROME: TEMPLE OF APOLLO AND THEATRE OF MARCELLUS

1209 *By John Aldridge, 1951* [Pl. XXVIII]

Oil on board, 57 × 75 cm (22½ × 29½ in), signed in red paint: *John Aldridge*, and on the back: *Roman Building, Aug. 51*

Presented by Sir Thomas Barlow, 1959

1210

ROME: TEMPLE OF PALLAS MINERVA

1210 *By Harry Williams, 1838*, lithograph, 37 × 26.4 cm (14½ × 10⅜ in), signed with monogram HW and inscribed: *Temple of Pallas – Rome*, probably from *Fugitive Sketches of Rome, Venice etc.* (1838).
Presented by the Ven. Michael Brown, 1979.

ST MICHAEL'S MOUNT AND THE ROYAL YACHT

1211 *By R. Wallis*, line engraving (Eng. A.I.33), plate in Dafforne, *Pictures by Clarkson Stanfield* (1855) after an oil by Clarkson Stanfield, 1846, in the Royal Collection (Millar 655).

ST RÉMY, PROVENCE

1212 *By Francis Ernest Jackson*

Oil on paper, 25.5 × 33 cm (10 × 13 in), uninscribed; ploughed field and two barns in foreground.

Presented by Mrs Ernest Jackson, 1947.

1217

ST RÉMY, PROVENCE

1213 *By Francis Ernest Jackson*

Oil on paper mounted on cardboard, 25.5 × 32.5 cm (10 × 12¾ in), uninscribed; olive grove with rocky hill background.

Presented by Mrs Ernest Jackson, 1947.

SALLANCHES, HAUTE-SAVOIE

1214 *By Charles March Gere, 1926* [Pl. XXVII]

Watercolour on flimsy paper, 33.5 × 46 cm (13¼ × 18 in), signed and dated with monogram: *CG 1926 - 1943.*

1216

SANCERRE

1215 *By W.H. Ansell, 1952*

Watercolour on card watermarked MAN 1951, 29.75 × 47 cm (11¾ × 18½ in), inscribed lower right in pencil: *Sancerre 7.8.52. W.H.A.*

Presented by the artist, 1956.

SEA SHORE

1216 *By Gwen Raverat,* wood engraving, signed in pencil: *G. Raverat.*
Presented by Mervyn O'Gorman, 1932.

SEBASTOPOL

1217 *By Captain Twopenny, 1855*

Sepia wash heightened with white on card: 28.4 × 41 cm (11¼ × 16⅛ in), inscribed lower left: *Sept. 9 1855,* and signed lower right: *RT*

'Sandford's Bird's Eye View of the Seat of War in the Crimea', a coloured sketch, was presented by E.H. Bunbury, 1855 (*Minutes* 19 Feb 1855), but is not yet located.
Presented by Lord Eversley, F.R.S., 1919.

SENNO

1218 *By Maurice Webb,*

Charcoal on buff paper, 25 × 19 cm (9⅞ × 7½ in), inscribed: *Senno [? Semio]*

Presented by Mrs Maurice Webb, 1940.

SMYRNA BAY

1219 *By William Holman Hunt, 1855* [Pl. XXV (b)]

Bistre wash, 13.5 × 26 cm (5¼ × 10¼ in), signed and dated lower left: *Smyrna Roadstead WHH 1855*, and under the mount in pencil: *When I did the last touch to this sketch on board the Tancredi I put down my pencil to take up a sword to help quell a furious mutiny by Bashi Bazooks – Novr 1855*.

Presented by Mrs Holman Hunt, 1930

SNOWDRIFT

1220 *By Sir Frank Short, 1904*

Mezzotint, 17 × 37 cm (6⅝ × 14½ in), after a watercolour by Peter de Wint in the V&A Museum (Short-Hardie I, 83).

Presented by the artist, 1931.

SPANISH LANDSCAPE

1221 *By Gerard Chowne, 1914*

Watercolour, 24.5 × 34.5 cm (9⅝ × 13⅝ in), signed and dated lower left: *Chowne 1914*.

Presented by Sir John Rothenstein.

STRATHEARN

1222 *By Sir David Cameron*

Watercolour on cartridge paper, 24 × 36.5 cm (9½ × 14⅜ in), signed lower left: *Strathearn / D.Y.C.*

Presented by the artist, 1939.

TALLOIRES, LAC D'ANNECY

1223 *By Charles March Gere, 1934*

Pencil and orange wash on off-white paper, 20 × 31 cm (10¼ × 18 in), signed and dated: *C.M. Gere 1934*.

Presented by the artist, 1934.

TASMANIA: NELSON'S HAVEN IN TASMAN'S GULF

1224 *By T. Allom, 1841,* coloured lithograph (Ath. Folio II. 8) from a drawing by C. Heaphy, Nov. 1841 (draftsman to the New Zealand Company).
Presented by the New Zealand Company, 1842.

TOWNELEY MUSEUM, see **Groups, No. 953**

TREYARNON BRIDGE: LOW TIDE

1225 *By Sir Francis Newbolt, 1931,* etching, 18.5 × 29 cm (7¼ × 11¼ in), signed in pencil: *F Newbolt*.
Presented by the artist, 1932.

TYNEMOUTH

1226 *Attributed to Edward Dayes, c.1787* [Pl. XXIV (b)]

Pencil and watercolour on white paper, 14.2 × 21.6 cm (5⅝ × 8½ in), inscribed indistinctly top right: *26 June 87 Tynemouth / from the sea*; ruined abbey, barn and church on a cliff top, brig at sea to left.

The drawing was formerly listed as by Turner but clearly untenably and the attribution to Dayes has been suggested by Andrew Wilton.
Presented by Thomas Cannon Brookes, 1939.

ULM

1227 *By Augustus Hare*

Pencil and white body colour, 18 × 26 cm (7⅛ × 10¼ in), inscribed in pencil: *Ulm*, and on the back: *Heidelberg*.

Presented by Sir Theodore Chambers, 1934.

THE VALLEY FARM

1228 *By A. Brunet-Desbaines,* etching, 50 × 42 cm (19¾ × 16½ in) after the oil by Constable, 1835, in the Tate Gallery; G. Reynolds, *Later Paintings & Drawings of John Constable* (Yale 1984), 35.1.
Lucas bequest, 1918.

VAUCLUSE

1229 *By Sir Reginald Blomfield, 1927*

Charcoal on paper watermarked AL in buckle, 27.5 × 38 cm (26 × 37 in), signed and dated in pencil: *Reginald Blomfield / Vaucluse - Sept 20-27*.

Presented by the artist, 1933.

1236

VENICE: LILY COLUMNS, ST MARK'S

1230 *By Reginald Barratt, 1911* [Pl. XXIX]

Watercolour on 'ordinary pasteboard faced with fine 72lb imperial O.W. paper', 54.5 × 41 cm (21½ × 16 in), signed and dated: *Reginald Barratt 1911.*

Presented by the artist, 1917.

VENICE: FISHING BOATS

1231 *By J.H. Bradley,* etching, 17.5 × 36 cm (7 × 14⅛ in) Lucas bequest, 1918.

VENICE: LA PIAZZETTA

1232 *By G. Pagani,* lithograph (Eng. C.I.37), after a picture by L. Sacchi.

WAXHAM, TITHE BARN

1233 *By H.C. Bradshaw, 1929*

Watercolour on card, 21.5 × 32 cm (8½ x 12½ in), signed and dated: *H C Bradshaw WAXHAM: 1929,*

Presented by Mrs H C Bradshaw, 1943,

WEST STOW HALL, SUFFOLK

1234 *By J.D. Harding, 1843,* lithograph (Eng. A.I.25), after W. Müller, with the relevant excerpt from the VCH.

WEST WITTERING, INLAND HARBOUR No.1

1235 *By Albert Rutherston, 1937*

Watercolour, 25.5 × 35.5 cm (10 × 14 in), signed and dated lower right in pencil: *Albert R. 1937.*

Presented by the artist, 1938.

WHITBY CLIFFS

1236 *By Alfred William Hunt*

Watercolour, 28 × 38.5 (11 × 15⅛ in), inscribed on the back in pencil: *by Alfred Hunt (given me by his daughter Violet) D S MacColl.* See No. 436 for MacColl's portrait of Hunt.

Presented by D.S. MacColl, 1940.

WHITE CHAPEL ROAD, *see* Satires No. 1030

WITHAM, ESSEX: BEACON HILL

1237 *By W.S. Lacey,* lithograph (Eng. C.I.31). Beacon Hill is near Wickham Bishops. Presented by J.H. Pattisson, *c.* 1830.

WITHAM, ESSEX: VIEW FROM BEACON HILL

1238 *By W.S. Lacey,* lithograph (Eng. C.I.32). Presented by J.H. Pattisson, *c.* 1830.

IV ARCHITECTURAL AND RELATED DESIGNS AND SCULPTURE

(a) JOHN HENNING'S FRIEZE FOR THE ATHENAEUM

IAN JENKINS
British Museum

The Athenaeum was founded in 1824 as a 'Club for Literary and Scientific men and followers of the Fine Arts'.[1] The building rose in 1827–30 as part of the new civic architecture in Greek style by which London was embellished after the Battle of Waterloo.[2] Following the defeat of Napoleon, whose ambition had been to transfer Rome to Paris, *Britannia Victrix* had sought a different model from Antiquity by which to shape her capital city. She found it in the democratic society of Periclean Athens.[3] On the balcony over the porch of the Athenaeum, Pallas Athena – a close replica by E.H. Baily of the Athena Velletri – was set up to preside over Waterloo Place. She was the warrior goddess of wisdom and patron deity of ancient Athens. Inside, on the staircase, a copy of the Apollo Belvedere, commander of the nine Muses, stands watch over the entrance to this modern *mouseion*. In niches in the flank walls of the entrance hall were casts of two female statues then, as now, in the Louvre, the so-called Venus Genetrix and the Diane de Gabies[4] (Nos. 1255, 1258–60 and Plate XVII).

The gods for the Athenaeum were chosen with care. The Henning frieze, being a copy of the frieze of the Parthenon, is likewise more than mere ornament. Democratic Athens, that ancient 'School of Hellas', had been declared the model of a new London.[5] The heroes of Marathon and Salamis were a paradigm for the victors of Waterloo and Trafalgar. Parliamentary consideration of whether or not to purchase the Elgin Marbles for the nation was interrupted in 1815 by the Battle of Waterloo. The eventual decision to acquire them was directly influenced by the idea that, just as the Parthenon had once commemorated Athens's victory over the Persians at the Battle of Marathon, so now its

sculptures would commemorate England's triumph.[6]

The Athenaeum's replica of the Parthenon frieze, carved by the Scottish sculptor John Henning (1771–1851) and his son John junior (1802–57), is perhaps more famous than Decimus Burton's Greek Revival building itself (No. 1239). Certainly there are few subjects more famous than the sculpted Ionic frieze of the Parthenon that inspired it. The Parthenon frieze was carved around 438–432 BC as part of the architectural ornament of the famous temple in Athens.[7] The greater part of what survived was recovered by agents working for Lord Elgin in the opening decade of the nineteenth century, and brought to England with the rest of the so-called Elgin Marbles.[8] Henning came to London from Paisley in Scotland on 9 July 1811.[9] The Parthenon Sculptures were then displayed in Lord Elgin's makeshift museum on the corner of Park Lane and Piccadilly. Struck by their beauty, Henning applied to Elgin for permission to draw and model from the sculptures. The artist was no stranger to London Society and already enjoyed a considerable reputation as a wax-modeller and portrait medallionist.[10]

Gaining access to the sculptures, Henning was one of a privileged few artists. These included Benjamin West, President of the Royal Academy, and Benjamin Robert Haydon, whose disastrous attempt to revive the painting of historical subjects in the Grand Manner ended in his suicide in 1846. Haydon saw the Elgin Marbles as the totem of his *real art* movement and was one of the first to make drawings of them.[11] Another was Charles Robert Cockerell, the architect, who made some rough sketches before departing for his Mediterranean tour in 1810.[12] In the course of his travels, Cockerell became involved in the discovery of another great body of Classical sculpture that was to preoccupy Henning. This was the frieze of the Temple of Apollo Epikourios at Bassae in the western Peloponnese, known in Henning's day as the Phigaleian Marbles after the nearest town to the ancient site.[13]

The Bassae frieze, along with some fragmentary metopes and pieces of a cult statue, was acquired for the

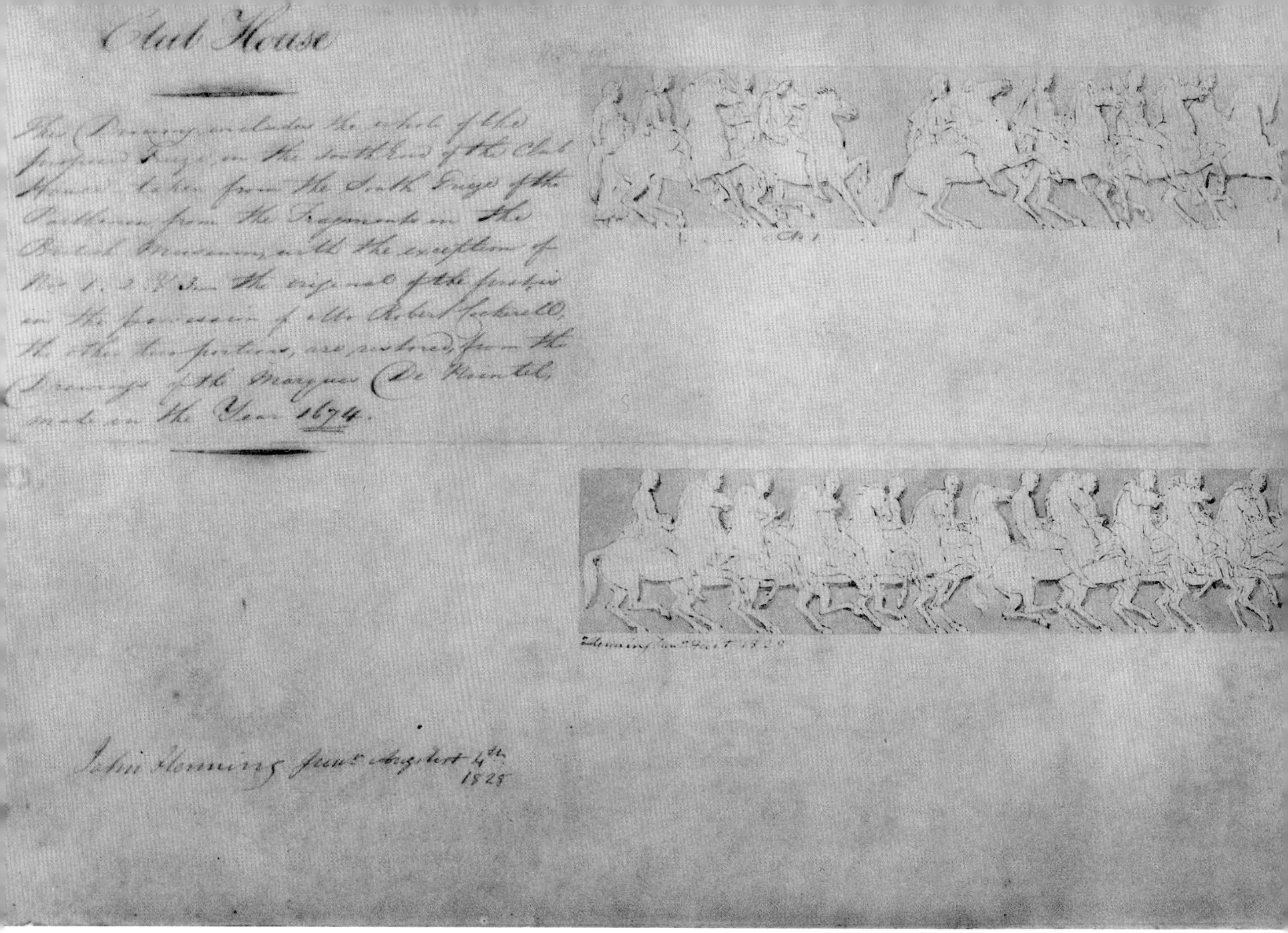

Fig.1. (below right) South façade section of the Frieze

Museum in 1814, two years before the acquisition of the Elgin Marbles. From February 1817 the Elgin and Phigaleian Marbles were displayed in connecting compartments of a temporary shed erected in the grounds of the British Museum.[14] Henning made careful drawings eight inches high and then tried his hand at sculpting miniature replicas of them in ivory.[15] This proved unsatisfactory. Accordingly, he gave up replicating the sculpture in cameo and carved it instead as an intaglio in slate. By reversing the original image these slate negatives could afterwards be cast in plaster as positives. It is said that Henning got the idea of carving moulds out of slate while teaching arithmetic to his reluctant son John. Inattentive to the lesson, John junior had picked up one of his father's sculpting knives from the table and carved a doodle, ruining the slate but inspiring his parent to a task that was to take him six years between 1816 and 1822.[16]

From his exquisite moulds, which are now in the British Museum (Fig. 2), Henning reproduced the Parthenon frieze in sections two inches high and six long, totalling some thirty-four feet. Each boxed set sold for thirty guineas.[17] Among his first customers were HM King George IV, the Duke of Devonshire and the Marquess of Lansdowne.[18] A set is to be found in the Athenæum (Nos.1253–4). Henning's own satisfaction in his achievement was soured by a profusion of pirated editions that were all too easily reproduced from his own casts. On 18 January 1837 the Trustees of the British Museum were read a letter of complaint from Mr J.G. Grace, abused in the Elgin Room by an emotional Henning, who had witnessed this complainant buying pirated casts in the Gallery itself from an Italian *formatore*. Ironically the complaint was not against Henning, but the Museum custodian, who had stood by and watched the incident without intervening.[19]

The production of a frieze in miniature was the prelude to the monumental Athenaeum frieze. In a letter to

Decimus Burton, dated 28 July 1828, John Henning Junior confirmed that he would 'execute in Bath stone for the Athenaeum Club a continued frieze about two hundred and sixty feet in length, to extend round three sides of the Club House erecting in Waterloo Place, the same to be an exact copy of such parts of the frieze of the Parthenon, taken from Marbles in the British Museum as far as they may be sufficient, as the Committee may decide upon, and the remainder of the frieze to be executed and the mutilated parts restored, from drawings which I agree to make from those made of the east frieze on the spot by the artists employed by Lord Elgin, and from fragments in the British Museum'. The cost was to be £1,300. [20]

Although it is the same height (3 feet 3 inches), the Athenaeum frieze, incorporating scenes from the north, south and east sides of the Parthenon frieze, is about half the length of the 524 feet long original. John Henning Junior chose to show a cavalcade on the flanks of the building (Fig. 1.). His signed drawing for the horsemen of the south frieze of the Parthenon, assigned to the *south* flank of the Athenaeum, survives in the Club's collections (No. 1252), and is dated 4 August 1828. The principal east façade carries a selection of figures from the pedestrian procession of the north, south and east sides of the Parthenon. These converge on the seated gods and, at the very centre, the scene of the handling of the sacred robe or *peplos* for Athena. (Pl. XVIII (a))

The original frieze of the Parthenon is battered, fragmentary and discoloured, while Henning's partial replica is a complete image. Henning states his intention to restore the missing parts of the frieze for the Athenaeum with the aid of drawings made on the spot by artists employed by Lord Elgin. These are principally the drawings made around 1800–1802 by Feodor Ivanowitsch (1765–1832) that came to the Museum with the Elgin Marbles. [21] It is a little disingenuous of Henning Junior to mention them at a time when his father had already restored his frieze in miniature using these and a number of other documentary sources. Foremost among them were the drawings attributed to the Flemish artist Jacques Carrey, travelling in the entourage of Marquis Olier de Nointel, French ambassador to Ottoman Constantinople. [22] They were executed in November – December 1674, and importantly preserve a record of the Parthenon and its sculptures before the explosion that destroyed it and many of its sculptures in 1687. The original drawings are in the Bibliothequè Nationale in Paris and, on acquiring the Elgin Marbles, the British Museum immediately commissioned a set of exact copies. [23] Henning will also have

consulted engravings after drawings by William Pars. [24] He was chosen by the Society of Dilettanti in 1764 as artist to Richard Chandler's expedition to Asia Minor. In 1762 the Society had already published the first volume of James Stuart and Nicholas Revett's *Antiquities of Athens*. This was the pioneering work of the eighteenth-century Greek Revival and reproduced architectural drawings by Revett and drawings of sculpture and some general views by Stuart. Pars was to contribute a great many drawings to successive volumes, including in the second volume one of the earliest published records of the Parthenon frieze. Its only rival is the set of engravings published in 1751–52 by Richard Dalton, which Henning may also have known. [25]

Pars's drawings were again engraved by Sir Richard Worsley (1751–1805) who had been the British diplomatic representative at Venice. [26] He travelled in Greece and Asia Minor and both studied and collected antiquities there. From 1794 he began to publish his *Museum Worsleyanum*, which appeared piecemeal in a limited edition that eventually comprised two handsome folio volumes. Engraved illustrations are in sepia and the text is by E.Q. Visconti. Pars's drawings are engraved in Volume II. [27]

Carrey, Dalton and Pars were the three sources that Henning could consult in his restoration of the frieze. He, however, had what these artists had not, namely close and constant access to the original sculpture. While their task, moreover, was simply to draw the frieze, Henning's was the greater challenge of recreating it as a bas-relief. Later in the century W. Watkiss Lloyd was to remark upon how Henning's restored copy of the frieze gave the modern spectator the 'best opportunity for studying its design'. Lloyd was an able scholar, who made a number of important contributions to nineteenth-century understanding of the Parthenon and its sculptures. Among them was the first written explanation of how the horsemen of the frieze were designed so as to fall into ranks, each rank marked by a horsemen placed nearest the spectator and not overlapped by any other. Lloyd discovered this while looking up at Henning's frieze on the Athenaeum. [28] Henning will have pondered the disposition of the horsemen as a practical problem and the Athenaeum frieze is itself an unspoken explanation of the question.

Decimus Burton contracted John Henning Junior in 1828 to carry out the frieze in Bath Stone. Already in 1827, father and son had completed a frieze loosely based on that of the Parthenon for the Screen at Hyde Park Gate also designed by Burton. [29] Both the Screen and the Athenaeum's friezes are remarkable achieve-

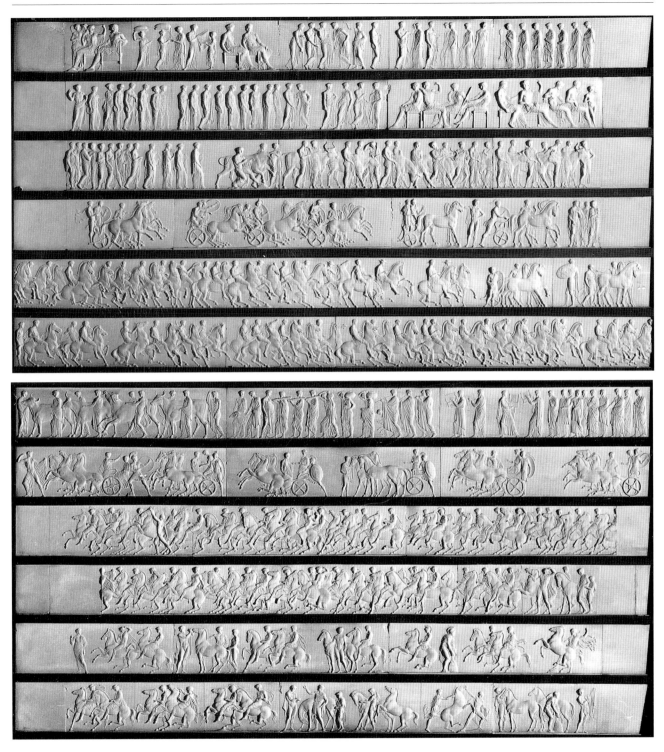

1253-4

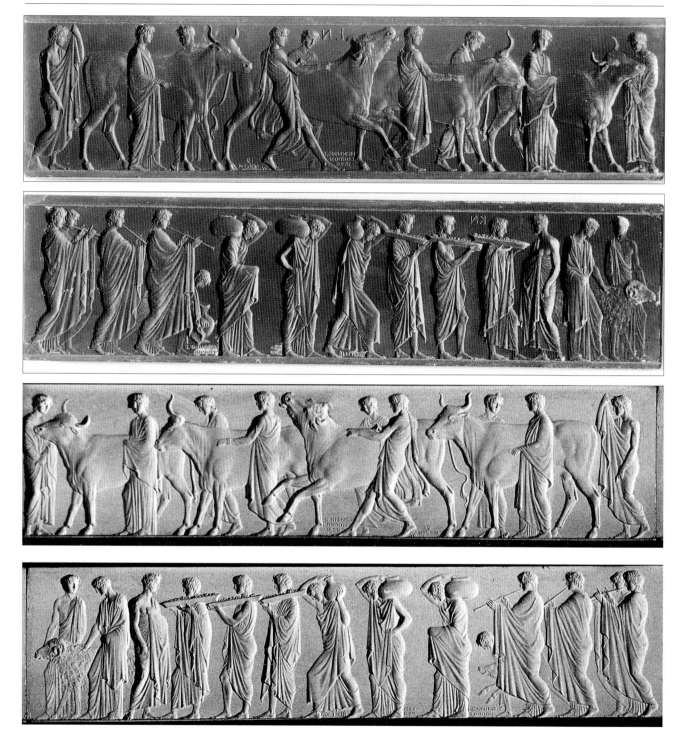

FIG 2 (above) Two of the slate moulds, carved in intaglio by Henning; the entire set is now in the British Museum
(below) The two corresponding details from the set of plaster reliefs in the Club's Collection (No. 1253).

ments when we consider that neither of the two sculptors seems to have done any comparable stone-carving before. The design was sketched directly onto the stone and then worked without the usual process of pointing.[30]

Henning wanted his achievements to last. Aware of the detrimental effects of weather on exposed limestone, especially Portland stone, he experimented with an attempt at coating the surface of his friezes with wax.[31] He took a piece of polished marble and partially coated it in wax. He warmed it until the wax was absorbed. The marble was then exposed for a winter on top of his house. Only where the wax had been applied was the polish preserved. On marble he found that the wax when warm penetrated up to one sixteenth of an inch. It would go further if the wax were mixed with turpentine and if the stone itself were heated with irons. Something similar was done with the friezes of the Athenaeum and Hyde Park Gate. The process is reminiscent of ancient encaustic painting and of *ganosis*, the polishing of marble with wax, as described in Vitruvius's treatise *On Architecture*.[32]

Whether or not the experiment was effective is now impossible to say. The Portland stone of the Hyde Park frieze has a weathered, raw look partly attributable to subsequent cleaning, while the Athenaeum's frieze is painted. Today the background of the frieze is blue, with figures standing out against it in the cream of the architecture. The result is a pleasing contrast reminiscent of a Wedgwood plaque. It is also consistent with the original manner of treating the pediment of the British Museum, where – although the colour has now all but disappeared – Richard Westmacott had the background tinted ultramarine contrasting with the natural colour of the figures in Portland stone.[33] The British Museum's pediment was painted around 1850 in response to the contemporary revival of ancient polychromy.[34] It might be thought that the Athenaeum frieze would have been coloured about the same time. It seems, however, that it did not receive its first coat of blue until 1950.[35] The frieze was painted before this date, first in 1845, but this was to restore the ground of the sculpture to the original colour of the stone.[36]

The Henning frieze of the Athenaeum holds testimony to the energy and ingenuity of its creators, on the one hand, and on the other it represents a substantial document in the history of the reception of the Elgin Marbles. It is an eloquent reminder of the role played by the sculptures of the Parthenon in England after the Napoleonic Wars as paradigms of a new cultural and political identity.

The Athenaeum was founded to provide a meeting place for Londoners who as new Athenians could identify their community with that of the procession shown in the frieze paying homage to Athena, eponymous goddess of the Club. No better subject than the Parthenon frieze could have been chosen for this haven of liberal and learned conviviality.

NOTES

The author wishes to thank Sarah J. Dodgson for supplying information from The Athenaeum's archives and Ivor Kerslake and Philip Nicholls for photography.

(1)   See Ward, pp. 9–10 for the letter from John Wilson Croker to Sir Humphry Davy, President of the Royal Society, March 13, 1823; also quoted by G.Nares, 'The Athenaeum', *Country Life*, 6 April 1951, 1018.

(2)   Nares, 1018–1022; J. Mordaunt Crook, *The Greek Revival* (London 1972) *passim*.

(3)   I. Jenkins, 'Athens Rising near the Pole – London, Athens and the Idea of Freedom' in C.Fox (ed.), *London – World City 1800–1840* (London and New Haven 1992) 143–53.

(4)   For the Athena, see F. Haskell and N. Penny, *Taste and the Antique* (London and New Haven 1981) 284–86, cat. 69, fig.150. Since 1803 the original had been, as it is now, in the Louvre. The statue had been moulded in Rome, before its departure for France. The Prince Regent donated a cast of it to the Royal Academy, where presumably E.H. Baily had access to it. For the place of the Apollo, a Demosthenes had been tried and rejected. For the Apollo, see *Taste and the Antique*, 148–151, cat. 8, fig. 77. For the Venus, see Margarete Bieber, *Ancient Copies – Contributions to the History of Greek and Roman Art* (New York 1977) 46 f., fig. 124. For the Diana, see *Taste and the Antique*, 198, cat. 31, fig. 103.

(5)   Jenkins, *op. cit.* note 3.

(6)   I. Jenkins, *Archaeologists and Aesthetes in the Sculpture Galleries of the British Museum 1800–1939* (London 1992) 15–19.

(7)   I. Jenkins, *The Parthenon Frieze* (London 1994).

(8)   A. H. Smith, 'Lord Elgin and his Collection', *Journal of Hellenic Studies* 36 (1916) 163–372; W. St Clair, *Lord Elgin and the Marbles* (3rd ed. Oxford 1998) *passim*.

(9)   J. Malden, *John Henning 1771–1851, '... a very ingenious modeller'* (Paisley 1977), catalogue of an exhibition organised by Paisley Museums and Art Galleries. The valuable introduction to this catalogue is misprinted and the pages are not numbered.

(10) John Henning's evidence given to the Select Committee on Arts and their Connection with Manufactures, 17 August 1835. Published Report in Parliamentary Papers IX .I (1836) minutes 849–907.

(11) F. Cummings, 'B.R. Haydon and his School', *Journal of the Warburg and Courtauld Institutes* 26 (1963) 367–80;

id. 'Phidias in Bloomsbury etc.', *The Burlington Magazine* 104 (July 1964) 323–8; R.W. Liscombe, 'The Commencement of Real Art', *Apollo* 103 (January 1976) 34–9.

(12) J. Rothenberg, *Descensus ad Terram – the Acquisition and Reception of the Elgin Marbles* (New York and London 1977) 222, pl.61.1.

(13) F.A. Cooper, *The Temple of Apollo Bassitas*, 4 vols. (Princeton 1992–96).

(14) Jenkins, *op. cit.* note 6, 78–9.

(15) *Op. cit.* note 10, minute 870.

(16) Malden, *op. cit.* note 9.

(17) Malden, note 9.

(18) *Op. cit.* note 10, minute 871.

(19) British Museum Archives Minutes of the Standing Committee of Trustees, C4443.

(20) quoted by Ward, pp. 37–8; also Nares, *op. cit.* note 1, 1020–21.

(21) Gisler-Huwiler in E. Berger and M. Gisler-Huwiler, *Der Parthenon in Basel, Dokumentation zum Fries* (Mainz 1996) 23.

(22) T. Bowie and D. Thimme, *The Carrey Drawings of the Parthenon Sculptures* (Bloomington and London 1971); Gisler-Huwiler, 21.

(23) British Museum Archives Minutes of the Standing Committee of Trustees, C2634, 15 June 1816; C2634, 19 July 1816.

(24) Gisler-Huwiler, *op. cit.* note 21, 21–22.

(25) *Ead.* 21.

(26) *Ead.* 22–23.

(27) I. Jenkins and K. Sloan, *Vases and Volcanoes: Sir William Hamilton and his Collection* (London 1996) 101–102.

(28) Lloyd is quoted by W.R. Lethaby in *The Builder*, 3 June 1927, p.896.

(29) *Op. cit.* note 10, minute 850. (See also Nos. 1131–2)

(30) *Ibid.*

(31) *Ibid.* minutes 894–907.

(32) Vitruvius, 7.9.3. G.M.A. Richter, 'Polychromy in Greek Sculpture', *The American Journal of Archaeology* 48 (1944) 327–8; P. Dimitriadou, *The Polychromy of Greek Sculpture: to the beginning of the Hellenistic Period* (UMI dissertation service Ann Arbor Michigan, degree date 1950) 123–25.

(33) I.Jenkins and A. Middleton, 'Painted Pediment', *British Museum Magazine* 11 (1992) 9.

(34) Jenkins, *op. cit.* note 6, 44–54.

(35) Nares *op. cit.* note 1, 1021. Sarah Dodgson informs me that the work was executed by T Kenyon and Sons in August 1950 at a cost of £1,237.14.0. The Athenaeum Committee agreed to it at the suggestion of M.Tudsbery Tudsbery Esq. in April of that year (see also Nos 869–70).

(36) Athenaeum General and Building Committee Minutes 4 November 1845.

(b) THE ATHENÆUM: THE EXTERIOR

(arranged chronologically)

1239

1829, 'THE NEW ATHENÆUM: WATERLOO PLACE'

1239 *By J.Tingle*, mezzotint after T.H. Shepherd, plate 189 from Shepherd's *London and its Environs in the Nineteenth Century (Nov. 1, 1829).*

c.1832-3, THE ATHENÆUM AND THE DUKE OF YORK COLUMN, *see* No. 1126–8

1832–38, THE ATHENÆUM FROM THE EAST

1240 *Unknown artist, 1832–38* [Plate XIX (a)]

Pencil and wash, 48.5 x 72.5 cm (19 x 28½ in), uninscribed.

Elevation of the east façade from across Waterloo Place, garden and Carlton House Terrace to left, packman and old gentleman with dog to left.

The Club Minutes record that Decimus Burton 'produced a model and drawings' on 18 August 1824. These have disappeared. In May 1828 'the building was proceeding with all possible speed', and Burton kept his promise to finish it by 1830. Indications towards a more precise dating of this drawing are: the buff-coloured stucco of the facade, the Bath stone of the porch, the uncoloured frieze, and Athena painted white. Athena has no spear, there are no gas jets on the balconies, and the Travellers' Club next door (completed 1832) appears

1243

to be finished, whereas the Reform Club facade (completed 1838) has not been begun. The Minutes of 1903 record John May's presentation: 'A watercolour drawing, framed and glazed, of the Athenaeum painted for Decimus Burton, the architect, shortly after the building of the House, in 1830. This picture was on the wall of Mr Burton's Drawing Room until his death'.

Literature: Club Minutes, vol I, p.44; Cowell p.15; Boucher 1999, p. 21 where the drawing is reproduced in colour and appears misleadingly as by Decimus Burton, *c.*1830.
Presented by John May, 1903,

*c.*1840, THE ATHENÆUM, PALL MALL

1241 *By Thomas Shotter Boys*
Coloured lithograph, from *Original Views of London* (1842, republished by James Laver 1954).

Literature: J. Roundell, *Thomas Shotter Boys* (1974), p. 160.

1852, FUNERAL PROCESSION OF THE DUKE OF WELLINGTON

1242 *By Read & Co.*, mezzotint, from *Views of Mighty London* (c.1854).

*c.*1853–5, THE ATHENÆUM FROM SOUTH EAST

THE ATHENÆUM THIRD STOREY

1243 *By E.J. May*, reproduction of a drawing. Plans for a third storey had been proposed in 1855 by Decimus Burton but rejected in 1865. The presence of Sir John Franklin's statue, erected in November 1866, suggests that this drawing was part of a scheme related to Barry's 1887 plans, resulting in the additional storey finally built in 1899 (see Appendix III).

Presented by E.J. May, a pupil of Decimus Burton.

1860-64, WATERLOO PLACE

1244 *By E. Anscombe* [Plate XIX (b)]

Oil on canvas (relined lately), 37 × 60 cm (14½ × 23½ in) sight size, signed lower right in white paint: *E. Anscombe 1860* (or *1864*), and inscribed on a lamp post in centre: *IV WR* under a crown. The Club to right, Senior to left, Duke of York column in background.

E. Anscombe, as an artist, does not appear in the usual reference books but may have been a member of a family of architects working in Brighton in the 1860s.

Condition: cleaned by Paul Mitchell, 1986.
Acquisition uncertain, possibly through E.J. May.

1863, WEDDING PROCESSION OF THE PRINCE AND PRINCESS OF WALES

1245 *Unknown artist, 1863*, coloured lithograph (two copies), 23 × 34 cm (9 × 13⅛ in), lettered: *Plate 12 Waterloo Place & Pall Mall March 7th 1863.* A view from Lower Regent Street, the procession moving east along Pall Mall, the Athenæum balconies fitted with red and white awnings and full of spectators, Athena ungilded.
Presented by R.W. Burkitt, 1970.

1894, LAND REGISTRY MAP OF THE CARLTON HOUSE AREA, *see* LONDON No. 1103

c.1910, THE SIEGE OF THE ATHENÆUM, *see* Satires, No. 973

1924, THE ATHENÆUM AND PALL MALL

1246 *By Hanslip Fletcher, 1924*

Ink and wash, 24.5 × 47 cm (9⅝ × 18½ in), inscribed: *The Atheneum Hanslip Fletcher 15 Feb. 1924*
Presented by Viscount Kemsley, 1942.

1931, THE ATHENÆUM FROM SOUTH-EAST

1247 *By Frank Lodge, 1931*
Ink drawing, 21 × 25 cm (8¼ × 9⅞ in), signed and dated:

F. Lodge. 31; illustration in *The Observer*, 14 August 1932. Presented by J.L. Garvin, 1932.

1949, THE ATHENÆUM

1248 *By Nevile Wallis, 1949*

Ink on white paper, 25.5 × 35.5 cm (10 × 14 in), inscribed: *The Athenaeum in Winter, 1949.* A drawing for *The Sunday Times.*
Presented by Viscount Kemsley.

1953, THE ATHENÆUM, TRAVELLERS AND REFORM CLUBS, BY OSBERT LANCASTER, *see* Satires No. 979

1961, THE ATHENÆUM, LADIES ANNEXE, No.6 CARLTON GARDENS, *see* No. 1294

1963, THE ATHENÆUM FACADE,

1249 *By Geoffrey Fletcher, 1963*

Ink and wash drawing, 37 × 45.5 cm, signed and dated: *G S Fletcher 1963.*

Bought from *The Illustrated London News* archive, 1989, together with Nos. 1273–4.

1991, THE ATHENÆUM FROM SOUTH-EAST

1250 *By David Lloyd, 1991*

Ink and wash, 23 × 18.5 cm (21 × 17 in), signed and dated: *David Lloyd, 1991,* and inscribed: *The Athenaeum.* Corner view with statue of Sir John Franklin to left.

Bought from the artist, 1991.

1996, THE ATHENÆUM, PORCH AND FRIEZE

1251 *By David Grech, 1996*

Ink and watercolour, 23.5 × 16.5 cm (9¼ × 6½ in), signed and dated: *The Athenæum CP* (monogram) '*96*. Copy of an original watercolour sketch made for Kingswood.

Presented by Kingswood Conservation (London) Ltd, following the external repairs, re-decoration and replacement of the copper roof, summer 1996.

1828, THE ATHENÆUM FRIEZE

1252 *By John Henning Junior, 1828*

Ink and watercolour on buff (discoloured) paper, 28 × 76.5 cm (11 × 30⅛ in) signed left: *John Henning Junr· August 4th 1828*, and right: *July 31 Approved as stated on the other Drawing by the Building Committee JW Croker Chairman 31 July 1828*, and inscribed by the artist top left: *Athenaeum Club House / This Drawing includes the whole of the proposed Frieze on the south end of the Club House taken from the South Frieze of the Parthenon from the Fragments in the British Museum with the exception of Nos. 1, 2 & 3. The original of the first is in the possession of Mr Robert Cockerell, the other two portions are restored from the drawings of the Marquis De Nointel, made in the Year 1674.* On the back is inscribed: *Drawing of the Frieze on the South side of the Building / JH 1831*

Literature: Ward 1926, pp. 37–8; Cowell 1975, pp. 16–18; J. Malden, *John Henning 1771–1851, '… a very ingenious Modeller'* (Paisley 1977); and see Ian Jenkins above; illus. on pp. 150–1
Presented by E.J. May, 1900.

c. 1828, THE ATHENÆUM FRIEZE

1253 -4 *By John Henning*
Plaster models, twelve strips, 5 × 70 cm (2 × 27½ in) each, mounted in two frames. Other copies are known; see Ian Jenkins above; illus. on p. 153.
Purchased by the Club, *c.*1905

ATHENA

Daughter of Zeus, goddess of wisdom, and patroness of learning and the arts. Her statue on the porch dominates the east front of the Club.

1255 *By Edward Hodges Baily, 1829* [Plate XVII]

Gilt stone statue, 27.5 m (9ft) high, commissioned by Decimus Burton, probably at the suggestion of J.W. Croker and Sir Thomas Lawrence. The Club paid Baily £100 in 1829 (Minutes 11 December 1829, p. 68) and the statue was placed on the portico in 1830. It appears *ungilded* in the drawing of 1832–38 (No. 1240) and again (faintly, without spear, 1834) in Maclise's drawing of Theodore Hook (Ormond NPG, 1973, p. 231, plate 444). It was gilded during the redecoration of the Club 1889–92, and in 1899, according to the Rev Frederick Waugh, Athena holds out her prone hand as if welcoming worshippers into her temple (Waugh 1899, p. 13); see, also, Ian Jenkins above, p. 149.

1256 *By Lumb Stocks*, engraving (Eng. C. I. 35), of 'the statue of Athena on the Acropolis, to be restored by George Knowles'.
Presented by E.P. Colquhoun, 1849.

1257 *By H. Corbould, 1834*, lithograph after a statue of Athena by J. Thomson, 'in the Collection of Earl De Grey, publishd Society of Dilettanti, Feb 1834, plate XXXVIII'.

THE CLUB SEAL, see Nos. 1279–81, 1461–6

(c) THE ATHENÆUM: THE INTERIOR

arranged chronologically; see Appendix III for architectural drawings, 1840–1902 and Appendix IV for the re-decoration, 1889–1908

1828, APOLLO

One of the many sons of Zeus, looked on by the Greeks as the ideal of manly beauty. He was specially associated with music, archery, prophecy and medicine, and the higher reaches of civilization.

1258 Plaster cast, *c.*10 ft high, of the Apollo Belvedere in the Vatican (K. Kerényi, *Apollo* (1953); K. Clark, *The Nude* (1956); Campos & Calvesi, *Treasures of the Vatican* (1962), p.2; B. Ashmole, *Architecture and Sculpture in Classical Greece* (1977). pp. 46–7. The statue stands in a commanding site on the main staircase. A figure of Demosthenes was originally intended, placed on the staircase but almost immediately removed (*London Interiors* op cit. p.166).

The statue of Apollo, one of a variety of casts of classical sculpture readily available, was presented by Decimus Burton and its position on the staircase approved by the Building Committee in 1830 (Minutes 2 March 1830, p. 111). It is described in *London Interiors* of 1841 (see No. 1266). It was ostentatiously gilded at the redecoration of the Club in 1891, and the Club cypher (the Greek letters *alpha, theta, eta* within a wreath, placed on the plinth beneath at a later date. It was re-painted white in 1966.

Literature: Minutes op cit. and 2 March 1830; *New Monthly Magazine* (1 June 1828) p.256; *London Interiors* (1841); Gunnis 1953, p. 318; and Ian Jenkins above.
Presented by Decimus Burton, 1830, with special thanks from the Committee (Minutes 2 March).

VENUS

1259 Plaster cast, 183 cm (6 ft) high, of an antique marble statue, now in the Louvre. In her hand she holds the apple given her by Paris.

1258

1259

Literature: Waugh 1893, p. 306; Cowell 1975, p. 19; and Ian Jenkins above (p. 149).
Part of the original building and said to have been specially chosen by Sir Thomas Lawrence. The cast, with those of Apollo and Diana (Nos. 1258, 1260), was one of many classical sculptured figures readily available to architects and decorators of the time.

DIANA

1260 Plaster cast, 183 cm (6 ft) high, of the antique marble

statue in the Louvre, originally from Gabii and a Roman copy of a lost 4th century Greek original.

Literature: Waugh 1893, p. 306; Cowell 1975, p. 19; and Ian Jenkins above (p. 149).
Part of the original building and specially chosen by Sir Thomas Lawrence.

NIGHT AND DAY, BY BERTEL THORWALDSEN, *see* Nos. 1407-8

1829, THE ATHENÆUM DRAWING ROOM

1261 *By Decimus Burton, 1828-9* [Plate XX (a)]

-2 Watercolour drawings on discoloured white paper, 39 × 50 cm (15½ × 19½ in), initialled *DB* and captioned: WEST SIDE OF LIBRARY/EAST SIDE OF LIBRARY, and scale (at lower edge) Two

1260

suggestions for decorative schemes in the library (now drawing room), east and west walls showing curtains, low bookcases with numerous pictures above, (see *Survey 1960*, p. 399).

For three other Drawings of decorative schemes, see Appendix III. Commissioned by the Club.

1836, THE ATHENÆUM DRAWING ROOM

1263 *By James Holland, c.1836* [Plate XXI]

Oil on canvas, 31.5 × 45.5 cm (12½ × 18 in), two labels inscribed on the back indistinctly: *Holland … Club … 1836.*

This extremely interesting view shows the drawing room with its dome, with a number of the library busts, and with the original bookcases which, Crabbe

Robinson said, on waking from a post-prandial nap, reminded him of a magistrate's court. Decimus Burton's classical bookcases were subsequently replaced with the present more austere ones. A closely related pencil and ink drawing, is also in the collection (No. 1265). For Holland's drawing (and possibly oil) of Burton's arch at Hyde Park Corner, see Nos. 1131–2.

Condition: cleaned by Tom Lindsay, 1968.

Literature: Houfe 1972, pp. 293–4; Cowell 1975, illustrated opposite p.101.

1264 *By Weld Taylor after James Holland, 1841*, coloured steel engraving lettered: J. Holland / W. Taylor / The Athenaeum Drawing Room / L'Athenaeum Le Grand Salon / Das Athenaeum Clubhaus -Der Grosse Saal. Another version, without the French and German gloss, is a plate illustrating *London Interiors with their Costumes & Ceremonies* (1841–44), p.121. No. 21 of that work, the Reform Club, was presented by the Proprietors of *London Interiors,* in 1843 [Minutes 4 April 1843, p. 365].

1265 *Attributed to James Holland, 1843*

Pencil on off-white paper, 14.3 × 17.2 cm (5¾× 6¾ in), inscribed along top edge: *The Athenaeum Club House – Principal Drawing Room Feby 1843*

The drawing has been attributed to Thomas Hosmer Shepherd but appears to be similar (except for variations in the furniture and the introduction of figures in the foreground), to No. 1263 above, by James Holland. Presented by T.W. Hill, Assistant Secretary.

1841, THE HALL

1266 *By W. Radclyffe after G.B. Moore;* steel engraving, lettered: 'Hall of the Athenaeum / La Salle del Athenaeum / Der Saal des Athenaeum', Plate 21 to *London Interiors* (1841–44), p.165, showing the staircase, three statues, and scagliola columns imitating white marble, the capitals after those on the Choragte Monument of Lysistratus, Athens. The statues were the Venus (No. 1259) and two by J.G. Lough, Milo and Samson (Nos 1406 and 1413), moved from the Hall to Manchester in 1846 (Minutes 3 March 1846, pp. 32, 42).

Presented by the Proprietors of *London Interiors,* 1843.

1889–1908, DESIGNS FOR REDECORATION BY ALMA-TADEMA, POYNTER AND LUCAS *see* Appendix IV

The Athenæum Club House ~ Principal Drawing Room   July

1265

**1892, BALLOT DAY AND VARIOUS VIEWS BY
WALTER WILSON, see No. 956**

1897, MAIN STAIRCASE

1267 *By George Thomson, 1897*

Pencil on drawing–board, 39 × 33.5 cm (15⅝ × 13⅛ in),
signed: *George Thomson*. Interesting details include the clock,
statue of Apollo, original gas chandelier, coat hangers, banisters, stair carpet, floor decoration, etc.

Presented by the artist, 1897.

1897, LOWER SMOKING ROOM LOOKING
THROUGH TO BILLIARDS ROOM

1268 *By George Thomson, 1897*

Pencil on drawing board, 34.5 × 40 cm (13½ × 15¾ in), signed
and dated: *George Thomson / 1897*. View with impressive tiled
stove in foreground and large stuffed 'Eagle Owl' in glass case
given by John Gould (see **Memorabilia** No. 1457).

Presented by the artist, 1897.

1897, DOORWAY IN COFFEE ROOM

1269 *By George Thomson, 1897*
Pencil on cardboard, 39.5 × 27 cm (15½ × 10¾ in), signed
and dated: *George Thomson / 1897*.
Presented by the artist, 1897.

1266

1935, SCHEME FOR RE–DECORATING THE COFFEE ROOM

1270 *By Sir Albert Richardson, 1935* [Plate XIV]
Watercolour sketch, 35 × 47 cm (13¾ × 18½ in), signed and dated: *AER / 17 March 1935.*
Presented by the artist.

1939, COFFEE ROOM WINDOW (DICKENS'S TABLE)

1271 *By A.M. Hind, 1939* [Plate XV]
Watercolour, 33.5 × 26 cm (13⅛ × 10½ in), signed and dated *A.M.Hind / 1939,* and inscribed below the mount in ink: *641 A M Hind / Coffee Room Window, Athenaeum,* and dated in pencil: *Spring 1939.*
Presented by Sir Hugh (later Lord) Molson, 1942.

1951–75, INTERIOR SCENES BY FOUGASSE, AND SIR OSBERT LANCASTER, *see* Satires

1961, BILLIARDS ROOM

1272 *By John Ward, , 1961*

Ink and watercolour, 32 × 64 cm (12½ × 25¼ in), signed and dated: *John Ward 1961,* and inscribed above the cue rack: *William Makepeace Thackeray's 1851 Billiards Cue 1863* (see **Memorabilia** No. 1453).

Commissioned by the Club to mark the demolition of the billiards room in 1961. Three further items in the Collection are evocative of this lost aspect of the Club's social life: the silver Billiard Table Trophy (No. 1454), the Billiard Champions wall-plaque (No. 1455) and the humourous exchange in 1933 (No. 1456).

1268

1963, HALL AND STAIRCASE

1273 *By Geoffrey Fletcher, 1963*

Ink and grey wash drawing, 37 × 42 cm (14½ × 16¼ in), signed and dated: *Athenaeum - Entrance Hall / G S Fletcher / 63.*

Bought from *The Illustrated London News* archive, 1989.

1963, THE DRAWING ROOM

1274 *By Geoffrey Fletcher, 1963*

Ink and wash drawing, 34.5 × 25 cm (13½ × 9⅞ in), signed and dated: *G.S. Fletcher 1963.*

Bought 1989, together with Nos. 1249, 1273

1992, JOHN ROSS'S LIBRARY TALK ON ERASMUS, *see* Groups No. 971

1994, FOUR CLUB INTERIORS

1275 *By Hugh Lane-Davies*

-8 Ink and black wash drawings, two of the Kitchen and two of the Coffee Room.

Presented by the artist, 1994.

1272

(d) THE DESIGN FOR THE CLUB SEAL

HEAD OF ATHENA

1279 *By Sir Thomas Lawrence, 1824* [Plate I (a)]

Pencil and watercolour, oval 4 × 3.3 cm (1½ × 1¼ in), set in a gilt gesso relief, 13.4 × 11 cm, decorated with suitable emblems – tree of knowledge, quill and inkpot, open book, star globe, and artist with easel – signed lower right: *E.F. Watson / del et sculpt.* [Plate I (b)]

This drawing is one of the utmost delicacy and is one of the few examples of Lawrence's work as a miniaturist (another is his self-portrait at Croft Castle). It was done as a model for the Club seal (engraved by William Wyon – see Nos. 1461–2). On 6 July 1824 'Francis Chantrey Esq offered to execute and present to the Club a Seal for its use after a design by Sir Thomas Lawrence' (Minutes II, p.26). On 13 July Chantrey was thanked and the Committee 'Ordered that a letter be written to Sir

Thomas Lawrence acquainting him with Mr Chantrey's proposal and requesting that he will be pleased to give Mr Chantrey a Design for the seal …' (Minutes II, p.28). There is, however, no mention of this medallion in the Chantrey Ledgers (*Walpole Soc. Journ.* LVI, 1994). Five months later, the Committee resolved that 'a head of Minerva be adopted for the seal of the Club', 28 Dec. 1824 (Minutes I, p.97).

Literature: 1939 Inventory p.40; Lawrence's work as a miniaturist is discussed by Daphne Foskett (Foskett 1987, pp. 31, 311), but the Athenaeum Athena is not mentioned, nor does it appear in Dr Kenneth Garlick's *Sir Thomas Lawrence* (Phaidon 1989).
Presented by Sir Thomas Lawrence, PRA , 1824. The frame by E.F. Watson, was presented by Messrs Colnaghi & Sons (Minutes 18 March 1828, p.136).

1280 *By R. Lane, 1830,* line and stipple eng. (Eng. C.I.1), after W. Wyon's Club seal.

1281 *By J. Bate, 1840,* line engr. (Eng. C.I.11), after W. Wyon's Club seal.

1294

(e) OTHER BUILDINGS

BERLIN: OPERA HOUSE

1282 *By P. Herwegen, 1846*, lithograph (Eng I. 16a) after a drawing by E.F.A. Rietschel. Tympanum of the new opera house, Berlin.

CAMBRIDGE: HOLY SEPULCHRE

1283 *By J. Deason, 1842*, lithograph (Eng C. I. 25), the church as restored in 1842 by A. Salvin, architect, after a drawing by Deason himself.
Presented by the Cambridge Camden Society, 1842.

CAMBRIDGE: ST EDWARD'S CHURCH

1284 *By T.J. Rawlins*, engraving (Eng. C. I. 24) after a drawing of the font by F.A. Paley, MA.
Presented by the Cambridge Camden Society, 1842.

1298

CLIFTON OBSERVATORY

1285 *By J.S. Prout,* lithograph (Eng. C. I. 18) after a design by W. West, with proposed additions.

DARTMOUTH: PLAN OF BROOKHILL HOUSE AND ESTATE

1286 *By Decimus Burton,* engraving (Eng. C. I. 17), scale 1¼ inches to 20 feet, showing its situation on the River Dart.

DARTMOUTH: VIEW FROM BROOKHILL

1287 *By P. Gauci,* lithograph (Eng. C. I. 16) after a drawing by A. Holdsworth Esq. MP.

DEWLANDS, ESSEX

1288 *By W.S. Lacey,* engraving (Eng. C. I. 30), 'the residence of John Ray Esq, Black Notley, Witham Hundred'. Presented by J.H. Pattisson, *c.* 1830.

EDINBURGH

1289 *By T. H. Shepherd,* line engraving (Eng. I. 6), 'view with connection of old & new town as proposed by Alexander Trotter Esq of Dreghorn' *c.* 1829. Presented by Alexander Trotter, *c.* 1830.

ELGIN CATHEDRAL: CHAPTER HOUSE

1290 *By David Roberts, 1848* [Plate XXV (a)]

Pencil and watercolour on prepared paper, 34.75 × 25 cm (13⅝ × 9⅞ in), inscribed lower left: *Entrance to the Chapter House, Elgin Cathedral, Sept. 13ᵗʰ 1848,* and signed right in red paint: *David Roberts RA.* The drawing was made on the spot and worked up later into the oil of 1853 in the V&A Museum (see Helen Guiterman & Briony Llewellyn, *David Roberts* (1986), no. 30, colour plate 23).

Presented by Mrs Arthur Acland Allen, 1940.

HOLWOOD, NEAR KESTON, KENT

1291 *By T. Scandrett, 1825,* lithograph (Eng. C. I. 15), 'formerly the seat of William Pitt, after …sketches & measurements by Decimus Burton'.

KEMERTON CHURCH

1292 *By C.T. Heartley, c.1856,* coloured lithograph (Eng. I.19), view of the chancel.

LLANTRITHYD PLACE HOUSE

1293 *By A.F. Rolfe, 1846,* lithograph (Eng. C. I. 33) 'the property of Sir T.D. Aubrey Bt.' after a drawing by Mrs Traherne.

LONDON: THE ATHENÆUM, LADIES' ANNEXE, NO. 6 CARLTON GARDENS

1294 *By Sir Henry Rushbury*

Watercolour on prepared card, 36.5 × 46 cm (14⅜ × 18⅛ in), inscribed: *Carlton Gardens – Henry Rushbury – 1961.* View looking west towards Marlborough House. The building was formerly lived in by Mr Gladstone and acquired by the Club in 1936 as the first Ladies' Annexe. The lease expired in 1961 when the Crown Estate Commissioners declined to renew and the Club created alternative space by sacrificing the Billiard Room and nearby area.

Commissioned by the Club, 1961.

LONDON: BANK OF ENGLAND

1295 *By George Rennie,* lithographs (Eng. A. I. 8–10), designs for sculptural decoration (Mercury, Britannia, Ceres, Neptune, Ariadne, and a muse).

1296 *By C.R. Cockerell, 1835,* lithograph (Eng. A. I. 7), 'section through the new Dividend Pay & Dividend Warrant Offices … at the Bank of England'.

LONDON: CARLTON HOUSE AREA, 1894,
see No. 1103

LONDON: COLOSSEUM, REGENT'S PARK

1297 *By G. Hawkins, c.1823,* lithograph (Eng. A. I. 6), after a design by Decimus Burton.
Presented by Decimus Burton, 1839.

LONDON: G.B. GREENOUGH'S VILLA, REGENT'S PARK

1298 *By J. Roffe,* line engraving (Eng. C. I. 10), after a design by Decimus Burton.

1299 *By H. Winkles, 1825,* steel engraving (Eng. C. I. 12), after Decimus Burton, plate to *Edifices of London – Private Buildings.*

LONDON: IMPERIAL CLUB

1300 *By G.E. Madeley,* lithographs (Eng. A. I. 28–9), section and elevation after designs by E.W. Trendall, architect.

LONDON: ISLINGTON

1301 *By R.B. Grantham, engineer,* 'Isometric View of Islington Cattle Market, Meat Market and Lairs'. (Ath. Folio II. 17).

LONDON: ROYAL GARDENS, KEW

1302 *By Vincent Brooks, 1862,* lithographs (Eng. A. I. 31), plans of the palm house and conservatory, by Burton, Turner & Nesfield, 1844–48.

LONDON: ROYAL THEATRE AND ATHENÆUM,
see London, No. 1146

LONDON: THAMES TUNNEL

1303 *By M. I. Brunel, 1825-40,* coloured plan and transverse section of the River (Ath. Folio III. 13).
Presented by Sir Marc Isambard Brunel, 1841.

LONDON: TOWNELEY GALLERY, *see* Groups No. 953

LONDON: TRAFALGAR SQUARE

1304 *By L. Haghe,* lithograph (Eng. I. 13), design for 'A National Naval Monument' by T. Bellamy.

LONDON UNIVERSITY (NOW UNIVERSITY COLLEGE)

1305 *By W. Wilkins, 1826,* engraving (Eng. C. I. 22), 'Design adopted by the Council', completed 1828.

OXFORD: ASHMOLEAN MUSEUM

1306 *By J. Coney, 1816,* line engraving (Eng. C. I. 4), 'From a Drawing in the Possession of Thos. Dunbar Esq'. Presented by Thomas Dunbar.

PARIS: CHAMBER OF DEPUTIES

1307 *By P. Herwegen, 1846,* lithograph (Eng. I. 16b), the tympanum sculpture by Cartot (cf. Berlin No. 1282)

PLYMOUTH: ROYAL WILLIAM DOCKYARD

1308 *By L. Haghe, c.1832,* lithograph (Eng. I. 12), after a drawing by Charles Purser, dedicated to William IV by George & John Rennie, architects of the Yard (see Richardson & Gill, *Regency Architecture of the West of England* (1924), pp. 59–63).

ROME: FORUM

1309 *By J. Coney, 1829,* line engraving (Ath. Folio III. 10), 'from a drawing by C.R. Cockerell, architect'. Presented by Colnaghi & Co. 1829.

ROME: VIEW TAKEN FROM THE JANICULAN HILL

1310 *By F. Smith, c.1830,* engraving (Eng. A. I. 26), 'reduced from Vasi's large print, with recent improvements and additions'. A numbered panorama extending from St Peter's to left, to the Fountain of Paul V to right, Tivoli in background. Giuseppe Vasi, the master of Piranesi, published his *Prospects of Rome* in the 1740s.

V. MISCELLANEOUS

(a) PRINTS, DRAWINGS AND THEATRE DESIGNS

THE ADAM & EVE

1311 *By Edwin Edwards, 1872*, etching 28.5 × 22 cm (11¼ x 8⅝ in), dated '72., from *Old Inns.* Waterside scene with Norfolk wherry and 'Adam & Eve' public house in background (Beraldi VI p.85).

AGAMEMNON BREAKING UP

1312 *By Sir Francis Haden, 1870*, etching with drypoint, 20 × 41.5 cm (7⅛ × 16⅜ in), signed and dated: *Seymour Haden 1870* (Beraldi VIII, no.128; Haden-Schneiderman, no.133).
Lucas bequest, 1918.

AMELIA AWAITING THE RETURN OF HER HUSBAND

1313 *By J.C. Bromley, 1836*, mezzotint (Ath. Folio II.1), from a picture by Edward Prentis, exh SBA 1835, 'from the Original Picture in the Collection of P. Hesketh Fleetwood Esq.' The subject illustrates Fielding's *Amelia,* book IX.

ARAGONESE STRING MAKERS

1314 *By Sir William Russell Flint*

Dry point, 24 × 36.5 cm (9½ × 14½ in), inscribed in ink: *Trial Proof "Aragonese String Makers" to the Athenaeum / W Russell Flint.*

Presented by the artist, 1931.

ARMORIALS AT COURT RHYDHIR, NEATH

1315 *By A.F. Rolfe, 1846*, lithograph (Eng. C.I.34), after a sketch by Mrs Traherne.

1314

ATHENA AND GODDESSES WITH PUTTI

1316 *By H.C. Shenton*, line engraving (Eng C.I 7), after T. Stothard.

BARROW MONUMENT

1317 *By M.J. Starling, c.1850*, engr. (Eng. A.I.25) of Sir John Barrow's memorial tablet, Ulverston, Cumbria.

BATE PROCESS

1318 *By J. Freebairn,,* engraving (Eng. A.1.23-24), specimens of John Bate's patent process of anaglyptograph engraving including a medallic portrait of Henry of Navarre, and the 'Gate Beautiful', No. 1319 (for the Bate process see *Art Union* 1846, p. 14).

THE BEAUTIFUL GATE OF THE TEMPLE (ACTS III. 6)

1319 *By J. Freebairn, 1837*, Bate's patent anaglyptograph after a plaster bas-relief by John Henning, 1820-22, after the cartoon by Raphael, one of the famous set in the V&A Museum. The Athenaeum Collection also has a silvered electrotype of this Henning relief, signed and dated John Henning, 2 May 1821, the gift of Paul Paget Esq. 1976.

BELSHAZZAR'S FEAST

1320 *By John Martin*, mezzotint (Ath. Folio III. 2), inscribed: 'To the Athenaeum from the Artist'. A letter accompanies the print from Martin, Allsop Terrace, 5 June 1833, listing Fall of Nineveh, Belshazzar, Fall of Babylon, Deluge, and Joshua (*qqv*), the first half of illustrations to the Bible, and his 'Plan for Improving the Air & Water of the Metropolis'.

Literature: Thomas Baldwin, *John Martin 1789-1854* (1947); M.J. Campbell, *John Martin* (1992).

CANTERBURY PILGRIMAGE: CHAUCER 1400

1321 *By A. Collas, 1836*, Collas process engraving (Eng. A. I. 21), after a plaster bas-relief by Samuel Henning after the oil by T. Stothard in the Tate Gallery.

CARNE MONUMENT

1322 *By G.S. 1848*, engraving (Eng. C.I.35) of Sir Edward Carne's monument, Llandough Castle, Glamorgan, based on the atrium of San Gregorio in Monte Celi, Rome.

CAVALIER

1323 *By John Petter, 1880*, silk engraving no.7, 51 × 33 cm (20 × 13 in), signed and dated 1880, after an oil by C.P. Slocombe.

CHARTERHOUSE STUDY

1324 *By Sir Hubert von Herkomer*, etching, 15 × 10 cm (5¾ × 4 in), proof signed *S.H.H. Sculp / Hubert v Herkomer*. Presented by the artist, 1900.

CHILDREN

1325 *By Sir Edward Poynter Bt. PRA, 1897*

Pencil on greenish-grey paper, 35 × 24.5 cm (13¼ × 9⅝ in), stamped with monogram *EJP* and inscribed by C.F. Bell: *studies for the attendant genii and for the hands of Peace and*

1325

Painting in the allegorical frontispiece to the address presented by the Royal Academy to Queen Victoria on the occasion of her Diamond Jubilee, 1897.

Presented by C.F. Bell, 1931.

CHRIST CARRYING THE CROSS

1326 *By H. Andrew Freeth*, etching, 27 × 37 cm (10¾ × 14½ in), signed in pencil.

COINS

1327 *By B. Thorwaldsen*, engr. (Eng. C.I.20–21), Sicilian tetradrachma (Thorwaldsen Museum K2487, illustrated in Thorwaldsen Exhibition, Rome 1989-90, no. 195).

COLLAS PROCESS

1328 *By Achille Collas, c.1833*, engraving (Eng. A.I.18-20),

specimens of his *procédé Collas* from C. Lenormant, *Le Trésor de Numismatique et de Glypyique* (1836-50), including an ivory Madonna and Child, medallions of Caesar Augustus, Louis XIV and Diana, and Henning's 'Canterbury Pilgrimage'.

CORNWALLIS MONUMENT

1329 *By G. Dawe, 1803,* mezzotint (Ath. Folio III. 8; O'D 26), painted by Dawe from the statue by J. Bacon jun. in Calcutta.

1330 COTTAGE INDUSTRY, *see* **Portraits** No. 1

CRIMEAN WAR: SEBASTOPOL, *see* No. 1217

CRIMEAN WAR: DEPARTURE OF THE GRENADIER GUARDS FROM TRAFALGAR SQUARE, 22 FEBRUARY 1854

1331 *By D.J. Pound, 1854,* steel engraving after a picture by J. Künzley, London Printing & Publishing Co.

CRIMEAN WAR: HER MAJESTY TAKING LEAVE OF THE FUSILIER GUARDS

1332 *By T. Sherrett, 1854,* steel engraving after a picture by J. Benwell.

CRIMEAN WAR: THE QUEEN RECEIVING THE GUARDS AT BUCKINGHAM PALACE ON THEIR RETURN FROM THE CRIMEA

1333 *By G. Greatbach, 1854,* steel engraving after a picture by R. Hind.

CRIMEAN WAR: HER MAJESTY DISTRIBUTING THE CRIMEAN MEDALS AT HORSE GUARDS, 18 May 1856

1334 *After R. Hind,* steel engraving page 142 in …

CRUCIFIXION

1335 *By H. Andrew Freeth,* etching, 28 × 37.5 cm (11 × 14¾ in), signed in pencil.

DEATH OF THE FIRSTBORN

1336 *By Frederick, Lord Leighton, PRA*

Pencil and white chalk on coarse green paper, 49 × 22 cm (19¼ × 8⅝ in), uninscribed; Tate Gallery, no. 4012. a study for an illustration in Dalziel's *Bible Gallery* (SPKG 1881).

Formerly in Douglas Freshfield's collection, sold Christie's 2 November 1934 (32); presented by D.R.H. Williams, 1934.

1337

DEERHOUND OF SIR WALTER SCOTT

1337 *By Sir Edwin Landseer, RA , c.1824*

Pencil on off-white paper, 24.5 × 20 cm (9⅝ × 7⅞ in), signed: *Edwin Landseer,* and inscribed: *A Favorite old Deerhound of Sir Walter Scott.*

Landseer first visited Scott at Abbotsford in 1824. Scott had several deerhounds over the years, all called either Bran or Maida. For Landseer's portrait of Scott, with eagle and horse's heads on reverse, see Nos. 762-3.

Literature: Letters of Sir W. Scott, VIII, p.392.

THE DELUGE

1338 *By John Martin, 1827,* mezzotint (Ath. Folio III. 5), see above, No. 1320.

THE DIGGERS

1339 *By Jean-François Millet*, etching, 23 × 32 cm (9 × 12½ in), printed in Paris, as 'Les Creuseurs'.
Lucas bequest, 1918.

ECLIPSE 1927

1340 *By F.W. Dyson*, signed photograph of the total eclipse of the sun, 29 June 1927, taken by the astronomer royal at Giggleswick, Yorkshire.

ELM TREE

1341 *By Alfred Thornton*

Sepia wash on card stamped: Dixon's David C - Drawing, 24.5 × 28 cm (9⅝ × 11 in), signed heavily: *THORNTON*.

Presented by the artist, 1938.

EVE OF THE DELUGE

1342 *By John Martin, 1827*, mezzotint (Ath. Folio III. 7), see above No. 1320.

THE EXHUMATION OF POPE FORMOSE

1343 *By P. Teysonniere, 1874*, etching 21 × 32 cm (8¼ × 12½ in), inscribed: *Etienne VII a fait exhumer le corps du pape Formose pour lui faire subir un gorgement. C'est au avocat nommé l'office qui doit reponde pour le mort*, after an oil by Jean-Paul Laurens, 1870 (Beraldi XII, p. 108). Lucas bequest, 1918.

THE FALL OF BABYLON

1344 *By John Martin, 1827*, mezzotint (Ath. Folio III. 4), see above No. 1320.

THE FALL OF NINEVEH

1345 *By John Martin, 1829*, mezzotint (Ath. Folio III. 6), see above No. 1320.

GENTIANS

1346 *By Edna Clarke Hall*

Watercolour, 34.5 × 25.5 cm (13½ × 10⅞ in) sight size.

THE GENTLE SHEPHERD

1347 *By Lumb Stocks 1862*, steel engraving after an oil by Wilkie, then in possession of James Gibson Craig, now in the Forbes-Leith Collection.

THE GLEANERS

1348 *By Jean-François Millet*, etching, 19 × 23 cm (9½ × 9⅞ in), printed in Paris as 'Les Glaneurs'.
Lucas bequest, 1918.

HALS (after): GOVERNORS OF THE ST ELIZABETH HOSPITAL, HAARLEM, *see* **Groups No. 950**

HALS (after): OFFICERS OF THE SHOOTING COMPANY OF ST GEORGE, see **Groups No. 949**

LE HAUT D'UN BATTANT DE PORTE

1349 *By Felix-Henri Bracquemond, 1865*, etching, 28 × 38 cm (11 × 15 in), dead birds of prey and a bat nailed to a door, inscribed *Ici, tu vois instement perdre Oiseaux pillards …* (Beraldi II. 110).

THE INFANT SAMUEL

1350 *By J. Brett, 1829*, mezzotint (Eng. I.11), after the oil by Reynolds in the Tate Gallery.

IN THE STUDIO OF A FRIEND

1351 *By H.J. Lucas, 1871*, etching, signed and dated with monogram, and exhibited RA 1871 (864).

ISLAY

1352 *By Sir Edwin Landseer, RA, 1849*

Ink and brown wash, 17.5 × 10.5 cm (6⅞ × 4⅛ in), signed and dated with monogram: *EL 1849*.

Possibly a copy of the skye terrier, Islay, in Landseer's oil, 'Islay, Tilco, a Macaw and two Love-birds', painted for Queen Victoria in 1839. A chalk drawing of Islay was etched by Landseer in the presence of the Queen in 1842.

Literature: Ormond 1981, p.148; Millar 1992, no. 421.
Presented by Lord Kilbracken, 1949.

1352

ITALIAN GIRLS PREPARING FOR A FIESTA

1353 *By D. Lucas, 1830,* mezzotint (Eng. I.7 and Eng. A.I.2), after a painting by P. Williams.
Presented by Colnaghi & Son, *c.* 1830.

JONES MONUMENT

Statue of Sir John Thomas Jones, Bt. KCB (1783-1843).

1354 *By Corbould,* after a lithograph by Edward Morton from the statue by Behnes, erected in St Paul's Cathedral by his surviving brothers of the Royal Engineers.

JOSHUA COMMANDING THE SUN TO STAND STILL

1355 *By John Martin, 1827,* mezzotint (Ath. Folio III. 3), see above No. 1320.

LUDLOW, WEST WINDOW OF THE CHURCH OF ST LAWRENCE

1356 *By Thomas Willement* FSA, chromolithograph 59 × 29 cm (23¼ × 11½ in).
Presented by Beriah Botfield Esq MP and his wife Isabella, 1860.

LYONS BRASS

1357 *By J. Nethercliff,* lithograph coloured to imitate brass (Ath. Folio III.14), from the memorial brass in Harrow Church of John Lyon and his wife, the founders of Harrow School.

MADONNA AND CHILD

1358 *By T. Vernon,* engraving (Eng.A.I.32) for *The Royal Gallery of Art,* vol I, after the picture by W. Dyce, 1845, in the Royal Collection (Millar 227).

MEDALS

1359 *By C. Chabot,* engraving (Eng. I.17), Andrews Medals, Royal Manufacturor of Linen and Damask Table Linen, Ardoyne, Belfast, 1834–45.

THE MORNING WALK BY GAINSBOROUGH, *see* Portraits No. 366

MOTHER AND CHILD

1360 *By John Wheatley*
Ink and chalk on grey squared paper, 31 × 20.5 cm (12¼ × 8⅝ in), uninscribed.
Presented by the artist, 1944.

MOTHER AND CHILD

1361 *By J.G. Wille,* line engraving after a picture by his son, P.A. Wille.
Presented by Dr M.T. Morgan, MD, MC, 1938.

NUDE

1362 *By Barry J. Martin, 1962*

Unfinished pencil drawing, 40 × 30 cm (15¾ × 11¾ in), signed and dated: *B.J. Martin* 62.

Presented by the artist, 1962.

ORIENTAL

1363 *By Sir Hubert von Herkomer, 1895,* herkomertype 23 × 18 cm (9 × 7⅝ in), signed and dated '95.
Presented by the artist, 1901.

THE PEACOCK'S FEATHER

1364 *By Robert Anning Bell, 1930*

Watercolour, 18.75 × 14 cm (7⅜ × 5⅛ in), signed and dated: *R. An. Bell '30.*

Presented by the artist, 1933.

1364

PHILIPPA, DAUGHTER OF HENRY IV, *see* PORTRAITS No. 680

PHILOSOPHER AT A WINDOW

1365 *By Sir Frank Dicksee, PRA*

Watercolour , 11.5 × 13 cm (4½ × 5⅛ in), inscribed: *sketch made at the Langham Sketching Club* (see E.R. Dibdin, *Frank Dicksee,* 1905)

Presented by Herbert Dicksee, 1933

1365

THE PIED PIPER

1366 *By R.W. Macbeth,* etching, 30 × 53.5 cm (12 × 21 in), after a watercolour by G.J. Pinwell, 1869, caricatured by G.R. Halkett in *Gladstone Almanack* 1885, showing Gladstone piping the children to oblivion (see G.C. Williamson, *George Pinwell* (1900), p. 65).

PORTRAIT OF A CHILD

1367 *By F.C. Lewis,* engraving imitating a pencil drawing (Ports I. 25), after Lawrence aged 20, 1790.
Presented by the publisher, Colnaghi & Co, *c.* 1830.

PORTRAIT OF A YOUTH

1368 *By A.P. Martial,* etching, after an oil by J. Goupil.
HL seated in profile to right, 18th century dress and cocked hat.
Lucas bequest, 1918.

THE RECORDING ANGEL

1369 *By William Boscombe Gardner,* wood engraving 29 × 21 cm (11⅜ × 8⅜ in), after an oil by G.F. Watts at Compton. Given by Watts to a member of the Bolitho family (AVB initials) and presented to the Club by Hector Bolitho.

THE REFUSAL

1370 *By Sir Frank Dicksee*

Ink on card, 17 × 12 cm (6¾ × 4⅜ in), signed: FD. Two well-dressed admirers and a toffee-nosed lady holding a prayer book.

Presented by the artist, 1933.

REMBRANDT (after): CHRIST BEFORE PONTIUS PILATE

1371 *By Charles Albert Waltner,* etching (Beraldi XII, 103), after the oil by Rembrandt in the National Gallery.
Lucas bequest, 1918.

REMBRANDT (after): HEAD OF A RABBI

1372 *By L. Lenain,* etching, after an oil attributed to Rembrandt; a variant of Lucian the philosopher (KK527)
Lucas bequest, 1918.

REMBRANDT (after): THE NIGHT WATCH

1373 *By C.H.* Waltner, etching (Beraldi XII.116) after an oil by Rembrandt in the Rijksmuseum.
Lucas bequest, 1918.

REMBRANDT (after): RABBI

1374 *By Charles Albert Waltner, 1887,* etching, after an oil by Rembrandt in the Metropolitan Museum, New York.
Lucas bequest, 1918.

REMBRANDT (after): RABBI

1375 *By Charles Albert Waltner,* etching, after an oil by Rembrandt in the National Gallery.
Lucas bequest, 1918.

REMBRANDT (after): RABBI

1376 *By Leon Richeton, 1889,* etching, published March 1889 by Arthur Lucas, after an oil by Rembrandt in the Royal Collection.
Lucas bequest, 1918.

RICHMOND MONUMENT

1377 *By Alfred Brown,* lithograph after a silver table-centre by Hunt & Roskill, ? at Goodwood, 'Presented on June 21st 1851, the thirty-eighth anniversary of the Battle of Vittoria to His Grace the Duke of Richmond, Lennox and D'Aubigné by the Recipients of the War Medal …'

ROVER

1378 *By W.D. Taylor,* line engraving (Eng. I.9), after a picture by J. Ward, 'A favourite Dog: the Property of the Rt Honble The Earl of Powis'.
Presented by Colnaghi & Son, 1830.

SCOTT MONUMENT, EDINBURGH

1379 *By Brown & Somerville,* lithograph (Ath. Folio II. 19), from a drawing by the architect, C.M. Kemp, 1840.
Presented by Major Jelf Sharp.

SEALS

1380 *By J. Freebairn,* Bate's patent anaglyptograph (Eng. I.14), 'The Great Seal of England', after B. Wyon.
Presented by Benjamin Wyon and W. Brockedon, 1839.

1381 *Unknown engraver, c.1830,* engraving (Eng. C.I.5), seal of Margam Abbey, Glamorgan, 1518.
Presented by the Rev J.M. Traherne, 1832.

SHAKESPEAREAN SCENE(?)

1382 *By Alfred Elmore, RA*

Watercolour, 21.5 × 14 cm (8½ × 5¾ in), uninscribed.

A young man in a red cap, buff jerkin, green trousers, pointed slippers, implores the hand of a young woman in white supported by her father and uncle, women retreating in background.
Presented by Philip James, 1942.

THE SMOKER

1383 *By Paul Adolphe Rajon,* etching 37 × 28 cm (14½ × 11 in), after an oil by John Seymour Lucas.
Lucas bequest, 1918.

1382

A VISIT TO AESCULAPIUS

1384 *Berlin Photographic Co. Berlin, 1891,* photogravure of the oil by Poynter (1880) in the Tate Gallery.
Presented by the artist, 1894.

WAYFARERS

1385 *By Charles Albert Waltner,* etching, after an oil by Fred Walker exhibited Gainhart's Gallery 1866.
Lucas bequest, 1918.

THE WITCH'S PET

1386 *By Sir Hubert von Herkomer, 1891,* etching 15 × 9.8 cm (5¾ × 3¾ in), signed and dated '91.
Presented by the artist, 1901.

1388

WOMAN AND CHILD ON A BEACH

1387 *British School*

WOMAN SEWING

1388 *By William Mulready, RA, 1824*

Pencil, 20.5 × 9.4 cm (8 × 3¼ in), signed and dated: *W. Mulready 1824*. A later variant is at Eton College.

Literature: K.M. Heleniak, *William Mulready* (1980), pp. 78–9.
Presented by Professor Thomas Bodkin, 1945.

THE WOOD SAWYERS

1389 *By William Hole*, mezzotint 46 × 67 cm (18 × 26¼ in), published 1 Feb 1890 by Dowdeswell, after an oil by Jean-François Millet in the V & A Museum.
Lucas bequest, 1918.

FIVE THEATRE DESIGNS

CHARLES JOHN KEAN AS 'MACBETH'

1390 *By A.E Chalon, 1840*, [Pl. XIII (b)] watercolour 44 × 30 cm (17¼ × 11¾ in), signed and dated: *A.E. Chalon, R.A &c. 1840*. Costume design for a production of Macbeth. Chalon was a founding member of the Club. Kean was elected in 1845.
Presented by Edward Croft-Murray, 1948

PAVLOVA AS 'AN AMAZON'

1391 *By Albert Rutherston, 1914* [Pl. XII (b)]

Watercolour on yellowish-brown paper, 34 × 23 cm (13¾ × 9 in), signed and dated: *Albert R. 14,* and annotated: *No.23 Amazon, Madame Anna Pavlova. No.2 Dress for War Dance.*

Presented by the artist, 1939.

PAVLOVA AS 'LA POUPÉE'

1392 *By Albert Rutherston, 1914* [Pl. XII (a)]

Watercolour on yellowish brown paper, 32.5 × 18.25 cm (12¾ × 7¼ in), signed and dated *Albert R. 14,* and annotated: *No.24, Poupée Mme Pavlova*, with colour details. Costume design for a production of Clustine's 'The Fairy Doll'.

Presented by R.A. Walker, 1938.

PRINCE FLORIZEL

1393 *By Charles Ricketts, RA* [Pl. XIII (a)]

Watercolour on discoloured off-white paper, 38 × 39.5 cm (115 × 15½ in), inscribed in pencil: *Winter's Tale / Prince Florizel.*

1394

Costume design for a production of The Winter's Tale.
Presented by Mrs Winslow in memory of Robin de la Condamine, 1966.

'SIEGFRIED'

1394 *By Charles Ricketts, RA*

Watercolour on discoloured white paper, 51 × 35.5 cm (20 × 14 in), uninscribed.Costume design for a production of *Götterdämmerung* in … (letters from Brig. Charles Swift, 30 Dec 1966, in Art File).

Presented by Mrs Winslow in memory of Robin de la Condamine, 1966.

(b) SCULPTURE

Portrait busts are not included here and will be found in the Portrait section.

APHRODITE

1395 *By Sir Charles Wheeler, PRA, c.1944*

Portland stone statuette, 32 cm (12½ in) high, on a greenish porphyry base.

A small version of Wheeler's 'Aphrodite II', *c.*1944, bought for the Tate Gallery from the Chantrey Bequest, 1944.

Literature: Wheeler's *High Relief* (1968), p.123, and as frontispiece the life-size version in English alabaster, 'Aphrodite I'.

Presented by the artist, 1968.

APOLLO, see No. 1258

ARIEL

1396 *By Sir Charles Wheeler, 1947*

Bronze head, 18cm (7 in) high, incised: CW 47. Head from the WL figure commissioned by Sir Herbert Baker for the Bank of England, 1945 (repr. Wheeler, *High Relief* (1968), p. 29).

Presented by W.E. Gelson, 1972.

1395

1398

ATHENA, BY EDWARD HODGES BAILY, *see* No. 1255

ATHENA

1397 *Unknown sculptor*

Statuette in coloured plaster (gold helmet and breastplate, green dress, white robe with traces of red paint), 17.5 cm (7 in) high, on an ebonised plinth in a glass case. A spear is fitted in a hole in the base.

Condition: her right hand is missing, several diagonal fractures across the feet.
Presented by Arthur Lucas, 1901.

ATHENIAN DEMOCRACY

1398 *By Jacqueline Stieger, 1992*

Circular bronze medal, 7 cm (2¾ in) diameter, commemorating the 2500th anniversary of Democracy. Obverse: slightly convex with the figure of Athena, right arm raised in a welcoming gesture, Acropolis below her elbow, to left incised: *2500 year;* above her hand, globe with continents, to left in relief: *ΔΕΜΟΧΡΑΤΙΑ* (democratia). Reverse: slightly concave with American continents and Pacific Ocean; to left in high relief: *508/507 BC 1992/1993 DEMOCRACY;* below a crowd of people in three groups. There are three small punch marks: *CS* on circumference below Athena.

A commemorative medal designed by J. Stieger to mark the 2500th anniversary of the reforms which led to the establishment of democracy in Athens by Cleisthenes in 508–507 BC. A celebration party was held in the Athenaeum on 24 June 1993.
Given by Sir David Hunt, 1993.

BARROW MONUMENT, *see* No. 1317

BATE PROCESS, *see* No. 1318

THE BEAUTIFUL GATE OF THE TEMPLE, *see* No. 1319

BOY SEATED EXTRACTING A THORN FROM HIS FOOT

1399 Modern copy of the Roman bronze in the Capitol Museum, Rome; no longer in the Collection.

CANTERBURY PILGRIMAGE: *see* No. 1321

CARNE MONUMENT, *see* No. 1322

COLLAS PROCESS, *see* No. 1328

CORNWALLIS MONUMENT, *see* No. 1329

DIANA ROBING, *see* No. 1260

1402

EVE AT THE FOUNTAIN

By Edward Hodges Baily

1400 Cast of a statue made for the British Literary Institution in 1818; a version dated 1822 is in the Bristol Art Gallery. Baily was specially thanked by the General Committee in 1830, for 'Presents of Statuary – Eve, Poetry and Painting, and a bust of Flaxman'.

Literature: Literary Gazette, 24 June 1826, pp. 396, 682 and 13 Feb 1830, p. 105; Minutes 9 Feb 1830, p. 94, and 26 July 1927, p. 13.
Presented by the artist, 1830, placed in the Gallery at the top of the main staircase, and 'disposed of' in 1927.

1401 *Unknown artist,* stipple engraving (Eng. A.I.1), 'from the Statue in the Bristol Institution'.
Presented by E.H. Baily, 1829.

THE HAWK OF HORUS

1402 Carved and painted wood, (length of base 18 cm). an Egyptian antiquity attributed to the 25th dynasty (c. 712–663 BC) and preserved in a glass case.
Presented by W. Wyatt-Paine, 1925.

JONES MONUMENT, *see* No. 1354

LAOCOÖN

1403 Bronze, no foundry mark, 70 × 60 × 30 cm (27½ × 23½ × 11¾ in), a modern copy of the classical original in the Vatican Museum, a masterpiece of the Pergamene school (2nd cent, BC). The subject was frequently reproduced throughout the centuries, especially in France; for instance a sumptuously mounted but smaller version is at Corsham Court, acquired by Lord Methuen in 1774 (exh. *Treasures Houses of Britain*, 1985, no. 254). A full-scale marble copy, attributed to Joseph Wilton, is at Sledmere (Sir Christopher Sykes).

Literature: Haskell & Penny, (1981), pp.243–7; Tessa Murdoch, 'Roubiliac and his Huguenot Connections', *Proc. of the Huguenot Soc. of London* (1983), pp. 26–45. Presented by Professor Edward Paolozzi, RA, 1988.

LION

1404 *By Alfred Stevens*

Bronze casting, 34 cm (13⅛ in) high) of a lion seated on a very small square plinth reputedly based on a drawing, by Sidney Smirke, of a lion at the foot of a staircase in the Bargello, Florence, and first used to ornament the railings protecting the gatekeepers' lodges at the newly finished British Museum (see Mordaunt Cook, *The British Museum* (1972), pp. 141–2), and also round the Wellington monument in St Paul's Cathedral. The Lion functions at present as a doorstop in the Club drawing room.

MEDALS

By C. Chabot, engraving see No. 1359; and *also* Franqueville No. 298, Athenian Democracy No. 1398, and Prince Taffari No. 1414

MERCURY IN FLIGHT

1405 *by Alessandro Nelli*

Bronze statue balanced on breath from a zephyr's mouth, 53cm (21 in) high including socle, incised: *Nelli. Roma;* small modern copy of the famous Mannerist statue by Giambologna made for a fountain at the Villa Medici in 1564, and now in the Bargello, Florence. A similar copy, made by Giacomo Zoffoli in the 1760s, is at Aske Hall (Marquess of Zetland). Other examples are at Woburn Abbey, the Royal Palace, Stockholm, and Schloss Wörlitz, Dessau, and modern replicas proliferate.

Literature: Elizabeth Dhanens, *Jean Boulogne* (Brussels 1956), pp. 125–35; Hugh Honour, 'Bronze statuettes by

Giacomo and Giovanni Zoffoli', *Connoisseur* 148 (1961), pp. 200–5; Avery & Radcliffe, *Giambologna 1529–1608*, exhition catalogue 1978–9, pp. 14 and 85–8. Presented by the Rev Canon John Kerruish, 1986.

MILO

1406 *By J.G. Lough, 1827*, marble statue formerly in the hall, *see* No. 1266.

NIGHT AND DAY

1407 *By Bertel Thorwaldsen, 1815*

-8 Two circular plaster medallions, 61 cm (24 in) diameter, from the 1815 originals in the Thorvaldsens Museum, Copenhagen. 'Morning' scattering flowers, 'Night' holding infants and with a bat below her wings. Since the redecoration of the Club House 1889-92 (see Appendix IV), these two roundels have been set in either side of the main staircase; their earlier history is unknown.

Literature: H.W. Janson, 'Thorwaldsen in England', *Bertel Thorwaldsen* (Cologne 1977); Majo, Jørnaes & Susinno, *Bertel Thorwaldsen 1770–1844, Scultore Danese a Roma* (Rome 1989), p. 163, nos 31–2.

POETRY AND PAINTING

1409 *By Edward Hodges Baily*

-10 Two plaster casts, (the marbles exh RA 1827), presented by the artist in 1830 and disposed of in 1927 (*see* No. 1400).

Literature: Literary Gazette, 22 June 1826, p.395, and 13 Feb 1830, p.105; Minutes 4 Feb 1830, p.94.

POMPEIAN YOUTH

1411 Bronze head, 18 cm (7 in) high, a copy, probably 19th cent., of the original marble bust from Herculaneum.

Literature: D. Comparatti & G. da Petra, *La Villa Ercolanese dei Pisoni* (Turin 1883). Presented by Dr Emanuel Miller, 1971.

PSYCHE

1412 *By Bertel Thorwaldsen*

Marble statue, with wings attached, 127 cm (50 in) high, unsigned.

Thorwaldsen's treatment of the Cupid and Psyche

PSYCHE

1412

theme, dating from 1806 to 1841, is displayed in Room II of the Thorvaldsens Museum, Copenhagen. The earliest version, made in Rome in 1806, has no wings (Thorvaldsens Museum, inv. no. A26). Later versions with wings attached include the example formerly in the Hope Collection at Deepdene, Surrey – and, therefore, probably dating from the first quarter of the nineteenth century – and subsequently purchased at

the 1917 auction of 'The Deepdene Hope Collection' by the Thorvaldsens Museum. Another winged example in England, formerly in the possession of Robert Barclay, Dorking, Surrey, was recorded in the 1960s in the collection of Captain Evelyn H.T. Blackwood, where the Barclay family tradition that it had been 'finished by one of Thorvaldsen's best pupils' had been preserved.

Literature: E. Hannover, *Thorvaldsens Vaerke* (Copenhagen, 1907) p. 14, no. 27; *The Thorvaldsens Museum Catalogue* (in English, Copenhagen, 1995), A. 821; letter from Dr Margrethe Floryan of the Thorvaldsens Museum (dated 3rd March 2000). Presented by Percy H. Fitzgerald, 1912.

SAMSON

By J.G. Lough, marble statue formerly in the hall, *see* No. 1265.

SEALS, *see* Nos. 1276–81

TAFFARI MEDAL

1414 *By J.C. Chaplain*

Gold medal, carat mark 30R, 39 mm (1½ in) diameter; obverse: image of the Lion of Judah, signed J.C. Chaplain; reverse: inscribed in relief: *S.A.I. & R. Le Prince TAFFARI Héritier de la Couronne et Régent de l'Empire d'Ethiope / Mai 1924.*

Presented by the Prince, 1924, in acknowledgment of honorary membership.

TEUCER

The best archer in the Greek army *(Iliad)*

1415 *By Sir Hamo Thornycroft*

(a) Bronze head; another version in the Tate Gallery. Presented by Lady Thornycroft, 1939

(b) Statuette. Presented by the artist's nephew, Malcolm Donaldson, 1970

Both are no longer in the Collection.

VENUS

1416 Marble, 87 cm (34¼ in) high, a modern reduced copy of the Venus de Milo in the Louvre. Presented by E.R.P. Moon, 1939.

VENUS, plaster cast, *see* No. 1259

VI ORIENTAL

ORIENTAL

RALPH PINDER-WILSON

(a) Sir Alan Barlow's gift of Turkish pottery

Before describing the pottery, readers may wish to be reminded of the donor of this generous gift (No.55). Sir Alan Barlow (1881–1968) was a man of impressive achievments. The son of Sir Thomas Barlow, physician extraordinary to Queen Victoria, Edward VII and George V and president of the Royal College of Physicians (No. 54), he was educated at Marlborough and Corpus Christi College, Oxford where he took a first in *literae humaniores*. He had a distiguished career in the Civil Service, becoming second secretary at the Treasury in 1938. He was, however, much more than a civil servant in that he was actively interested in the arts, science and the academic world. Above all he was an art collector whose two collections, the one of Islamic pottery and the other of Chinese pottery and porcelain, were of national importance. He started collecting at eighteen when he purchased a piece of Persian pottery; and went on to Turkish pottery from Iznik which had been keenly sought after by collectors since the third quarter of the nineteenth century. It was not until the first decade of the twentieth century that the pottery of Persia aand the other countries of the Miiddle East came on the market as a result of archaeological excavations; and with few exceptions, examples of early Islamic pottery were extracted from beneath the ground.

Barlow turned to collecting Chinese art after the first World War. It was only then that western taste turned from the blue and white porcelain and the enamelled wares of the Kangxi period and later to the much rarer ceramics of the Tang and Sung periods. This was due to the influence of the small circle of collectors led by George Eumorfopoulos, who formed the Oriental Ceramic Society in 1921. Barlow joined the Society in 1932 and in due course served as president from 1943 to 1961.

The great collections of Chinese and to a less degree Islamc art were formed in the first half of the century. Only rarely are we informed of the impulse that drove the collectors. Sir Alan Barlow was exceptional when in 1937 he delivered a paper to the Oriental Ceramic Society entitled: 'The Collector and the Expert', which is at once a defence of collecting and a critique of the role of the expert.

He believed that collectors, often taken to task for being exclusive and jealous possessors of works of art, on the contrary complement the function of public collections; for example the collector can afford to make mistakes in purchasing controversial pieces which is not possible for the museum curator who has to account for his acquisitions. He also provides the opportunity for the handling and studying of objects which is hardly encouraged in the case of museum collections. Again private collections, besides advancing knowledge have raised public awareness of quality and he cites the improvement in taste in contemporary ceramic production of this country. Above all, the signal benefit that has accrued from the collector is the generous donation of works of art and indeed whole collections to our national and public collections. As for the expert, Barlow had in mind the scholar with a lifetime's devotion to the study of Chinese ceramics to whom the collector or, as he preferred, the amateur, might appeal for guidance. The scientific expert however must be treated with caution and questions put to him should be formulated within the narrow limits of his expertise.

These views expressed over sixty years ago may seem to have little relevance today when there are so few collectors in this country and the availability of works of art is limited by the restrictions on the export of works of art from China and the countries of the Middle East. In one respect, however, Barlow has certainly vindicated what he called the main contribution of the collector, the donation of works of art to museums. Here Sir

55

Alan Barlow acted with exemplary generosity. His collection of Chinese art was donated to the University of Sussex and the collection of early Islamic pottery was given largely to the Ashmolean Museum and the remainder to the British Museum, the Victoria and Albert Museum, the Fitzwilliam Museum and the Perceval David Foundation in the University of London. The later Islamic pottery including the Iznik pottery was divided beween members of the family, the Athenaeum Club and the Savile Club. The selected pieces of Iznik were handed over to the Club's General Committee by the Chairman, Sir Alan Barlow himself, on the 21st September, 1953. These, according to the minute, were placed in the Annexe Drawing Room which at that time was in the Ladies Annexe at no 6 Carlton House Terrace (No. 1294). Today they are displayed in the Gallery of the Garden Room.

Iznik, the ancient Nicaea, is situated about one hundred miles south east of Istanbul astride the east – west trade route across Anatolia. It has come to be associated with its pottery industry which flourished under the patronage of the Ottoman Sultans from the end of the fifteenth to the seventeenth century and has undergone a revival in the twentieth century. Pottery of a provincial nature was already being manufactured there in the fourteenth cetury but it was not until about 1480 that the potters adopted an entirely new ceramic technology. This comprised a hard white frit body on which was applied a white slip also containing frit; and on this was painted the decoration consisting of up to seven glaze colours. Finally came the application of the overglaze compounded of both lead and tin oxide and which resulted in the brilliant transparent glaze which is a characteristic of the Iznik wares. Production included tiles which were destined for the walls of religious buildings and palaces in Istanbul and in the provincial centres of the empire. The range of vessel shapes was increased and there is an assured mastery in the handling and potting particularly in the case of oversize vessels. Styles of decoration responded to changes in taste and their development has been demonstrated from decade to decade.

In the earliest period, decoration, exclusively in blue on white or white on blue and later with addition of turquoise, oscillated between the *hatai* or "chinoiserie" floral scrolls in the Chinese manner and *Rumi*, that is, classical arabesque ornament. Around 1540 yet another decorative style was developed in which flowers both naturalistic and fantastic were rendered in a palette that included sage green and purple. About twenty years later,these two colours were replaced by a virulent green

and a red derived from Armenian *bole*, aptly described as sealing wax red. This new palette represents the high point of Iznik, and was continued into the seventeenth century. The decoration in this new palette consists of the Turkish flora which aroused such interest in Europe.

The sudden efflorescence of the Iznik ceramic industry owed of course much to the patronage of the Imperial Court. But an undoubted stimulus was provided by competition from the imported Yuan and Ming porcelain and celadon which was highly regarded by the Sultan and of which the collection which has survived in the Topkapi Saray is among the most important. This was carefully protected and reserved for occasional use; and it seems that Iznik pottery supplied the daily needs of the court which may explain the dearth of Iznik in Turkey today since much must have been destroyed in the frequent fires that occurred in the Palace area. Fortunately the products of Iznik were being exported to the West and it is no accident that the best representation of Iznik is in the public collections in Europe.

Evidence for the value attached to Iznik pottery in contemporary Europe are those pieces which on their arrival were supplied by their new owners with mounts of precious metal. Quite a number of examples reached England in the reign of Queen Elizabeth I. The date and maker's mark on the mounts have contributed to establishing the chronology of Iznik pottery. One such is that on a polychrome Iznik jug of about 1585 in the British Museum; its fine English silver-gilt mounts are dated 1597–8 and bear the maker's mark "HB" (Fig. 3)[1]. The mounts are an embellishment due to the goldsmith's imagination.

The Iznik pieces displayed in the Club are all interesting and worthy of comment. They range in date from about 1580 to the third quarter of the seventeenth century. An added interest in some of these is that although unmistakeably Iznik, their decoration is uncommon in the Iznik repertoire and goes to show the wide range of Ottoman decoration. In the two dishes (nos 1417–8) the decoration consists of a central radiating figure, a style of ornament aptly termed kaleidescopic. In the centre of no 1417 is a rather complex geometric figure of a hexagram composed of two intersecting triangles forming a knot in the middle, all within a geometrical rosette. This feature is unusual at the date of the dish 1570–80 and seems rather to be a revival of the Iznik style of the early sixteenth century, but is in fact much older in Islamic art since a precisely similar geometric figure is found in metalwork of the

Fig. 3

Courtesy of the Trustees of the British Museum

eighth century in eastern Persia. The lotus leaves that radiate from the roundel are a borrowing from the decoration of Chinese blue and white porcelain of the Yuan and Ming periods. In no 1418, the central roundel is in the form of a fantastic flower which is also an example of the imaginative inventiveness of the Iznik potter. Centrally composed decoration is not common at Iznik but was almost standard in Islamic pottery of the fourteenth century.

In the dish painted in green, red and black (no 1419) the composition is also radial while the rows of half palmettes are those found in the earliest style of Iznik blue and white, of which the classical Islamic arabesque is a characteristic. The animals of no 1420 are commonly found in Iznik pottery of the second half of the sixteenth century when they are taken to represent animals of the chase suitably set against a turquoise ground as here. This may be a survival of representations of the chase characteristic of Seljuq art of the twelfth century and later. A Balkan origin has also been suggested where animals such as these are to be found in *repoussé* metalwork. The chequer board on no 1422 is unusual but the rim decoration needs a comment. This is known as the "rock and wave" motif and is derived from the stylised waves dashing against the rocks, a common rim ornament in Yuan and Ming blue and white porcelain and frequently used by the Iznik potters.

While figures occur in the early periods of Iznik, those such as the lute player in no 1421 cannot be earlier than the 1660s. The source for such figures was the costume books that were produced from the sixteenth century onwards. No 1424 is decorated with tulips and floral sprays which is a reminder of the great period of Iznik floral decoration and shows the developments that took place in the seventeenth century.

In three of the dishes (nos 1422–4) there are touches of gilding which are detailed below. Gilded decoration was used on tiles in the fifteenth century and gold leaf was a feature of *mina'i* pottery of Persia in the Ilkhanid period and was adopted in tile work in Timurid Samarqand. In Ottoman Turkey gilding was used in the monochrome tiles of 1421 in the Yesil Cami in Bursa. Gilding was very occasionaly used by the Iznik potters in the sixteenth century but seems to have enjoyed a certain popularity in the seventeenth century. It will be noticed that in the three dishes in the Club the gilding is reduced to somewhat haphazard touches, with the possible exception of no 1424 where the gilding is applied to some of the petals of the tulips. One may wonder if this somewhat meretricious kind of embellishment was not designed to attract the eye of possible purchasers.

A description of the eight surviving dishes in the Barlow Gift now follows:[2]

1417   Shallow dish with curving side; painted in polychrome: inside, a lotus petal roundel in blue and green and in the centre a hexagram in white reserved in red; in the cavetto, a series of half rosettes; on the outside, flower and cloud patterns in blue and green.
Diam. 27.7 cm (10.9 in)
Turkey, Iznik, 1570–80. [Plate XXX (a)]

Published *BC*, no 252, p.166 and pl.101a

1418   Dish with flanged rim; painted in polychrome: on the inside, a thirteen petalled lotus blossom in blue and on the rim twenty one petals in white and blue on a green ground; on the outside, flowers and leaves in blue and green. Diam.28.5 cm (11.3 in)

Turkey, Iznik, last quarter of 16th century.

[Plate XXX (a)]

Published *BC*, no 243, p.164 and pl.100c

1419   Dish with flanged rim; painted in polychrome: on inside, a whorl of half palmettes in red and white radiating from a central eight-petal flower in blue and arranged in three concentric circles all on a green ground; on the rim, outlined in black, Chinese "rock-and-wave" pattern in black and white; on the underside of rim, blue spots. Diam. 30.0 cm (11.8 in)
Turkey, Iznik,about 1580

Published: *BC*, no 239, p.163, pl.99c. There were two other related dishes in the Barlow collection (*BC*, nos 236 and 238)

1420   Dish with flanged rim; painted in polychrome: on the inside within a roundel with a petalled border, three animals – a lion, gazelle and a hound – in a circular chase, and two birds and leaves all on a light blue ground; on rim a band of overlapping petals; on the outside, patches of green and blue.
Diam. 31.0 cm (12.2 in)
Turkey, Iznik, 1580–85 [Plate XXX (b)]

Published *BC*, no 258 p.167f and pl.104b

1421   Dish with flanged rim; painted in polychrome: on the inside a standing man in a green coat and short black trousers playing a sitar; in the background, flower

1422. 1419, 1423

sprays, a bird and a lidded ewer; on rim Chinese "rock and wave" pattern, touches of gilding on the flower spray; on the outside, patches of blue and green.
Diam. 26.0 cm (10.2 in)
Turkey, Iznik, 1650–75 [Plate XXX (b)]

Published *BC*, no 256, p.167 and pl.103c

1422 Dish with flanged rim; painted in polychrome: in centre a chequer board pattern divided into eight vertical zones, the diamonds alternately green and white with a red central spot, touches of gilding on the red spots; on rim alternately rosettes and leaves with touches of gilding; on the outside, blue spots. Diam.27.5 cm (10.8 in)
Turkey, Iznik, 1650–75

Published *BC*, no 291. p.282 and pl. 113b; *Iznik* no 659 p.283

1423 Dish with flanged rim; painted in green and blue with black outlines: in the centre within a roundel, a hexagram of two intertwined triangles with a rosette in the middle and a half rosette between the points; on the rim a series of white petals with red centres; on the outside, blue spots. Diam.25.0 cm (9.9 in)
Turkey, Iznik, late 17th century

Published *BC*, no 284 p.173 and pl.112b

1424 Dish with flanged rim. In the centre three tulips in a vase within a circular flower spray traces of gilding on

the petals; on rim half rosettes within a chevron border. On outside, leaves in blue. Diam. 26.5 cm (10.4 in)
Turkey, Iznik, 1660–75
Published *BC*, no 288 p.174 and pl.114c; *Iznik* no 660

FOOTNOTES

1.   Height 33.2 cm (12.9 in); formerly in the collection of F.G.Sambrooke; lent to the South Kensington Museum Exhibition, 1862, no 3280; and published *Carswell*, p.101, fig.82 (in colour); *Iznik*, fig.774 (in colour); *Read & Tonnochy*, p.10 and plate XV
2.   A ninth piece of Iznik pottery, a jug, and four more Iznik dishes were part of the Gift, but are no longer in the Collection.

REFERENCES

BC: Geza Fehervari, *Islamic Pottery: a comprehensive study based on the Barlow Collection*, London, 1973
Carswell: John Carswell, *Iznik Pottery*, British Museum, London, 1998
Iznik: Nurhan Atasoy and Julian Raby, *Iznik: the Pottery of Ottoman Turkey*, London, 1989
Read & Tonnochy: Sir Hercules Read & A.B. Tonnochy, *Catalogue of the silver plate, mediaeval and later, bequeathed to the British Museum by Sir Augustus Wollaston Franks, K.C.B.*, British Museum, London, 1928

(b) Sir Clarmont Skrine's gift of a Chinese carved jade junk

Sir Clarmont Skrine (1888–1974) had a distinguished career in the Indian Political Service. His posts included Consul General in Chinese Turkestan (1922–24), in Seistan and Kalaf (1927–29) and in Meshed (1942–46).

1424

Apart from articles in the Journal of the Royal Central Asian Society, he published *Chinese Central Asia*, London, 1926 and *Macartney in Kashgar*, London, 1973.

Sir Clarmont Skrine, who was elected a member in 1953, presented the jade junk to the Club in 1969.

1425 Jade boat, pale green jade with russet markings on a hardwood stand. China, dated 1766 [Plate XXXI (a)-(b)]

Length (of jade carving) 27.6 cm (10.8 in)

The boat is flat bottomed and single masted and riding across the crested waves rendered with skill by the carver of the hardwood base. On the base is inscribed a poem signed by the Qing Emperor Qian Long and dated 1766, of which the following is a translation:

> A whole family afloat
> The pleasure of a life afloat should be enough.
> Why sun the nets and catch the carp for sale?
> With money thus earned they buy a brave kite and a flute.
> In the night their melodies clash with the barking of dogs.
> How sad for me to be brought to realize that, in harmony and sincerity, such men can achieve their ambition like kings!

The Qianlung emperor wrote at least 75 poems which were inscribed on individual jade carvings; and in the National Palace Museum, Taipei, there are 19 jades carved with his poems.

In the Ming and Qing periods, the principal jade carving centre was in south China at Suchou where

1425

1426

there were also commercial establishments working for the court, in addition to jade carvers in the imperial workshops in the Palace at Peking. The advance of the Chinese into Central Asia and the defeat of the Khojas of Kashgaria in 1860 opened up the jade mines of Khotan, so that in the last part of the Qianlong emperor's reign there was a marked increase in the production of jades of which many were carved from exceptionally large boulders.

The jade junk was said to have been acquired in the looting of the Summer Palace, Peking in 1860; it subsequently passed into the hands of Colonel John Stewart, laird of Ardvorlich (1833–1914), who, reputedly purchased it from a French colonial soldier together with a red lacquer chest. Stewart served with Probyn's Horse in the China expedition of 1860. The jade was bequeathed to Colonel Stewart's daughter and mother of Skrine; and the red lacquer chest passed to a nephew of Colonel Stewart and then to his son John William Stewart who has published *Envoy of the Raj : the Career of Sir Clarmont Skrine, Indian Political Service*, Maidenhead, 1989.

(c) Sir Eric Pridie's gift of a Japanese Embroidered Picture

The framed picture was presented in 1975 to the Club by Sir Eric Pridie KCMG, DSO, OBE (1896–1978), who was elected a member of the Club in 1949. Unfortunately, there is no record of how he came to acquire the embroidered picture.

1426 'SCENE ON LAKE BIWA'

Embroidered in coloured silks

Dimensions H. 15.3 cm × W. 34.4 cm (6 in × 13½ in)

Japan, about 1880

Embroidered pictures such as this were given to industrial firms working in Japan as good will presents or souvenirs. Lake Biwa is the largest inland stretch of water in Japan and is famous for its scenic beauty. Its temples, too, are a favourite subject with Japanese poets.

VII MEMORABILIA AND SELECTED OBJECTS

MEMORABILIA AND SELECTED OBJECTS

HUGH TAIT

With so much to choose from and so little space left in this volume, each successive decision to exclude became both more necessary and more difficult.

The Club, for example, still preserves in an individual case of mahogany and glass the remaining bones (vertebrae and humerus) of a mammoth discovered accidentally in October, 1927, while digging beneath the basement floor of the Club House. Undoubtedly, a similar sense of history had led to the mounting (on a wooden panel) of those fragments of shrapnel and splintered glass that had been gathered up after a German air raid on 29 September, 1917, during which the central skylight lantern was damaged and "a piece of an aerial shell" was retrieved from the roof.

In 1912, this concern for the Club's history had resulted in Mr. T. W. Hill, then Assistant Secretary (see No. 409), acquiring for the Club's Collection a piece of masonry salvaged from the demolition of the northwest side of Waterloo Place. It was a volute from the capital of one of the columns decorating the Nash facade of No.12, Waterloo Place – the Club's first home from 1824 to 1830. This weighty relic "made of Roman cement" measured 15 in. x 14 in. and was last recorded in the Basement Strong Room. By contrast, the iron key-ring engraved "Edwd Magrath, 12 Waterloo Place" (see No. 571) was highly portable and so disappeared – along with other items of memorabilia and curiosity – from the display case in the Drawing Room over one weekend in February 1987.

In the early days, the Club's snuff-boxes were frequently very simple, being round, black and made of papier-mâché; only the legend, 'Athenæum' (in gold) on a green garter label, made them distinctive. The one example still kept in the display cabinet had been much used and rubbed before it was finally 'withdrawn'. In its place, a conspicuous horn, complete with thistle-decorated silver mounts, has occupied a prominent position since its presentation to the Club in 1935 by Sir Buckston Browne. Despite the engraved inscription (below the rim), which reads "Presented to John Douglas by his brother Alexander, 1850", nothing is known of its history. Indeed, the indistinct set of London hall-marks (on the tip of the horn) merely confirms that the horn had been mounted by a London goldsmiths shortly before, probably in 1845. Even less is known about the Indian (?) ivory column with screw-top lid and silver finial (H.22 cm; 8½ ins), which Colonel Henry A. Ouvry presented in 1885 for use in the Smoking Room.

These seven disparate examples typify much of the Club's memorabilia and associated objects. Within the space available therefore, only some of the more significant could be adequately presented; however, these do serve to illustrate very diverse aspects of the Collection and range from the earliest days of the Club to the Coronation Year (1953) and the building of the Ladies' Annex in 1961.

1427 THE CROKER CUP AND COVER

Acquired in 1975 under the terms of the bequest of Miss G. M. Pennell with the stipulation that it be cherished for all time in memory of her great, great uncle, John Wilson Croker.

Silver; struck (close to the handle) with Dublin hall-marks for 1804; also, the maker's mark: 'RS' (for Richard Sawyer Jnr., of 2 Salls Court, Fishamble Street, Dublin, who was registered in 1797 and died in 1812 – see D. Bennett, *Irish Georgian Silver*, London 1972, no. 209).

The cover is also struck with at least two Dublin hall-marks but, because they are on the flange, they have become extremely faint with the frequent rubbing.

This tall two-handled covered cup (H 42 cm; 16.5 in.) is in the neo-classical style and has few decorative details, apart from the engraved armorials (on the front) and an engraved inscription (on the reverse),

1427

"The Principal Merchants & Owners Concerned
in the SHIP FRIENDS of LIVERPOOL and her Cargo
which had been Wreck'd at Balbriggan
        in Decr. 1803
have presented this Cup to
        JOHN CROKER ESQr
Surveyor Genl of the Port & District of Dublin
in Testimony of their Grateful recollection
of His prompt Effectual & disinterested Exertions
in the preservation of a Great proportion of their property
on that Awful & critical Occasion
    and also as
a mark of Respect & Esteem for Him
    As an Able Officer of the Revenue
        & a Friend to
            The Fair Trader."

This lengthy inscription is most carefully laid out and expertly engraved in a flowing script, with the occasional flourish; only the name of the ship and the Surveyor General himself (No. 190) are given greater prominence.

On the other side of the bowl, the finely engraved armorial decoration comprises a shield bearing the

Croker arms; *argent*, a chevron engraved *gules* between three ravens *ppr*. The shield is surmounted by the helm and the Crest. The Crest is most distinctive, having been first granted by Edward IV to Sir John Croker, who had accompanied the King as the royal cup and standard bearer in the expedition to France in 1475: "A drinking cup *or*, with three *fleurs* of the same issuing therefrom and charged with a rose *gules*." (see B. Burke, *The General Armory of England, Scotland Ireland and Wales*, London 1878.) On the Croker Cup of 1804, the engraving of the Crest is, from the heraldic point of view, incorrect because the three *fleurs* of gold issuing from the cup have been transformed into a sizeable bunch of flowers and foliage. Furthermore, the engraver has failed to depict the "rose *gules*" on the side of the cup and, finally, he has made the drinking cup resemble a two-handled vase. Most probably, the engraver was faithfully copying from a design supplied by those who placed the commission in 1804, but, as yet, the source of this debased version of the Croker Crest has not been traced, either in England or in Ireland.

The motto of the Crokers, DEUS ALIT EOS, is accurately engraved beneath the shield. However, two non-heraldic motifs have been introduced on either side of the shield – presumably on the specific instructions of the owners of the ship that had been lost in December, 1803, at Balbriggan (a small town about 35 kilometers north of Dublin). To the right of the shield, the engraver has depicted the stern of this three-masted sailing vessel, even including its name: 'FRIENDS OF LIVERPOOL'; to the left of the shield, the ship's prow with its winged figure-head and an anchor form an elegant and harmoniously balancing composition. It seems likely, therefore, that an artist was specially commissioned to prepare a finished design incorporating these unique elements and that the engraver was then given this design to copy onto the convex surface of the Cup.

This handsome Presentation Cup was, irrefutably, destined for John Croker (1743–1814), the father of John Wilson Croker, the so-called 'founder' of the Club. His family, the Crokers of Tallow, Co. Waterford, were descended from the long-established medieval family of Crokers in Devon and Cornwall, one branch of which had in the early seventeenth century acquired an estate in Ireland. Fortunately, John Croker late in life had his portrait painted by the London artist, William Haines (1778–1848), and the Club possesses a rare print by Edward Scriven, after Haines (*see* No. 190), probably dating from *circa* 1810. John Croker, after a long career in the Revenue Service, had been chosen in 1800 by the newly appointed Lord Lieutenant of Ireland, Lord

1427-1428

Hardwicke, to be Surveyor General of Customs and Excise, with a salary of £800 p.a. and spacious accommodation in Dublin's palatial new Custom House, designed by James Gandon on the north bank of the River Liffey.

When John Croker retired in 1807, Walter, his only son by his first wife, Catherine, took over the post of Surveyor General but within a few months he had died. John Croker had three children by his second wife, Hester, and he now decided to live in London with his son, John Wilson, who from 1808 to 1832 was MP for Down Patrick and was to become a Privy Councillor for Ireland. Indeed, at the age of seventy-one, John Croker was to die in London (on 29 April, 1814) and to win from Edmund Burke (see No. 118) this tribute: "a man of great abilities and most amiable manners, an able and upright public steward, and universally respected and beloved in private life" (see M. F. Brightfield, *John*

Wilson Croker, Berkeley, California, 1940, p. 2).

In 1814, the passing of the 'Croker Cup' to his son, John Wilson Croker, would under these circumstances seem to be a most likely occurrence and, since John Wilson had married a Miss Pennell, it is not in the least improbable that, in due course, his great, great niece, Miss G. M. Pennell, should have become the owner of both the 'Croker Cup' and the 'Croker Salver' (see No. 1428).

1428 THE CROKER SALVER

Acquired in 1975 under the terms of the bequest of Miss G. M. Pennell with the stipulation that it be cherished for all time in memory of her great, great uncle, John Wilson Croker.

Silver; struck (on the reverse) with the London hall-marks for

PLATE XVII: 1255: Athena, by E.H. Baily, 1829 (spear added later).

PLATE XVIII: (a) John Henning's frieze above Athena, 1829 (pp. 149–156).

(b) 1047: The Acropolis, Athens, by W. Curtis Green.

PLATE XIX: (a) 1240: The Club House, by an unknown artist, "painted for Decimus Burton", 1832–8.

(b) 1244: Waterloo Place, by E. Anscombe, 1860–64.

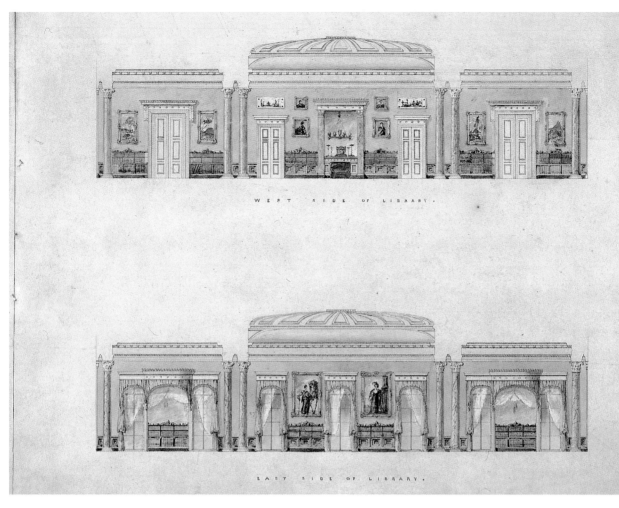

PLATE XX: (a) 1261–2: "West Side of Library" and "East Side of Library", both by Decimus Burton, 1828–9.

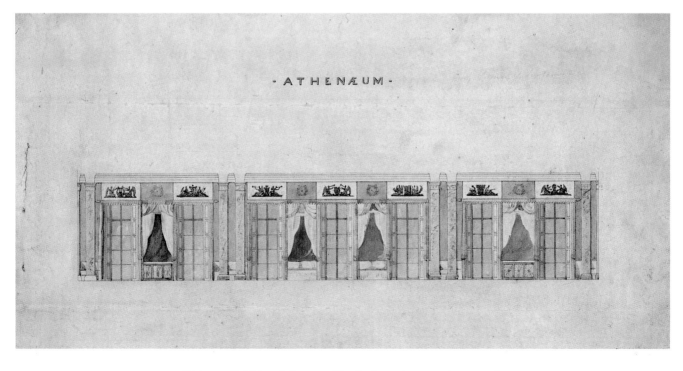

(b) Appendix III (1829): "Approved by the Committee on 25 June, 1829".

PLATE XXI: 1263: The Drawing Room, by James Holland, *c.* 1836.
The final result has been developed from Decimus Burton's designs,
three of which are illustrated opposite on Plate XX.

PLATE XXII: Appendix IV: Re-decoration, 1889–1908.
(a) No. 1: Staircase, with the two Thorwaldsen roundels, by Arthur Lucas.
(b) No. 4: South side of Hall, by Arthur Lucas.

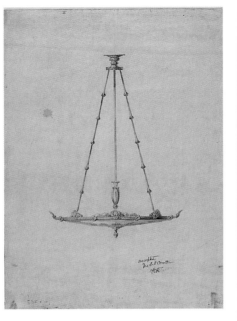

PLATE XXIII: Appendix IV: Re-decoration, 1889–1908.
(a) No. 32: "panel, Coffee Room ceiling", by Sir Ambrose Poynter.
(b) No. 24: Electrolier, by Alma-Tadema.
(c) No. 26: "narrow panel, Coffee Room ceiling",
    by Sir Ambrose Poynter.
(d) No. 23: "frieze for Dome, Drawing Room", by Alma-Tadema.
(e) No. 22: "frieze, Drawing Room", by Alma-Tadema.

PLATE XXIV: (a) 1156: St. James's Square, by David Cox.

(b) 1226: Tynemouth, attributed to Edward Dayes, *c.* 1787.

PLATE XXV: (a) 1290: Elgin Cathedral, by David Roberts, 1848.

(b) 1219: Smyrna Bay, by Holman Hunt, 1855.

PLATE XXVI: 1052: Carros, Var, by Augustus Hare.

PLATE XXVII: 1214: Sallanches, Haute-Savoie, by Charles March Gere, 1926.

PLATE XXVIII: 1209: Temple of Apollo and Theatre of Marcellus, Rome, by John Aldridge, 1951.

PLATE XXIX: 1230: Lily Columns, St Mark's, Venice, by Reginald Barratt, 1911.

PLATE XXX: (a) 1418 and 1417: Two Iznik dishes, last quarter of 16th century.

(b) 1420 and 1421: Two Iznik dishes, c. 1580–5 and c. 1650–75.

PLATE XXXI: (a) 1425: Jade carving, on a hardwood stand, China, 1766.

(b) 1425: Jade carving (another view), China, 1766.

PLATE XXXII: 1429–1448: The Club's first "Private Dinner Service", made of Spode's 'New Stone', Staffordshire, 1830. This selection comprises a 'covered dish' (No.1433), a 'salad bowl' (1434), a 'sauce tureen and stand' (1431) and a 'stand' for a soup tureen (1430).

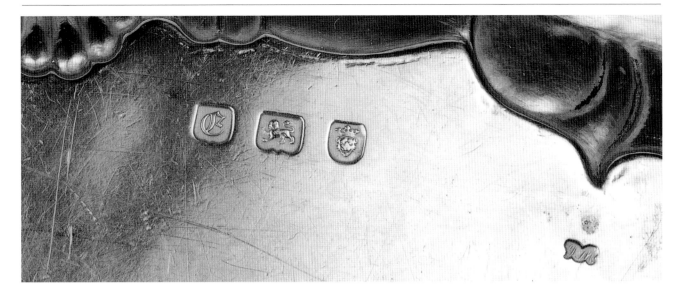

1428

1760 and the maker's mark, 'J.M.' (for James Morrison, who registered his mark in 1740 and whose son was apprenticed to him in 1776 – see A. Grimwade, *London Goldsmiths 1697–1837*, London 1990, No. 1534).

This ornate salver (diam. 36 cm; 14.2 in.) has a raised border in the rococo style and rests on three small 'ball-and-claw' feet. The engraved arms in the centre of the salver are those of Croker, accompanied by the Crest and the Motto (for a description and brief discussion of the heraldry, see the preceding entry, No. 1427). The engraving of the Crest on this salver differs from the version on the 1804 Croker Cup: firstly, the side of the drinking cup is "charged with a rose *gules*" and, secondly, there are only three flowers of gold issuing from the cup. The latter have been given the form of the fleurs-de-lys because, according to family tradition, Louis XI had in 1475 authorised their use by Sir John Croker. In addition the engraver of the Crest on the salver has created a two-handled drinking cup that does not resemble a flower-vase; on the other hand, its design fails – most unexpectedly – to correspond with the style prevailing in London circa 1760 when this salver had been made.

Indeed, the style of engraving on the salver in general, but more especially the decorative cartouche surrounding the shield, is far more characteristic of the nineteenth century than of the rococo period. This London-made salver of 1760 seems, therefore, to be yet another example of that common Victorian practice of engraving the family coat-of-arms on a much older piece of domestic silver plate. Regrettably, nothing was

recorded about its history between 1760 and its putative association with John Wilson Croker (died 1857) when his great, great niece bequeathed the salver to the Club.

1429 CROKER AND THE CLUB'S FIRST "PRIVATE -48 DINNER SERVICE" [PLATE XXXII]

By 17 May, 1824, the task of equipping the infant Club at No. 12, Waterloo Place with the best – but not necessarily the most expensive – furnishings and other essentials was well advanced, largely due to the energy and shrewdness of John Wilson Croker (1780–1857) whose detailed report to the Sub-Committee has been printed *in extenso* (see Ward, pp. 22–5)

The next hundred years was to take its toll and in 1933 the Committee, not surprisingly, decided to retain for posterity no more than a small selection of the best pieces that had survived from the Club's first special dinner and dessert services, along with a representative group of the original drinking-glasses and engraved silver plate used at the dining tables. The remainder of the dinner service – even those items that were chipped or cracked – were to be offered for sale to the members "as mementoes, not more than two pieces to be allowed to any one member" (*Minutes* 26 Sept., 1933). After the more damaged items had been withdrawn, there were still some 96 pieces suitable for sale and these were offered to members at fixed prices.

The Club had retained only a modest selection from the dinner service for the Collection (see below for a detailed list, with measurements) and, today, most of these items are to be seen in an illuminated display cabinet. They were made at the Spode Pottery in Stoke-on-Trent, Staffordshire, with the 'New Stone china body' (to quote the term used in the firm's later recipe book). Indeed, all the Club's items of flat-ware (plates, stands and dishes) bear on the reverse the factory's impressed mark:

SPODES
NEW STONE

This mark was first introduced *circa* 1822, when the improved formula was adopted and New Stone replaced Stone China.

Most of the Club's specimens still bear the Spode Pattern No. 4623 (either in gold or in enamelled red on the reverse). In the archives at the Spode Works in Stoke-on-Trent, this No. 4623 is recorded as a particularly rich version of the highly successful 'Frog Pattern'. Indeed, the firm has preserved one comparable example of the 'Frog Pattern' elegantly inscribed on the reverse: "Used at the Coronation of His Majesty George The 4th – 19th July, 1821" (see L. Whiter, *Spode*, London 1970, pp 195–6, col. pl. IX). A royal association of this kind might be good for business but there is no suggestion that the Club was influenced by this claim.

In meeting the Club's order for this dinner service, Spode created a special mark (in transfer-printed blue): ATHENÆUM. It was applied to the reverse of every piece – even the covers of the tureens and dishes – before firing in the kiln. This clear and bold form of indelible marking was an effective way to make identification easy at a glance and, without doubt, it would have been far less costly than introducing a well-designed, enamelled and gilded 'Athenæum Badge' onto the obverse of each piece, especially if that solution necessitated modifying the expensive 'Frog Pattern, No. 4623', in any way.

Until today this dinner service has always been described as one of the Club's earliest purchases in 1824 and that it was intended for general use in the members' dining-room at 12, Waterloo Place, which Croker reported had been furnished with "twenty dinner tables and five dozen of chairs of the same pattern and the same price… "(Sub-Committee, 17 May, 1824). Recent research in the Club's archives has uncovered evidence that casts doubts on the correctness of these assumptions.

Firstly, there is an invoice dated "Feby 11th, 1830" and a receipt dated "March 4th, 1830" establishing beyond doubt the exact date when the Club received and paid for this dinner service. Not only is the Pattern No. 4623 included by the clerk listing the pieces on the invoice

1435

but the quantities of each article and their total cost are itemised; for example,

"48 plates.. £9-0-0
2 Soup tureens & Stands................... £4-4-0
1 Salad Bowl...................................... £- 18-0

Secondly, all the quantities correspond exactly with the Club's 1830 inventory of "the Private Dinner Service". Furthermore, the valuations given in the Club's 1830 inventory are identical; for example, each plate was valued at 3s.9d, which, when multiplied by 48 totals £9; similarly, a single soup tureen was valued at £2:2s and the single salad bowl at 18s.

The "Private Dinner Service" (as it was termed in the 1830 inventory) was, therefore, ordered and delivered to the Club to coincide with the completion and celebratory opening of Decimus Burton's Club house in the spring of 1830. Indeed, the first General Meeting was held there on 30th May and Croker, the originator and *primum mobile* (as Joseph Jekyll most accurately described him), was in the chair.

Looking at the extant specimens of this special dinner service, there can be little doubt that they had never been subjected to the hard daily 'wear-and-tear' of the members' dining-room. The gilding, for example, shows little sign of the heavy scratching that results from the regular use of knives and forks. This 'Private Dinner Service' was evidently intended for use on intimate occasions when probably no more than eighteen persons would have been present. In listing the specimens preserved by the Club, it was decided that the wording of the original invoice (11th Feby, 1830) should be used:

1429 ONE 'SOUP TUREEN & STAND':

The tureen has survived complete with its cover (Max width, incl. two projecting handles: 33 cm; 13 in.). The stand has moulded flowers on the projecting rims at either end to match the knob on the cover (max. length: 40.5 cm 16 in.).

1430 ONE 'STAND':

identical to the preceding (max. length: 40.5 cm; 16 in.).

This stand originally belonged to the second soup tureen that was supplied as part of this 1830 'Private Dinner Service'.

1431 TWO 'SAUCE TUREENS & STANDS':

-32 Both tureens have survived complete with covers designed to accommodate a ladle or spoon, although Spode seem not to have supplied ceramic ladles or spoons. Both stands have also survived (max. length 20 cm; 7.9 in.).

1433 ONE 'COVERED DISH':

There were originally four of these covered dishes supplied in February, 1830; two were sold in 1933 and, presumably, one had already been broken and lost (max. length 28.5 cm; 11.2 in.).

1434 ONE 'SALAD BOWL':

The invoice only lists the one (H 13 cm; 5.5 in.; diam. of rim 28.1 cm; 11 in.).

1435 EIGHT 'PLATES':

-42 In 1933 thirty plates were offered for sale but it seems no record of their sizes was kept. Each of these eight plates measures the same (diam. 22 cm; 8.75 in.).

1443 TWO 'PLATES':

-44 These specimens differ from the preceding eight plates in being slightly larger (diam. 25.5 cm; 10 in.).

1445 TWO 'LARGE DISHES';

-46 In 1933, nine meat dishes (as they were then called) were offered for sale and their sizes ranged from 12 to 25 in. The Club retained none of the largest but has two of the slightly smaller size (L.51 cm; 20 in.).

1447 TWO 'DISHES':

-48 Although their precise function in 1830 is not clear, they were classified in 1933 as examples of the smallest size of the so-called 'meat dishes' (L.30.5 cm; 12 in.).

Misleadingly, the Club's purchase in 1830 has been described recently as a 'Spode and Copeland' dinner service. This partnership, however, did not concern the Spode factory in Staffordshire but only the London retail business at Portugal House, Lincoln's Inn, where there were show-rooms and offices – and, of course, the printed stationary (bill-heads, receipts, etc.) that bore the words: "Spode & Copeland". The terms of the partnership agreements (made in 1812, 1824 and 1826) are most explicit and, for that reason, the name of Copeland does not appear on any Spode products until after 1833, when W. T. Copeland gained control of the Spode works.

1449 THE BENNETT CUP

Silver; struck with London hall-marks, 1879, and the maker's mark, HH (for H. Holland). This typically Victorian goblet, with its beaded pedestal foot, measures 20.5 cm; 8 in. high and was engraved with the following inscription:

> "Presented by The Establishment of the Athenaeum
> in token of their high respect and affectionate esteem
> to Mr. John Bennett
> House Steward of The Club
> on his retirement after completing fifty-six
> years' service. 26 April, 1880."

1450 A rare photograph of John Bennett, dating from the same time, has been preserved in the Club's archive. It was decided that it should be reproduced alongside the Bennett Cup, the stand of which (*not illustrated*) bears a silver plate engraved with the inscription:

> "Presented to the Club in 1954
> By Mr. W. J. Andrews
> A Member of John Bennett's Family"

John Bennett died in 1883, within three years of his retirement from the Club, where he had started as a page-boy in 1824. He had been the Club's butler for a number of years when, in 1868, the post of Steward

Mr John Bennett.
HOUSE STEWARD OF THE ATHENAEUM
WHO HAVING FAITHFULLY SERVED THE CLUB FOR FIFTY-SIX YEARS
RETIRED IN 1880 WITH ALL HONOUR AND CREDIT,
CARRYING WITH HIM THE RESPECT AND AFFECTIONATE ESTEEM,
OF THE
WHOLE ESTABLISHMENT.

1449-1450

became vacant and, almost immediately, a memorial was sent to the Committee by no less than 106 members (including Browning, Dickens, Matthew Arnold, Archbishop Thomson, Huxley, Tyndall and Wilkie Collins) asking that John Bennett should be appointed. The Committee, even if it had wished otherwise, could not fail to take note of the strength of support and appreciation expressed by so many distinguished members (see Ward, p.72).

1451   THE MICHAEL FARADAY INVALID'S CHAIR:

Early in 1824, the young Michael Faraday (1791–1867), having been introduced at one of the preliminary meetings by Sir Humphry Davy, rashly agreed to act as the Club's earliest Secretary. Within months, he realised that the demands of his scientific research left him insufficient time to deal with the affairs of a new Club of 500 members. In May, 1824, he therefore resigned; the Committee expressed their thanks and without delay, Faraday was admitted a founder member of the Club.

On his recommendation, Edward Magrath, an assistant at the Royal Institution, was appointed his successor; however, for the next thirty years or so Faraday continued to play an important role in the Club's affairs, not least by inventing an apparatus to minimise the ill-effects of the open-gas flare-burners. The sudden deterioration of the leather bindings of so many books in the Club's expanding library may, with the installation of Faraday's 'Perfection Ventilation Apparatus', have been halted (as reported by the Committee in 1844) but members' complaints about fumes led to yet further trials and improvements in 1848 (see Cowell, pp 24–5).

In 1858, Queen Victoria placed a house at Faraday's disposal near Hampton Court and, until his death in 1867, he spent much of his time there, especially after ill-health had forced his resignation from the Royal Institution in 1861. Aware of a now failing memory, he decided to give his last public lecture in June, 1862.

The wooden chair, with its cane panelling is adjustable as a chair, a couch or a bed, and was designed for Faraday by his friend, Thomas Twining, the tea merchant. The wheels originally had an additional handrail so that the occupant could both propel the chair and alter its direction.

The chair was presented to the Club by Dr. J. Rudd Leeson on 28 October 1908, and bears a brass plate with the following inscription: "*Michael Faraday died in this chair, August 25, 1867*". He was buried in Highgate Cemetery.

1452   THE CHARLES DICKENS CHAIR

Gad's Hill Place, an eighteenth century house in a hamlet about 3 miles north-west of Rochester, Kent, was known to Charles Dickens (1812–70) from his boyhood. In 1856, he realised his ambition to own it and set about building a tunnel under the main road that ran through the property so that the garden around the house could be attractively linked to the 'wilderness' in which he had decided to place the Swiss chalet (a present from the actor, Charles Fechter). In the following year, he worked both in the chalet and in the study on the ground floor of the house, writing *Great Expectations* and *The Uncommercial Traveller* (both published in 1860), *Our Mutual Friend* (1865) and the unfinished *Edwin Drood*. Dickens died here suddenly in June, 1870 following an apoplectic fit.

Later that year, an auction sale was held and one of the items sold was the chair that Sir William Fraser Bt. bequeathed to the Athenæum on 21 January 1899. It bears a brass plaque with the following inscription: *This chair was used, when writing, by Charles Dickens, author of the 'Pickwick Papers' It was bought at Gad's Hill Place, August 10*th *1870, by Sir W. Fraser, Bart. Lot 277.*

The chair, with its frame of bird's eye maplewood and its cane back and seat, is on castors. It is said to have been in the Swiss chalet – not in the study in the house. *The Empty Chair* by Sir Luke Fildes, RA (1843–1927), was inspired by the tragic event at Gad's Hill but the two chairs are not the same. In 1970, the Victoria and Albert Museum included the Club's chair in a special exhibition and published it in the Catalogue: '*Charles Dickens: An Exhibition to commemorate the centenary of his death, June–September, 1970* (London, 1970), p. 105, no. N.1. Also in the V&A Exhibition was a print *after* the painting by Fildes, see cat. no. M.42 (pl.89).

1453   THACKERAY'S BILLIARD CUE

This cue, a cherished relic of the Club's underground Billiard Room, was duly inscribed *William Makepeace Thackeray's Billiard Cue, 1851–1863* and measures L. 145.5 cm (57¼ in.). It was given a place of honour above the cue-rack, as can be seen in John Ward's pictorial record of a typical evening's game in progress in 1961 (see No. 1272).

Later that year, the demolition of the Billiard Room began; it was a necessary part of the plans to create a

1452, 1453, 1451 (left to right)

Ladies' Annexe within the Club house itself and, on completion, it was decided that Thackeray's Billiard Cue should be re-hung near to the spot where, for more than one hundred years, members had been able to enjoy this most relaxing of pastimes on two full-sized tables. As a result, the north-east corner of the Ladies' Annexe is to this day adorned – some might say, incongruously – with this, and several other, reminders of this colourful (but now firmly closed) chapter in the history of the Club.

In Thackeray's own life-time, members "could no more smoke in the Athenæum than they could smoke in church" (Ward, p. 67) – and the Billiard Room was no exception. Later in the 1860s, the first concessionary establishment of a 'Smoking Room' (on the top floor) led to demands for the privilege to be extended, not least from those frequenting the Billiard Room; in time, they prevailed and the ante-room soon became known as 'The Lower Smoking Room' (see No. 1268, for George Thomson's detailed sketch of 1897).

An illustration of Thackeray's early self-portrait (No. 840) has also been included, together with a brief reference to his troubled election to the Club in 1850–1.

1454   THE BILLIARD TROPHY OF THE ATHENÆUM

Silver, struck with the London hall-marks for 1908; also, the maker's mark H.L. (for H. Lambert). In addition, the firm's oval mark (stamped inside the lid): LAMBERT 12 COVENTRY ST. Dimensions (with plinth) 15.5 cm × 39.1 cm × 25.3 cm; 6.1 in. × 15.5 in. × 10 in.)

Made in the form of a billiard table, this silver trophy has its six pockets made of a fine mesh of silver threads (added individually to the table). On the top two silver cues are placed so that the one lies across the other and thereby almost hides the fine line of the join between the two halves of the table top, both of which have been hinged at the far ends of the table. On lifting up each half, a shallow compartment, lined with wood, and extending the length of the table, is revealed – presumably for cigars.

The silver billiard table is mounted on an ebony plinth, to which are fixed inscribed silver plaques recording the name of the member declared each year to be the Club's Billiard Champion from 1909–1913, 1919–1939 and 1947–1960.

Also inscribed on silver (on the plinth): *Presented to the Billiard Room of the Athenaeum by Sir Hubert E. J. Jerningham, 1909*. Indeed, the trophy was normally left on the mantelpiece in the Billiard Room. Sir Hubert

Jerningham KCMG, FSA, FZS, DL (1842–1914) was elected a member in 1877 and, after his career in the Diplomatic Service ended in 1900, he lived principally in London and Berwick-on-Tweed. He was author of several works, copies of which are in the Library, but, alas, he seems never to have won the annual Billiard Championship of the Athenæum, although he was to inspire the creation of a memorial sculptural relief (see the following entry, No. 1455).

1455   THE BILLIARD CHAMPIONS WALL-PLAQUE OF 1914

This unsigned polychrome and gilded glazed relief (62 cm × 43.4 cm; 24 in. × 17 in.) depicts the standing figure of Athene holding a laurel wreath over the rectangular tablet, on which has been painted – presumably in, or soon after, 1947 – a chronological list of those members who had been declared winners of the Club's Billiard Trophy (awarded annually) in 1909–1913, 1919–1939 and in 1947.

The incised (and coloured) Greek inscription above the figure of Athene may be translated as follows:

> 'A crown to identify here in the amphitheatre of the Athenæum he who is best with ball against ball.'

A second inscription, also incised and coloured, is in English (near the base of the relief): "*In memory of our old and generous friend, Sir Hubert Jerningham from Lord Charles B. Bruce*".

In 1914 the death of Sir Hubert Jerningham, the donor of the silver Billiard Trophy (No. 1454), caused Lord Charles Frederick Brudenall Bruce (died 1935–6), who had been elected a member in 1882 just five years after his old friend, to commission this evocative relief. Significantly, its artistic merits were more widely enjoyed when in November, 1922, the loan of this plaque to the Arts and Crafts Exhibition was requested (and approved by the Club's Executive Committee).

As a postscript, reference should be made to an item preserved (and framed) in the Club's archive:

1456   *A humorous exchange in 1933* between "the Library Sub-Committee" (apparently composed of "S.H." and "A.M.H.") and "the Billiard Players of the Athenæum".

(i) THE ATHENÆUM
Resolution of the General Committee proposed by the Library Sub-Committee and, in the absence of any billiard player, passed unanimously, on 1ˢᵗ April 1933: that

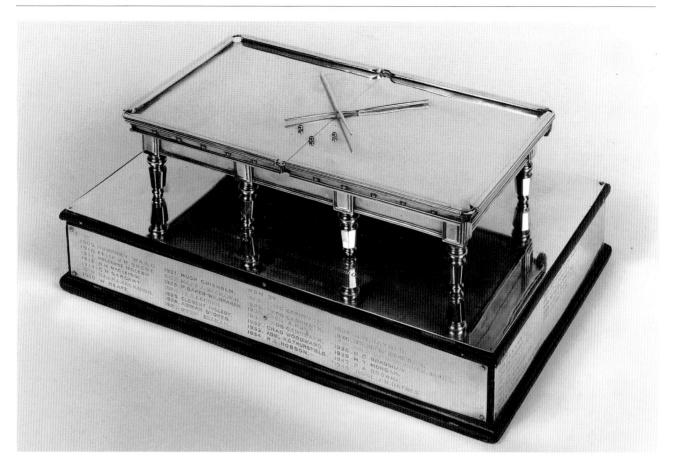

1454

the accompanying extract be placed on permanent exhibition in a prominent place in the billiard room as a constant reminder to players of the futility and fatuity of their
proceedings

> NOR ENVY WE aught more their idle sport,
> Who pant with application misapplied
> To trivial toys, and, pushing iv'ry balls
> Across a velvet level, feel a joy
> Akin to rapture when the bauble finds
> Its destin'd goal, of difficult access.

> William Cowper
> *The Task*, IV, 272–294

(ii) *The Billiard Players are deeply sensible of the kindly
interest that doubtless prompted the 'Resolution' of the
Library Sub-Committee, now upon the Billiard Room
mantle piece, the "futility and fatuity" of which are indeed
worthy of its date. They desire to refer the Authors of this
Resolution to the following extract from the same poem of
William Cowper and to express their opinion that this
extract might with advantage be placed on permanent
exhibition in the Drawing Room or South Library*

> Books are not seldom talismans and spells,
> By which the magic art of shrewder wits
> Holds an unthinking multitude enthrall'd,
> Some to the fascination of a name
> Surrender judgement hoodwink'd. Some
> the style
> Infatuates, and through labyrinths and wilds
> Of error leads them, by a tune entranced.
> While sloth seduces more, too weak to bear
> The insupportable fatigue of thought,
> And swallowing therefore, without pause
> or choice,
> The total grist unsifted, husks and all.

> William Cowper
> *The Task*, IV 98–108

1457 GOULD'S 'EAGLE OWL' AND THREE
–59 'TEMPLE OWLS' (*Athene Noctua*)

1457 John Gould FRS (1804–1881), the distinguished
ornithologist and creator of those highly-prized volumes on the birds of the world, was elected a member

ΣΦΑΙΡΑΝ ΕΠΙ ΣΦΑΙΡΗΙ ΙΟΥΝΕΙΝ ΟΣΤΙΣ ΑΡΙΣΤΟΣ
ΕΝΘΑΔ' ΑΘΗΝΑΙΗΣ ΑΜΦΙΘΕΤΩ ΣΤΕΦΑΝΟΝ

1909	HVMPHREY WARD
1910	FELIX J·H·SKENE
1911	HOLCOMBE INGLEBY
1912	N·M·MACLEHOSE
1913	C·H·SARGANT
1919	MAJ. P·A·MACMAHON
1920	W·HEAPE
1921	HVGH CHISHOLM
1922	MAJ. P·A·MACMAHON
1923	P·BAKER·WILBRAHAM
1924	W·A·LOCKER
1925	CLEMENT INGLEBY
1926	ADRIAN STOKES
1927	OWEN SEAMAN
1928	THOS·CARNWATH
1929	THOS·CARNWATH
1930	CECIL A·HVNT
1931	THOS·CARNWATH
1932	CHAD WOODWARD
1933	ADML. H·G·THVRSFIELD
1934	R·L·HOBSON
1935	J·N·DAYNES
1936	BISHOP OF WORCESTER
1937	SIR P·BAKER-WILBRAHAM BART
1938	H·C·BRADSHAW
1939	M·T·MORGAN
1947	P·A·BROWNE

IN MEMORY OF OVR OLD AND GENEROVS FRIEND SIR HVBERT JERNINGHAM
FROM LORD CHARLES B BRVCE

1455

under Rule II in 1854 and, subsequently, presented a large specimen of the 'Eagle Owl'. In 1874, its prime location in the Drawing Room was questioned and, later that year, it had been moved into the ante-room of the Billiard Room, later known as the Lower Smoking Room; indeed, it dominates the foreground of George Thomson's sketch of 1897 (No. 1268). Seven years earlier, Sir William Flower, Director of the Natural History Museum, had arranged for essential repairs to be expertly carried out but, thereafter, Gould's 'Eagle Owl' seems to have attracted no official attention. By 1961, when the demolition of the Billiard Room and its environs would have required its removal, the noble bird failed to receive even the briefest mention. Its fate remains shrouded in uncertainty.

1458 Two 'Temple Owls' (*Athene Noctua*), preserved together in the one glazed case (32 cm × 20.3 cm; 12.6 in. × 8 in.), were presented in 1902 by H.E. Dresser, who was also the donor of an oil painting, *A Golden Eagle and an Arctic Hare* (by von Wright) in 1908–9. This painting was

recorded, as late as 1932, hanging in the Billiard Room but it is no longer in the Collection. Dresser was author of a 9-volume work on the *History of the Birds of Europe* (1871–96), a copy of which is in the Club's Library, together with several other related books by this distinguished authority.

1459 One 'Temple Owl' (*Athene Noctua*), presented by Dr. F. William Cock FSA in 1919, is preserved in a slightly smaller glazed case.

1460 THE 'CORONATION BOWL' WITH ATHENA'S OWL

Silver centrepiece in the form of a circular bowl with a central domed boss supporting the silver figure of a 'Temple-Owl' (*Athene Noctua*). Around the inside of the bowl (below the rim), the Homeric Greek inscription, taken from *The Odyssey* (Book 6, line 149), is decoratively engraved and may be translated:

'Whether you are mortal or divine, I now supplicate thee, O! Queen'

On the underside of the bowl, a finely engraved inscription has been added by the maker:

'Made for the Athenæum in the year of the Coronation of Queen Elizabeth II./Designer and maker Leslie Durbin' (Diam [of rim] 31.9 cm; 12.5 in.)

Made in London in 1953 by Leslie Durbin (born 1913).

On Tuesday, 16th March, 1954, the Club held a formal Dinner chaired by Sir Frederick White, to celebrate the completion of 'The Coronation Bowl' and the guest of honour, Leslie Durbin, spoke about his experiences as a practising goldsmith and artist. The Dinner, which was attended by those members who had subscribed to 'The Coronation Bowl', was a fitting inaugural occasion for this fine modern work of art.

Leslie Durbin, a Londoner, was trained at the Central School of Arts and Crafts and, in 1929, was apprenticed to Omar Ramsden (1873–1939). He won the competition for the Chapel of Chivalry's plate at the new Guildford Cathedral and the results of this major commission were to be seen at Goldsmith's Hall in the 1938 Exhibition of Modern Silverwork.

During World War II, Leslie Durbin served in the Royal Air Force but in 1943 he was given indefinite leave to work on the famous 'Stalingrad Sword', the Sword of Honour with which King George VI was determined to commemorate the heroic defence of Stalingrad. Designs from the four successful competitors (R.M.Y. Gleadowe, Percy Metcalfe, Leslie Durbin and Cyril

1458

Skinner) had been submitted to the Palace and on 31 March, 1943, the King chose the meticulous line drawing by Gleadowe, the former Slade Professor at Oxford (No. 331).

Gleadowe, however, was not a craftsman and so Leslie Durbin was given the task of executing all the gold and silver parts. Sadly, Gleadowe's health deteriorated as the tight schedule advanced and Leslie Durbin's role correspondingly grew. By October, 1943, the Sword was ready for exhibition: at Goldsmith's Hall (3 days), at the V & A Museum (2 days) and at Westminster Abbey before leaving London to be shown (for one day only) in Belfast, Cardiff, Edinburgh, Glasgow, Birmingham, Bristol, Coventry, Derby, Liverpool, Manchester, Newcastle, Plymouth, Sheffield, Stoke-on-Trent and Winchester. Long queues of people formed at each place and everywhere it was accompanied by Leslie Durbin. His name became well known and in October, he was invested with the MVO. (He was awarded, in 1976, the CBE.)

Significantly, the City of Volgograd (formerly Stalingrad) graciously allowed the Sword to return to London in 1982 to be included in the *Leslie Durbin Retrospective Exhibition* held at Goldsmith's Hall (cat. no. 1, with illustrations).

When being presented with an honorary degree at Cambridge in 1963, Leslie Durbin was praised as a craftsman "inspired by Minerva" – but, perhaps, the Orator should have preferred, "by Athena".

1461 THE CLUB SEALS AND GAVEL
-7

In the past, there has been confusion about the role played by Sir Francis Chantrey (No.155) in the creation of the Club's seal in 1824–5 (see Cowell, p.13, where it is stated to be both "executed by Chantrey and engraved by William Wyon").

Although Chantrey, a member of the first working Sub-Committee (set up on February 16, 1824), offered "to execute and present a seal for the Club after a design by Sir Thomas Lawrence" (*Minutes*, 6 July, 1824), there is no evidence that Chantrey engraved any seal for the Club or, indeed, that he was ever the donor of a Club seal.

Furthermore, no Lawrence design seems to have existed at the time of Chantrey's offer, because a week later the Committee had a letter sent to Sir Thomas Lawrence informing him of Chantrey's proposal and expressing the hope that he might "give Mr. Chantrey a Design for the seal" (*Minutes*, 13 July, 1824). The reply has not been preserved. However, it would seem that by the following December Sir Thomas Lawrence, PRA and Trustee of the Club, had chosen his subject and completed his design (No.1276; Pl. I(a)) but, instead of giving it to Chantrey, he showed it to the Committee. As a result, the Committee "resolved that a head of Minerva be adopted for the seal of the Club" (*Minutes*, 28 December, 1824).

Eleven months later, the task of making the Club seal appears to have been completed and, once again, the Committee considered the matter. Omitting any mention of Chantrey, the Committee expressed complete satisfaction with the finished seal (No. 1461), and, without hesitation, they decided to commission a smaller, but otherwise identical, seal: "*Resolved that Minerva's Head according to the design of Sir Thomas Lawrence, executed by Mr. Wyon, be adopted as the Seal of the Club...That a seal of half dimensions after the same design be executed by Mr. Wyon.*" (*Minutes*, 8 November, 1825)

Any remaining doubts about Chantrey's early withdrawal from this project are dispelled by the conclusive evidence in 1826 that Chantrey did not make a present to the Club of either seal: "*An account from Mr. Wyon amounting to £90 for engraving two seals was presented and ordered for payment.*" (*Minutes*, 20 May, 1826)

1460

1461 THE CLUB SEAL (larger size) by William
Wyon, 1825

Steel, oval, engraved with the head of Athena to right
(after the design by Sir Thomas Lawrence, PRA); signed
below the truncation: W. Wyon. (H. 4.4 cm (1.7 in.);
Total L. (with handle) 10.1 cm (4 in.), The handle of
turned ivory has a flat surface at the top; probably made
and attached in October/November, 1825.
Commissioned by the Club, 1825.

1462 THE CLUB SEAL (smaller size) by William
Wyon, 1826

Steel, oval, engraved with the head of Athena as in No.
1461 but "of half dimensions" (as quoted above from
Minutes, 8, Nov. 1825). Its handle was made of turned
ivory.

Commissioned by the Club; no longer in the
Collection following the theft in February, 1987.

William Wyon, RA (1795–1851), chief engraver at the

Royal Mint, was elected a member in 1830 (see No.
941)and later made a youthful portrait of Queen
Victoria for the coinage. He belonged to a famous family of seal-engravers, the first of whom probably came to
this country from Cologne in the reign of George II; for
a history of the family, see L. Forrer, *The Wyons*
(London, 1917; reprinted from Vol. VI of the
Biographical Dictionary of Medallists).

1463 IMPRESSION (from the Club seal,
No. 1461) by Sir Emery Walker, FSA

Plaster, oval, ivory-coloured and preserved in a specially
made glazed-top box. Presented by Sir Emery Walker, 1928.

Sir Emery Walker (1851–1953), a prominent figure in
the new Arts and Crafts Exhibition Society, was elected
a member in 1924 and was knighted in 1930. He is said to
have made this impression of the Club's seal when he
was engraving the plate for the Club's new book-plate, a
skill he had acquired as a young printer and engraver. At

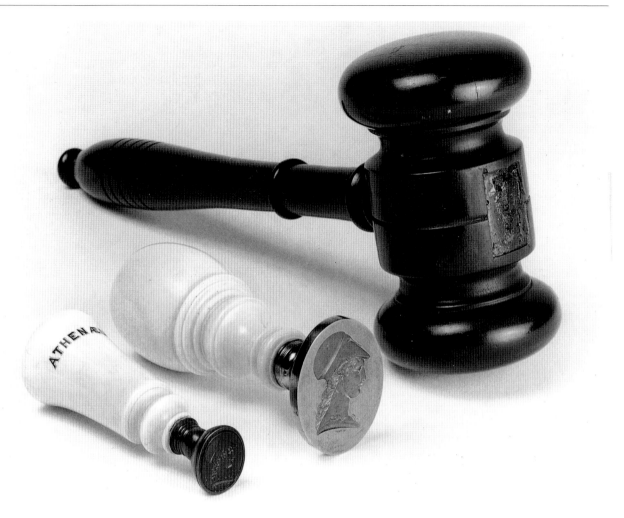

1465, 1461, 1467 (left to right; 1467 photographed without the later silver plaque).

the same time, he made and donated a version of the Club seal in brass (No. 1464).

1464 COPY OF THE CLUB SEAL
by Sir Emery Walker, FSA, 1928

Brass, oval, with the head of Athena; mounted with an ivory handle. No further details or dimensions can be given as the object is no longer in the Collection nor has any photographic record of it been found.
Presented by Sir Emery Walker, FSA, 1928.

1465 THE CLUB SEAL FOR MEMBERS' USE

Origin uncertain; attributed to William Tassie (1777–1860) or to his partner and (after 1840) successor, John Wilson.

Glass, of a blackish appearance, with the head of Athena to right and (below the truncation) W. WYON; and, behind Athena's head and neck, a second inscription: 'Athenæum' (in Greek).

This glass-paste *intaglio* is set in a silver mount attached to a turned ivory handle inscribed (in black) 'ATHENÆUM'. H. 2.1 cm (0.75 in.); Total L (with handle) 8.4 cm (3.3 in.) Probably commissioned by the Club soon after the Club House opened in 1830, it was withdrawn from the Writing Room in 1892 and, thereafter, kept with the Club's memorabilia. Subsequently, it was described as a cast made from the smaller Club seal (No. 1462) but if that statement is correct, then the second inscription (in Greek) must have been added after the cast had been made in glass. Certainly, the lettering of the second inscription seems slightly less assured.

1466 IMPRESSION OF THE CLUB SEAL (larger size)

Origin uncertain; made of a white plaster, oval and mounted in an elaborate gilt-wood picture-frame (under glass) dating from mid-19th century. At the time of presentation, this gift was described as "a Replica of a Tassie after the Club Seal" (Annual Report of the Committee, 6 May, 1940) but, more probably, it is a good quality impression taken directly from the larger Club seal (No. 1461), since no Tassie glass-paste of the corresponding size has been recorded (4.4 cm; 1.7 in.). Presented by Arthur Jaffé, 1939.

1467 THE CLUB GAVEL 1902

Ebony, turned and polished; (L. 25.4 cm; 10 in.)this gavel was used by the Chairman, Lord Avebury, at the dinner given by the Athenæum to celebrate the institution of the Order of Merit by King Edward VII on 26 June, 1902.

The dinner was held on 25 July and the twelve members of this high Order were the invited guests. Many of them were members of the Club and most were able to accept, although ill-health prevented two from staying after the reception. The dinner was attended by 150 members and among the speakers were the veteran Lord Roberts and the Rt Hon Arthur Balfour, MP, who on behalf of the twelve proposed a vote of thanks to the Chairman.

The telegram sent by HM the King, together with the seating plan and the menu cards signed by those present, have been preserved in the Club archive. Set in the head of the gavel, an engraved silver plaque (not illustrated) bears the inscription: THE ATHENÆUM / DINNER TO MEMBERS / OF THE ORDER OF MERIT / 25 JULY 1902.

1468 A DIFFRACTION GRATING RULED WITH 22,139 LINES TO THE INCH by Archibald Campbell, 1st Baron Blythswood, circa 1900

The polished speculum-metal mirror (or plate) is securely mounted under glass within a shallow, hinged case of wood fitted with lock and key. H. of wooden case 13.4 cm (5½ in) An engraved plate (beneath the mirror) is inscribed:

Presented by
Lord Blythswood
to the Athenæum Club, Sept. 1903
on his being elected.
22,139 lines. Cut at Blythswood, Scotland

1468

Born in 1835, he was the son of Archibald Douglas, 17th laird of Mains, Dumbartonshire, who assumed the name of Campbell in 1838 on succeeding his cousin as 12th laird of Blythswood. He retired from the army in 1868, having been severely wounded at Sebastopol (see No. 1217), and embarked on a political career, becoming an MP before being raised to the peerage in 1892.

He also devoted much of his wealth to the advancement of science under the guidance of his friend, Lord Kelvin (No. 483), and others. The resources of his splendidly equipped laboratory at Blythswood were made freely available to this circle of scientists. Much of his own time and expertise in the last decades of the century were concentrated upon the construction – and perfecting – of precision instruments, especially his great dividing engine for ruling diffraction gratings. He published, with H. S. Allen, *Effects of Errors in Ruling on the Appearance of a Diffraction Grating* (Phil. Mag. Jan. 1902 and Nov 1903). A diffraction grating is able to disperse a beam of various wavelengths into a spectrum of associated lines because of the principle of diffraction. It is hoped soon to display Lord Blythswood's gift with a special light source so that its optical effects can be observed and its purpose more clearly appreciated.

One year before his death in 1908, he was elected FRS in recognition of his contribution as a specialist and a 'patron'. The 'Blythswood Collection' of instruments and related apparatus were deposited by his widow with the National Physical Laboratory at Teddington.

1469

lived for a long time in London, where the head of his firm had for many years been the Swiss Consul-General. He was, however, the first member of his family to become British Consul-General in Switzerland. He was noted for his antiquarian interests and played an important role in ensuring that the new Swiss National Museum should be sited in his native city of Zurich. His principal service to Britain on the eve of the Boer War was to discover that the Boers had planned – but had failed to pay in advance, as contracted – for maps of the uncharted Transvaal to be secretly made at Winterthur. Henry Angst, having informed our War Office, quickly purchased the maps and had them conveyed to London. In 1902, he was made CMG and, some years later, KCMG. His election to the Club took place in 1903 and his death occurred in 1922; in the following year, the silver ewer came to the Club.

The form of this ewer had been popularised in England by Josiah Wedgwood, who first produced it in 1775 in his new black basalt ware at his Staffordshire factory of 'Etruria'. Wedgwood marketed it as one of a pair of ewers: "Sacred to Bacchus" and "Sacred to Neptune" but, more usually, they became known as the "wine and water" ewers. Wedgwood was indebted on this occasion to John Flaxman (1726–95), who had sent him two plaster models; both survive, together with Flaxman's invoice for 3 guineas (dated 25 March 1775), in the Wedgwood Museum. However, the assumption that Flaxman was the creator of the highly original design of these ewers is disputed because the French sculptor, Clodion (1738–1814), is also credited with producing models of this design (see M. Thiron, *Les Adam et les Clodions*, Paris, 1885, p. 355). In England, the success of Wedgwood's 'wine and water' ewers led to their design being copied in silver and other highly prized materials, even malachite, throughout the nineteenth century.

1469 THE ANGST EWER

Silver; struck (under the lip) with London hall-marks, 1904; also, the maker's mark: E Barnard & Sons. H. (excl. plinth) 41 cm; 16.1 in.; Total H. 52.2 cm; 20.6 in.

Mounted on a high wooden plinth, to which are attached two silver plaques, each struck with the London hall-marks for 1916 and engraved *Presented by His Majesty's Government to Sir Henry Angst, KCMG, his Britannic Majesty's Consul-General at Zurich in recognition of his long career of distinguished service under Three British Sovereigns*. The plaque on the reverse bears the Royal Coat-of-arms and is inscribed *JULY* 1916.

Dr. Henry Angst (1847–1922)) was of Swiss birth but

1470 THE BANCROFT CUP AND COVER

Silver, struck (close to the left handle) with the Dublin hall-marks but without a date-letter mark. The maker's mark, 'R.T.' (for Richard Tudor, of 20, Skinner Row, Dublin, who was registered in 1784 – see D. Bennett, *Irish Georgian Silver*, London, 1972, no 252). The second maker's mark, 'J.L.' (in script and within a cusped oval) was used by John Locker, a leading Dublin silversmith, whose workshop was at its most productive in the 1770s. The National Museum of Ireland possesses five marked examples of his work bearing date-letters ranging from 1773–79.

1470

The cover is also struck with the Dublin hall-marks and has a date-letter mark, 'X' (for 1794); The maker's mark is largely illegible but resembles the R.T. mark (for Richard Tudor). H. 37.5 cm (14.7 in.; W. (incl. handles) 33 cm (13 in.).

1470

50

The foot-rim bears an engraved inscription:

Presented to the Athenæum by George Pleydell Bancroft in memory of his Father, Sir Squire Bancroft, Obit 19 April, 1926.

The gift was made in 1927.

Eleven years later, George Pleydell Bancroft presented a portrait in oils of his father painted by W W Ouless in 1881 (No. 50). Both gifts are illustrated here, side by side.

The silver cup has (on either side) an embossed oval medallion, one of which is blank whereas the other is engraved with the head of Athena – perhaps added just prior to the presentation of the cup to the Club.

The rococo style of the cup itself is typical of Dublin silver of the 1770s; for another example, see the two handled cup (without cover) made in Dublin in 1775 by Richard Williams (National Museum of Ireland, no. 386 1887; illustrated in *Irish Silver from the Seventeenth to the Nineteenth Century* (Smithsonian Institution, 1982, p. 44, no. 46). The cover of the Bancroft cup (with the date letter, 1794) may, therefore, be a later replacement or an addition in matching style. The Cup itself would, therefore, be best described as the work of John Locker in the 1770s, to which was probably added in 1794 the mark 'R.T.' The Cup would have been in Richard Tudor's workshop while he was making the new cover for it.

APPENDIX I

AN ALBUM OF ETCHINGS BY MARY DAWSON TURNER

Etchings by Mary Dawson Turner (1774–1850). She was second daughter of William Palgrave of Coltishall, married Dawson Turner 1796, and had eleven children of whom five were daughters, skilled artists themselves. They were taught by John Sell Cotman, and Mrs Dawson Turner's *Hundred Etchings* were presented to the Club by Dawson Turner in 1830, in a bound album lettered: TURNER'S ETCHINGS. Twelve sets of her *Fifty Etchings* were specially bound by her husband in 1823, as presents for his friends. In most of the plates she had help from her teacher, the engraver William Camden Edwards

Literature: Minutes 29 August 1830, p. 227; C.J. Palmer & S. Tucker, *Palgrave Family Memorials* (Norwich 1878), pp. 90–4; Warren R. Dawson, *Journ. of Soc. for Bibliography of Natural History* III (Dec 1958) pp. 303–10; A.N.L. Munby, *The Cult of the Autograph Letter in England* (1962), chapter III, 'Dawson Turner'.

1 **Alderson. James,** MD, of Norwich and father of Mrs Opie, from a drawing by John Opie, 1800

2 **Anglesey, Marquess of** (see No. 23), from a drawing by Chantrey, 1819

3 **Aubrey, John** (1626–97), antiquary, from a drawing in the Ashmolean Museum, 1665

4 **Banks, Sir Joseph, Bt.** 1743–1820, PRS, from a drawing by Thomas Phillips, 1816

5 **Banks, Sir Joseph,** from a medal by Pistrucci, 1819

6 **Bidder, George** 1806–78, 'the calculating boy', from a drawing by J.S. Cotman, 1819

7 **Bird, Edward** 1772–1819, artist, from a drawing by Chantrey, 1816

8 **Blagden, Sir Charles** 1748–1820, physician, from a drawing by Thomas Phillips, 1816

9 **Burchell, William John** c.1782–1863, explorer and naturalist, from a drawing by J.S. Cotman, 1816

10 **Burney, Rev Charles** (see No. 120), from a drawing by Thomas Phillips, 1816

11 **Cambridge,** Richard Owen 1777–1802, author of satirical verse, from a drawing by Ozias Humphry, 1781

12 **Canning, George** (see No. 138), from a drawing by Chantrey, 1821

13 **Canova, Antonio** 1757–1822, sculptor, from a drawing by Thomas Phillips, 1816

14 **Clarke, Edward Daniel** 1769–1822, traveller and Cambridge University librarian, from a painting by John Opie, 1807

15 **Coke, Thomas William** (see No. 518), from a drawing by R.R. Reinagle, 1817

16 **Coster, De,** guide to Napoleon at Waterloo, from a drawing by C.A. Stothard, 1820

17 **Cotman, John Sell** 1782–1842, author of *Antiquities* and landscape painter, from a drawing by J.P. Davis, 1818

18 **Baron Dominique Nenon** 1747–1825, French artist and first Director of the Louvre, from a drawing by H.J. Hesse, 1816

19 **Decandolle, Augustin Pyrame** 1778–1841, Professor of Botany, Montpellier, etching 1816

20 **Dibdin, Rev Thomas** (see No. 230). from a drawing by Mrs F. Palgrave (Elizabeth Turner), 1821

21 **Edwards, Edward** 1738–1806, etcher and author of *Anecdotes of Painters,* from a drawing by Ozias Humphry, 1777

22* **Edwards, William Camden** (see No. 258), finished by Edwards himself, 1817, from a drawing by J.P. Davis, 1815

23 **Englefield, Sir Henry, Bt.** 1752–1822, antiquary, from a drawing by J.S. Cotman, 1815

24 **Flaxman, John** 1755–1826, sculptor, from a drawing by Ozias Humphry, 1778

25 **Foscolo, Ugo** 1778–1827, Italian poet, from a picture by H.J. Fradelle, 1816

26 **Fraser, Miss Susanna,** from a drawing by Thomas Phillips, 1817

27 **Gooch, Thomas Sherlock** 1761–1851, MP for Suffolk, from a picture by G.H. Harlow, 1818

28 **Graham, Maria, later Lady Callcott** 1785–1842, author of *Journal of a Residence in India, Little Arthur's History of England, &c.* from a drawing in Rome by Eastlake, 1818

29 **Gunn, Rev William** 1750–1841, translator of Nennius, from a drawing by Mrs F. Palgrave (Mrs Turner's second daughter, Elizabeth), 1821

30 **Gurney, Hudson** 1775–1864, MP, antiquary and Dawson Turner's banking partner, from a picture by Opie, 1797

31 **Gage, Sir Thomas, Bt.** 1781–1820, of Hengrave, from a miniature by Charles Jagger, 1806

32 **Hales, John** d.1571, founder of the Free School at Coventry, from a picture given to the school in 1704

33 **Hall, John** 1739–97, Historical Engraver to His Majesty, from a drawing by Ozias Humphry, 1782

34 **Harrington, James** 1611–77, author of *Oceana*, from a portrait after Lely in the possession of Colonel Samuel at Upton Hall (now NPG)

35 **Haydon, Benjamin Robert** 1786–1846, painter, from a drawing by Wilkie, 1815

36 **Heath, James** 1757–1834, Historical Engraver to His Majesty &c., from a drawing by W. Behnes, 1819

37 **Heath, Charles** 1785–1848, engraver, from a drawing by H. Corbould, 1822

38 **Heber, Reginald** (see No 395), from a picture by T. Phillips

39 **Hooker, W.J.** (see No. 425), from a drawing by J.S. Cotman, 1813

40 **Hooker, Mrs** (formerly Miss Turner), from a drawing by T. Phillips, 1814

41 **Hoole, John** 1727–1803, translator of Tasso, from a drawing by Ozias Humphry, 1784

42 **Humboldt, Alexander von** 1769–1859, German traveller, from an original sketch by T. Phillips, 1815

43 **Johnson, Samuel** (see No. 466), from a drawing by Ozias Humphry. 1773

44 **Lowry, Wilson** 1762, 1824, engraver, from a drawing by Mrs Hemmings, 1818

45 **Manby, George William** 1765–1854, inventor of life-saving apparatus, from a drawing by S. De Koster, 1810

46 **Mansel, William Lort** 1753–1820, Bishop of Bristol, from a drawing by G.H. Harlow, 1815

47 **Marsden, William** 1754–1836, author of *History of Sumatra*, from a drawing by T. Phillips, 1815

48 **Miller, William**, publisher (see No. 596), from a drawing by T. Phillips, 1814

49 **Opie, Amelia** 1769–1853, novelist, from a picture by J. Opie, 1798

50 **Palgrave, William**, father of Mrs Dawson Turner, from a picture by S. Lane, 1810

51 **Palgrave, Elizabeth, Lady**, formerly Miss Elizabeth Turner, d. 1852, from a drawing by J.P. Davis, 1816

52 **Perkins, Jacob** 1766–1849, American inventor of siderography, from a drawing by C.R. Leslie, 1821

53 **Phillips, Thomas** 1770–1845, portrait painter and friend of the Turner family, from a self-portrait, 1815

54 **Phillips, Mrs,** wife of Thomas Phillips, from a drawing by T. Phillips, 1814

55 **Phillips, Miss and Miss Fraser,** from a drawing by T. Phillips, 1817

56 **Pitt, Ann,** sister to the Earl of Chatham, from a drawing by Ozias Humphry, 1777

57 **Potter, Rev Robert** 1721–1804, translator of Aeschylus, from a drawing by A. Payne, 1789

58 **Rigby, Edward,** 1747–1821, physician and mayor of Norwich, from a picture by M. Sharp, 1815

59** **Roberts, Richard** (Jones) of Liverpool, etched by Mrs Turner, 1819, to illustrate Roscoe's *Memoirs of R.R. Jones of Aberdaron* (1822)

60 **Roscoe, William** 1753–1831, Liverpool historian, from a cast of a medallion by J. Gibson, 1813

61 **Scott, Sir William** (later Lord Stowell see No. 809), from a drawing by T. Phillips, 1816

62 **Serres, Dominic** 1722–93, maritime painter, from a drawing by Ozias Humphry, 1778

63 **Sharp, Thomas** 1770-1841, *author of Coventry Mysteries,* from a drawing by J.S. Cotman, 1823

64 **Siddons, Mrs Sarah** 1755–1831, actress, from a drawing by G.H. Harlow, 1813

65 **Siddons, Mrs,** from a drawing by G.H. Harlow, 1813

66 **Sims, John** 1749–1831, botanist and physician, from a medallion by Pistrucci, 1817

67 **Smith, Sir James Edward** 1759–1828, botanist, founder of the Linnean Society of London, as a child, from a drawing by T. Worlidge, 1763

68 **Southey, Robert,** poet laureate (see No.789), from a drawing by T. Phillips, 1815

69 **Staël, Madame de** 1766–1817, novelist, from a drawing by T. Phillips, 1814

70 **Sowerby, James** 1787–1871, botanist, from a drawing by J. Heaphy, 1818

71 **St John, Sir Oliver** 1598?–1673, Lord Chief Justice, from a picture by Jameson, in the possession of Lady Olivia Sparrow

72 **Stokes, Charles,** secretary of the Geological Society, from a drawing by Chantrey, 1821 (but not listed in Chantrey ledgers, *Walpole Soc.* LVI).

73 **Talma** 1763–1826, French actor, from a drawing by J.P. Davis, 1817

74 **Teniers, David** 1610–90, Flemish painter, from a self-portrait in the Collection of Dawson Turner

75 **Tresham, Henry** 1749?–1814, historical painter, from a drawing by Chinnery, 1802

76 **Turner, Rev Joseph,** Dean of Norwich, from a drawing by Schipper, 1817

77 **Turner, Miss Hannah Sarah,** b. 1808, m. 1839 Thomas Brightwen of Yarmouth, from a drawing by Elizabeth Turner (Lady Palgrave), 1818

78 **Twiss, Richard** 1747–1811, traveller, from a drawing by G.H. Harlow, 1814

79 **Wellington, Duke of** (see No. 892), from a drawing by Chantrey, 1822

80 **Wilkie, David** 1785–1841, artist, from a drawing by G.H. Harlow, 1812

81*** **Wingfield, Sir Anthony** 1485?–1552, Comptroller of the Household, from a picture then at Letheringham in the possession of R. Rede

Duke of Wellington

Chantry Esc 1822

Appendix I, 79

*   This plate, though begun by Mrs Turner, was finished by Mr Edwards himself; a long illness having prevented her completing it. It commemorates an excellent artist, and a most worthy man, to whose teaching she is principally indebted for whatever success may have attended her in this department of art, and whose assistance is more or less to be traced in every plate in this collection.

**   This plate was etched to accompany the Memoirs of his Life, published by Mr Roscoe in 1822.

***   The portrait mentioned by Horace Walpole in a letter to Richard Bentley, 28 August 1755

APPENDIX II

DECIMUS BURTON'S ALBUM OF PORTRAITS

A large quarto album lettered BURTON PORTRAITS ALBUM.

Flyleaf inscription: "This Album of Portrait engravings, formerly belonging to Decimus Burton, was presented to the Club by Miss Constance M. Poll, June 1929. Duplicate prints were taken out, with the donor's approval, for sale or exchange.

29 prints left in the Album.

2 lithograph portraits (Lutwidge & D'Israeli) have been added to a volume of Drummond's *Athenaeum Portraits.*"

1   **William Davies**, director of Phoenix Fire Insurance
By G. Zobel, 1852, mezzotint (O'D 1) after E.U. Eddis, 'from a Portrait painted at the request of the Directors of the Phoenix Fire Insurance Company'.

2   **Thomas Drummond** (1797–1840), captain of Engineers; elected in 1838.
By H. Cousins, 1841, mezzotint (O'D 1) after H.W. Pickersgill.

3   **Portrait of a Man**, possibly Austrian, c.1840
Unknown artist, lithograph, TQL standing in tail coat, grey trousers, striped waistcoat, left hand on back of chair, right pointing to letter on table.

4   **Chevalier B. Schlick,** *see* No. 75, another copy inscribed: *To Decimus Burton Esq with B. Schlick's friendly remembrances.*

5   **Lord Brougham,** see No. 105
By J.S. Templeton, lithograph (O'D 29), after Templeton.

6   **Sir Walter Scott,** see No. 760
By J.S. Templeton, lithograph after Templeton, HS vignette to right, black bow tie.

7   **Lord Althorp** (later 3rd Earl Spencer), 1782–1845; elected in 1830.
By J.S. Templeton, lithograph 'from life by J.S. Templeton'.

8   **Portrait of a Man,** c.1830–40
By J.S. Templeton, lithograph vignette after Templeton, HS to left, balding, coat with black velvet collar.

9   **Lord John Russell,** see No. 738
By J.S. Templeton, lithograph vignette after Templeton, HS to left holding a roll of paper.

10   **Thomas Murdoch,** FRS see No. 617
By M. Gauci, 1832, line engraving (O'D 1), after a drawing by

W. Behnes, 1818.

11   **Richard Burke,** see No. 118, another copy, inscribed: *Decimus Burton Esq with T.H. Burke's best compliments.*

12   **Thomas Tredgold** (1788–1829), engineer and architect's clerk. Unknown artist, line engraving vignette (O'D 1), with engraved holograph: 27 May 1828, *Dear Sir, The best plan you can adopt will be to clay the bottom and the back of the walls to above the height of the water – To Matt. Habershon esq. Architect, London / Yours most obt*[y]*, Thomas Tredgold.*
"One hundred impressions of this engraving of the late Thomas Tredgold M.J.C.E are taken off and presented to eminent men, professors of Civil & Mechanical Engineering, and of Architecture in Great Britain, and is Inscribed to Them by their grateful and humble servant, John Weale"

13   **Mr Stanhope,** probably Col the Hon James Hamilton Stanhope MP (1788–1825), a founding member of the Club.
By J.S Templeton, lithograph, HL to right, short curly hair, left arm on books, aged *c.* 35.

14   **Thomas Telford,** see No. 838
By W.C. Edwards, etching, after a portrait by S. Lane in Institute of Civil Engineers.

15   **George Bellas Greenough,** FRS, see No. 347
By C. May, 1845, satirical etching, WL to right in chair, reading newspaper.

16   **Sir Charles Wheatstone,** FRS (1802–75), musical instrument maker, inventor of the concertina, and professor of experiment physics, King's College, London; elected in 1838 under Rule II.
By C.H. Jeens, stipple engraving (O'D 2) after a photograph by Mayall, published by Macmillan in *Nature,* 27 April 1876.

17   **Benedetto Pistrucci** (1784–1855), gem engraver and medallist; elected in 1842 under Rule II.
By ? J.S. Templeton, lithograph vignette, lettered: *Pistrucci to his friend Schassi, London 1 Feb 1824, printed by Hullmandel.*

18   **Friedrich Gottlieb Klopstock** (1724–1803), German poet.
By F. Müller, line engraving after a drawing by Gerdt Hardorff.

19   **Goethe** (1749–1832), German poet.
By Moritz Steinla, line engraving after a portrait by Ferdinand Fagermann, 1806.

20   **Gottfried August Bürger** (1747–84), German poet.
By Gottschick, line engraving after a drawing by Baumann of a portrait by Fiorillo.

PISTRUCCI,
to his friend
SCHIASSI.
London 1· Feb.ᵗ 1824.
Printed by C. Hullmandel

Appendix II. 17

21 **Friedrich von Schiller** (1759–1805), German poet
By Moritz Steinla, engraving after a portrait by Frau Simonawitz.

22 **Johann Gottfried Herder** (1744–1803) German philosopher.
By Moritz Steinla, line engraving after a portrait by Friedrich Rehberg.

23 **Lord Glenbervie,** Sylvester Douglas (1743–1823), politician.
By C.S. Taylor, stipple engraving (O'D 1), after a portrait by Adam Buck published in *New European Magazine,* 1823.

24 **Christopher Martin Wieland** (1733–1813), German poet.
By Moritz Steinla, line engraving after a portrait by Ferdinand Fagemann.

25 **J.C.C.M. Fenner von Fennerberg** (1774–1849), German physician.
Unknown artist, 1838, lithograph, HS to right, black band over left eye.

26 **Thomas Phillips** (1770–1845), portrait painter and a founding member.
By Mrs Dawson Turner, c. 1814, etched vignette (Walker NPG p. 389).

27 **Lord Howden,** John Hobart Caradoc (1799–1873), diplomat; elected in 1837.
By Juan Antonio Lopez, c.1830, lithograph, WL standing in ? Basque costume with thumbstick, inscribed: *For Decimus Burton Esq with the kind regards of the original.*

28 **Edward Magrath,** *see* No. 576, another copy.

29 **[Karl Friedrich] Schinkel** (1781–1841), German architect.
By Tiechel, engraving from a bust by C.F. Tieck, printed by G. Gropius, Berlin.

ARCHITECTURAL DRAWINGS, 1829–1901

1829 Drawing Room walls, colour schemes

By Decimus Burton

(1) see Nos. 1261–2

(2) Watercolour 39 × 49.5 cm (15¼ × 19½ in), scaled and lettered at top: – ATHENÆUM –

(a) top, the west side of drawing room with two colour schemes (buff and green), two sopra porte reliefs, electrolier reflected in glass over fireplace.

(b) bottom, the east wall with two similar colour schemes, lunettes with winged 'muses' above pelmets, low bookcases or cupboards between windows.

(3) watercolour [Pl. XX (b)] 32.5 × 49.5 cm (12¾ × 19½ in), scaled and lettered at top – ATHENAEUM – and inscribed: *Approved by the Committee, E Magrath Sec^y 25 June 1829*. East wall of drawing room , pale green, gold and pink, rectangular reliefs of winged 'muses' representing music, wisdom, learning, etc.

Presented by E.J. May, 1901

1840, Plans of the Athenaeum

By Decimus Burton

A bound volume, 49 × 66 cm (19¼ × 26 in), containing 16 pages of ink drawings, dated January 1840, including situations of gas and water pipes, ventilating shafts, the basement showing drains, and proposed bookcases in the Committee Room. The book also shows some alterations, proposed in 1845 and 1887 but not executed.

1853–62, Various plans &c

By B.B. Sapwell & Co. and Decimus Burton

A bound volume, 66 × 50 cm (26 × 20 in), containing 103 pages of various drawings: a New Room for books (Sapwell), attic storey (DB 21 March 1854), front elevation showing the glass dome and ventilation system (DB 25 June 1854), elevation with additional storey (DB 25 April 1855), section of south library with bookcases (DB 28 June 1854), east elevation (DB April 1854).

1856, Miscellaneous Plans

A bound volume, 64 × 50 cm (25 × 19½ in), containing 47 pages of various plans and elevations and a *Statement for the Enlargement of the Club House*, submitted at the AGM, 13 March

1856. At the end (pp. 46–7) are two watercolour elevations of the Army and Navy Club.

1864, Plans for Alterations

A bound volume, 74 × 55 cm (29 × 22 in), containing 12 pages of ink plans and two interesting watercolour elevations of the Club House from Pall Mall and Waterloo Place, dated May 1864.

1882, Charles Barry – Architect

A bound volume, 68 × 56 cm (27 × 22 in), containing 12 pages of miscellaneous plans, all signed *Charles Barry Arch^t 1882,* including interesting views of the drawing room lantern light.

1886–88, Charles Barry – Architect

A bound volume, 50 × 35 cm (18¾ × 14 in), lettered: *Athenæum Building Plans 1887–8*, containg a photograph of the Club House from the south-east, fourteen signed and dated (some 1886) architectural drawings, and a copy of No. 1243 with a scaled plan of the second floor.

1887, Charles Barry – Architect

A bound volume, 64 × 47 cm (25½ x 18½ in) lettered: *Athenæum Club Proposed Alterations* 1887 and containing the printed Report of the Building Special Commission 30 March 1887, Charles Barry, Report, 25 March 1887, and eighteen pages of coloured elevations and plans, signed and dated *Charles Barry March 1887*.

1891–93, Uncoloured Drawings

A bound volume, 69 × 102 cm (27 × 40 in), containing 12 pages of ink drawings, 3 showing elevations of the main staircase with skylight, Apollo, clock, and the Thorwaldsen roundels, pp. 7–9.

1899–1901, Plans of the Attic Storey

By T.E. Collcutt, FRIBA

A bound volume, 66 × 48 cm (26 × 19½ in), containing 11 pages of watercolour drawings including a Roof Plan showing the lantern light (no.4) and elevations from Waterloo Place.

AN ALBUM OF DESIGNS BY LUCAS, ALMA-TADEMA & POYNTER, 1889–1908

1   **The Staircase** [Pl. XXII (a)]
By Arthur Lucas

Watercolour on discoloured white paper, 67 × 50 cm (26½ × 19¾ in), inscribed: *ATHENÆUM,* and copiously annotated in pencil. A view of the main staircase showing Apollo, scagliola columns, clock, Thorwaldsen roundels, and stair carpet.

2   **Electrolier**
By Sir Lawrence Alma-Tadema

Watercolour on white paper, 48 × 32 cm (19 × 12½ in). Plan and elevation of a chandelier, annotated: *No. 8741 / Echelle 0.20 PIM (not used).*

3   **Front Hall, North Side**
By Arthur Lucas

Watercolour, 50.5 × 75 cm (19 × 29½ in), scale ½ in = 1 ft. View showing the north wall painted buff-yellow, two doors, scagliola panels, and niche with cast of 'Venus' (No. 1259).

4   **Front Hall, South Side**   [Pl. XXII (b)]
By Arthur Lucas

Watercolour, 49 × 77 cm (19¼ × 30¼ in), scale ½ in = 1 ft, annotated: *the marble to be the same as on the North Side – further on drawing, cancel this 11/1/91.* Similar view and colouring , with 'Diana' in the niche (No. 1260).

5   **Hall, Frieze and Column**
By Sir Lawrence Alma-Tadema

Watercolour, 46 × 52.5 cm (18¼ × 20¾ in), dated 1891 and annotated in pencil.

6   **Hall Ceiling**
By Sir Lawrence Alma-Tadema

Watercolour, 57.5 × 55 cm (22½ × 21¾ in), annotated in pencil: *Hall Wagon Roof (Tadema) / This dimension was calculated from drawings as the ceiling at this point in inaccessible for measurement. This panel is arched and 15 ft 4 in is about the dimension if it were developed.*

7   **Hall Ceiling**
By Sir Lawrence Alma-Tadema

Watercolour, 71 × 44 cm (28 × 17¼ in), annotated: *centre line.* A single decorative motif of the side panels.

8   **Hall Ceiling**
By H. Davison

Pencil drawing, 67 × 105 cm (26¼ × 41¼ in), (one watercolour motif), annotated in pencil: *A Red, B Blue C Gold D Green E*

Black, and signed and dated: *H. Davison 20/8/91.*

9   **Hall**
Attributed to Alma-Tadema

Pencil drawing, 67 × 92 cm (26¼ × 36¼ in), two plans of panel enrichment and a wide elevation of the south wall and staircase.

10   **Morning Room Ceiling**
By Sir Edward Poynter

Pencil and watercolour, 66 × 88.5 cm (26 × 34¾ in), annotated: *No. 9 Morning Room Poynter / Approved by Sub Committee June 14 92 Edward Poynter / Lawrence Tadema / Arthur Lucas.* A circular panel with a single segment painted in watercolour.

11   **Morning Room, West Wall**
By Sir Edward Poynter

Watercolour and pencil, 66.5 × 100 cm (26 × 39 in), inscribed: *Approved by Sub Committee June 14. 92.*

12   **Morning Room, Ceiling & Cornice**
By Sir Edward Poynter

Watercolour and pencil, 54 × 76.5 cm (21¼ × 30 in), annotated: *No. 10. Light Blue, Umber 1 White etc. / Elevation / Profile.*

13   **Coffee Room**
By Sir Edward Poynter

Watercolour, 67 × 79 cm (26 × 31 in), annotated: *No. 3 / Panel enrichment practically the same as on staircase.* Brightly coloured black, red, purple and yellow.

14   **Coffee Room: West Wall**
By Sir Edward Poynter

Watercolour, 66 × 90 cm (26 × 35¼ in), annotated: *No. 2. Athenaeum = West Wall of Coffee Room 1 inch = 1 foot (Poynter).* Panels painted orange with buff, red and black borders.

15   **Coffee Room: West Wall**
By Sir Edward Poynter

Watercolour and pencil, 67 × 91.5 cm (26½ × 36 in), annotated: *No 1 annotated & approved by Sub Committee June 14. 92 – Lawrence Tadema, Edward Poynter, Arthur Lucas.* Brilliantly coloured and includes enrichment details, sunflower, and Club cypher.

16   **Coffee Room: Part Plan of Ceiling**
By Sir Edward Poynter

Pencil and watercolour, 67 × 100 cm (26½ × 39¼ in), annotated: *No. 4 – approved by Sub Committee June 14 92.*

Photograph of one of the Club's electroliers executed by Balshaw
after a design by Alma-Tadema [Pl. XXIII (b); see Appendix IV 24).

17   Coffee Room: Cornices & Mouldings

By Sir Edward Poynter

Ink and pencil, 67 × 100 cm (26½ × 39¼ in), annotated: *Athenaeum Club / No. 5 Cornice in Coffee Room – about 1/3 full size.*

18   Drawing Room: North Side

By Sir Lawrence Alma-Tadema

Ink drawing, 67 × 49.5 cm (26½ × 19½ in), scaled and annotated: *Half Elevation of North Side.*

19   Drawing Room: West & East Sides

By Sir Lawrence Alma-Tadema

Ink and watercolour, 50 × 68.5 cm (19 × 27 in), annotated and showing bookcases.

20   Drawing Room: North West Side

By Sir Lawrence Alma-Tadema

Ink and watercolour, 67 × 50 cm (26½ × 19⅝ in), annotated and showing bookcases and scagliola columns.

21   Drawing Room: Ceiling North & South Ends

By Sir Lawrence Alma-Tadema

Ink and watercolour, 49 × 61 cm (19¼ × 24 in), section through cornice annotated: *Quarter Plan of Drawing-room Ceiling North and South Ends.*

22   Drawing Room: Frieze [Pl. XXIII (e)]

By Sir Lawrence Alma-Tadema

Watercolour, 38.5 × 105 cm (15 × 41¼ in), complete page of brilliant blue, yellow and red.

23   Drawing Room: Frieze for Dome [Pl. XXIII (d)]

By Sir Lawrence Alma-Tadema

Watercolour, 36.5 × 47.5 cm (14 × 18¾ in), 5ft of frieze in yellow and pale green.

24   Electrolier [Pl. XXIII (b)]

Designed by Alma-Tadema, executed by Balshaw Watercolour, 54 × 41.5 cm (21¼ × 16¼ in), *Accepted Dec. Sub Com^{ee} HRT [edder].*

25   Drawing Room: Cornice

By Sir Lawrence Alma-Tadema

Watercolour, 33 × 146 cm (13 × 57½ in), folded and annotated: *Squares & Modillions round Cornice* (more annotation on verso).

26   Coffee Room: Ceiling [Pl. XXIII (c)]

By Sir Ambrose Poynter

Watercolour, 58 × 105 cm (22¾ × 41¼ in), a single white floral motif on buff ground, signed and dated; *AP 15.ix. 08.*

27   Coffee Room: Ceiling

By Sir Edward Poynter

Ink, 66 × 104 cm (26 × 41 in), similar floral motif with colour notes, signed and dated: *EP 15. ix. 08.*

28   Drawing Room: Panel of Dome

By Sir Lawrence Alma-Tadema

Watercolour, 65 × 89 cm (25½ × 35 in), annotated.

29   Drawing Room: Dome

By Sir Lawrence Alma-Tadema

Watercolour, 62 × 88 cm (24 × 34 in), sketch, folded, and dated: *Autumn 1893.*

30   Coffee Room

By Sir Ambrose Poynter

Black ink, 52 × 73 cm (20¼ × 28¾ in), signed and dated: *AP 18.ix. 08.*

31   Coffee Room: Ceiling

By Sir Ambrose Poynter

Ink on tracing paper, 100 × 156 cm (39½ × 61½ in), pricked for stencil, folded, signed and dated: *15. ix. 08,* and also on verso.

32   Coffee Room: Ceiling [Pl. XXIII (a)]

By Sir Ambrose Poynter

Dark brown watercolour touched with white, on brown paper, 80 × 104 cm (63¼ × 41 in), floral designs and inscribed: *Angle of large panel only.*

APPENDIX V

POLITICAL AND SOCIAL SATIRES

POLITICAL AND SOCIAL SATIRES, CARTOONS AND ILLUSTRATIONS

SARAH DODGSON

INTRODUCTION

The oldest piece of satirical art in the Club is a folded leaf, dated 1748, illustrating a work by "Baron Huffumbourghausen" entitled *The congress of the beasts under the mediation of the Goat to which is prefixt a Large Curious Print of the last scene of the Drama being the General Conference.* (Morton Pitt Collection 43/7). The interest of the members in satirical art is shown in the subscriptions maintained by the Club to McLean's Political Sketches by H.B. from 1829–1850, and by the retention of an almost complete run of Punch from 1841 to June 1975.

However, in 1866, the Club acquired its first mounted album of cartoons originally published as individual prints.

(A) JAMES SAYER'S CARTOONS

SAYER, (or sometimes Sayers) James b. Gt Yarmouth 1748, d. Mayfair 1823

Album of cartoons, 57 x 44 cm (19 x 13 ins), red quarter leather, lettered *Sayer's Caricatures 1780–1807.*

This volume contains 154 plates mounted on 75 pages. The earliest print dates from 6th April 1782 forming the beginning of a set of 37 (Nos. 2a–11a) depicting individual members of the Fox administration. The identities of these individuals have been added to each print in pencil in a later hand, possibly that of Spencer Hall, the Club's librarian from 1833–1874. This set continued to appear until June 1789. Published by Charles Bretherton of New Bond Street, they form an introductory 'vade mecum' to the identification of characters in the rest of the collection.

Sayer was a supporter of Pitt. Fox is supposed to have said that Sayer's cartoons did him more harm than all the attacks made on him in parliament or the press (DNB VL.p.392)

Even the Clubs were not immune; No. 23a depicts *The Head Quarters: Brookes's* 18 July 1785.

Not all the satires relate to British politics; No. 47a shows '*Master Priestly and the National Assembly*' recording the future president of the Royal Society and a bottle of Phlogiston from Hackney College appearing before a revolutionary council, 18 June 1792. The French revolutionaries were particular targets and are featured in a second series (Nos. 51a–54b) entitled *Illustrious Heads designed for a new History of Republicanism in French and English,* 2 May 1794. Sayer was fond of lampooning the output of the republican press in a series of fake Frontispieces such as No 57a *Frontispiece to Citizen Nicholl's Parliamentary and Unparliamentary Letters, Speeches and Visions,* 15th Dec. 1797.

The later satires include more social than political subjects such as No. 66a *Coke and Gas: Coal and Oil,* 9th March 1808. This is the last dated item in the collection, which ends with 14 prints initialled by Sayer but having no other imprint.

(B) SIEGE OF PARIS 1870-71

At a meeting of the Committee of the Athenaeum held Tuesday July 25th 1871, the Librarian drew the attention of the Committee to "a collection of caricatures published during the Siege of Paris and the reign of the Commune, about 900 in number, ... the whole collected and submitted by Messrs Dulau of Soho Square".

The list was "produced, considered and it was resolved that the caricatures be purchased at a cost of £15, the outlay being, with the assent of the members of the Library subcommittee present, charged to the Library Fund".

Thus the Club acquired a collection of material, which is now very frail. These cartoons were sold as a collection, not, as with other material held by the Club, assembled by the Club itself. The acquisition, together with some bound issues of back numbers of French newspapers from this period, suggests the Club was deliberately investing in the material in the expectation that it would be of lasting interest to the members. As the Library Committee minute of December

See p. 226 for caption

8th 1871 suggests, the Club was interested enough to build on this initial purchase by the acquisition of a number of individual volumes, listed below, which had been assembled by Mr Dulau to supplement the first collection. These are distinct from the original material, which is now bound up in ten volumes, in that most of the material, in the volumes with titles, is clearly attributable. The first cartoons acquired are not bound in a coherent order. Some volumes start with sequences bearing such vague titles as *La Musée Comique* or *L'Eclipse: Supplement*, only to peter out after 7 or 8 issues; later issues of these series are scattered haphazardly throughout other volumes. Some titles, such as *Actualité* or *Actualités*, seem to have been used for several different series, by the same artist, or by the same publisher.

The utility of this collection lies in the opportunity it offers to juxtapose cartoons of similar appearance, one innocuous, signed and clearly attributed, with one bordering on the scurrilous, hiding in anonymity. Comparisons thus made possible will enable the serious student to venture identifications and attributions that would be difficult where such cartoons are held as individual items. The jokes and even the identities of the subjects portrayed, may be beyond the comprehension of the non-historian. However, the depiction of events from three sides, French, Belgian and German allows an insight into the characteristics and attitudes that informed both the Siege of Paris itself and late nineteenth century assumptions of nationality. The same joke on the title of '*Sire de Fisch Ton Kan*', a popular music hall ballad, appears in both the French and Belgian collections. There is a running joke on accents in a significant part of the French material. Current scientific interests are satirised in a series entitled Phrénologie Politique.

The sale of the 1870–1871 set also suggests a deliberate investment on behalf of certain publishers. The number of printers and publishers involved in the production is far smaller than the range of artists and lithographers whose work is included. For example, of the 92 Belgian cartoons 68 originate with the firms of Emile Breyer and L. Jaugery. One short series in this collection, '*Les genies de la mort*' by E. Cheval, rises above the lightweight sketch and approaches the quality of a modernist work with an anti-war message. Finally the one cartoon of English origin rounds off the collection – summarising the events depicted as *"An awful lesson to the world for all time to come"* – designed, etched and published by George Cruikshank June 1871.

Caricatures published during the Siege of Paris and the Government of the Commune 1870–1871 in ten volumes : Paris Brussels and Berlin 1870–1871. quarter leather, purple rexine and green cloth. French caricatures seven vols, Belgian caricatures one vol, German caricatures two vols.

Cham et Daumier : *Album du Siège.*
Draner : *Paris Assiège* 1870–1871.
Draner : *Les Soldats de la République* 1870–1871
Draner : *Souvenirs du Siège de Paris* 1870–1871
Le Petit, Alfred : *Fleurs fruits et légumes du jour Paris* 1871
Marrons Sculptés : caricatures de 1870–1871
La Ménagerie Impériale 1870–1871
Profils politiques 1870-1871
Les Ruines de Paris 1871 (illustrated).
Souvenirs comiques de l'Armée de l'Est en Suisse 1871

(C) THE DREYFUS AFFAIR

The policy of acquiring material relating to current affairs was continued with the formation of a collection on the Dreyfus Affaire, bound in 32 volumes and including one volume (22) containing 35 satirical sheets relating to the scandal published between 1894 and 1899. This appears to be the only occasion in which satirical material in the Club includes moving parts and pop up flaps.

(D) THE BOER WAR

The Boer War collection consists of 86 volumes of material (approx. 2,000 items) in English, French, Dutch, Afrikaans and German relating to the conflict of 1899–1901, which was formed by purchase by the Club during the war. Its unusual completeness was noted in the *National Review* of December 1903, in which it is described as follows :

"[The Athenæum] has brought together with great labour a remarkable series extending to 86 volumes of various sizes consisting of pamphlets, fly sheets, placards, postcards and songs in all languages and pictorial productions and caricatures of all kinds relating to the late war in South Africa. The collection includes the coarsest effusions of Germany, Belgium, France and all European countries. All kinds of ephemeral productions about the war are found in it whether historical or critical whether in praise or blame".

The satirical material is scattered throughout the collection, but the following volumes contain material of relevance here:

vol. 14 No 6 *The Westminster Cartoons* vol. IV: a pictorial history of Political Events connected with South Africa 1899–1900 by F. Carruthers Gould.

vol. 16 No 4 *Dum Dum's Der Publieke Opinie: Een Honderdtal Caricaturen op den Transvaalsch-Engelschen Oorlog.*

vol. 28 : Labelled "Caricatures" on the spine but actually

contains 200 pages of the 1900 editions of *Die Nederlandsche Spectator*, 16 editions of *Eigen Haard* and 12 editions of *Uilenspiegel*.

vol. 29 No 1 A set of nine pictorial postcards with cartoons of the war.

vol. 44 Bound editions of *Le Rire* from 8th July to 23rd Sept 1899, 23rd Nov. 1899 and 9 June 1900.

vol. 54 No 1 A set of 61 pictorial postcards with caricatures.

vol. 69 Bound editions of *Lustiger Blätter* and *Kladderadatsch* for 1901 and 1902

One volume in this collection deserves particular mention for consisting entirely of illustrated material. Vol 45 is a quarto volume lettered on the spine Caricatures (French). It commences with 12 pictorial postcards with caricatures lithographed in primary colours by Julio. The next item is a blank school exercise book with a lurid scene of English Atrocities at Ladysmith (for the instruction of school pupils). The remainder of the volume consists of the Boer War issues of the current satirical and illustrated magazines, which indicate the extent of the French press at the turn of the century and the quality of the art work and photography used to represent the war. The illustrations in this volume are largely anglophobic, ending with a copy of Jean Veber's Les Camps de Reconcentration au Transvaal a publication entirely critical of the concentration camps of Lord Kitchener. The following titles are represented in this volume : *Le Petit Illustré Amusant, Le Bon Vivant, l'Actualité, Le Journal Amusant, La Vie Pour Rire, La Caricature, Chari-vari Album, L'Assiette de Buerre, La Vie Illustrée, L'Illustré National*, and *Le Monde Illustré*.

The collection also includes (vol. 32) 10 calendars for 1901, with coloured illustrations in a very high quality chromolithography, although with no imprint. They are dramatic scenes from the war, and, although not satirical, deserve to be noted as good examples of the ephemeral works of art retained in the Club's collections.

(E) THE FIRST WORLD WAR

The interest in satirical material, in the form of individual prints or cards, seems to have declined after the turn of the 19th/20th century. Only one volume of satirical material survives in the First World War collection, in magazine format, and with the tone of propaganda rather than satire.

The Club has continued to acquire satirical material in the 20th century, but has concentrated on individual pieces in their original sketch or watercolour format, framed and hung as works of art, rather than mounted into albums or bound into volumes. These later acquisitions are included in the main catalogue.

Caption to illustration on p. 221

Appendix V (a) : Title page of *Les Ruines de Paris, Journées du 22 au 28 Mai 1871*; published by J. Grognet, the publisher or distributor of about 10 percent of the material of Parisian origin in the Siege of Paris collection. The engraver, Marks, may be the W. Marks noted in Bénézit as the engraver of Watteau's paintings, (1850). *Les Ruines* contains 13 plates by three different artists, none now identifiable. The scenes are not particularly satirical, except in the choice of buildings portrayed in flames or in ruins, such as the Town Hall, the Finance Ministry or the Prefecture of Police.

APPENDIX VI

AN ALBUM OF ENGRAVINGS BY JAMES WARD, R.A.

A giant folio album of twenty-seven mezzotints and lithographs lettered:

WORKS OF JAMES WARD R.A. and presented by the artist in 1825 (Minutes 22 March 1825, p. 126). The manuscript contents list reads:

1 George III on his charger, Adonis, by Sir William Beechey, R.A.
2 H.R.H. the Duke of Clarence, by Archer Shee, R.A.
3 Rt Hon General Sir William Fawcett, by Sir Joshua Reynolds.
4 Mrs Billington as St Cecilia, by Sir Joshua Reynolds (*see* No. 78).
5–6 blank pages [as noted 29 March 1853]
7 Cornelius the Centurion, by Rembrandt
8 Christ taken down from the Cross, by C.W. E. Dietricy (after Rubens)
9 Diana and her Nymphs, by Sir P.P. Rubens
10 Studies from Nature, drawn and engraved by J. Ward
11 Dogs of the Dalmatian breed, drawn and engraved by J. Ward.

Lithographs of Horses
12 Nonpareil, a Favourite Charger of George IV.
13 Adonis, a Favourite Charger of George III.
14 Soothsayer, a Celebrated Race-horse of George IV.
15 Monitor, a Blood-horse, property of George IV.
16 Copenhagen, a Horse rode by the Duke of Wellington at Waterloo
17 Marengo, a favourite Barb Charger, rode by Napoleon at Waterloo.

18 Persian Horse, property of the Duke of Northumberland.
19 Cossack War Horse, property of the Duke of Northumberland,
20 Primrose, A Brood Mare and Foal, property of the Duke of Grafton.
21 Walton, a celebrated Race-horse, property of Sir John Shelley, Bt.
22 Leopold, a celebrated Race-horse, property of J.G. Lambton, Esq.
23 Phantom, a celebrated Race-horse, property of Sir John Shelley, Bt.
24 Little Peggy, a Horse brought from the Thibet Mountains, height 33 inches, 9 years old.
25 Doctor Syntax, a celebrated Race-horse, property of Ralph Riddel, Esq.
26 Princess Royal, property of Sir T. Mostyn, Bt.

***

27 Shepherd's Dog, drawn and engraved by J. Ward
28 Shepherd Boy, drawn and engraved by J. Ward.
29 Rover, a favourite Dog, property of the Earl of Powis, by W.D. Taylor after James Ward (see No. 1378, presented by Colnaghi, 1830).

Literature: Ath. Cat. vol I (1845), pp. 263–6, where these prints are published.

Authors' note: this album was only available for inclusion in the Catalogue in July 2000.

BIBLIOGRAPHY

Most of these volumes are in the Club library, but asterisks*
indicate those exclusively so.

Dictionaries

Archibald E.H.H. Archibald, *Dictionary of Sea Painters* (Woodbridge 1980)

Bénézit E. Bénézit, *Dictionnaire des Peintres, Sculpteurs, Dessinateurs et Graveurs* (14 vols Gr,nd, Paris 1999)

Beraldi Henri Beraldi, *Les Graveurs du XIXe Siëcle* (12 vols Paris 1885–92)

Bryant & Mark Bryant & Simon Heneage, *Dictionary of British* **Heneage** *Cartoonists and Caricaturists 1730–1980* (Scolar 1994)

Clark Alan Clark, *Dictionary of British Comic Artists, Writers & Editors* (1998)

DNB *Dictionary of National Biography*

Engen Rodney K. Engen, *Dictionary of Victorian Engravers and Print Publishers* (1979)

Forrer L. Forrer, *Biographical Dictionary of Medallists* (7 vols 1902-22)

Gunnis Rupert Gunnis, *Dictionary of British Sculptors 1660–1851* (London 1953)

Hardie Martin Hardie, *Watercolour Painting in Britain* (3 vols 1967–9)

Hollstein F W H Hollstein, *Dutch & Flemish Etchings &* **Dutch** *Engravings* (52 vols Amsterdam 1949-98)

Hollstein F W H Hollstein, *German Engravings Etchings and* **German** *Woodcuts* (46 vols in progress, Amsterdam 1954-99)

Houfe 1978 Simon Houfe, *Dictionary of British Book Illustrators and Caricaturists, 1800–1914* (1978)

Houfe 1996 Simon Houfe, *Dictionary of 19th Century British Book Illustrations and Caricatures* (1996)

Hunnisett Basil Hunnisett, *Illustrated Dictionary of British Steel Engravers* (1989)

Ingamells John Ingamells, *The English Episcopal Portrait 1559–1835* (1981)

Johnson & *Dictionary of British Artists 1880–1940* (Woodbridge **Greutzner** 1976)

Malalieu H L Malalieu, *The Dictionary of British Watercolour Artists up to 1920* (3 vols 1976–90)

O'D F. O'Donoghue, *Catalogue of Engraved British Portraits ... in the British Museum* (6 vols 1908–25)

Pyke E.J. Pyke, *Dictionary of Wax Modellers* (1973) and *Supplements* (1981,

Sauer K G Sauer, *Allgemeines Künstler-Lexicon* (22 vols in progress, Munich 1992–)

Singer Hans Wolfganger Singer, *Allgemeiner Bildniskatalog* (14 vols, Leipzig 1930–36)

Stewart Brian Stewart & Mervyn Cutten, *Dictionary of* **& Cutten** *Portrait Painters in Britain up to 1920* (Woodbridge 1997)

Thieme-Becker *Algemeines Lexicon der Bildenden Künstler* (37 vols Leipzig 1907–50)

Waterhouse 1981 Ellis Waterhouse, *Dictionary of British 18th Century Painters* (Woodbridge 1981)

Waterhouse 1988 Ellis Waterhouse, *Dictionary of 16th & 17th Century British Painters* (Woodbridge 1988)

Wood 1987 Christopher Wood, *Dictionary of Victorian Painters* (1987)

Special books and albums in the Club library

*Ath Cat Catalogue of the Athenaeum Library, 2 vols 1845–50 and 1851–80, with Supplement and Annual Additions from 1859, printed for Members

*Ath Folio Three albums of engraved portraits and miscellanous subjects, large folios lettered ATHENAEUM FOLIO I, II and III.

Ath Inv 1830–66 Athenaeum Inventories; two large quarto vols 1830–39 and 1856–66, in manuscript

*Ath Inv 1901 Inventory of Fixtures, Decoration, Household Furniture, Coppers, Domestic Utensils, Linen, Plate, Plated Articles and other effects ... revised November 1901

*Ath Ports *The Athenaeum Portraits,* 54 lithographs by William Drummond after portrait drawings by E.U. Eddis and others 1835–37, quarto vol bound in green and blue

*Ath Ports M Two albums of engravings of members of the Club, large folios lettered PORTRAITS MEMBERS I and II

*Ath Ports Red An Album of photographs, 1868-1931, quarto in red morocco, lettered ATHENAEUM PORTRAITS I

* Burton Portraits	An album of 29 engraved portraits, large quarto lettered BURTON PORTRAITS ALBUM (Appendix II)*
Cartoons, Boer War	An album of cartoons of the Boer War, large quarto lettered BOER WAR (Appendix Vc)
* Cartoons, Paris	An album of cartoons of the Siege of Paris, large quarto lettered RUINES DE PARIS (Appendix Vb)
*Eng I & II	Two albums of miscellaneous engravings, folios lettered ENGRAVINGS
*Eng A I	An album of 33 miscellaneousengravings, large folio lettered ENGRAVINGS A. I)
*Eng C I	An album of 40 miscellaneous engraving (folio lettered ENGRAVINGS C I)
*Eng Ports	Two royal folio vols of engravings lettered PORTRAITS
*Eng Ports Q	An album of 27 engraved portraits, quarto lettered PORTRAITS QUARTO I
* HB	Twenty folio albums of Political Sketches, 1829–51, by HB (John Doyle)
*Minutes	Bound volumes of the Club Minutes from 1824
* Plans 1840	An album of ink architectural drawings by Decimus Burton, 16 page folio (Appendix III)
* Plans 1853–62	An album of various architectural drawings by Sapwell & Burton, 103 page folio (Appendix III))
* Plans 1856	An album of various architectural drawings, 47 page folio (Appendix III
* Plans 1864	An album of ink architectural drawings, 12 page folio (Appendix III)
* Plans 1882	An album of watercolour architectural drawings by Charles Barry, 12 page folio (Appendix III)
* Plans 1887–8	An album of architectural drawings by Charles Barry (Appendix III)
* Plans 1889–1908	An album of watercolour drawings for the re-decoration by Lucas, Alma-Tadema, Poynter, and Richardson, 32 page folio (Appendix IV)
" Plans 1891–93	An album of ink architectural drawings, 12 page folio (Appendix III)
* Plans 1899–1901	An album of watercolour architectural drawings by T.E Collcutt, 11 page (Appendix III)
*Richmond Coll.	Five albums of engravings after portraits by George Richmond, specially bound and presented by Richmond himself in 1865 and 1889.
*Sayer Etchings	An album of etched political cartoons by James Sayer, 75 page large quarto lettered SAYER'S CARICATURES, – 1780 to 1807 (Appendix Va)
* Turner Etchings	An album of 101 etchings by Mary Dawson Turner, large quarto lettered TURNER'S ETCHINGS (Appendix I)
Ward Prints	An album of 27 Engravings by James Ward, R.A. (AppendixVI).

*Wells-Grillion	An album of 29 lithographs and 11 Autotype facsimiles of portraits drawn by H.T. Wells for Grillion's Club (see *Grillion's Club A Chronicle 1812–1913* (Oxford 1914)

General reference books

Adams 1983	Bernard Adams, *London Illustrated 1604–1851* (Library Association 1983)
Beerbohm-Hall	N. John Hall, *Max Beerbohm Caricatures* (Yale 1997)
Beerbohm -Davies	Rupert Hart Davies, *A Catalogue of the Caricatures of Max Beerbohm* (1972); see also Rothenstein and Lago
Beerbohm- Observations	Max Beerbohm, *Observations* (1923)
Boswell	James Boswell, *Life of Samuel Johnson* (ed. Hill & Powell 1934)
Boucher 1999	Bruce Boucher, 'Lawrence Alma-Tadema, Edward Poynter and the redecoration of the Athenaeum Club', *Apollo* (October 1999), pp. 21–9
Burchard 1987	Ludwig Burchard, *Corpus Rubensianum* (vol XIX by Hans Vliege 1987)
Chantrey Ledgers	Sir Francis Chantrey's Ledgers, MSS at the Royal Academy (1809-41), and the British Library (1809–23), *Walpole Society Journal* LVI (1994).
Cowell 1975	F.R. Cowell, *The Athenaeum: Club and Social Life in London 1824–1974*, (Heinemann 1975)
Creaton 1939	Heather Creaton, *Bibliography of Printed Works on London History to 1939* (Library Association 1939)
Delteil 1925	Loys Delteil, *Manuel de l' Amateur d'Estampes* (2 vols Paris 1925).
Egerton 1998	Judy Egerton, *National Gallery Catalogues The British School* (1998)
Esdaile 1924	Katherine Esdaile, *Roubiliac's Work at Trinity College, Cambridge* (CUP 1924)
Esdaile 1928	Katherine Esdaile, *The Life and Works of François Roubiliac* (OUP 1928)
Ganz 1950	Paul Ganz, *The Paintings of Hans Holbein* (Phaidon 1950)
Garlick 1989	Kenneth Garlick, *Sir Thomas Lawrence* (Phaidon Oxford 1989)
Garrick 1997	Geoffrey Ashton, *Pictures in the Garrick Club* (1997)
Haden -Schneiderman	Richard S Schneiderman, *Catalogue Raisonné of Prints by Sir Francis Seymour Haden* (1983 reprint 1997)
Haskell & Penny	Francis Haskell and Nicholas Penny, *Taste and the Antique* (Yale 1981)
Holloway 1977	Merlyn Holloway, *A Bibliography of 19th Century British Topographical Books with Steel Engravings* (Holland Press 1977)

Houfe 1972 Simon Houfe, 'The Athenaeum', *The Antique Collector*, Dec 1972, pp. 287–96

ILN 1893 *see* Waugh 1893

Jenkins 1994 Ian Jenkins, *The Parthenon Frieze* (1994)

Kerslake 1977 John Kerslake, *The Early Georgian Portraits* (NPG 1977)

Lago 1990 *Max Beerbohm and William Rothenstein their Friendship and Letters 1893-1945* (ed. Mary Lago and Karl Beckson, 1990).

Legros-Bliss *A Catalogue of Paintings, Drawings, Etchings and Lithographs by Professor Alphonse Legros, from the Collection of Frank E. Bliss Esq.* Preface to the etchings by Campbell Dodgson, CBE (1922)

Legros-Wright 'The Etchings, Drypoints and Lithographs of Alphonse Legros 1837–1914', *Print Collectors' Club*, XII (1934)

Leighton 1996 *Frederick Leighton 1830–1896*, RA Exhibition catalogue 1996

London Interiors *London Interiors … of the British Capital beautifully engraved on Steel* (2 vols 1841–4)

Marsh 1859 J.F. Marsh, 'On the Engraved Portraits and Pretended Portraits of John Milton', in *Trans. Hist. Soc. Lancs. and Cheshire*, vol 102, 1859–60)

Men & Memories Sir William Rothenstein, *Men and Memories* (3 vols 1933–39)

Millais 1899 J G Millais, *Life and Letters of Sir John Everett Millais* (2 vols 1899)

Miller 1992 Oliver Miller, *The Victorian Pictures in the Collection of Her Majesty the Queen* (1992)

Oppé 1950 Paul OppÈ, *English Drawings … at Windsor Castle* (1950)

Ormond 1973 Richard Ormond, *Early Victorian Portraits* (NPG 1973)

Penny 1986 Nicholas Penny, *Reynolds* (RA exhibition catalogue 1985-6)

Piper 1963 David Piper, *Catalogue of the Seventeenth-Century Portraits in the National Portrait Gallery* (Cambridge 1963)

Poole 1912 Mrs R.L. Poole, *Catalogue of Portraits in the Possession of the University, Colleges, City and County of Oxford* (3 vols 1912-25)

Reynolds 1984 Graham Reynolds, *The Later Paintings and Drawings of John Constable* (2 vols Yale 1984).

R [Rothenstein] Sir John Rothenstein, *Portrait Drawings of Sir William Rothenstein* (1926)

Russell 1987 Francis Russell, *Portraits of Sir Walter Scott* (1987)

Shepherd 1828 T.H. Shepherd & J. Elmes, *Metropolitan Improvements* (2 vols 1827–9)

Shepherd 1829 T.H. Shepherd, *London & its Environs in the Nineteenth Century* (1 Nov 1829)

Short-Hardie I-III Martin Hardie *Etched and Engraved Works of Frank Short* (3 vols: I The Liber Studiorum mezzotints after Turner, II mezzotints & aquatints, III etchings, dry-points, lithographs. Print Collectors' Club 1938–40)

Smith 1920 J.T. Smith, *Nollekens and His Times* (ed. Whitten 1920)

Strang-Binyon Laurence Binyon, *William Strang: Catalogue of His Etched Work* (Glasgow 1912)

Strang 1962 David Strang, *William Strang, Catalogue of his Etchings & Engravings* (xenograph, Glasgow 1962)

Strong 1969 Roy Strong, *Tudor & Jacobean Portraits* (2 vols NPG 1969)

Survey of London *Survey of London* XXIX. I (1960), pp. 386–99

Tait 1984 Hugh Tait (ed), *The Art of the Jeweller: a Catalogue of the Hull Grundy Gift to the British Museum* (2 vols 1984)

Tallis *John Tallis's London Select Views 1838–40* (London Topographical Society 1969)

V&A 1980 Lionel Lambourne and Jean Hamilton, *British Watercolours in the Victoria and Albert Museum* (1980)

Walker 1985 Richard Walker, *Regency Portraits* (2 vols NPG 1985)

Walpole Soc. *Journals of the Walpole Society* (1911 in progress)

Ward 1926 Humphry Ward, *History of the Athenaeum 1824–1925* (1926)

Waterhouse 1941 Ellis K. Waterhouse, *Reynolds* (1941)

Waugh 1893 Francis Gledstanes Waugh, 'In Clubland No. III The Athenaeum', *The Illustrated London News*, 11 March 1893, with cuts by J. Walter Wilson

Waugh 1899 F. G. Waugh, *The Athenaeum Club and its Associations* (c.1899, reprinted 1968)

Williams 1971 Iolo Williams, *Early English Watercolours* (1952, reprinted 1971)

Williamson 1908 G.C. Williamson, *Portraits, Prints and Writings of John Milton* (1908)

Wolstenholme & Piper 1964 Gordon Wolstenholme & David Piper, *The Royal College of Physicians of London: Portraits* (1964)

BIOGRAPHICAL NOTES & INDEX

chiefly of artists, architects and donors to the Collection. Portraits are excluded and appear alphabetically in Section I. For Satires see General Index. Numerals refer to Catalogue numbers except where page numbers are specially indicated.

1922, (after) 426–7

Francke, Johann Heinrich Christian (1738–92), German portrait painter, pp. xxiii–xxiv; 300

Fraser, Sir William Bt (1826–98), MP, donor, 1452

Freebairn, Alfred Robert (1794–1846), landscape engraver, 666, 880, 902

Freebairn, J. (*fl.* 1835–40), engraver, 1318–9, 1380

Freeman, Samuel (1773–1857), portrait engraver, 398, 419, 592, 788

Freeth, H. Andrew (1912–86), official war artist with the RAF; elected in 1955, p. xxvii, 121, 1326, 1335

Fremantle, the Hon Reginald (1863–1956), donor, 1014

Freyberg, Barbara, Lady (d. 1973), granddaughter of Joseph Jekyll (*see* No.463); she m. 1922 General Lord Freyberg and was donor of a large collection of engravings, p. xxvii; 30, 51, 56, 122, 133, 261, 271, 322, 343, 372, 702, 705, 817, 849, 859

Frith, W.P. (1819–1909), Victorian artist, (after) 230

Furse, C.W. (1868–1904), portrait painter, (after) 455

G, R. (*fl.* 1820–30), engraver, 781

Gade, Alfred (*fl.* 1854–91), Danish modeller, 130

Gahagan, Lawrence (*fl.*1756–1820), sculptor, 315

Gainsborough, Thomas (1727–88), painter, (after) 366

Gardner, Daniel (1750–1805), portrait painter, (after) 113

Gardner, W.B. (c.1849–1919), wood engraver, 1369

Garrard, Peter (b. 1929), artist, 55

Garvin, J.L. (1868–1947), editor of *The Observer*, donor, 1247

Gaselee, Sir Stephen (1882–1943), librarian of the Foreign Office and honorary librarian of the Athenaeum; elected in 1919, donor, 547

Gauci, Maxim (*fl.* 1810–46), engraver, 124, 169, 231, 248, 275, 347, 368, 389, 415, 459, 476, 490, 513, 520, 574, 599, 648, 673, 814, 887, 890, 943–5, Appendix II, 10

Gauci, Paul (*fl.* 1834–63), lithographer, 1287

Geller, W.O. (*fl.* 1830–57), mezzotint engraver, 136, 408

Gelson, W.E. elected in 1970 and a donor, 1396

Gere, C. M. (1869–1957), painter; elected in 1933, donor, 1214, 1223

Giambologna (1529–1608), Italian sculptor, (after) 1405

Gibb, Sir Alexander (1872—1958), engineer; elected in 1927, donor, 838

Gibbon, Benjamin (1802–51), animal and portrait engraver, 643

Gibson, John (1790–1866), medallist, *see* Appendix I, no. 60

Gilbert, P.N.G. (*fl.* 1989), a donor, 752

Giorgione (1477–1510), Venetian artist, (called) 329

Gladstone, W.E. (1809–98), Prime Minister, donor of a drawing attributed to Sebastian Ricci (*see* Palgrave and p. xxiii)

Glenbervie, Lord (1743–1823), politician and memoir writer, Appendix II, 23

Goethe, J. W. von (1749–1832), German poet, Appendix II, 19

Goetze, Leopold (*fl.* 1907–14), etcher, 544

Goff, Colonel Robert Charles (1837–1922), Royal Engineer; a friend of Charles Dickens, 1050

Golding, Richard (1785–1865), engraver, 133, 158, 372

Gordon, G.P. Pirie (*fl.* 1939), donor, 109

Gottschick, J.C.B. (1766–1844), German engraver, Appendix II, 20

Gould, John (1804–81), ornithologist, elected 1854, donor, 1457

Goupil, Jules (1839–83), French painter, (after) 1368

Goupil & Co, French photographers,

Grant, Alice (*fl.* 1879–1907), portrait painter, 798

Grant, Sir Francis (1803–78), PRA, elected in 1853 under Rule II, (after)

104, 506

Grantham, R.B. (19th cent), civil engineer, 1301

Gray, Ronald (1868–1951), portrait painter, 564

Graziani, G. (19th cent), sculptor, p. xxi, 601

Greatbach, G. (*fl.* 1854), steel engraver, 1333

Grech, David (*fl.* 1990s), architectural draftsman, 1251

Green, Christopher (*fl.* 1960), a donor, 1047

Green, William Curtis (1875–1960), President of the Architectural Association; elected in 1922, 1047

Grevedon, G. (*fl.* 1831), French artist, (after) 93

Gulland, Elizabeth (d. 1934), portrait engraver, 799

Gunn, Sir James (1893–1964), portrait painter, (after) 201

Gunther, R.W.T. (1869–1940), historian of science, elected 1915, donor, 353

Gurney, Hudson (1775–1864), 946–8, and *see* Appendix I, 30.

HB, *see* Doyle

Hacker, Arthur (1858–1919), portrait painter,

Haden, Sir Francis Seymour (1818–1910), surgeon, etcher, and Whistler's brother-in-law; elected in 1881, 1051, 1078, 1312

Haghe, Louis (1806–85), Belgian lithographer, 297, 1304, 1308

Haig (Hägg), Axel Herman (1835–1921), Swedish architect and etcher, 1094, 1180

Haines, photographer, 677

Haines, William (1778–1848), portrait painter and miniaturist, (after) 190

Hall, Edna Clarke, Lady (1881–c.1940), née Waugh, portrait painter, 1346

Hall, H.B. (1808–84), engraver, 383

Hall, John (1739–97), engraver to George III, 320

Hall, Spencer (1806–75), appointed Club librarian 1833, honorary member from 1875,

Hals, Frans (1580?–1666), Dutch painter, (after) 949–50

Hamilton, H.D. (c.1739–1808), portrait painter, (after) 372

Hanhart, M & N (19th cent.), lithographers, 777

Hardenberg, F.H. (*fl.* 1800–23), sculptor, 315, 683

Harding, J.D. (1797–1863), landscape painter and lithographer, 1234

Hardorff, Gerdt (1769–1864), German portrait painter, (after) Appendix II, 18

Hare, Augustus (1834–1903), watercolour artist, collector and author; elected in 1874, 1052, 1227

Harford, Miss (*fl.* 1957), great-niece of A.W. Kinglake, donor, 492

Harlow, George Henry (1787–1819), portrait painter, (after) 343, 354, 641, Appendix I, 27, 46, 64–5, 78, 80, 83

Harris, Mrs John (*fl.* 1939), a donor, 452

Havell, D.L. (*fl.* 1810–26), aquatint engraver, 1109, 1120, 1150

Hawkins, George (*fl.* 1809–52), lithographer, 1297

Hawkins, J.H., founding member and donor, 136

Hayles, W.H., photographer, 740

Hayter, Sir George (1792–1871), donor, *see* No.392 and 579, p. xxiii, 952

Heaphy, Charles (*fl.* 1840s), draftsman to the New Zealand Company, 1183, 1224

Heaphy, T. (1775–1835), portrait painter, *see* Appendix I, 70

Heartley, C.T. (*fl.* 1856), lithographer, 1292

Heger, Heinrich A. (1832–88), German architectural draftsman, 1043

Hemmings, Mrs (*fl.* 1818), portrait painter, *see* Appendix I, 44

Henning, John (1771–1851), modeller, sculptor, and founder of the

GENERAL INDEX